THE DISCOVERY
OF THE NILE

STEWART, TABORI & CHANG
NEW YORK

Text
Gianni Guadalupi

Editorial production
Marcello Bertinetti

Editorial coordination
Laura Accomazzo

Graphic design
Patrizia Balocco Lovisetti

Translation
Neil Frazer Davenport

© 1997 White Star S.r.l.
Via Sassone, 22/24, 13100
Vercelli, Italy

Published in 1997 and distributed by Stewart, Tabori & Chang, a division of U.S. Media Holdings, Inc. 115 West 18th Street, New York, NY 10011

Distributed in Canada by General Publishing Company Ltd. 30 Lesmill Road Don Mills, Ontario, M3B 2T6, Canada

Library of Congress Cataloging-in-Publication Data
Guadalupi, Giovanni
   [Scoperta del Nilo. English]
   The discovery of the Nile / by Giovanni Guadalupi.
      p. cm.
   Includes bibliographical references and index.
   ISBN 1-55670-600-6
   I. Nile Valley—Discovery and exploration. I. Title.
DT117.G813   1997
962—dc21   97-10738

Printed in Italy

10 9 8 7 6 5 4 3 2 1

CONTENTS

6

1 The island of Philae, not far from Aswan, with its great monumental complexes dedicated to the cult of Isis, was one of the most sacred sites of ancient Egypt. This evocative illustration is taken from Views of the Nile *by Owen Jones, London, 1843.*

2-3 Many of the murals that still decorate the tombs depict scenes of everyday life on the river and along its banks. This large painting from Tomb No. 2 in the Beni Hasan necropolis shows men fishing with nets and spears and provides examples of the aquatic and swamp fauna. (Karl Richard Lepsius, Denkmäler Aus Aegypten und Aethiopien, *Berlin, 1848–1859)*

4-5 The Nile and the Temples of Abu Simbel in an evocative illustration from Egypt and Nubia *by Giovanni Battista Belzoni, London, 1820.*

6-7 On this map from the Theatrum Orbis Terrarum *by Abraham Ortelius— an atlas published in Antwerp in 1592— the immense course of the Nile crossed almost the whole of the African continent, originating not only from a lake more or less corresponding to the position of Lake Tanganyika but also from a larger nonexistent stretch of water between Angola and southern Zaire. Another river, corresponding to the Zambesi, is also shown to drain from this lake.*

In what the geographers of the baroque period called the Great Theater of the World, the Nile Valley was a privileged stage on which myth, legend, and history were intertwined as the likes of Isis and Moses, the pharaohs and the Mamelukes, Caesar and Cleopatra, Saint Louis and Saladin, Napoleon and Mehemet Ali played out their roles. The millenary history of Egypt, punctuated with an apparently miraculous regularity by the highs and lows of the great river, was enriched in the nineteenth century by a unique

INTRODUCTION

8

8 *The long, winding Nile Valley is ideally suited to the bird's-eye views typical of the nineteenth century such as this panorama ranging from Abu Simbel to the Pyramids* executed by the French artist Nestor L'Hôte *and taken from his volume* Panorama d'Egypte et de Nubie, *published in 1841.*

chapter in which the Nile itself took center stage: the epic search for and eventual discovery of its sources.

It may seem strange that the long search for the origins of the river upon which so much of Egyptian life depended was conducted not by the Egyptians themselves but by Europeans. The first to question the phenomenon of the floods and the location of the sources was, in fact, a Greek, Herodotus. It was a Roman emperor rather than a pharaoh who organized the first expedition to search for the source, an expedition eventually defeated by impassable swamps. Two Portuguese Jesuits were the first to identify— erroneously—the ultimate sources of the Nile in its Abyssinian branch. Even Mehemet Ali who ordered the first Egyptian expedition to ascend the White Nile, was a European, an Albanian Muslim who had taken over Egypt by force. The explorers who during the nineteenth century finally resolved the enigmas of Nile hydrography were British, German, Italian, and French.

However, the concept of cataloging

8-9 *This view shows the course of the Nile southward from Cairo. Temples and monuments are shown out of proportion in the desert landscape while numerous* dahabieh, *typical Nile boats, can be seen wending their way along the river.*

(Nestor L'Hôte, *Panorama d'Egypte et de Nubie*, Paris, 1878)

10 top *Natives hunting an elephant near a small Nile tributary. The appeal of an exotic, savage world and the vicissitudes of those who ventured into the unknown characterized the stories of the explorers. This illustration is taken from the Livingstone biography,* The Life and Explorations of Dr. Livingstone the Great Missionary Traveller.

the world, which appeared rash to the Eastern mind—that urge to fill in at all costs the white spaces remaining on the globe, naming places, perhaps after oneself, laying claim in perpetuity to a mountain, a river, or a waterfall—was part of what without the slightest hint of irony was called the white man's burden. That term has a hollow ring today when considered within the context of the imperial obsessions of nineteenth-century Europe. Thus, early last century, a curtain that had until then been almost hermetically sealed at last rose—or rather was thrust aside—to reveal a brand-new scenario that for thousands of years had existed apart from, and relatively untouched by, the ruinous passage of history: Bilad es-Sudan, the Land of the Blacks, a mysterious mosaic of deserts and forests, swamps, and mountains from which flowed together

with and along the river an uninterrupted stream of ivory, gold, ostrich plumes, and slaves. It appeared to be, and indeed was, an ideal terrain for the ambitions of the founders of empires. A patchwork of minuscule kingdoms, sultanates, and tribes upon which to impose a single crown and from which to drain the fabled riches of Solomon: columns of blacks to be transformed into soldiers for further acts of conquest and entire fleets of more or less celestial Aïdas to place in harems throughout the Islamic world.

The mirage of an Egyptian empire extending from the Mediterranean to the Indian Ocean was inextricably linked with the European obsession with resolving the age-old geographical problem of locating on the map of Africa the unseen sources of the Nile and the legendary Mountains of the Moon, from

12-13 *This nineteenth-century print provides a bird's-eye view of the Congo and Nile basins from the Great Lakes region to the Mediterranean. In the top left are portraits of the two "heroes of Khartoum," General Gordon and his adjutant, Colonel Stewart, framed by laurels and palm fronds. On the right, views of Khartoum with the administrative buildings in the governorate, or mudiria (top), the gorges of Karaza in the Kordofan region, and the city of Al-Ubayyid (bottom).*

whose snowy slopes that benevolent stream was thought to rise.

This book reconstructs the singular and frequently incredible stories of the greats of African exploration—Burton, Speke, Livingstone, Baker, and Stanley—as well as those of many other less famous figures; their tenacious and successive attempts to reach an objective that at times appeared to shift mockingly within the extremely complicated labyrinth of Central African hydrography. At the same time we will be discussing the events taking place in the immense basin of the Blue and White Niles as the exploration progressed and amplified the sphere of influence of a highly questionable civilization.

The stories of those who risked their lives wandering among the Pygmies and cannibals, the swamps and jungles, the slavers and the tribal despots, are set within the context of broader historical developments such as the descent of the Egyptian army upon a Sudan devastated by the slave trade; the British expedition to the ambas of Abyssinia sent to crush an arrogant king; General Gordon's attempt to eradicate the slave trade and his death at Khartoum besieged by al-Mahdi, the last of the great religious prophets; the legendary resistance of a governor isolated in the heart of black Africa; one Emin Pasha "saved" against his will by an overzealous Stanley following a grueling march across the entire continent; and the exhibition of British logistical might in the reconquest of the Sudan, tackling the cataracts with steamboats and laying railways across the deserts.

In terms of the theatrical metaphor used earlier, that previously unknown and isolated corner of Africa was the setting for the most spectacular series of tragedies ever staged. Perhaps this book's greatest virtue is in having collected for the first time a comprehensive pictorial record supporting the text and illustrating the stories with images executed by the protagonists themselves or their contemporaries. These images have been taken from the most disparate and rarest of sources, and we feel that the history of Nile exploration has never before been shown with such depth and fidelity. We hope that in this way we have succeeded in rendering the drama and grandiosity of the enterprise.

13 *A number of Nubian slaves, in a felucca sailing up the Nile, dance to the sound of drums for the amusement of their masters. The river represented the main arterial route for the slaves captured in Central Africa and sent north to the market at Cairo.*
(Maximilian in Bayern, *Bilder aus dem Orient*, Stuttgart, 1846)

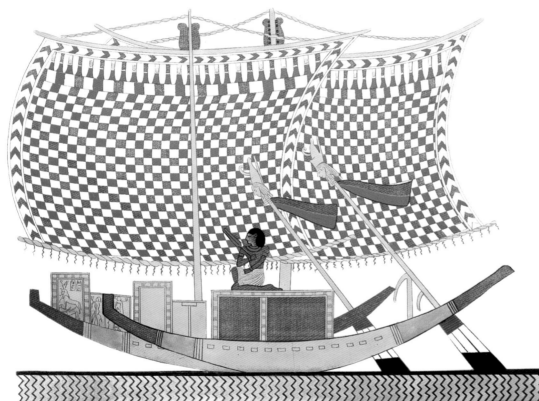

The first people to venture into the Nile Valley, probably by way of the Suez isthmus, would have encountered a landscape very different from that of today with its well cultivated fields and network of canals offering an image of cartographic precision. Left to its own devices the river continuously changed its course and during its periodic floods would inundate parts of the valley while leaving others untouched and infertile. Elsewhere the water would stagnate, forming pestilential crocodile- and snake-infested swamps.

The delta especially was an immense marsh dotted with sandy islands covered in a thick tangle of papyrus, lotus, and reeds through which the various branches of the Nile lazily wended their ever-changing way. On both banks the land spared by the annual floods was claimed by the desert. There was no transition between luxuriant swamp vegetation and arid sterility. The newcomers slowly learned how to curb and tame that unstoppable flow of life-giving water by building embankments, dams, and locks and by digging canals to irrigate the farthest corners of the valley. These labors lasted hundreds of years until, out of the mud, Egypt was born.

It is hardly surprising that the ancient Egyptian conception of the world—developed by their priests and handed down to us, thanks to the curiosity of the ancient Greeks—saw water as the fount of all creation, the primary element of the universe, and that this fecund mother of all nature was called, like the river itself, the creator of the country, Hepr or Hapi.

THE RIVER OF THE PHARAOHS

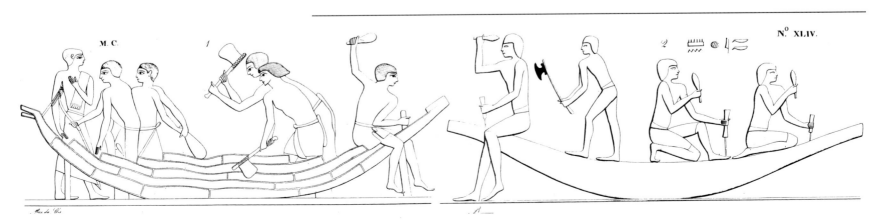

M. C.

14 top *The rudder of a royal boat is decorated with the sacred serpent, the naja, with a red crown on its head, a symbol of royalty. The eyes on the blade, on the other hand, are a propitiatory symbol intended to ward off ill fortune and can still be found painted on the boats of fishermen throughout the Mediterranean.* (Ippolito Rosellini, *I Monumenti dell'Egitto e della Nubia*, Pisa, 1832)

The origin of the word *Neilos* is uncertain. It was adopted from the Greek, with slight modifications, by every European language. It may have derived from the Egyptian *Neialu* or *Neilu*, names given to the branches of the river that separated to form the Delta.

The role of this river in everyday Egyptian life was too important for it not to have been deified and personified ever since the earliest of times. It was, in fact, represented as a man with regular facial features and a strong, slightly plump body symbolizing prosperity, wealth, and generosity. The figure had sagging female breasts in recognition of its power to produce nourishment. Its head was crowned with a wreath of water plants, and it held out either a frog or jars of delicacies and trays of flowers, fruit, geese, sheaves of grain, or fish. This was Hapi, the father of all gods who made

food sprout from the earth and flooded Egypt with his gifts. He gave life, banished poverty, and filled the granaries to bursting point.

Like the country itself, divided into Upper and Lower Egypt, the Nile was divided into Hap Reset, the southern section, and Hap Mehet, the northern section. The former, lined with papyrus, was a reddish color, while the latter, fringed with lilies, was a greenish blue like the river before and after a flood. The two Hapis were mirrored by two goddesses, Mirit Qimait and Mirit Mehet, personifying the two Egyptian regions. They were always depicted standing with their arms raised as if they were begging God for the water necessary to fertilize them.

The festivities celebrated in honor of the Nile were, of course, of fundamental importance in the Egyptian calendar, to

14 center *Two sailing vessels with a large central cabin and smaller ones at the bows decorated with royal symbols. The rudders feature crowned heads below which wave ostrich feathers.*

14 bottom *A group of carpenters building two boats of different types.*

15 *A royal sailing vessel decorated with horns at the prow and stern. The pharaoh's throne is located amidships with a kneeling servant behind it holding the royal scepter. The rudders are decorated with heads of the sun god, Ra.*

15

(I. Rosellini, *I Monumenti dell'Egitto e della Nubia*)

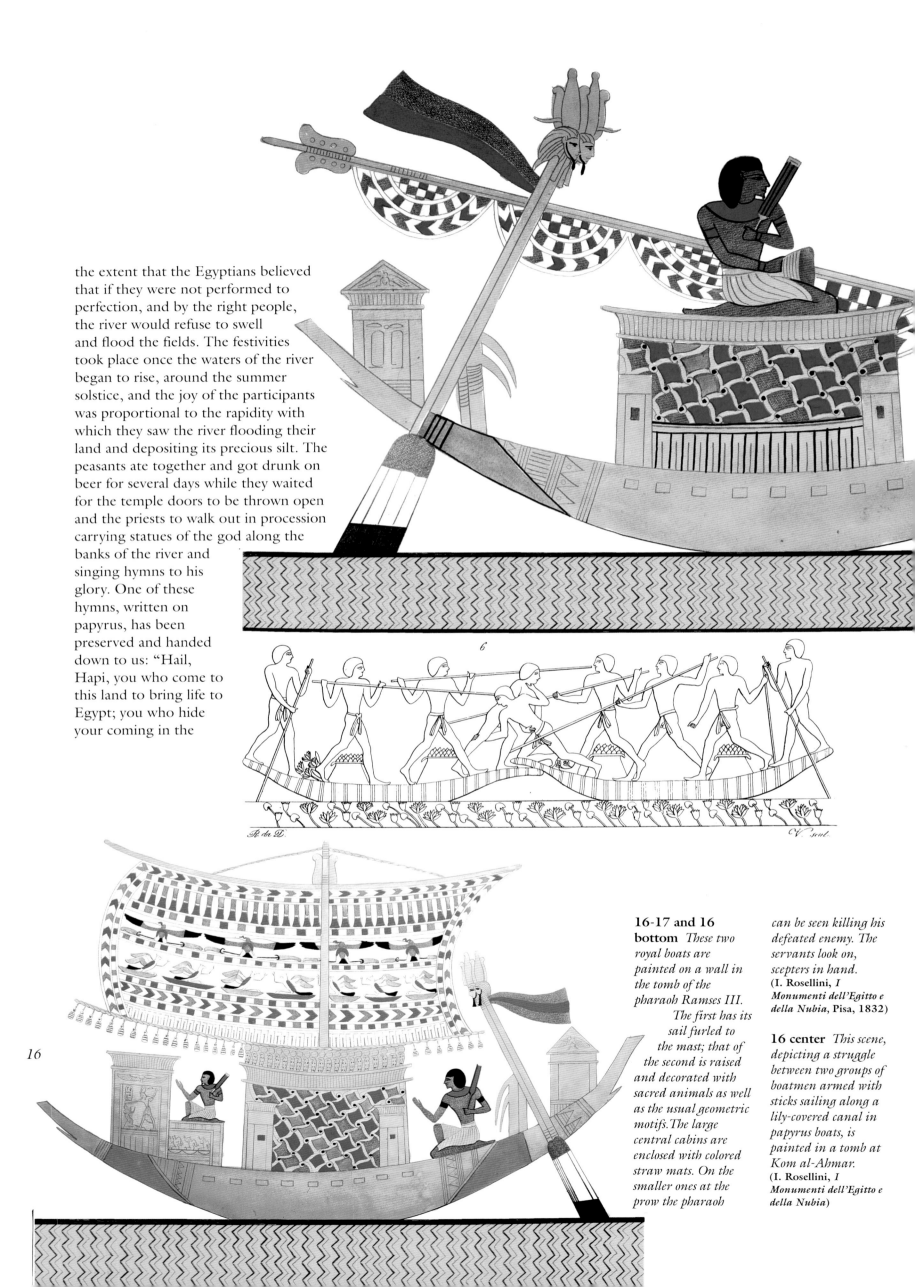

the extent that the Egyptians believed that if they were not performed to perfection, and by the right people, the river would refuse to swell and flood the fields. The festivities took place once the waters of the river began to rise, around the summer solstice, and the joy of the participants was proportional to the rapidity with which they saw the river flooding their land and depositing its precious silt. The peasants ate together and got drunk on beer for several days while they waited for the temple doors to be thrown open and the priests to walk out in procession carrying statues of the god along the banks of the river and singing hymns to his glory. One of these hymns, written on papyrus, has been preserved and handed down to us: "Hail, Hapi, you who come to this land to bring life to Egypt; you who hide your coming in the

16

16-17 and 16 bottom *These two royal boats are painted on a wall in the tomb of the pharaoh Ramses III. The first has its sail furled to the mast; that of the second is raised and decorated with sacred animals as well as the usual geometric motifs. The large central cabins are enclosed with colored straw mats. On the smaller ones at the prow the pharaoh* *can be seen killing his defeated enemy. The servants look on, scepters in hand.* (**I. Rosellini,** *I Monumenti dell'Egitto e della Nubia*, Pisa, 1832)

16 center *This scene, depicting a struggle between two groups of boatmen armed with sticks sailing along a lily-covered canal in papyrus boats, is painted in a tomb at Kom al-Ahmar.* (**I. Rosellini,** *I Monumenti dell'Egitto e della Nubia*)

17 *Both of these scenes, painted in a tomb at Beni Hasan, depict the transportation of a harem of women on boats rowed by slaves. The figures painted in ochre are the eunuchs guarding the harem. In both cases the boatmen at the bow are holding ropes in preparation for mooring. On the boat below, the owner can be seen sitting alone in a small cabin at the prow.*
(I. Rosellini, *I Monumenti dell'Egitto e della Nubia*)

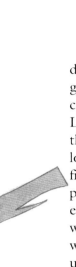

darkness of the very day in which you are greeted, wave that washes over the land created by Ra to revive the thirsty. . . . Lord of the fish, ever since you flowed through the cataracts, the birds have no longer fed on the fields. . . . When your fingers rest, we mortals wallow in abject poverty, the animals go insane, and the entire land is gripped by suffering. But when you hear the prayers of men the whole world comes alive with an unknown vigor, stomachs rejoice, mouths fill with youthful laughter, and teeth prepare to chew food."

The holiness of the river even extended to all the creatures that lived in, on, or about the river, from birds to crocodiles to fish and especially eels. When the body of a man was found floating in the river, whether drowned or torn apart by crocodiles, it was the responsibility of the city in the region in which he was found to take care of his embalming and burial in consecrated ground. No one was allowed to touch the corpse, not even relatives, only the priests of the Nile god, as if the victim of the river had, in dying, taken on a supernatural quality.

As Egypt gradually expanded southward, the location imagined to be the source of the Nile was placed farther away and was eventually believed to be situated on the very edge of the world which, for the Egyptians, meant in the circular range of mountains that enclosed the universe, from where it would cascade down, its furious current dragging the boat of the sun with it. One tradition, however, believed that the source—a bottomless chasm from which the impetuous river gushed forth—was located at present-day Aswan, near the First Cataract. This theory clearly fell out of favor as the regions comprising the

present-day Sudan were explored. It is probable that in a country where life itself depended on the regular flooding of the Nile, many brilliant minds wondered about the origins of this river and why its flow was so different from any other. There is no proof of this, however.

Fortunately, five centuries before the Christian era, Egypt was visited by a Greek traveler, Herodotus, whose appetite for knowledge was equaled only by his critical faculties. Herodotus was born in Halicarnassus between 490 and 480 B.C. and died in Athens around 424 B.C. The stories he wrote are a fascinating encyclopedic compendium of the knowledge and mentality of his time.

Herodotus was attracted by the Egyptian priests' reputation for learning and asked many questions about the floods, receiving, as far as we know, no particular explanation, perhaps because the natives considered this flooding such a natural event, like the sun rising each morning, that it just happened, and that was all there was to say. Herodotus then considered three hypotheses proposed by the Greeks and immediately confuted them. The first stated that the constant trade winds which blew southward during the summer prevented the river from flowing to the sea. The second said that the Nile had its source in the ocean surrounding the land, then rose, like the ocean, in a kind of fluvial tide during the summer. The third claimed that the river rose thanks to the snow melting near its source in the mountains in summer. This third idea outraged Herodotus, who considered it absurd "because the river comes from warmer lands" where it neither snowed nor rained. It was, of course, the correct answer and had been suggested by one of Herodotus' contemporaries, the philosopher and scientist Anaxagoras. This, like many other Greek intuitions, was a solution ahead of its time.

18-19 *The fertile silt deposited by the Nile floods being plowed with long-horned oxen in front of which a calf is romping. A second farmer follows the plow, sowing seeds in the furrows.* (I. Rosellini, *I Monumenti dell'Egitto e della Nubia*, Pisa, 1832)

18 bottom left
These lotus flowers, are typical of the Nile vegetation.

18 bottom right
A farmer drawing water from the Nile to irrigate a garden, symbolized by three plants: a sycamore, a tamarisk, and a doum palm.

19 top right *A date palm and a number of fruits that are difficult to identify.*

19 bottom *Two farmers carrying water in jars slung from a yoke to irrigate a kitchen garden. On the right a gardener is cleaning freshly picked garlic.*

19

(I. Rosellini, I Monumenti dell'Egitto e della Nubia)

20-21 *Birds of all kinds, domestic and wild, inhabited the banks and the islands of the great river, and in particular the delta with its rich swamp vegetation. The illustrations on these pages, reproducing details of the murals in the Beni Hasan tombs, show a wide variety. On the left from top to bottom: a heron, a kingfisher, a goose, an egret perching on a flower, and a duck. On the right: a shrike, a hoopoe in the branches of a mimosa, a duck, and an ibis between two geese.* (I. Rosellini, *I Monumenti dell'Egitto e della Nubia*, Pisa, 1832)

21

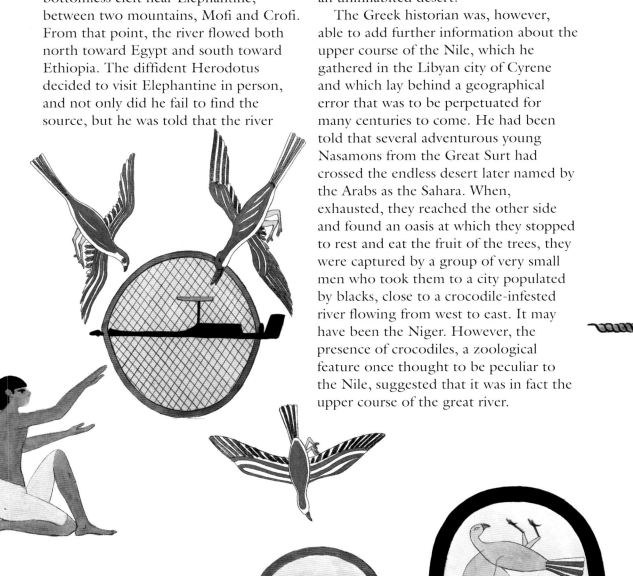

As far as the source of the Nile is concerned, Herodotus was no more successful; he was in fact teased by one of the scribes from the Temple of Saïs, who, reviving the ancient legend, confidently declared that the river had its origin in a bottomless cleft near Elephantine, between two mountains, Mofi and Crofi. From that point, the river flowed both north toward Egypt and south toward Ethiopia. The diffident Herodotus decided to visit Elephantine in person, and not only did he fail to find the source, but he was told that the river extended to the south for many days' walk, at least a hundred, passing close to a great city called Meroë. After that who knew where it went, as "Nobody has precise information as to the rest of the river as, due to the great heat, the land is an uninhabited desert."

The Greek historian was, however, able to add further information about the upper course of the Nile, which he gathered in the Libyan city of Cyrene and which lay behind a geographical error that was to be perpetuated for many centuries to come. He had been told that several adventurous young Nasamons from the Great Surt had crossed the endless desert later named by the Arabs as the Sahara. When, exhausted, they reached the other side and found an oasis at which they stopped to rest and eat the fruit of the trees, they were captured by a group of very small men who took them to a city populated by blacks, close to a crocodile-infested river flowing from west to east. It may have been the Niger. However, the presence of crocodiles, a zoological feature once thought to be peculiar to the Nile, suggested that it was in fact the upper course of the great river.

22 *These scenes illustrate the hunting of birds with various types of traps. At the bottom the hunters are returning home in a papyrus boat, some of their prey clutched in their hands and others closed in a cage.* (I. Rosellini, *I Monumenti dell'Egitto e della Nubia*, Pisa, 1832)

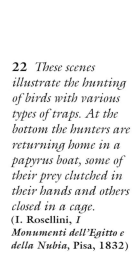

22-23 *In this painting from a Beni Hasan tomb two large hexagonal nets can be seen in which numerous ducks have been caught. The hunter has already removed one and is preparing to take another.*

23 bottom *This illustration depicts a nycticorax, an ibis, and an oyster catcher.*

(I. Rosellini, *I Monumenti dell'Egitto e della Nubia*)

23

24 top *Fishing was naturally one of the most important and profitable activities of the Nile dwellers. Top left, a group of four fishermen landing a net bursting with fish with the help of a fifth man in the water. On the right, fishing with a line, with and without a rod.* (I. Rosellini, *I Monumenti dell'Egitto e della Nubia*, Pisa, 1832)

24-25 *A man standing in a papyrus boat with two fish on his two-pointed spear.*

24 bottom *Among the most typical fish of the river were the* Lates niloticus *and the* Perca fluviatilis. (I. Rosellini, *I Monumenti dell'Egitto e della Nubia*)

25 top left *A fisherman carrying, perhaps to market, two creels full of fish.*

25 top right *This scene illustrates a moment during a crocodile hunt, with the animal being harpooned by a man in a papyrus boat controlled by two other men.*

25 bottom *A fisherman sitting near a papyrus plant begins to clean a fish.*

(I. Rosellini, *I Monumenti dell'Egitto e della Nubia*)

26-27 *In this painting from the ruined temple of Ramses II at Abu Simbel the pharaoh is sacrificing prisoners of various races— Libyans, Ethiopians, and Syrians—to the god Amon-Ra who is* *offering him his typical Egyptian sword. Ramses II grasps the bow and pulls back the victim's hair with the same hand while with the other he brandishes the sacrificial knife. The pharaoh is* *wearing a decorated breastplate and the double crown symbolizing his power over both Upper and Lower Egypt.* *(I. Rosellini,* I Monumenti dell'Egitto e della Nubia, *Pisa, 1832)*

27 top *A group of Nubians with Negroid features and bobbed hair dressed in long skirts and richly decorated cross belts.* *(I. Rosellini,* I Monumenti dell'Egitto e della Nubia)

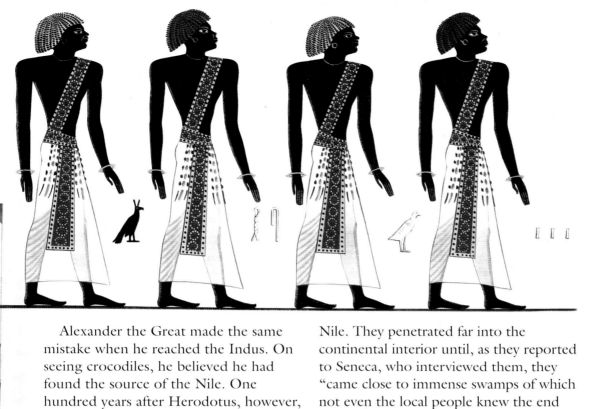

27 bottom *Nubians wearing leopard skins and tied to one another with cords around their necks. They are prisoners captured in battle by Pharaoh Ramses II and precede his carriage in a triumphal procession.*

27 right *This richly dressed Nubian was probably a chief or a wealthy merchant.*

Alexander the Great made the same mistake when he reached the Indus. On seeing crocodiles, he believed he had found the source of the Nile. One hundred years after Herodotus, however, Aristotle had already located the source of the Nile rather more precisely in an Argiros Oros, or Silvery Mountain, surrounded by great lakes in the heart of Africa, in an area inhabited by Pygmies, who he thought reared miniature horses.

Another century later, the geographer from Cyrene, Eratosthenes, was even more knowledgeable about the upper course of the Nile, which he believed to be composed of two rivers, the Astaboras and the Astapus—possibly the Atbara and the Blue Nile or perhaps the latter and the White Nile, as the Astapus was said to have its source in a lake far to the south. However, he also believed that it would be impossible to reach the source, as it was situated in such a hot, uninhabitable area. Throughout classical geography, not only in relation to the source of the Nile, this blend of invention and truth was commonly applied to the regions bordering the known world.

When Egypt was absorbed by the Roman Empire, the reigning emperor, a keen scholar, decided to make use of his immense power to discover the secret of the great river that now came under his jurisdiction. Nero was not really the wicked monster that history has made him out to be, but rather, as the philosopher Seneca said, "a prince, enthusiastically searching for truth." Two centurions were sent to Egypt to follow the course of the

Nile. They penetrated far into the continental interior until, as they reported to Seneca, who interviewed them, they "came close to immense swamps of which not even the local people knew the end and nobody could even hope to know it one day. So thick and tangled are the plants in the waters that it is impossible to proceed either on foot or by boat as the dense, slimy swamp can support but a single man in a small boat. In that place we saw two rocks from which gushed a great river. Whether this is the source of the Nile or of a tributary, whether it rose at the time, or came to light again after having been accepted by a previous course, do you not think that in any case it rises to the surface from some great under-ground lake?" The two Romans were blocked by the terrible swamps of the Sudd region.

According to Pliny the Elder who, adding a few more details, continued the story, the Roman expedition had military as well as scientific aims: Nero had designs on the Ethiopian kingdom of Axum. Even though on their return to Rome the explorers advised him against it, in A.D. 66 the emperor dispatched troops to Egypt with the intent of conquering that distant country, but the plan was eventually abandoned.

The long period of peace, ensured by the unification under Roman rule of the entire Mediterranean basin and the consequent economic prosperity also favored by the construction of a vast network of roads and safe sailing routes, saw the rise of a phenomenon that was not to be repeated until the modern era: traveling for pleasure. The great tourist attraction of the ancient world was the Nile Valley. It offered exotic landscapes, exotic monuments, exotic luxuries, and, above all, excellent communications.

(I. Rosellini, *I Monumenti dell'Egitto e della Nubia*)

28

28-29 *A sailing boat towing a barge on which an embalmed corpse lies surrounded by a number of priests.* (I. Rosellini, *I Monumenti dell'Egitto e della Nubia*, Pisa, 1832)

28 bottom left *The god Sobek could be portrayed either as a crocodile or as a man with a crocodile's head and was often depicted sitting on a throne. The cult of this god reached its apex during the twelfth and thirteenth dynasties.* (I. Rosellini, *I Monumenti dell'Egitto e della Nubia*)

From Rome the Nile was easily reached in comfort aboard the large grain-carrying vessel that sailed regularly between the ports of Ostia and Alexandria. On arriving in Egypt, the tourists would continue by boat, as everything of interest was to be found along the banks of the Nile. Even before landing in Egypt, travelers would encounter one of the Seven Wonders of the World: the tip of the Pharos of Alexandria could be seen from a distance of about 50 kilometers from the coast. This huge lighthouse was erected in front of the port on the island of Pharos (now a peninsula), the name being universally adopted to describe this type of construction.

28 top left and 29 bottom right *These two images are taken from scenes depicting funeral processions on the Nile. They depict the boats of the hired mourners who opened the funeral by chanting laments to which the onlookers on the banks and the friends and relatives of the dead on the other boats responded. The funeral barges were built in imitation of the vessel used for the funeral rites of the god Osiris, a model of which was conserved in the city of Abydos. They were long, slim, and light boats decorated at the extremities with metal lotus flowers. The procession was completed by smaller boats carrying the offerings and furnishings for the tomb.* (I. Rosellini, *I Monumenti dell'Egitto e della Nubia*)

As far as entertainment was concerned, Alexandria was both the Marseilles and the Hamburg of the ancient world, but there was also something of Vienna in its makeup. The inhabitants of the city, from the most uncouth fishermen to the most refined intellectuals, were music connoisseurs. In fact, during the famous lyre concerts, even the humblest members of the audience would be outraged by the slightest mistake and would protest furiously. The tourists mobbed the brothels, the markets, Alexander's tomb, and the city's many temples before leaving the riotously cosmopolitan city heading for the "real" Egypt farther south along the Nile, cities like Heliopolis and Memphis, ghost towns even in Roman times. At Memphis the travelers, after having adequately tipped the priest on duty, would be allowed to gaze through a small window at the sacred bull Apis in its holy stall. Memphis was also the point of departure if one was thinking of visiting another of the Seven Wonders, the Pyramids, then still covered with the original smooth facing decorated with hieroglyphics (today it can be seen only at the tip of the Chephren Pyramid).

Another great attraction was the so-called Labyrinth, an enormous tomb and temple complex near Lake Meride. Not far away was Crocodilopolis where tourists never failed to pay homage to the sacred crocodiles with tributes of roast meat and sweet cakes. The priests would call this reptile god, open its jaws, throw in the offering, and then wash it down with honey wine.

Continuing southward up the river, one reached Thebes, where still today one can visit the tombs in the Valley of the Kings. Thebes became the capital of Egyptian tourism in 27 B.C. when the so-called statue of Memnon (it was actually of Amenophis III), which had been cracked by an earthquake, started speaking. Ever since the upper section had collapsed, a hissing sound—like that of a stringed instrument—could be heard emerging from its remains at dawn. The firm belief that Memnon was speaking to his mother gradually spread. Crowds flocked to see and hear the statue, much to the delight of the local priests, guides, innkeepers, boat owners, and merchants. Three centuries later, however, Emperor Septimius Severus ill-advisedly ordered that the statue be restored, putting an end to a phenomenon probably caused by the rapid increase in temperature as the sun rose and by the expansion of the air in the cracks in the broken surface.

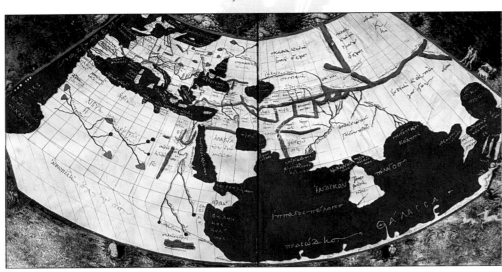

T he geographical knowledge of the classical world was organized and, so to speak, crystallized by Claudius Ptolemy, the Egyptian astronomer, geographer, and mathematician who lived in Alexandria from A.D. 130 to 184. The Egyptian capital's celebrated library, a monument to ancient knowledge, contained all the works of his predecessors, a resource Ptolemy used to compile a manual venerated as a geographical bible up to the threshold of the modern era when the great Portuguese and Spanish discoveries enormously expanded European horizons.

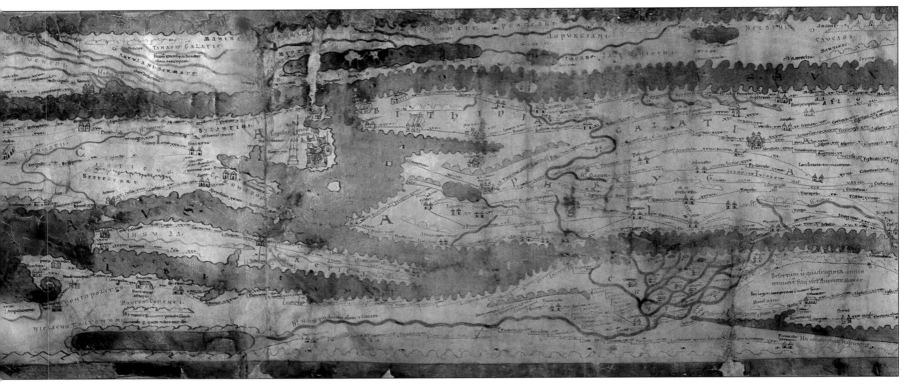

30 top *The world according to Ptolemy in a map drawn in the 12th or 13th century. The course of the Nile is fairly precisely plotted in the north but becomes very diagrammatic to the south while still retaining a semblance of accuracy. To the left of the Nile one can see the basin of the imaginary "Western Nile," probably the* *fruit of confused information and misunderstandings regarding the Niger, the Senegal, and Lake Chad.*

30 bottom *The Peutingerian table, a medieval copy of a Roman itinerary map, shows the Nile Delta in its lower section and the course of the river issuing from a great lake.*

THE IMAGINARY MAPS: NILE CARTOGRAPHY FROM PTOLEMY TO THE EIGHTEENTH CENTURY

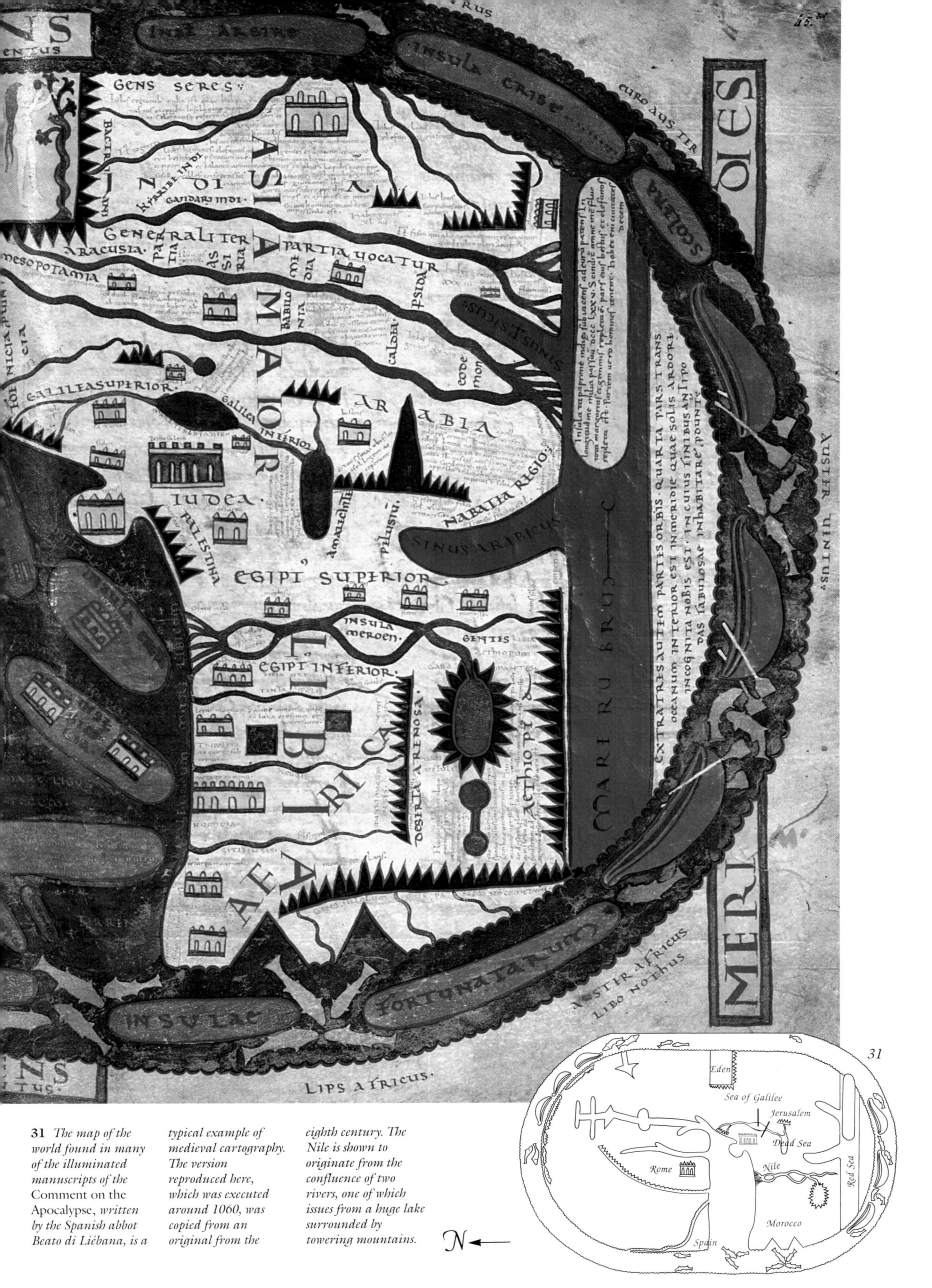

31

31 The map of the world found in many of the illuminated manuscripts of the Comment on the Apocalypse, *written by the Spanish abbot Beato di Liébana, is a* typical example of medieval cartography. The version reproduced here, which was executed around 1060, was copied from an original from the eighth century. The Nile is shown to originate from the confluence of two rivers, one of which issues from a huge lake surrounded by towering mountains.

32 *South is at the top of this map of the world drawn up in the twelfth century to illustrate the work of the Arab geographer al-Idrisi. It shows the White Nile and the Blue Nile streaming down from the Mountains of the Moon with one of the rivers flowing westward into the Atlantic.*

In his *Geography* Ptolemy was the first to reconstruct the entire course of the Nile, definitely rejecting the hypothesis of its rising in the west—Strabo (circa 60 B.C.–A.D. 20) had suggested that the great river originated in ancient Mauretania, in present-day Morocco—and correctly locating its sources in the Mountains of the Moon, so-called because the glare of their snow-capped peaks resembled or reflected nocturnal moonlight, in the Great Lakes region of central East Africa.

confirmed and redrawn as the first explorations of the region were completed. Up until the late fifteenth century, Europeans knew virtually nothing of East Africa—locating in the region the kingdom (perhaps a transfiguration of Ethiopia) of the legendary Christian monarch Prester John—about which only Marco Polo supplied even the vaguest information.

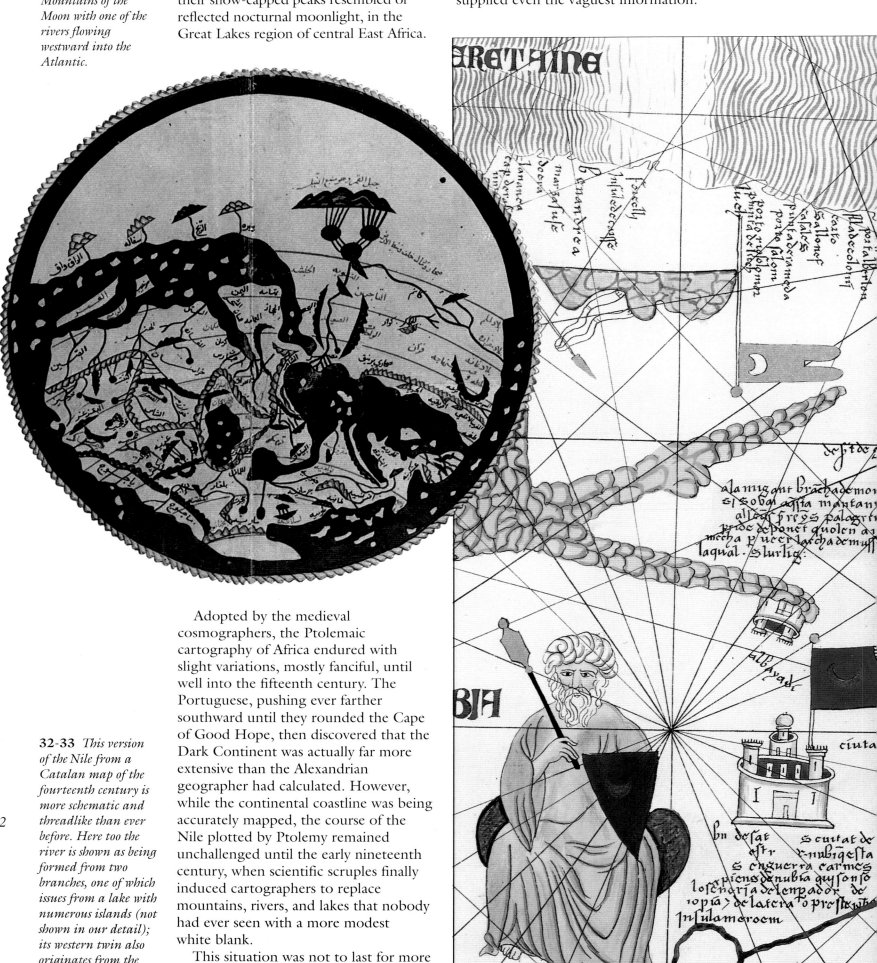

32-33 *This version of the Nile from a Catalan map of the fourteenth century is more schematic and threadlike than ever before. Here too the river is shown as being formed from two branches, one of which issues from a lake with numerous islands (not shown in our detail); its western twin also originates from the lake and flows into the Atlantic.*

Adopted by the medieval cosmographers, the Ptolemaic cartography of Africa endured with slight variations, mostly fanciful, until well into the fifteenth century. The Portuguese, pushing ever farther southward until they rounded the Cape of Good Hope, then discovered that the Dark Continent was actually far more extensive than the Alexandrian geographer had calculated. However, while the continental coastline was being accurately mapped, the course of the Nile plotted by Ptolemy remained unchallenged until the early nineteenth century, when scientific scruples finally induced cartographers to replace mountains, rivers, and lakes that nobody had ever seen with a more modest white blank.

This situation was not to last for more than half a century, for many of Ptolemy's geographical features were

33 right In this map of the world drawn on a psalter in England in the thirteenth century, the Nile appears on the right with its seven mouths greatly enlarged and with another river that branches off midway along its course and also flows, distant and isolated, into the Mediterranean. Above, to the right of the Red Sea, can be seen the mountain from which the river rises.

On the other hand, the Arabs, who dominated the African coastline as far south as present-day Mozambique, were far better informed about the continental interior, as they had established profitable trading relationships. One of the greatest Arab geographers, al-Masudi, born in Baghdad and a resident of Cairo during the tenth century, a highly inquisitive and indefatigable traveler, wrote a book entitled *Meadows of Gold and Mines of Gems* (alluding to gems of knowledge rather than jewels), in which he provided reasonably precise information relating to the sources of the Nile. The river, he said, was the fruit of twelve streams flowing down the slopes of Mount Qamar and converging into two lakes drained by a single river. Qamar, which in Arabic means "moon" would appear to correspond to the Ruwenzori Mountains from the slopes of which descend sixty-odd streams that flow into Lake Edward; its emissary, the Semliki, ends in Lake Albert, one of the principal Nile reservoirs. "Those mountains," wrote another Arab traveler of the time, "are known as the Mountains of the Moon thanks to their eye-catching splendor. It is said that someone has

climbed them and looked out onto the far side, seeing a turbulent black sea crossed by a light current that penetrates the northern flank of the mountain, passing close to the tomb of the prophet Enoch."

A blend of the probable and the imaginary is also to be found in the description of Nile hydrography written by al-Idrisi who lived at Palermo under King Roger II of Sicily. There he devoted many years to the construction of a great silver globe and the compilation of a geographical

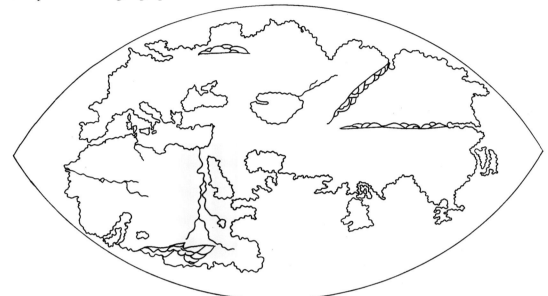

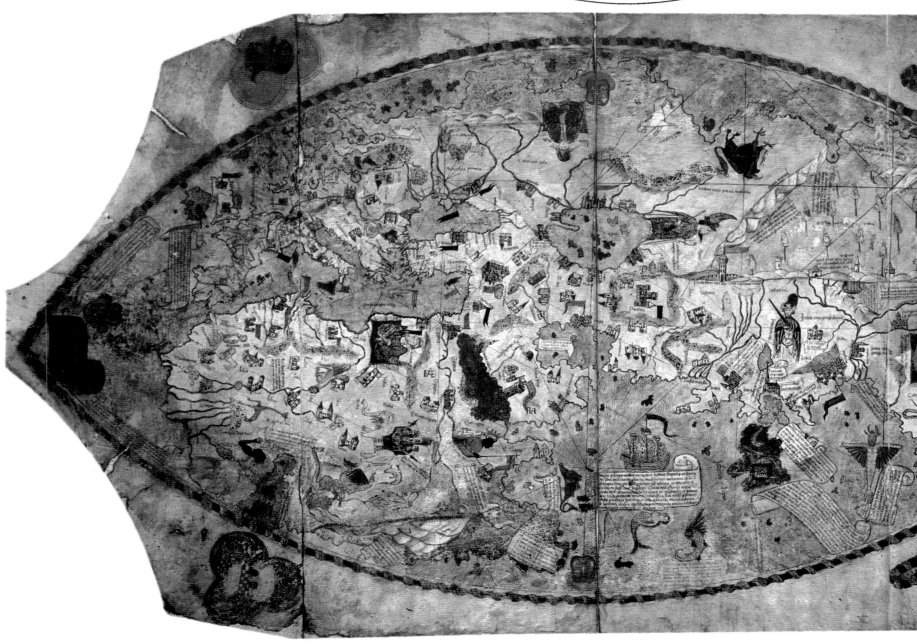

35 *These illustrations show a reproduction of a map of the world conserved in Hereford Cathedral, England, and executed by the scholarly clergyman, Richard of Haldingham, around 1290. The detail below shows the course of the Nile, near which can be seen imaginary fauna: a unicorn, a centaur, and a winged dragon. Walled and turreted cities are scattered all around. The river rises beyond a long chain of mountains through which it appears to flow as if in a tunnel.*

34-35 *White-capped and imposing, the Mountains of the Moon appear as the most important range in the world in this fifteenth-century planisphere. Two great lakes collect the waters of the White Nile, which then flow north toward Egypt, where they are joined by the current of the Blue Nile. Near the sources of the latter is depicted Prester John, the legendary Christian king of an Ethiopia that at times roughly coincided with its true position but which could also extend as far as India in the hazy geographical conceptions of the Middle Ages.*

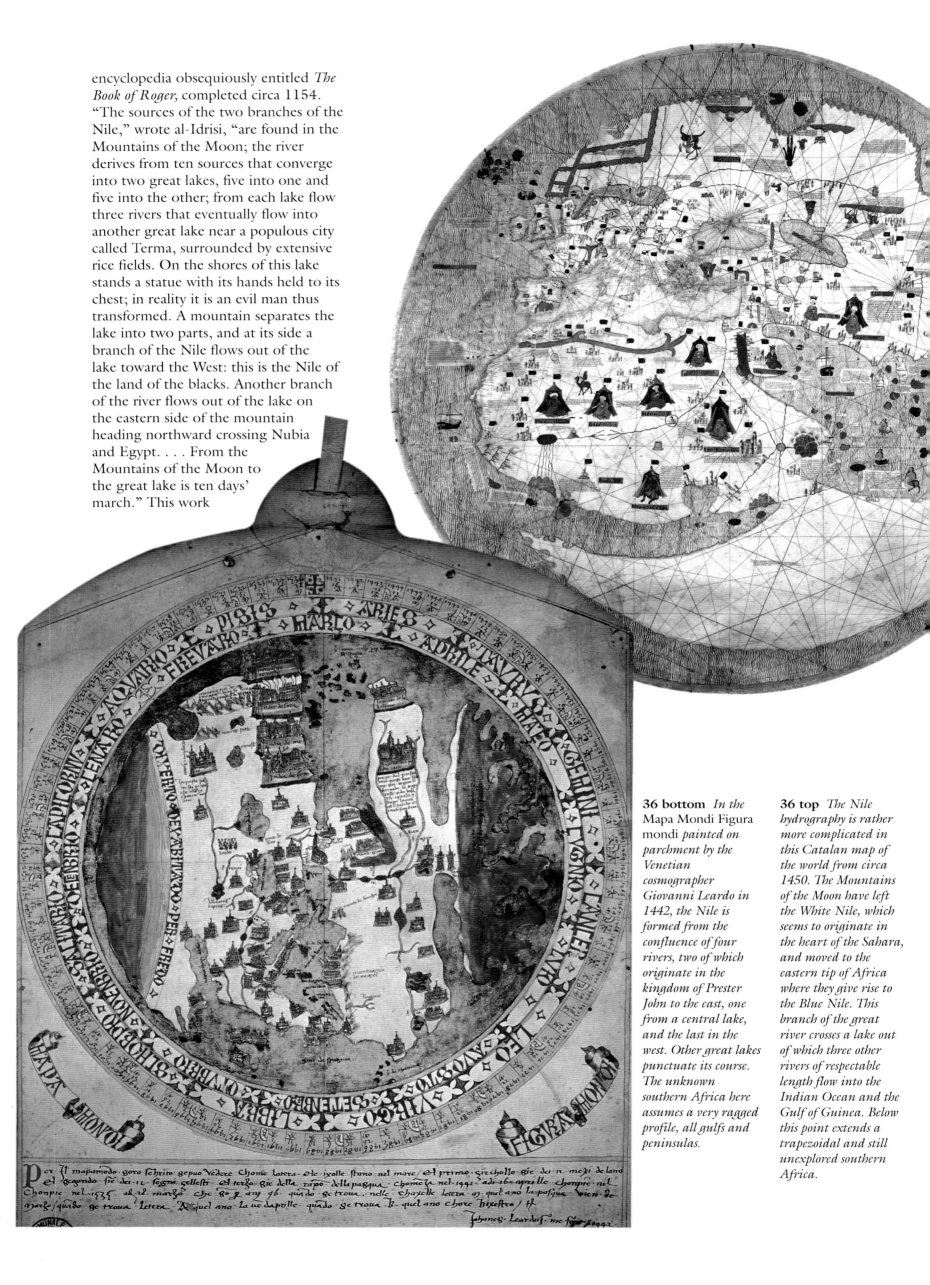

encyclopedia obsequiously entitled *The Book of Roger*, completed circa 1154. "The sources of the two branches of the Nile," wrote al-Idrisi, "are found in the Mountains of the Moon; the river derives from ten sources that converge into two great lakes, five into one and five into the other; from each lake flow three rivers that eventually flow into another great lake near a populous city called Terma, surrounded by extensive rice fields. On the shores of this lake stands a statue with its hands held to its chest; in reality it is an evil man thus transformed. A mountain separates the lake into two parts, and at its side a branch of the Nile flows out of the lake toward the West: this is the Nile of the land of the blacks. Another branch of the river flows out of the lake on the eastern side of the mountain heading northward crossing Nubia and Egypt. . . . From the Mountains of the Moon to the great lake is ten days' march." This work

36 bottom *In the* Mapa Mondi Figura mondi *painted on parchment by the Venetian cosmographer Giovanni Leardo in 1442, the Nile is formed from the confluence of four rivers, two of which originate in the kingdom of Prester John to the east, one from a central lake, and the last in the west. Other great lakes punctuate its course. The unknown southern Africa here assumes a very ragged profile, all gulfs and peninsulas.*

36 top *The Nile hydrography is rather more complicated in this Catalan map of the world from circa 1450. The Mountains of the Moon have left the White Nile, which seems to originate in the heart of the Sahara, and moved to the eastern tip of Africa where they give rise to the Blue Nile. This branch of the great river crosses a lake out of which three other rivers of respectable length flow into the Indian Ocean and the Gulf of Guinea. Below this point extends a trapezoidal and still unexplored southern Africa.*

37 *Among the world maps of the fifteenth century one of the most famous was produced by Fra Mauro for the Serenissima Republic of Venice shortly after 1450. The Nile, highlighted by the box, has a course marked by frequent voluptuous meanderings, as do all the other great rivers with which the author saw fit to irrigate the whole of Africa. Note also the "Western Nile" that runs along the coast of Guinea in two separate channels, issuing from a vast lake.*

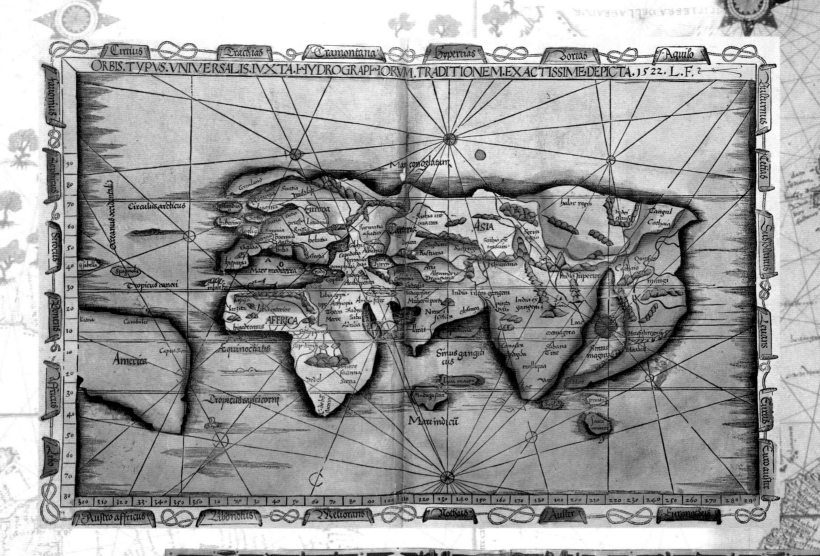

ORBIS.TYPVS.VNIVERSALIS.IVXTA.HYDROGRAPHORVM.TRADITIONEM.EXACTISSIME.DEPICTA.1522.L.F.

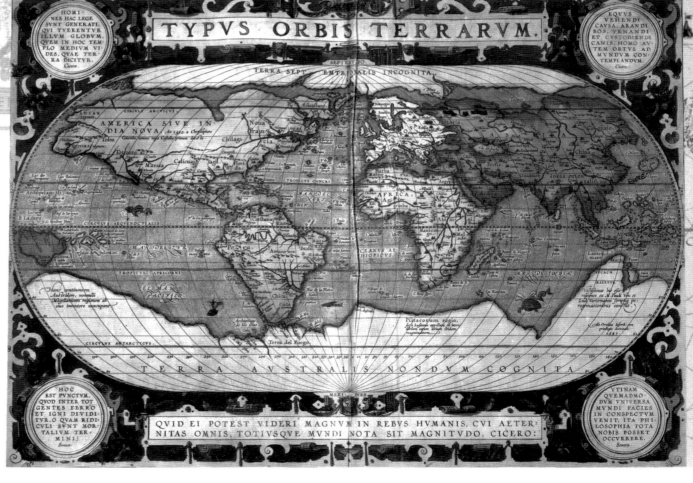

TYPVS ORBIS TERRARVM.

38 top *In this xylograph from 1541 the classic Ptolemaic planisphere has been largely corrected on the basis of the geographical discoveries made in the meantime. However, East Asia is still very far from accurate. The Nile is set in the middle of the African continent, slavishly repeating the schematic medieval model.*

38 bottom *The planisphere of the Theatrum Orbis Terrarum by Ortelius was published in 1592. While the profile of the African and Asian coastlines is much improved, the interiors of the continents are* still very fanciful. The Nile, however, is reasonably accurate, even though the White Nile thrusts diagonally across present-day Zaire.

38-39 *The course of the great river in this attractive map known as the Mappa Salviati after its owner, Cardinal Giovanni Salviati, was more decorative than geographical. The map was* presented by Emperor Charles V and was drawn around 1525 by a Catalan cartographer. The Mountains of the Moon have descended almost as far as the Cape of Good Hope.

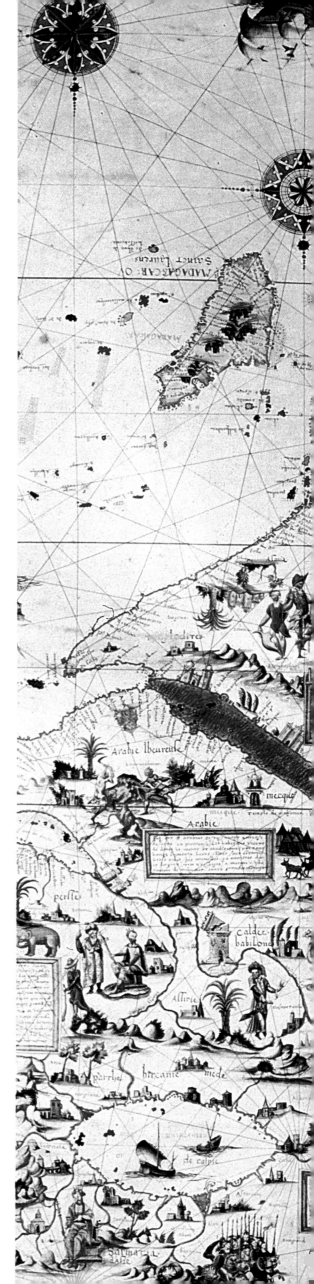

40 *The Atlas completed in 1559 by Diogo Homen, a Portuguese cartographer who emigrated first to London and then to Venice, is one of the most elegant and most accurate of the 16th century. The course of the Nile, which generally follows the Ptolemaic model, is dominated by the dignified figure of Prester John enthroned among the mountains of the Ethiopian plateau.*

40-41 *Pierre Desceliers, the author of this splendid planisphere from circa 1550, has scattered all sorts of finely drawn exotica throughout Africa. The sinuous lines of the Nile originate from an Arcadian mountain range situated far to the south and from other minor sources. Near the Ethiopian source we again find Prester John with a papal tiara on his head.*

marks the appearance, or reappearance, of the idea of two Niles that is found in various maps of Africa from the medieval period onward: this second river flowing to the west from the same mountain as the Nile has been identified as the Senegal, the Niger, and the Congo.

When early in the sixteenth century the ships of Europe began to venture throughout the globe, the Portuguese established a number of settlements on the African coast, staging posts supporting and supplying their ephemeral empire of the Indies. This led to a slow increase in knowledge of the interior, especially of those countries such as Angola and Mozambique in which a number of settlements were concentrated. However, fear of favoring rival colonial powers induced the Portuguese to maintain a veil of secrecy regarding this knowledge and to bury reports regarding their discoveries in the archives at Lisbon, many of them only coming to light centuries later.

42-43 *This map, taken from the* Nova et Accuratissima Totius Terrarum Orbis Tabula, *an atlas by Jan Blaeu (1662) devoted to the "Empire of Abyssinia or of Prester John," in reality covers the whole of central and eastern Africa from the Gulf of Guinea to the Indian Ocean and from the Mediterranean to Mozambique. Rich in affluents, the Nile winds majestically from the great lake "Zembre," collecting the waters of numerous and mainly Ethiopian tributaries.*

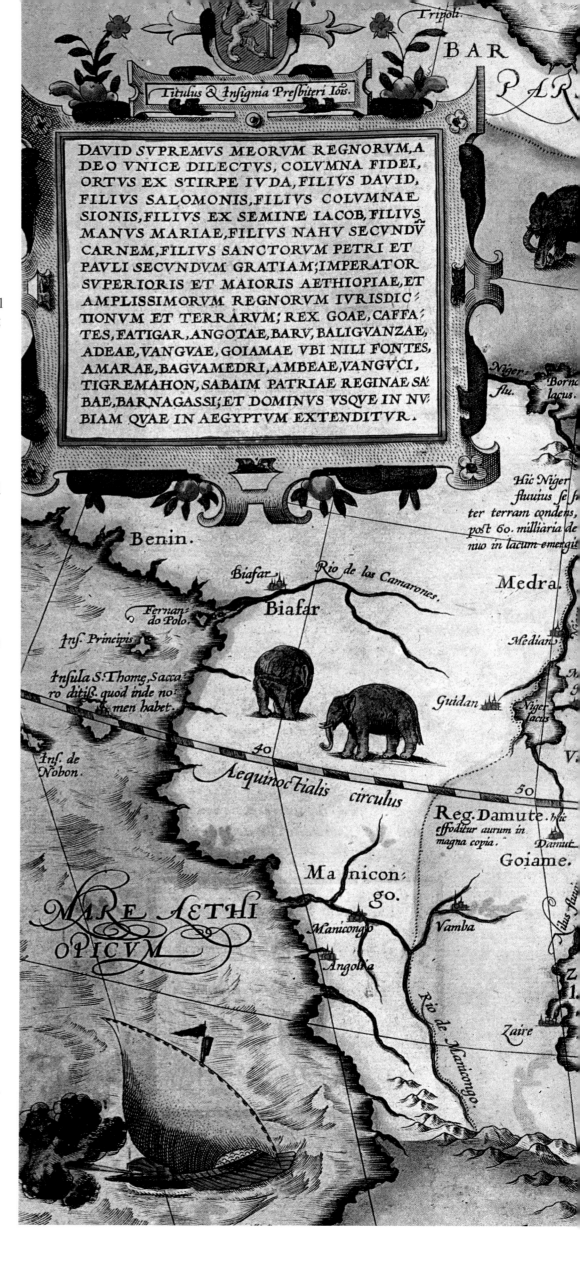

44 *The course of the river in a map of ancient Egypt, the* Theatrum Orbis Terrarum *by Ortelius, 1592. The cartouche, overlooked by an effigy of the Nile, records the contentment of a country "happy with its goods," trusting in the prosperity unfailingly brought by the periodic floods.*

45 top *In Mercator's planisphere of 1587 the Blue Nile, flowing from Abyssinia, and the White Nile, issuing from two great lakes, is joined by a third imaginary river that originates in the hinterland of Tripoli and crosses the Sahara.*

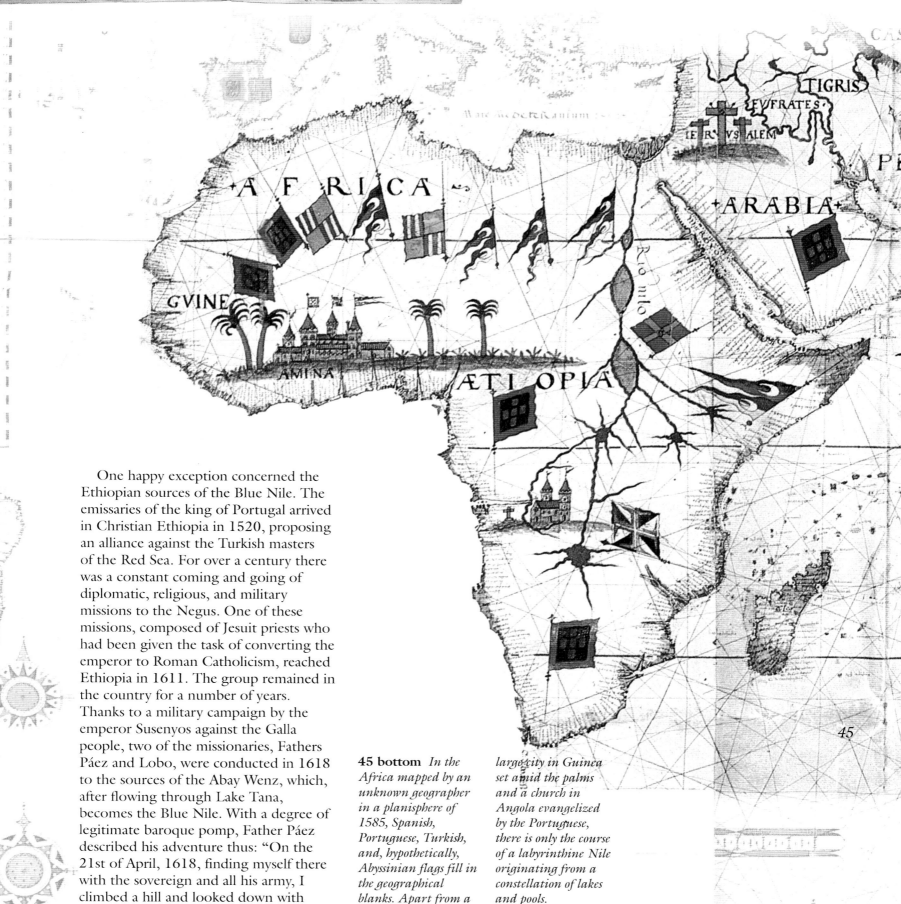

One happy exception concerned the Ethiopian sources of the Blue Nile. The emissaries of the king of Portugal arrived in Christian Ethiopia in 1520, proposing an alliance against the Turkish masters of the Red Sea. For over a century there was a constant coming and going of diplomatic, religious, and military missions to the Negus. One of these missions, composed of Jesuit priests who had been given the task of converting the emperor to Roman Catholicism, reached Ethiopia in 1611. The group remained in the country for a number of years. Thanks to a military campaign by the emperor Susenyos against the Galla people, two of the missionaries, Fathers Páez and Lobo, were conducted in 1618 to the sources of the Abay Wenz, which, after flowing through Lake Tana, becomes the Blue Nile. With a degree of legitimate baroque pomp, Father Páez described his adventure thus: "On the 21st of April, 1618, finding myself there with the sovereign and all his army, I climbed a hill and looked down with

45 bottom *In the Africa mapped by an unknown geographer in a planisphere of 1585, Spanish, Portuguese, Turkish, and, hypothetically, Abyssinian flags fill in the geographical blanks. Apart from a* *large city in Guinea set amid the palms and a church in Angola evangelized by the Portuguese, there is only the course of a labyrinthine Nile originating from a constellation of lakes and pools.*

45

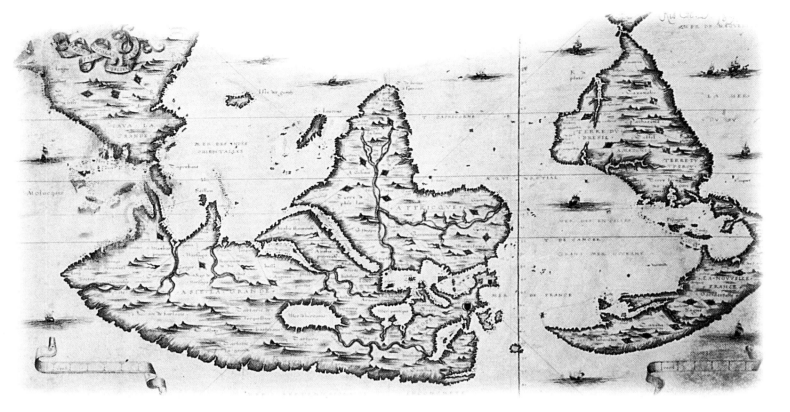

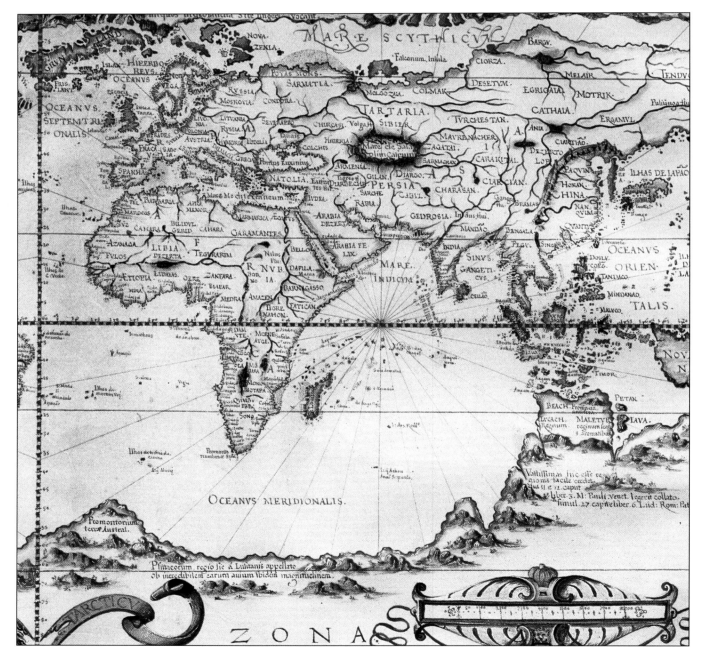

46 top *In the planisphere that the French cartographer Nicolas Desliens executed circa 1566, the Western Nile reappears, an imposing river that rises not from the Mountains of the* Moon but branches out from the true Nile in the region of the present-day Sudan and heads westward, forming large lakes and flowing into the sea in the region of Senegal.

46 bottom *Europe, Asia, and Africa in a map painted on parchment by the Portuguese cartographers Juan Lavanha and Luis Teixeira in 1612. The* Nile once again follows the Ptolemaic model while its western twin here has an independent source in a great lake in Angola.

46-47 *The Universal Hydrographic Map by Jean Guérand, 1634. In addition to showing the Western Nile originating in the region of the Great* Lakes, this map shows the imaginary Saharan affluent carrying copious amounts of water to Egypt.

48-49 *"The New Description of Africa" by the great Dutch cartographer Willem Blaeu, printed in 1617, shows in great detail the western affluent rising in the heart of the Sahara.*

The Nile itself is shown to have its source in the Mountains of the Moon and immediately forms a huge lake called both Zembre and Zaire, the latter being the name by which the natives called the Congo. Another branch of the Nile issues from a second large lake farther to the east, approximately in the position of Lake Tanganyika.

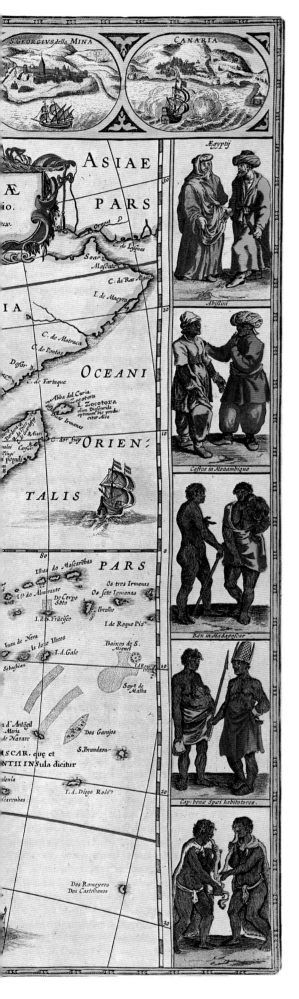

49 top *An elegant scroll embellishes the plate dedicated to Ethiopia in Blaeu's atlas, published in 1635.*

49 bottom *Egypt in Blaeu's atlas of 1662. The confluence of the two watercourses on the extreme right is not between the White and Blue Niles, but between the true Nile and its non-existent Saharan affluent. Moreover, in the Libyan desert toward the bottom, great lakes or swamps appear.*

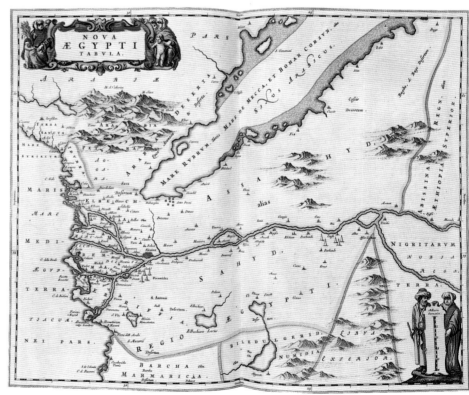

great attention. I saw two round springs, each of a diameter of about four palms, and I admired with immense joy that which neither Cyrus, King of Persia, Cambise, nor Alexander the Great and not even the famous Julius Caesar ever saw." His companion, Padre Lobo, noted the discovery in his *Historia da Ethiopia,* published in 1659, but it was appreciated only in the more erudite circles.

The general public, even the best informed members of it, preferred more spectacular stories. As late as 1704 King Louis XIV of France and his courtiers enjoyed the report delivered by the jeweler Paul Lucas on his return from a journey to the East. Lucas described how he pushed on as far as Aswan, where he saw the Nile cataract plunging down from a towering mountain. He made equally free with other similarly attractive inventions, claiming to have admired the native giants of Thessaly climbing mountains as if they were the rungs of a ladder and seen one-legged people who ran at breakneck speeds. He also related how in an unidentified desert he was pleasantly entertained by the philosopher-hermit Nicolas Flamel and his wife, both still very sprightly in spite of having been dead for three hundred years.

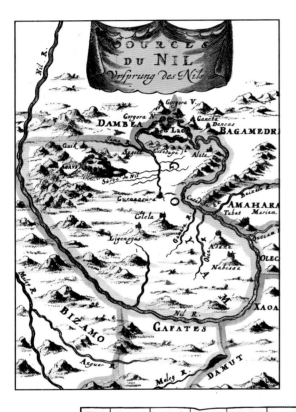

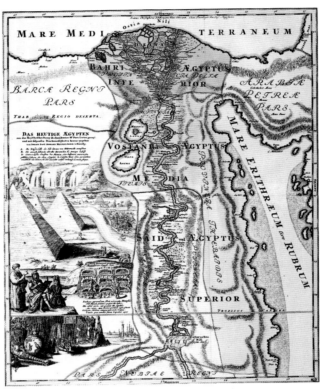

50

50 top left *This first map of the "Sources of the Nile (Blue)" is taken from a 1730 edition of Padre Lobo's book on Abyssinia. Note the broad spiral of the Abay Wenz that enters Lake Tana and completes a broad sweep before heading boldly toward the Sudan in the north.*

50 top right *A map of Egypt by Baptista Homann printed in 1710 in the* Atlas Novum Terrarum Orbis Imperia Regna et Status Exactis Geographie Demestrans. *On the left, the draftsman, here assisted in his work by two Mamelukes, has inserted a cataract, the pyramids, and various Egyptian antiquities.*

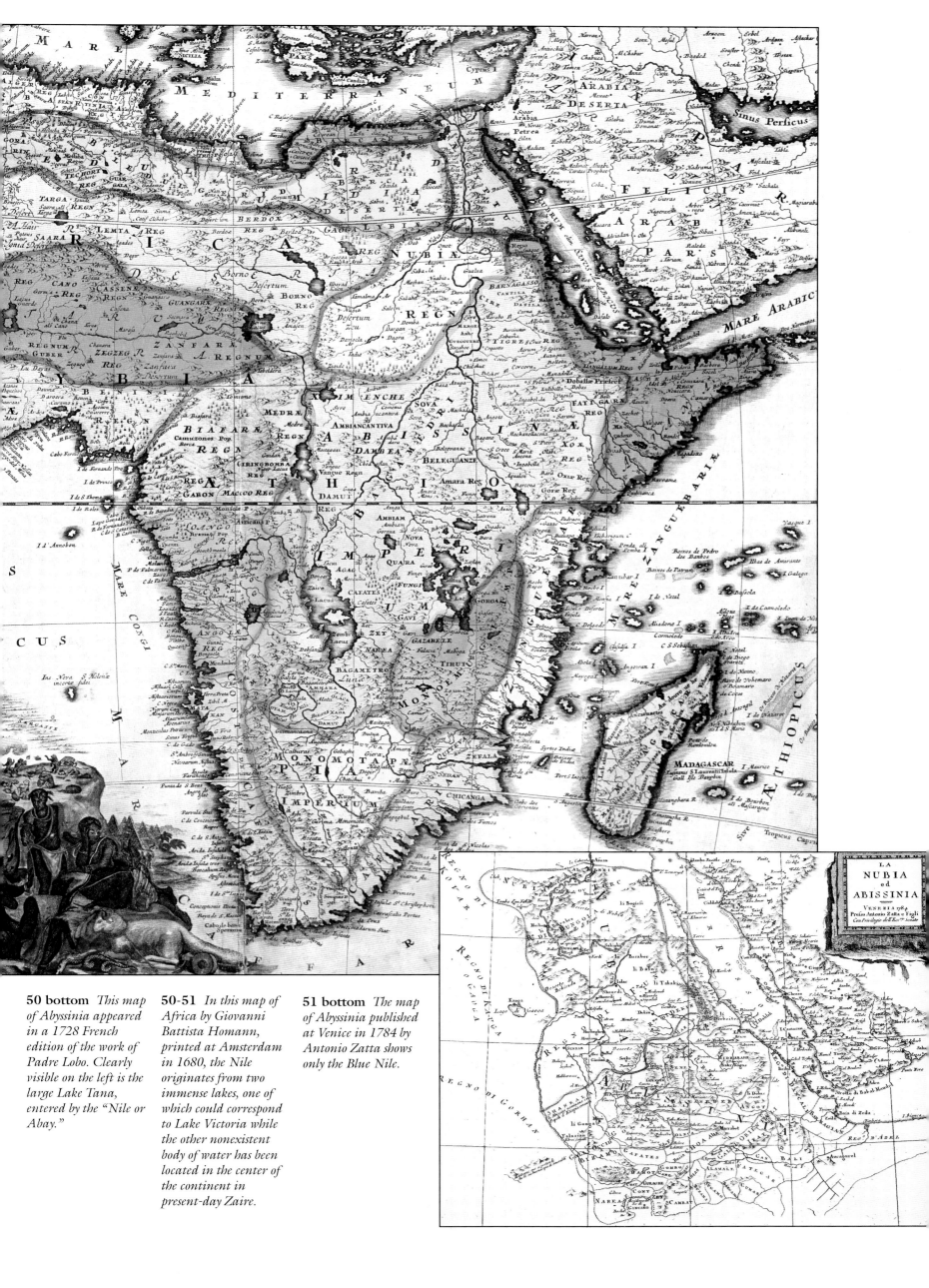

50 bottom *This map of Abyssinia appeared in a 1728 French edition of the work of Padre Lobo. Clearly visible on the left is the large Lake Tana, entered by the "Nile or Abay."*

50-51 *In this map of Africa by Giovanni Battista Homann, printed at Amsterdam in 1680, the Nile originates from two immense lakes, one of which could correspond to Lake Victoria while the other nonexistent body of water has been located in the center of the continent in present-day Zaire.*

51 bottom *The map of Abyssinia published at Venice in 1784 by Antonio Zatta shows only the Blue Nile.*

52-53 In this map of Africa by the French geographer Brué, published at Paris in 1828, the Mountains of the Moon have been located far to the north and are described as "a branch of the northern slopes of the great Ethiopian Alps."

53 top The course of the Nile according to the 1720 map of the Frenchman De Fer. As explained in the scroll at the bottom, this map is based on the discoveries of the Jesuits who visited Abyssinia in the seventeenth century. It indicates the Blue Nile as the principal stream and shows its sources, "Les Yeux du Nil," to the left of Lake Tana. Little importance is given to the White Nile, which is shown here to rise in a small lake in the "Kingdom of the Damot," again in Abyssinia toward the bottom of the map.

53 bottom This Venetian map of 1690 also considers the problem of the sources to have been resolved. It identifies them as those of the Blue Nile, as explained in the baroque scroll under which is a figure representing the Nile among papyri with a crocodile at its feet.

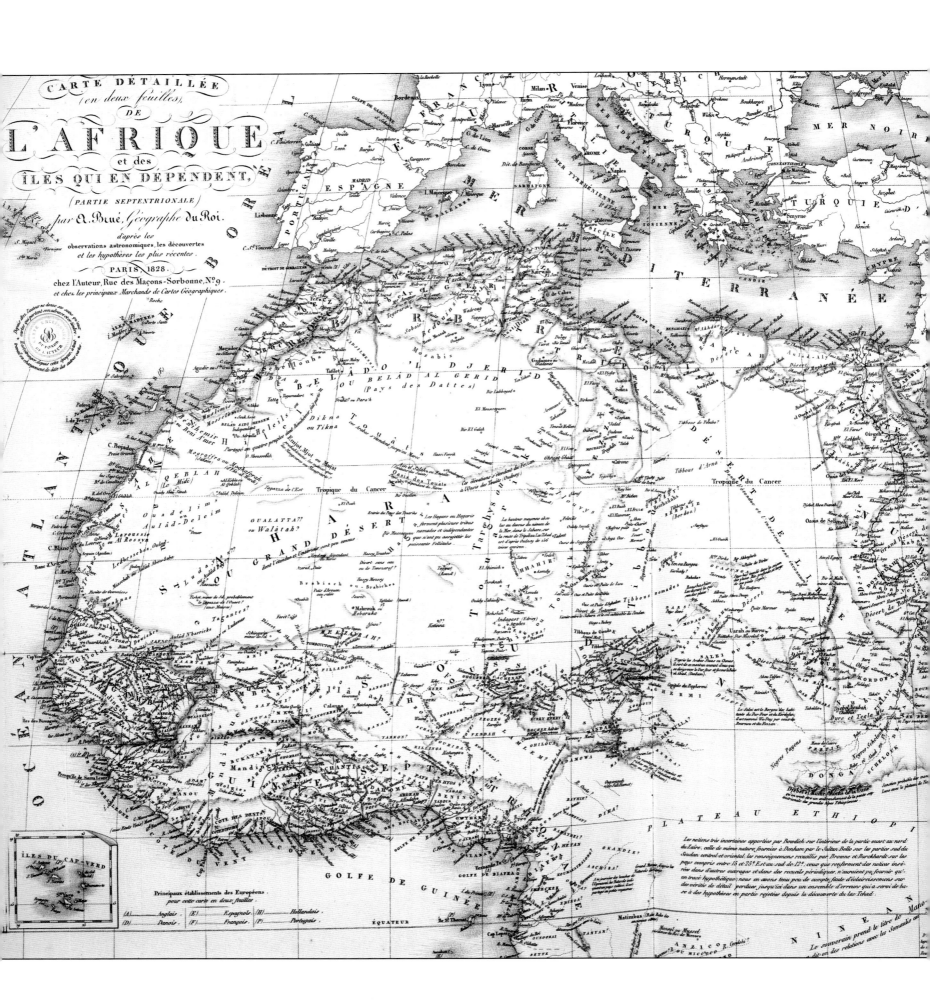

53

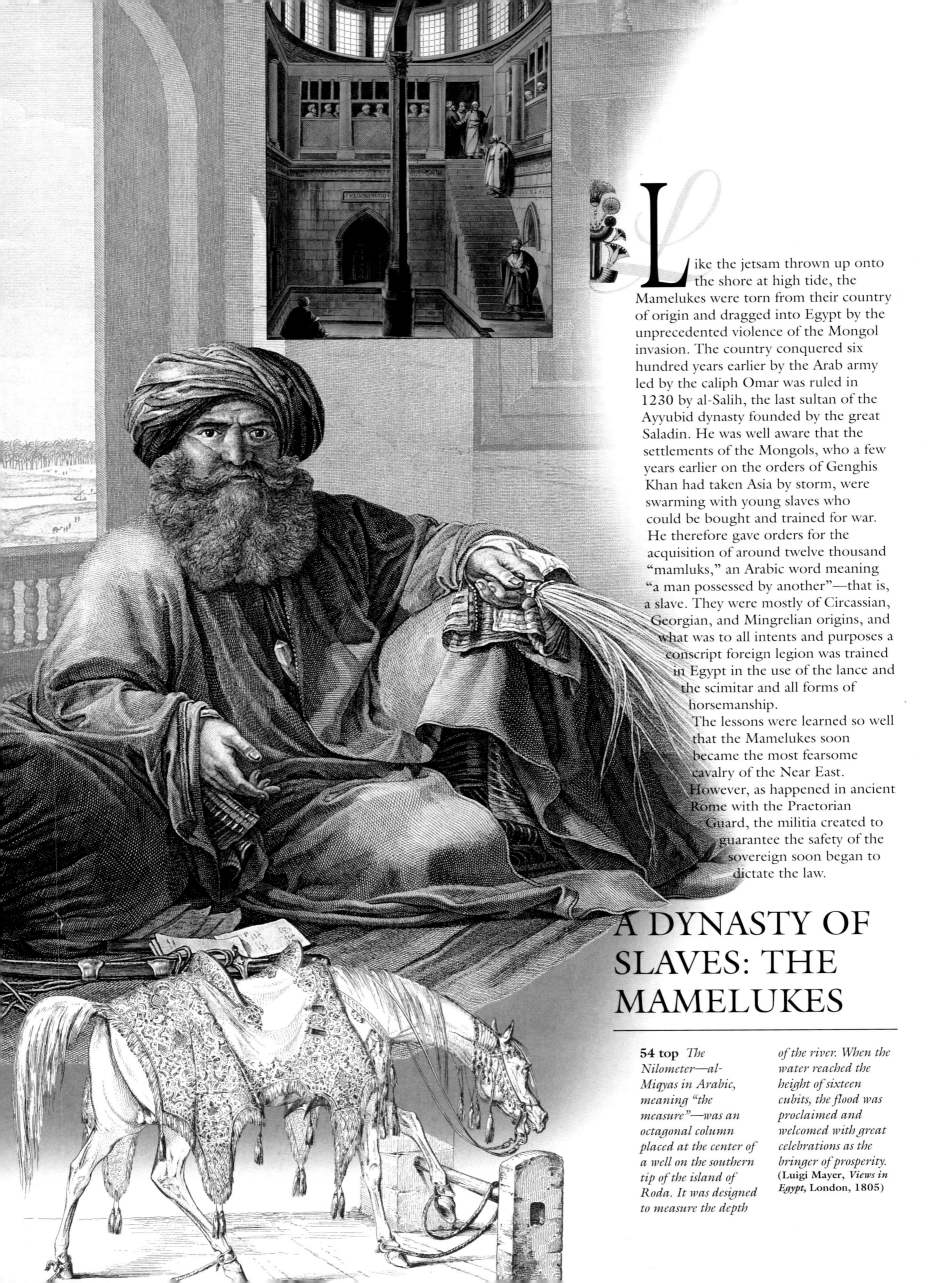

Like the jetsam thrown up onto the shore at high tide, the Mamelukes were torn from their country of origin and dragged into Egypt by the unprecedented violence of the Mongol invasion. The country conquered six hundred years earlier by the Arab army led by the caliph Omar was ruled in 1230 by al-Salih, the last sultan of the Ayyubid dynasty founded by the great Saladin. He was well aware that the settlements of the Mongols, who a few years earlier on the orders of Genghis Khan had taken Asia by storm, were swarming with young slaves who could be bought and trained for war. He therefore gave orders for the acquisition of around twelve thousand "mamluks," an Arabic word meaning "a man possessed by another"—that is, a slave. They were mostly of Circassian, Georgian, and Mingrelian origins, and what was to all intents and purposes a conscript foreign legion was trained in Egypt in the use of the lance and the scimitar and all forms of horsemanship.

The lessons were learned so well that the Mamelukes soon became the most fearsome cavalry of the Near East. However, as happened in ancient Rome with the Praetorian Guard, the militia created to guarantee the safety of the sovereign soon began to dictate the law.

A DYNASTY OF SLAVES: THE MAMELUKES

54 top *The Nilometer—al-Miqyas in Arabic, meaning "the measure"—was an octagonal column placed at the center of a well on the southern tip of the island of Roda. It was designed to measure the depth of the river. When the water reached the height of sixteen cubits, the flood was proclaimed and welcomed with great celebrations as the bringer of prosperity. (Luigi Mayer,* Views in Egypt, *London, 1805)*

56-57 *This engraving shows Cairo from the east. On the right is the Citadel, perched on a rocky crag; to the left is the aqueduct that carried water into the city from the Nile, and in the background are the Pyramids of Giza beyond the river.* (Dominique Vivant Denon, *Voyage dans la Basse et la Haute Egypte*, Paris, 1802)

57 top *The Mameluke chiefs built delightful villas with summerhouses and pavilions scattered in the shade of palm groves in these luxuriant gardens on the island of Roda.* (D. Vivant Denon, *Voyage dans la Basse et la Haute Egypte*)

58 top *A sumptuously dressed Mameluke horseman armed with a lance. The Mamelukes wore all their jewels in battle: necklaces, rings, bracelets, and belts ornamented with gold coins. When the French followed Bonaparte to Egypt in order to invade it, many of them got rich by plundering the corpses. One of them became famous because of a simple invention: he used to fold up his bayonet and use it as a hook to get the corpses that were floating in the Nile. This illustration appeared in the volume* Views in Egypt *by Luigi Mayer, London, 1805.*

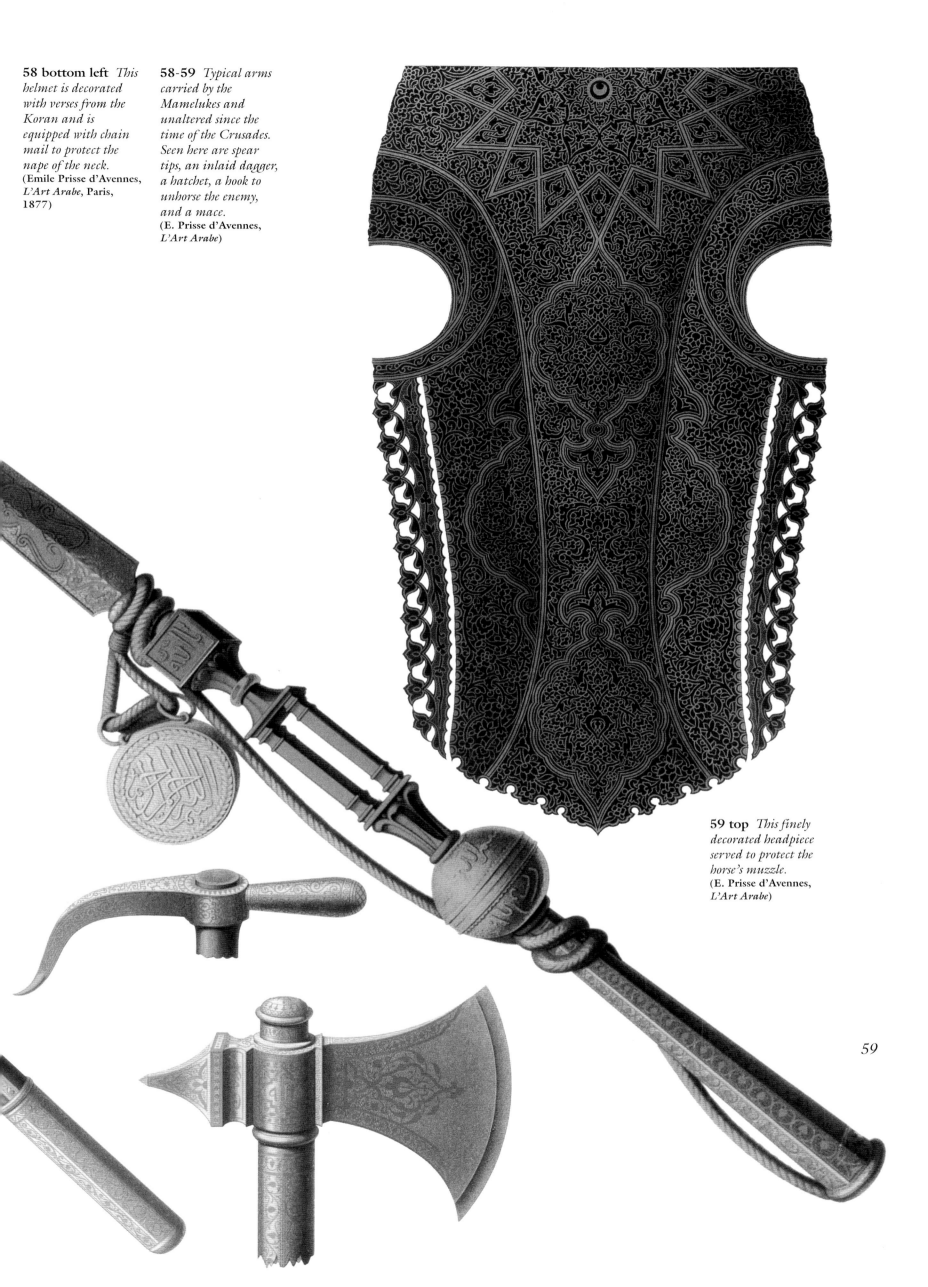

58 bottom left *This helmet is decorated with verses from the Koran and is equipped with chain mail to protect the nape of the neck.* (Emile Prisse d'Avennes, *L'Art Arabe*, Paris, 1877)

58-59 *Typical arms carried by the Mamelukes and unaltered since the time of the Crusades. Seen here are spear tips, an inlaid dagger, a hatchet, a hook to unhorse the enemy, and a mace.* (E. Prisse d'Avennes, *L'Art Arabe*)

59 top *This finely decorated headpiece served to protect the horse's muzzle.* (E. Prisse d'Avennes, *L'Art Arabe*)

60-61 *A throng of Mamelukes practicing fencing and spear throwing in the courtyard of Murad Bey's palace in Cairo, while a crowd of notables watches from the windows and galleries.*
(Luigi Mayer, *Views in Egypt*, London, 1805)

60 bottom *The faces of old bearded Mamelukes at Thebes.*
(Dominique Vivant Denon, *Voyage dans la Basse et la Haute Egypte*, Paris, 1802)

After al-Salih died in 1249, his widow Shajarat al-Durr reigned alone for a brief period—a remarkable example of a woman wielding power in a Muslim country—before marrying the Mameluke Aybak, who initially appeared content in the role of submissive prince consort. When Shajarat al-Durr discovered that he was in fact plotting a second marriage, she had him assassinated and was herself then beaten to death by her slaves.

Violence of this kind was to mark the entire history of the Mameluke dynasty: in 260 years, fifty-three sultans succeeded to the throne of Egypt, elected by the Mameluke emirs of just over twenty families. Only thirteen of them died in bed; the others were all deposed or assassinated. The most illustrious of these sultans was Baybars I, a Turkoman who reigned from 1260 to 1277. With his military campaigns in Syria he succeeded in defending the country from the Mongol invasion.

The most eminent of these sultans was al-Nasir, who had the singular destiny of being called to the throne three times, from 1293 to 1294, from 1298 to 1308, and from 1309 to 1340. He finally defeated the Mongols and made Egypt the most powerful Islamic kingdom; built mosques, schools, and aqueducts; and dug a canal to link Alexandria with the Nile. His reign was followed by plagues and famine, court intrigues, assassinations, and plundering.

True power was in the hands of the emirs; the elected sultan was nothing but a more or less depraved puppet; one of them, Yalbay, who reigned for a few months in 1467, was actually insane. Egypt was gradually squeezed dry by the capricious behavior of its rulers. One sultan had eleven thousand sugarloafs filled with candies prepared for the wedding of his daughter. He then repeated the gesture for each of her ten sisters. Another sultan undertook a pilgrimage to Mecca with a caravan of six hundred camels laden with geese and chickens for his kitchen and another forty camels laden with great chests of earth—a portable kitchen garden that each day, in the middle of the desert, supplied fresh vegetables. A third sultan donated vast portions of land in the delta to his physician, but had him decapitated when he attributed a slight indisposition to an overly strong purgative prescribed by the physician.

61 *This magnificently costumed Mameluke bey is standing near the balustrade of his balcony, below which can be seen a throng of peasants and, in the background, a mosque amid the palms. A page, also sumptuously dressed, is carrying his master's scimitar on his shoulder.* (**L. Mayer,** *Views in Egypt*)

62-63 and 62 bottom *In the image at the top, the waters of the flooding river surround an island on which stand a number of simple cabins made of woven straw mats. In them, sheltered from the heat of the sun, sit administrators employed by the wealthy landowners. Before them the peasants stack sacks of harvested crops, which will be loaded onto the waiting camels. Goats, oxen, and ducks wander here and there. Below, the Pyramids at Giza can be seen from the opposite bank of the Nile, where three Egyptians are calmly smoking and talking while two sailing boats pass by.* (Giovanni Battista Belzoni, *Egypt and Nubia*, London, 1820)

63 top *The peasants spent many working hours irrigating the fields by drawing water from the Nile and pouring it into the ditches that furrowed the land on either side of the river.* (**Bartlett,** *The Nile Boat*)

This dynasty of regal former slaves survived into the sixteenth century, when, in 1517, Egypt was invaded from Syria. The Ottoman Turks were equipped with all the latest techniques in the art of war and had mastered the use of firearms, thanks to well-paid European advisers. Sixty years earlier they had conquered Constantinople and had continued their expansion into Europe.

The writing was on the wall for the Mamelukes whose military strategy had failed to progress beyond the medieval cavalry charge and who lacked the knowledge to make best use of the few firearms they possessed. Their last sultan, Tuman, fought courageously at the gates of Cairo but was defeated, captured a few months later in the desert, and hanged. The victor, the Ottoman Sultan Selim I, spent a few months in the Nile Valley, visiting Pyramids and temples before

returning to Constantinople. From that point onward Cairo was but a remote provincial city governed by a pasha. The diffident Selim was reluctant to exterminate the Mamelukes, however, because their power counterbalanced that of his viceroy, preventing the latter from entertaining any thoughts of independence. He therefore constituted a divan, or regency council, composed of the pasha and seven of the leading Mameluke chiefs. The pasha was charged with the task of passing on the orders of the Sublime Porte (the Ottoman government) while the Mameluke representatives had the right to repudiate the decisions of the pasha on presentation of their reasons and could even depose him. Selim then decreed that the governors of the twenty-four provinces, the beys, should be chosen from among the Mamelukes and should be responsible for controlling the Egyptians, collecting taxes,

and ensuring public order. One of them was the sheikh of Cairo, a civil rather than military post.

This form of despotism, tempered by a limited tolerance of insubordination, allowed the Turks to govern Egypt for almost three hundred years. Selim's successors never returned to the country, and the pashas they dispatched were wholly ignorant of their domain. They only occasionally succeeded in imposing the will of their sovereigns, and they attempted to enrich themselves at the expense of their subjects. The Mamelukes tolerated the more malleable pashas, assassinated the most stubborn ones, and happily waited for Constantinople to send another.

64 top *Two barges on the Nile. These rafts were built for thousands of years using the same techniques used by the ancient Egyptians. They were made of bundles of papyri or palm stems.* (Jean-Jacques Rifaud, *Voyage en Égypte, en Nubie*, Paris, 1830)

64-65 *These two Nile sailing boats were drawn by the French sculptor Jean-Jacques Rifaud, one of the numerous "predators of antiquity" who invaded Egypt early in the nineteenth century. Rifaud remained in Egypt for forty years searching high and low, purloining antiquities, and executing around four thousand drawings that form an extraordinary corpus of images of Egyptian daily life as well as archaeological remains. The two fish reproduced below are also his work.* (Jean-Jacques Rifaud, *Voyage en Égypte, en Nubie*)

65 top *A number of potters after having completed their products attach them to a trellis to form a kind of raft, which they float to market exploiting the current of the river.* (J.-J. Rifaud, *Voyage en Égypte, en Nubie*)

65 bottom *Front and rear views of the costume of an Egyptian woman carrying a large jug on her head. The water of the Nile was so famed for its purity and goodness that, after the Turkish conquest early in the sixteenth century, it was carried by sea to Constantinople, where the sultans drank nothing else.* (J.-J. Rifaud, *Voyage en Égypte, en Nubie*)

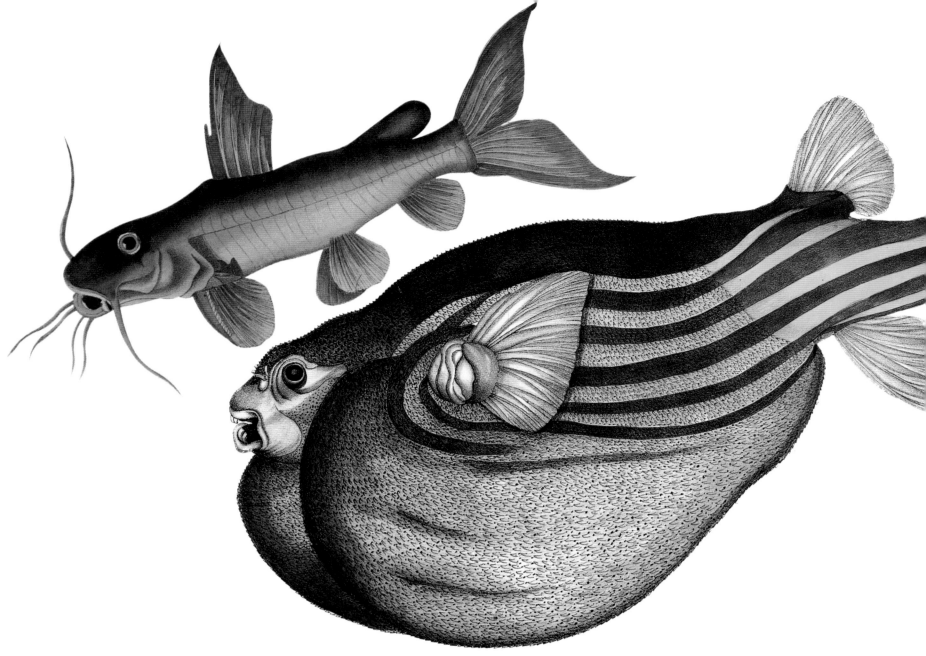

66 top *A catfish and a globefish from the waters of the Nile. In addition to being an archaeologist's paradise, Egypt was an extremely interesting country for naturalists, especially in the delta region, which was extremely rich in* *fauna and flora. Many Europeans came to study them early in the last century, subsequently publishing splendid albums of illustrations.* (Jean-Jacques Rifaud, *Voyage en Égypte, en Nubie,* Paris, 1830)

66-67 *These illustrations depict various methods of fishing that had remained unaltered since the times of the pharaohs. Two different types of nets were used; in shallow water in Nubia, fish were hunted with spears; and in the fish-filled delta, lines were used.*

(J.-J. Rifaud, *Voyage en Égypte, en Nubie*)

Participating in the divan flattered their love of display and ostentation: the immense courtyard of the Cairo Citadel was filled with horses with magnificent caparisons as the beys and emirs strove to outdo one another in the exhibition of precious fabrics, diamonds, sparkling saddle pistols, and imposing processions of richly costumed slaves. As the precious goods of Asia, silk and spices above all, that once reached Europe by way of Egypt were now carried by sea on the Cape of Good Hope route with the Portuguese—the Dutch, the English, and the French having established colonies and emporiums in the eastern seas—the Mamelukes were less wealthy than they had once been. However, they made amends by exploiting still further the poor fellahin, and the Nile rarely failed to fertilize the fields with its annual floods.

A French consul depicted the situation in Egypt in the mid-eighteenth century thus: "The cupidity of the Mamelukes finds its limit only when the farmers are absolutely unable to pay; and these poor souls have but escape as their only defense against their oppressors. A fellah who finds himself unable to satisfy the avidity of his master leaves his fields and his home, followed by his wife and children, and searches in another village for a piece of land to cultivate and a less voracious master. True servants of the glebe, the farmers are treated not as the descendants of the Arabs who conquered Egypt but as the lowest of the low in this realm. Incapable of courage or any bold action, their spirit, quelled by fear and baseness, prevents them from ever taking part in the numerous disturbances that so often shake the country. Their masters consider them animals necessary for cultivating the fields; they treat them without any form of indulgence, with none of the respect due to a human being; they have their goods and their very lives at their disposal, and the government makes no attempt to repress this tyranny. Far from correcting the situation, it encourages it by its own example. Frequently, on the basis of unfounded complaints, the pasha orders the sacking of a village and the extermination of all the inhabitants. At Cairo the life of a man is worth no more than that of a beast; the militia charged with patrolling the city day and night dispenses justice in the middle of the street, condemning and hanging the hapless criminal on the spot. On the accusation of any enemy whatsoever, those suspected of possessing any sum of money are called before the bey; if he refuses to appear, or if he denies the fact, he is thrown to the ground and receives two hundred lashes, or he is killed immediately

69 top right *Beside this tastefully dressed Egyptian noblewoman is an equally well dressed servant.* (L. Mayer, *Views in Egypt*)

69 bottom left *An Egyptian beauty in a nineteenth-century engraving. Again this is a girl from a noble family, made up, bejeweled, and dressed with elegance. She is leaning on an inlaid chest.*

68-69 *The slave market at Cairo was the largest and busiest in the whole of Africa. It was frequented by slave buyers from throughout the Islamic world, and the sultan of Constantinople bought the women for his harem there.*

69 top left *A meeting between Mameluke noblemen in the streets of Cairo. According to foreign travelers in Egypt, their elegance contrasted sharply with the extreme poverty of the Egyptian peasants who made up the vast majority of the population.* (L. Mayer, *Views in Egypt*, London, 1805)

69 center *The dragoman was the indispensable interpreter and guide who served as a factotum for the foreign travelers. Factotums were usually Greeks or Maltese rather than Egyptians.* (L. Mayer, *Views in Egypt*)

70-71 *In the last years of the Mameluke dominion, Egypt was visited by an Italian artist, Luigi Mayer, the first of many who* *would arrive to paint panoramas of the Nile Valley and its monuments. This illustration shows a summer palace and* *garden built near the ruins of the Minuf Canal, not far from Cairo.* (L. Mayer, *Views in Egypt*, London, 1805)

70 bottom left *A view of the city of Minuf, located between Cairo and Rosetta.* (L. Mayer, *Views in Egypt*)

70 bottom right *The illustration shows an Arabic dance.* (Giovanni Battista Belzoni, *Egypt and Nubia*, London, 1820)

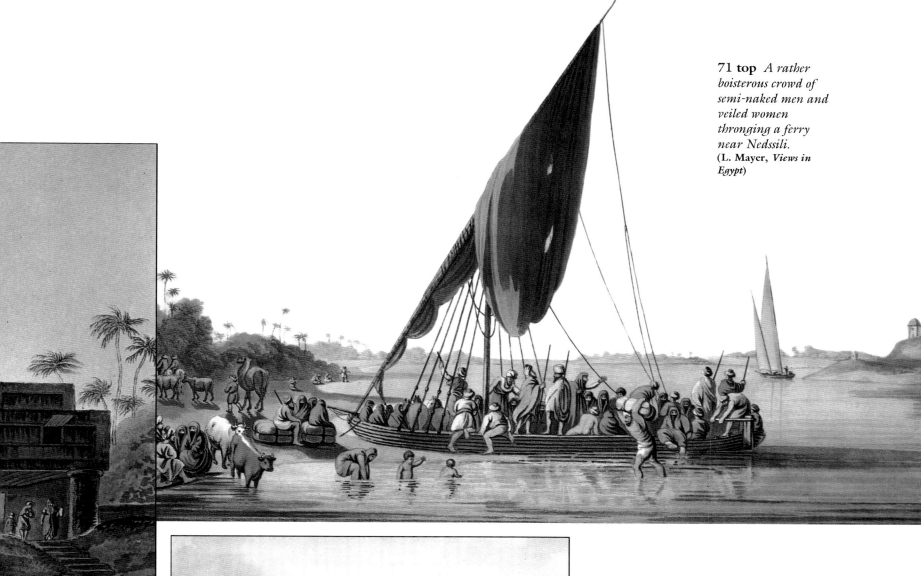

to provide an example for his fellows."

With these methods of government, and thanks to the recurrent plagues, the population of Egypt, which during the era of the Roman Empire had numbered some eight million, was reduced by one-third by the end of the eighteenth century. The pashas were increasingly impotent while the spirit of rebellion grew among the Mamelukes. In 1769 one of them, Ali Bey, who was said to be the son of a Christian priest from the Caucasus, threw out the latest pasha and proclaimed Egyptian independence from the Sublime Porte. Having raised an army, he put it in the capable hands of his lieutenant, Abu al-Dahab, who in July 1770 conquered Mecca, expelled the sharif, and replaced him with a trusty who conferred upon Ali the grandiloquent title of Sultan of Egypt and Sovereign of the Two Seas. The following year Abu al-Dahab marched on Syria and took Damascus. However, the Turks, masters of intrigue, succeeded in corrupting him and turning him against

his master. He then led his victorious forces to Egypt. Ali Bey fled to Acre, where obliging Russian ships (Catherine the Great was at war with Turkey) brought him reinforcements in the form of three thousand Albanians, with whom he returned to fight for his lost throne. Wounded in battle, Ali Bey died shortly afterward, perhaps poisoned. The traitor al-Dahab was rewarded with the title of sheikh of Cairo and pasha of Egypt.

This was the first time that a Mameluke had been appointed to the post of viceroy, and subsequently the government of Egypt passed into the hands of the two leading Mamelukes, the beys Ibrahim and Murad; they retained power for the next two decades. Ottoman power appeared to be increasingly precarious and was to collapse like a house of cards within a few years, due to the intervention of a European power and then to the birth of a new foreign dynasty out of the ashes of the Mameluke line.

In the meantime certain farsighted

parties began to look upon Egypt with renewed interest. In the year of the death of Ali Bey, 1773, a remarkable figure, James Bruce, returning from multiple adventures in Ethiopia, presented himself in rags at Cairo. The benevolent pasha sent him a chest of oranges and a bag of gold coins so that he could purchase new clothes. When Bruce refused the money the pasha asked what he could do for him. "Give my countrymen the right to carry their goods to Suez rather than oblige them to unload them at Jidda," replied the Scot. The privilege was granted and recognized for what it was worth by Baldwin, one of the most important British merchants trading with the Levant, who described it to the British government in enthusiastic terms: "We will thus unite the Ganges, the Nile, and the Thames, and at the top of the Pyramid we will drink to the prosperity of England." A new route to the Indies was now possible, but it was to take another century before it was practicable.

71

The veteran of Abyssinia who had asked that strange favor of the pasha was a truly remarkable man. The son of a Scottish nobleman who claimed to be a descendant of an ancient royal dynasty, James Bruce was born at Kinnaird in 1730. His mother died when he was just three years old, and at six he was sent to school in London. He then completed his education at the University of Edinburgh. At twenty-four years of age he married the daughter of a wealthy London vintner, but his beloved bride died in his arms just a few months later, a tragedy that was to remain with him throughout the rest of life. Subsequently he devoted himself to travel and study; he must have already harbored a desire to trace the course of the Nile, because he took the trouble while in Holland to learn Arabic and the Ethiopian language.

In 1762 the British government offered Bruce the post of consul at Algiers, the capital of one of those barbarian states that lived by piracy, preying on Christian-owned ships. It was a rather tricky posting, as the bey had little respect for diplomatic niceties, and, exemplary Oriental tyrant that he was, he did not hesitate to resolve controversy by throwing overzealous consuls in prison and beating their secretaries. During Bruce's presentation ceremony a courtier who made a false move was strangled in front of him.

The Scotsman made the best of his uncomfortable lot by studying the country's Roman antiquities. When he was finally able to leave Algiers, in August 1765, he followed up his archaeological investigations by visiting all the points on the North African coast in which he hoped to uncover traces of the past.

As his carping critics were later to say, Bruce had a clear predilection for the wonderful. He passed through Africa like a latter-day Marco Polo. His principal goal was to verify the existence

73 *This portrait of James Bruce has been superimposed on a map of the course of the Nile taken from his book* Travels to Discover the Source of the Nile, *Edinburgh, 1805. The route followed by Poncet is marked with a dotted line while that followed by Bruce is marked in red. Note at the bottom, in the center of Abyssinia, the sources of the Blue Nile at Lake Tana, held to be the true and sole sources of the great river. The White Nile has in fact been reduced to the rank of an insignificant tributary whose course is marked as running almost parallel with the Blue Nile and originating in the Ethiopian highlands a little farther to the south.*

A LATTER-DAY MARCO POLO:
JAMES BRUCE IN ABYSSINIA

72

72 top *The meeting between James Bruce and Ahmed, the grandson of the governor of Massawa, the port giving access to Turkish-controlled Abyssinia. Here the Turks detained the explorer at length in order to extort further money from him. This was common practice among the local* Ottoman authorities when dealing with foreigners.
(James Bruce, *Travels to Discover the Source of the Nile*, Edinburgh, 1805)

72 bottom *A canga, a large cargo boat, under full sail on the Nile.*
(J. Bruce, *Travels to Discover the Source of the Nile*)

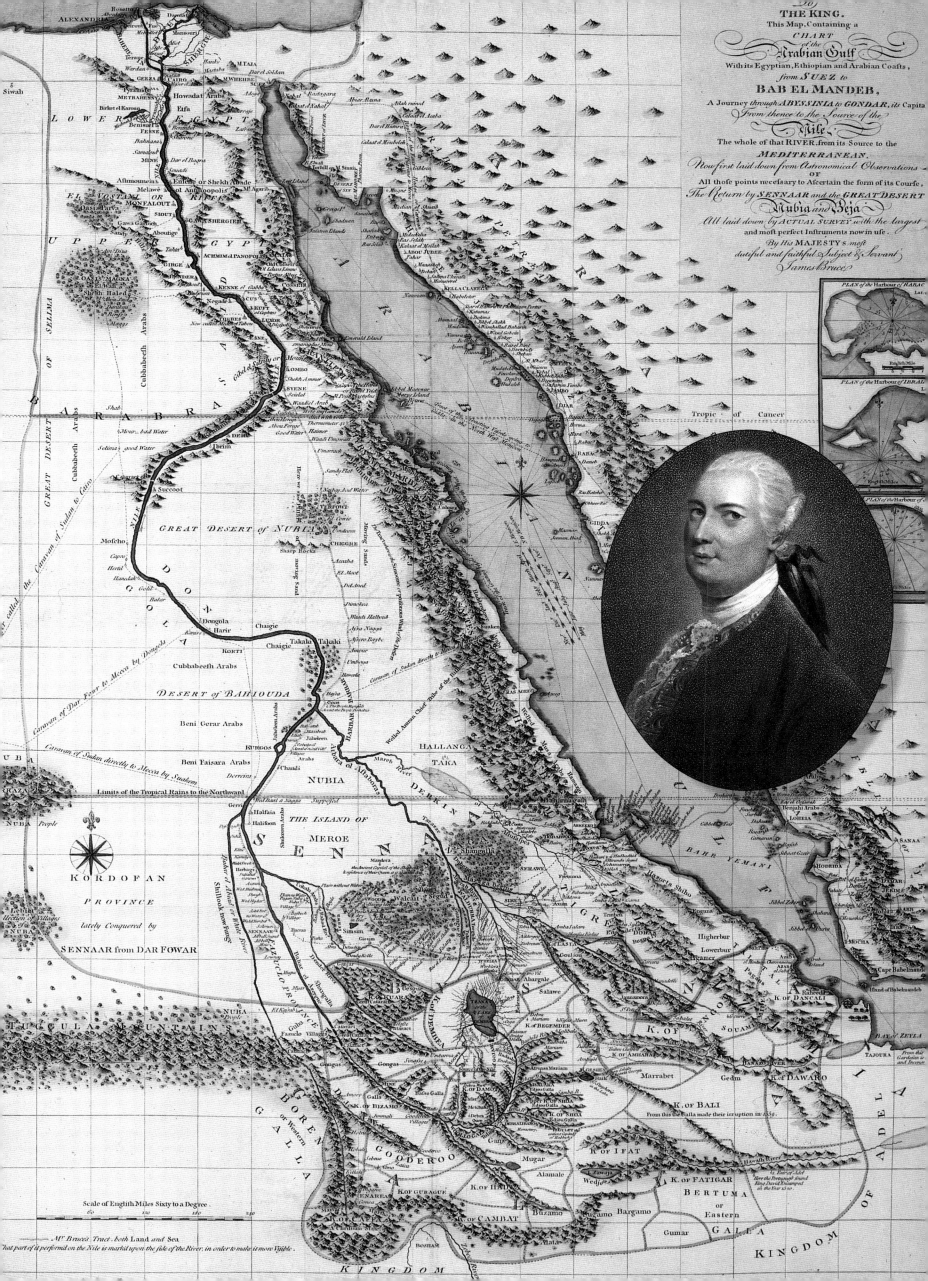

74 top When Bruce visited the Christian kingdom of Abyssinia, that country was enjoying a period of relative calm; there were, however, almost incessant wars against tribes that had converted to Islam and against those that had never embraced Christianity. There were also frequent internal conflicts between the great feudal chieftains. This tinted engraving shows an Abyssinian chieftain, Zogo—who had the rank of fitaurari, or commander of an army—on horseback, attacking a Galla warrior. Both men are armed with lances.

74 bottom Bruce on horseback crossing a bridge from which one can admire the imposing spectacle of the great waterfall at Alata on the Blue Nile near Lake Tana. Tending to exaggerate when describing his adventures, the Scotsman considerably inflated the size of the falls.
(James Bruce, *Travels to Discover the Source of the Nile*, Edinburgh, 1805).

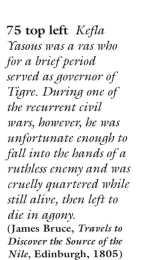

of Ras Sem, a desert village that was said to have been petrified in an act of divine retribution and whose inhabitants were believed to have been standing in the streets for centuries in the positions in which the heavenly ire had caught them. A French consul at Tripoli had offered a great deal of money for one of the stone figures but was brought a mutilated Roman statue.

Finally, after having visited Crete, Cyprus, and Syria, Bruce reached Egypt in 1768 accompanied by his young Italian secretary, Luigi Balugani. He had now decided that his life's great goal would be to discover the source of the Nile, and by this he meant the Blue Nile. The existence of the White Nile was of no concern to him; neither was the fact that the source of the Blue Nile had been reached and described 150 years earlier by the Portuguese missionaries, whose book he had read. A dutiful Scottish Protestant, Bruce hated "Papists," and even before he set foot in Ethiopia he had convinced himself that those contemptible, fanatical priests must have lied. After them few white men had ventured into Abyssinia, but late in the seventeenth century a French doctor, Jacques-Charles Poncet, accompanied by a Jesuit, had reached Gonder, where he treated the emperor. In recompense the emperor offered to have Poncet escorted to the Nile springs, but the Frenchman, who was unwell, declined the honor.

Bruce, who had during his Levant adventures acquired a useful grounding in medicine, also decided to present himself as a physician. On December 12, 1768, he embarked at Cairo with the intention of ascending the Nile in the company of Balugani and Strates, a Greek who, together with a Moor named Yasmine, acted as a majordomo to the expedition. Reaching Aswan after passing through all of Upper Egypt, which had impressed Bruce with the fertility of its terrain, the abundance of the harvests providing a striking contrast with the abject poverty of the inhabitants, the party was obstructed by the restless locals. This induced the Scotsman to choose the Red Sea route rather than continue along the river as he had initially intended. The group thus joined a caravan that in February 1769 was crossing the desert to reach the port of Kosseir, collecting along the way around twenty Turks who had recently been attacked by a band of Arabs. From Kosseir a felucca took them to Massawa where they disembarked in September and were immediately subjected to the rapacious attentions of the bey, in spite of Bruce's vain waving of his letters of introduction from the Turkish governor of Jidda. Only two months later did the group manage to escape the bey's

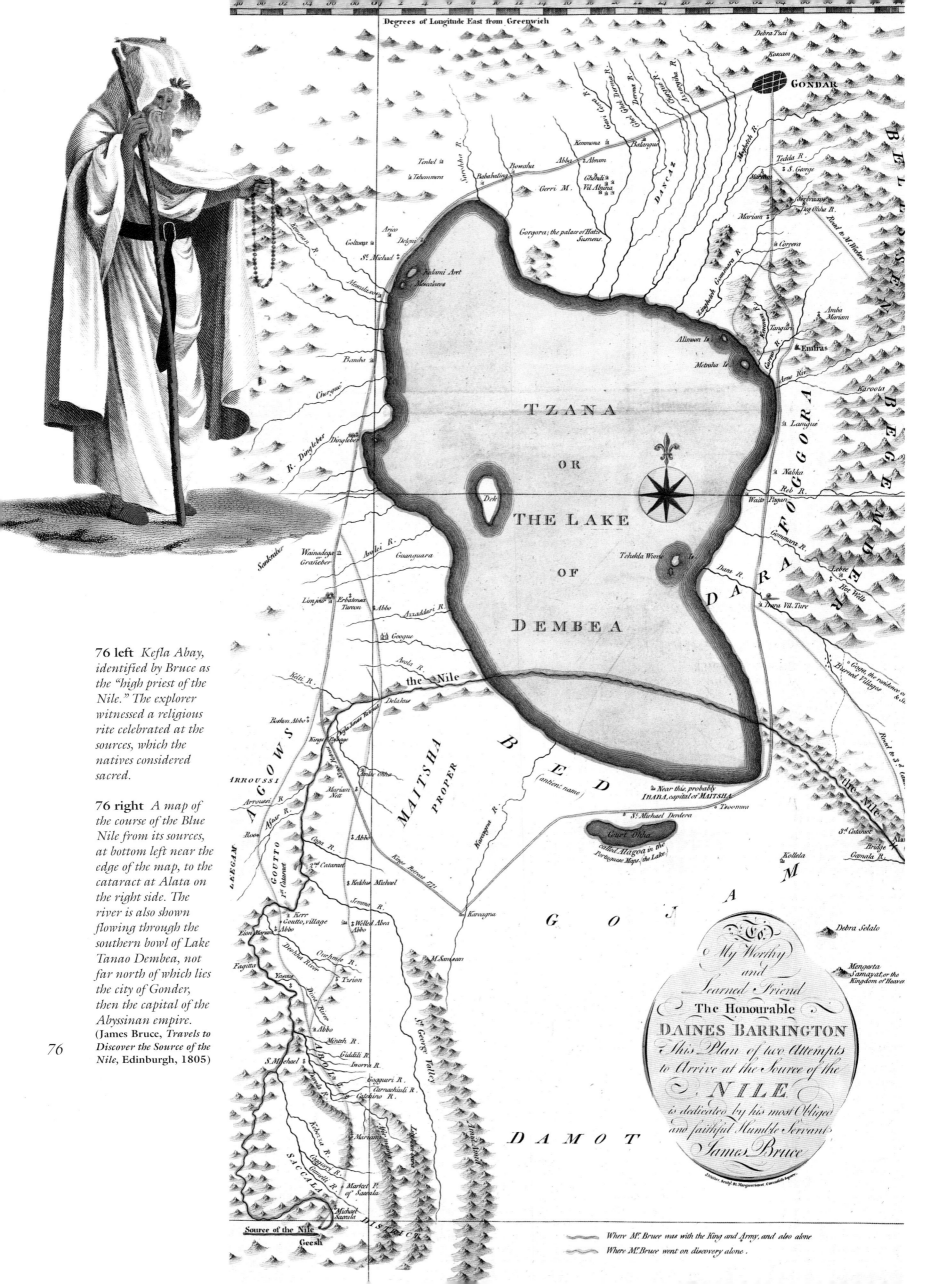

76 left *Kefla Abay, identified by Bruce as the "high priest of the Nile." The explorer witnessed a religious rite celebrated at the sources, which the natives considered sacred.*

76 right *A map of the course of the Blue Nile from its sources, at bottom left near the edge of the map, to the cataract at Alata on the right side. The river is also shown flowing through the southern bowl of Lake Tanao Dembea, not far north of which lies the city of Gonder, then the capital of the Abyssinan empire.* (James Bruce, *Travels to Discover the Source of the Nile*, Edinburgh, 1805)

76

clutches and head toward the Ethiopian highlands and the mountains that our hero, perhaps influenced by the idea of being close to fulfilling his dream, rashly numbered among the highest on the globe.

The party reached Adik'eyih, described as the capital of the Abyssinian kidnappers: its inhabitants trafficked in children, and kidnappers from throughout the country came to its market to sell their pitiful goods. The expedition then proceeded to Adwa, where they saw numerous debtors locked in special cages while their relations collected the funds with which to pay their creditors, and lastly to Axum, where they admired the ruins of the ancient capital of the realm, punctuated by obelisks and crumbling churches.

Before arriving in Gonder, the home of the court, Bruce witnessed a scene that he was later to describe in his book to the disbelief of the right-thinking people of the United Kingdom. He saw three wayfarers who, after having stunned their

cow, skillfully carved a steak from the flank of the living animal. Having eaten the raw meat and applied a poultice of clay to the wound, they happily went on their way, all three of them plus the cow.

At Gonder, Bruce unexpectedly found himself before a great turreted castle resembling those of medieval Europe set among the straw huts. The minute king Tecla Haimanot and his prime minister, the wily old Ras Michael, were absent, engaged in a punitive expedition against rebellious subjects, but the queen mother received them cordially. When Bruce presented himself as a doctor, she immediately had him treat her children and grandchildren, who were suffering from smallpox. The Scotsman achieved significant results through the simple remedy of hygiene and ventilation of the rooms and thus earned the respect of the women of the court, possibly the only stable source of power in the country in those turbulent times. Thus when Ras Michael and the king returned, Bruce obtained a hearing, immediately after having witnessed the entrance into the city of the victorious army, the testicles of the defeated enemy swinging from their lances.

Having entered the good graces of the king and, above all, his omnipotent vizier, Bruce was honored with almost daily invitations to the court, the barbaric customs of which were as repulsive to him as to his scandalized future readers. His account of a typical celebration like the Polyphemus banquet clearly shows the Abyssinian roughness. A long table is set in the middle of a large room with benches beside it for a number of guests. Servants approach the table and place a great slice of bloody raw meat on a round slab of unleavened bread that serves as both plate and tablecloth. Each man, sitting in such a way as to be facing two women, cuts a large piece of meat with the same knife he uses in war and then sheathes the blade. The women then take the meat, cut it with minuscule knives into strips as long as a little finger and then into chunks, which they wrap in the bread after having covered them with a layer of salt and black pepper. In the meantime the men place their hands on the knees of both their female neighbors and, with their bodies thrust forward and their mouths wide open like perfect idiots, turn first to one and then the other to be stuffed with mouthfuls so large that they risk suffocation from one moment to the next. According to the rules of etiquette, Bruce writes, he who

77 left *During his journey through Abyssinia, Bruce found numerous remains that provided evidence of the ancient relationship between Abyssinia and the Egypt of the pharaohs—for* example, this fragmentary standing stone covered with hieroglyphics, which he discovered in the holy city of Axum. (James Bruce, *Travels to Discover the Source of the Nile*, Edinburgh, 1805)

77 right *One of the obelisks standing in the little Abyssinian Rome. It is evidence of the great influence of Egyptian culture.* (J. Bruce, *Travels to Discover the Source of the Nile*)

78 left *The Ethiopian flora and fauna attracted the attention of the Scottish traveler, a keen naturalist. From top to bottom, a cuckoo, a plant known as a wanzey, and a fennec, a small fox with long ears, in drawings taken from Bruce's book.* (James Bruce, *Travels to Discover the Source of the Nile*, Edinburgh, 1805)

swallows the largest mouthful and makes the most noise chewing it is considered to be the politest. And a proverb says, "Only beggars and thieves eat small pieces or without making a noise." The man will drink only when he has finished eating, and before drinking he wraps two chunks of meat in bread and presents them simultaneously to the two women who have fed him; this is his way of thanking them. He then quaffs the entire contents of a large bull's horn while the women eat; lastly they all drink and abandon themselves to song and merrymaking. In the meantime, the unhappy victim of their appetite, the still living ox from which the butchers have the cut the devoured flesh, is still moaning on the floor of the hut, where it eventually bleeds to death. Those who have dined are at this point extremely aroused.

His account goes on to describe what happens after the meal, when love begins to make itself felt. The altar of Bacchus immediately becomes one dedicated to sacrifices to Venus. There is no modesty, there is no restraint, they have no need of secret and mysterious havens in which to satisfy their desires. This is again proof of their absolute freedom and lack of decency. A pair of lovers slides down from the bench the better to give vent to the passion overwhelming them.

Immediately the two men closest raise a cloak to hide them from the eyes of the others; silence when making love is considered as shameful as when eating. When the lovers have taken their place at table once again, all the other guests drink to their health, and their example is immediately followed by others. All this takes place without the slightest scandal and even without jokes or licentious comments. Striking enough is that the women who take part in these banquets are almost always persons of distinguished birth or character.

When obliged to witness such events, Bruce gritted his teeth and firmly insisted that they

should be allowed to proceed to the source of the Nile, or rather the Abay Wenz, the river that flowed into Lake Tana and gave rise to the Blue Nile. Despite the reproaches of the queen mother who had grown fond of him and considered his insane desire to be unworthy of an educated intelligent person, a caprice through which he could even lose his life, Bruce finally obtained the long-awaited permit, together with the honorary title of governor of the province of Ras el-Feel. This last would serve as protection against diverse ill-intentioned brigands.

The caravan departed on April 4, 1770, for Lake Tana, reaching the Tisisat falls, which the Abyssinians considered the second Nile cataract and which Bruce exalted as one of nature's greatest spectacles. He gave the lie to Padre Lobo's claim of having climbed a spur of rock under the cascading water. Dismissing the feats of his predecessors was Bruce's only means of claiming primacy for himself, and he tried to prove that Lobo could not have reached that point. The Portuguese Jesuit had visited the falls during the dry season, however, when the underlying rock was accessible.

Forced to interrupt the journey by a revolt in the region, Bruce had to return to Gonder, where he fell ill. He departed once again in October with Balugani and Strates, revisited Lake Tana, and followed the Abay Wenz upstream until finally, on November 4, 1770, in the company of just Strates and a guide, Bruce reached a point from which a marsh was pointed out to him that had an island in the middle: the source of the Nile. "Throwing my shoes off," he wrote, "I ran down the hill toward the little island of green sods, which was about three hundred yards distant; the whole side of the hill was thick grown over with flowers, the large bulbous roots of which, appearing above the surface of the ground, and their skins coming off on treading upon them, occasioned two very severe falls before I reached the brink of the marsh; I after this came to the island of green turf,

79 top left *Gonder, the Abyssinian capital of the time, was a walled city perched on a crag. Bruce, on horseback, accompanied by an escort of Abyssinians armed with lances,* *and followed by camels carrying his baggage, climbs the steep road leading to the city gate.* (James Bruce, *Travels to Discover the Source of the Nile*, Edinburgh, 1805)

79 bottom left *Bruce, in Arab costume with a scimitar at his side and a turban on his head, prostrates himself on the steps of the throne at the feet of the king of kings, the emperor of Abyssinia, who is wearing a simple tunic and an unusual twin-horned crown. One of* *the traveler's servants, on his knees to the right, is carrying a tray on his head with gifts for the sovereign: bolts of colored fabric. The courtiers on either side of the monarch wear expressions suggesting a mixture of shock and satisfaction. One of them, on the left, is* *indicating Bruce, clearly asking for the benevolence of his powerful master on the Scotsman's behalf.*

79 right *Another Ethiopian animal illustrated by Bruce, a serboa, a small rodent with an unusual disproportionate tail.*

(J. Bruce, *Travels to Discover the Source of the Nile*)

which was in the form of an altar, apparently the work of art, and I stood in rapture over the principal fountain which rises in the middle of it."

Following a suitably rhetorical passage ("It is easier to guess than to describe the situation of my mind at that moment—standing in that spot which had baffled the genius, industry, and inquiry of both ancients and moderns, for the course of near three thousand years. Kings had attempted this discovery at the head of armies, and each expedition was distinguished from the last only by the difference in the numbers which had perished, and agreed alone in the disappointment which had uniformly, and without exception, followed them all"), Bruce once again launched into an unworthy tirade against the unfortunate Portuguese Jesuits whose only crime was to have preceded him. The Scotsman treated them as braggarts, declaring that they had made mistakes throughout with place-names, dates, and distances. In the face of this patent injustice to two modest men who had narrated their extraordinary adventure with great simplicity and humility, one is inclined to feel that the ironic incredulity with which Bruce's book was received was nothing more than he deserved. The incredible tales he told about the Abyssinians led many to suspect that he had never set foot in Africa.

Having at last bathed in the headwaters of the Nile, Bruce turned his attention to the journey home. A civil war was raging in Abyssinia, and travel was impossible. While the Scotsman waited for a chance to leave, Balugani, suffering from a fever, died at Gonder. Not until December 1771, a year after his return from the Nile springs, was Bruce allowed to leave the country.

Because his earlier experience at Massawa had been so disagreeable, this time he chose to go by way of Sudan. The caravan set off confidently, laden with gifts supplied by the Abyssinian court with which to pay the chiefs through whose terrain they would have to travel. Once the party had descended

80

80-81 *On these pages we can admire a number of examples of Abyssinian fauna in the drawings illustrating Bruce's book that dealt not only with hydrography but with all aspects of the countries through which he traveled. As a naturalist he earned the respect of the most eminent zoologist of the eighteenth century, Comte Georges Buffon, whom he met at* *Marseilles on his return journey. Buffon was so struck by the explorer's tales that he wanted to present him to Louis XVI. At the top left we can see a bird known to the Abyssinians as a houbarra and, in the bottom left, a lynx. At top right is a species of vulture known as a nifser werk, in the center a turtle, and at the bottom a snake.*

from the highlands onto the disease-ridden plain, however, malaria and the tsetse fly soon took their toll and the rapacious natives proved increasingly eager to lay their hands on the party's treasures. On more than one occasion Bruce came close to losing his life at the hands of brigands.

Finally, in April 1772, the group reached Sennar, which in 1699 Dr. Poncet had described as the capital of a great kingdom but which Bruce found to be a desolate, ruined jumble of human misery and animals. Its young king, Ismail, received Bruce by having his body smeared with elephant fat, protection against insect bites and a source of magical strength. They had an almost philosophical discussion about the Scotsman's journey and his efforts as a kind of penance for his sins.

He then went to pay homage to the true master of the country, the sheikh Aslan who commanded the famous Black Riders of Sennar, four hundred men who were the terror of the Sudan and wore helmets and chain mail like the knights of Charlemagne. The stay at Sennar, during which Bruce was robbed of virtually all his belongings, dragged on into September when he could at last leave the hated city and press on to Shendi on the Nile, from which caravans left for Cairo. That village, near which he saw an expanse of ruins which were all that remained of ancient Meroë, was governed by a queen, an attractive forty-year-old dressed in silks and a gold crown who, when Bruce gallantly kissed her hand, said that nothing similar had ever happened to her before.

After another two months and a disastrous crossing of the desert from Berber to Aswan, Bruce, reduced to a shadow of his former self, entered Cairo once again. He remained in the city from December 1772 to March 1773 to regain strength and recover from the various illnesses he had contracted, including the so-called worm of the pharaohs, or guinea worm, a parasite that burrows into the flesh of the legs or arms.

Back in Europe after an absence of ten years, he delayed at length his return to his homeland, first stopping in Marseilles and Paris with Buffon, who presented him to Louis XVI to whom Bruce presented the seeds of Ethiopian plants, and then in Italy where he challenged

81

(James Bruce, *Travels to Discover the Source of the Nile*, Edinburgh, 1805)

to a duel the Florentine marquess who had married Bruce's Scottish fiancée. The latter had decided to take this momentous step after a period of a dozen years during which she had received no news of Bruce. The duel never took place because the presumed offender expressed his profound regret.

In June 1774, Bruce finally reached London. He was initially received in the salons with serious interest, but once his Abyssinian stories had been heard and considered incredible, he was invited for his entertainment value as a kind of yarn-spinning Baron von Münchhausen. The offended Scotsman retired to his estate, married an attractive girl twenty-four years his junior, built an astronomical observatory in which he spent his nights peering through a telescope while wearing Ethiopian costume, and produced a number of children. These were perhaps his happiest years but unfortunately they were not to last: in 1788 his second wife died, and Bruce sought refuge in his work. On the basis of his diaries he began writing an account of his travels in Abyssinia: five large volumes that saw the light of day in 1790, arousing a new wave of incredulity and facile irony. Surprised and humiliated, the author retreated to his Scottish haven, pining away in bitter isolation. He died a few years later, on April 27, 1794, after falling downstairs and hitting his head.

82 and 83 bottom left *These figures were met by Bruce during his return journey across the Sudan: an Arab sheikh and a woman from Laheia, both of the Beni Koreish tribe. In spite of the incredible and revolting customs he had witnessed in Abyssinia, the Scotsman described the*

Sudanese Arabs in far darker tones, seeing them as a rabble of predators intent on robbing travelers in a country lacking resources and impoverished not only by the accidents of nature but also by the wickedness of man. (James Bruce, *Travels to Discover the Source of the Nile*, Edinburgh, 1805)

83 top *Formerly the capital of a great kingdom, Sennar was in severe decline by the time Bruce visited it. This engraving shows a slave caravan from Ethiopia in the vicinity of the royal palace.*

83 center *Bruce paying tribute to the favorite of the king of Sennar. The opulence of the lady demonstrates that in the Sudan women were appreciated for their weight.* (James Bruce, *Travels to Discover the Source of the Nile*, Edinburgh, 1805)

83 bottom *Bruce traveling through the desert with a large caravan. The return journey was a grueling odyssey, especially from Berber to Aswan. The heat was unbearable, the wind raised columns* *and waves of sand, and before they could approach the wells, the party had to fire their guns to disperse the predators watering there. All the camels died, one of the men was driven insane, and the Scotsman's* *baggage was abandoned in the desert and recovered later only because of the courtesy of the governor of Aswan.* (J. Bruce, *Travels to Discover the Source of the Nile*)

he idea of a French conquest of Egypt has a curious and remote history. It was the German philosopher Gottfried von Leibniz, then just twenty-six years old, who conceived of it in 1671 as an intelligent means of distracting the France of Louis XIV, the Sun King, from its wars to ensure its Rhine borders. He suggested a more glorious objective worthy of the Crusades and of the king's predecessor Saint Louis IX, who had made an unsuccessful attempt to set foot in Egypt four centuries earlier. Armed with a letter of introduction

THE GREAT SULTAN:
BONAPARTE IN EGYPT

84 *The victorious young general Napoleon Bonaparte on horseback, surrounded by his officers. Bonaparte was only thirty years old at the time of his conquest of Egypt. Two years earlier, with his victorious Italian campaign of 1796–97, he had proved himself* the most outstanding general in the army of the French Republic. With the Egyptian expedition he was perhaps counting on destroying the already declining Ottoman Empire and conquering the East like a second Alexander the Great.

84-85 *The Armée d'Orient, as the French expeditionary force was called, advances with difficulty along the Nile, raising clouds of dust, flanked by cavalry detachments. The march from the coast to Cairo was a horrendous experience for the French soldiers. Wearing bulky* uniforms and weighed down by rifles and backpacks, they were tormented by the burning sun, thirst, insects, and attacking Bedouins, who killed anyone who lagged behind. (Dominique Vivant Denon, *Voyage dans la Basse et la Haute Egypte*, Paris, 1802)

85 top *Rosetta in the Nile Delta was one of the first cities to be occupied by the French, seen here parading before the stupefied Egyptians.* (Dominique Vivant Denon, *Voyage dans la Basse et la Haute Egypte*)

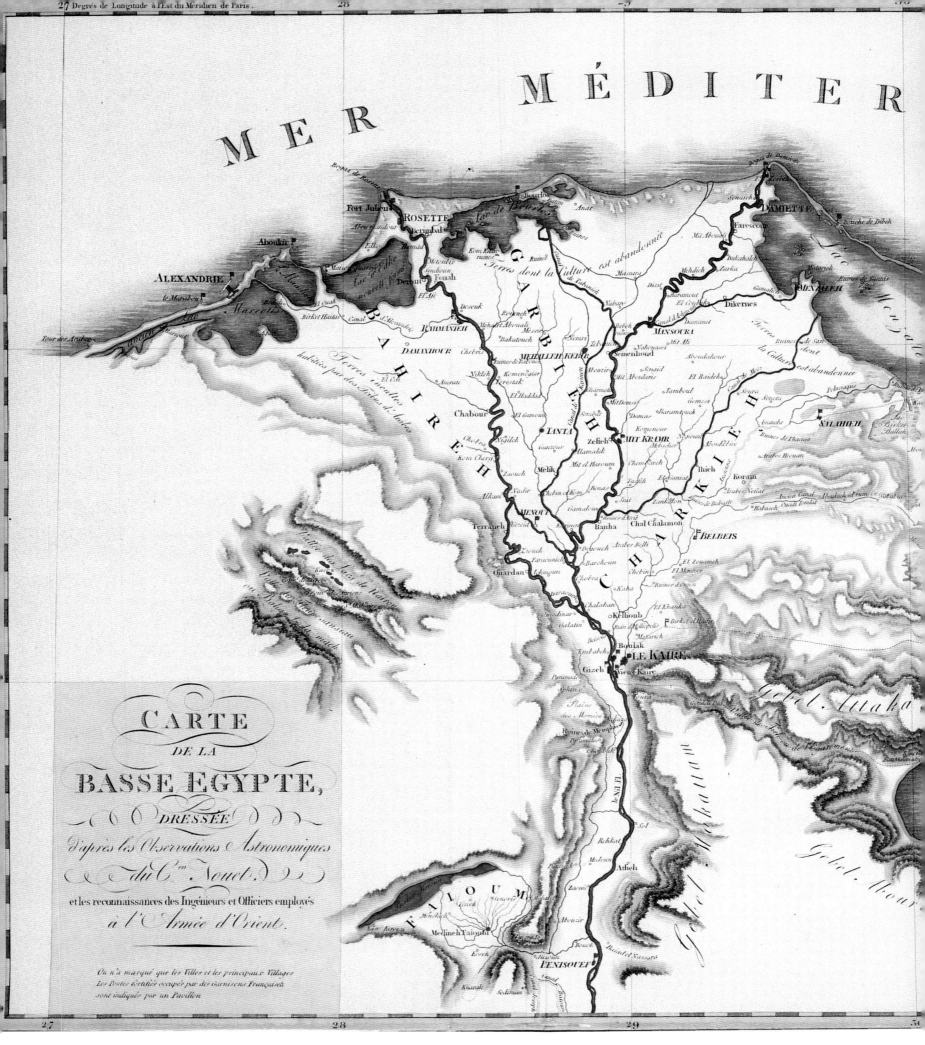

MER MÉDITER

CARTE
DE LA
BASSE EGYPTE,
DRESSÉE
d'après les Observations Astronomiques
du C.ᵉⁿ Nouet
et les reconnaissances des Ingénieurs et Officiers employés
à l'Armée d'Orient.

On n'a marqué que les Villes et les principaux Villages
Les Postes fortifiés occupés par des Garnisons Françaises
sont indiqués par un Pavillon

86-87 *A map of the delta region from Dominique Vivant Denon's book* Voyage dans la Basse et la Haute Egypte, *published in Paris in 1802. The book did much to enhance its author's reputation as a preeminent archaeologist and artist. Denon was perhaps the most distinguished and adventurous of the savants who accompanied the French expedition. He went as far south as he could in search of Egyptian monuments, which he drew meticulously and unhurriedly even under enemy fire.*

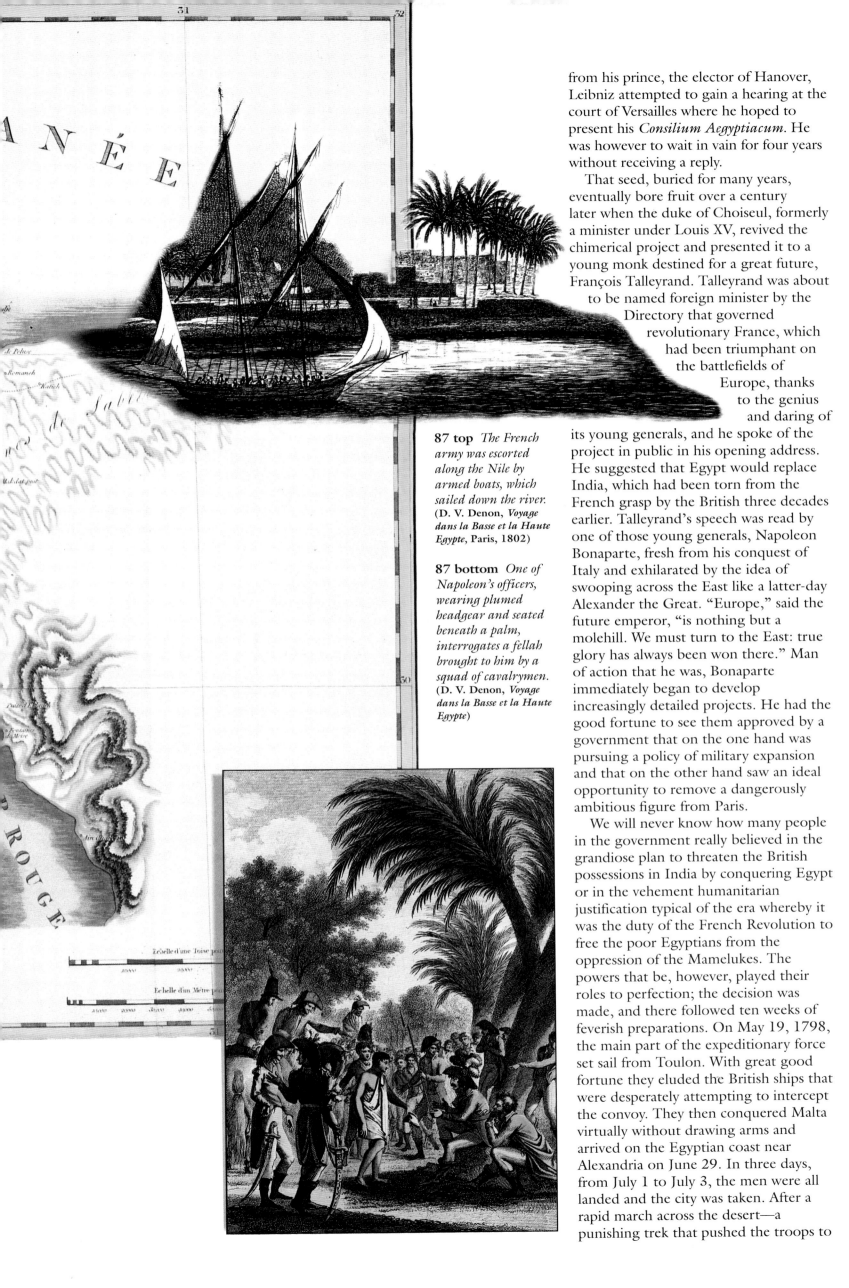

from his prince, the elector of Hanover, Leibniz attempted to gain a hearing at the court of Versailles where he hoped to present his *Consilium Aegyptiacum*. He was however to wait in vain for four years without receiving a reply.

That seed, buried for many years, eventually bore fruit over a century later when the duke of Choiseul, formerly a minister under Louis XV, revived the chimerical project and presented it to a young monk destined for a great future, François Talleyrand. Talleyrand was about to be named foreign minister by the Directory that governed revolutionary France, which had been triumphant on the battlefields of Europe, thanks to the genius and daring of its young generals, and he spoke of the project in public in his opening address. He suggested that Egypt would replace India, which had been torn from the French grasp by the British three decades earlier. Talleyrand's speech was read by one of those young generals, Napoleon Bonaparte, fresh from his conquest of Italy and exhilarated by the idea of swooping across the East like a latter-day Alexander the Great. "Europe," said the future emperor, "is nothing but a molehill. We must turn to the East: true glory has always been won there." Man of action that he was, Bonaparte immediately began to develop increasingly detailed projects. He had the good fortune to see them approved by a government that on the one hand was pursuing a policy of military expansion and that on the other hand saw an ideal opportunity to remove a dangerously ambitious figure from Paris.

We will never know how many people in the government really believed in the grandiose plan to threaten the British possessions in India by conquering Egypt or in the vehement humanitarian justification typical of the era whereby it was the duty of the French Revolution to free the poor Egyptians from the oppression of the Mamelukes. The powers that be, however, played their roles to perfection; the decision was made, and there followed ten weeks of feverish preparations. On May 19, 1798, the main part of the expeditionary force set sail from Toulon. With great good fortune they eluded the British ships that were desperately attempting to intercept the convoy. They then conquered Malta virtually without drawing arms and arrived on the Egyptian coast near Alexandria on June 29. In three days, from July 1 to July 3, the men were all landed and the city was taken. After a rapid march across the desert—a punishing trek that pushed the troops to

87 top *The French army was escorted along the Nile by armed boats, which sailed down the river.* (D. V. Denon, *Voyage dans la Basse et la Haute Egypte*, Paris, 1802)

87 bottom *One of Napoleon's officers, wearing plumed headgear and seated beneath a palm, interrogates a fellah brought to him by a squad of cavalrymen.* (D. V. Denon, *Voyage dans la Basse et la Haute Egypte*)

88-89 *A number of Mamelukes sent by Murad Bey board the British ships after the battle to congratulate the victors.* (**William Cooper,** ***A Voyage up the Mediterranean,*** **London, 1802**)

88 bottom *British boats comb the waters of the anchorage and exchange gunfire with the French troops from another boat.* (W. Cooper, *A Voyage up the Mediterranean*)

89 top *During the battle of the Nile, Horatio Nelson, depicted here in a nineteenth-century print, was wounded by shrapnel. His adversary, Brueys, died during the battle.*

the threshold of mutiny and induced a number to commit suicide—Bonaparte reached the Nile at Rahmaniyeh. There his party joined a flotilla that had sailed up the river, and on July 13 they routed the fifteen thousand men of the Mameluke chief Murad Bey. A week later the Frenchmen were in sight of the Pyramids and Cairo. Murad was waiting for them with another army that met with the same end as the first. The survivors fled into the desert and on July 24 the victor entered the Egyptian capital, which the other Mameluke chief,

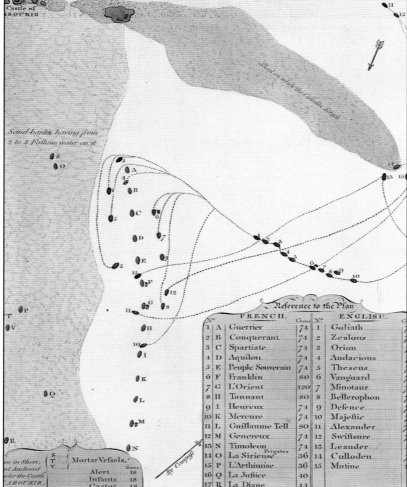

89 center *Admiral Nelson, the commander of the British Mediterranean fleet, tried in vain to intercept the French squadron heading for Egypt. This map shows the routes followed by the two fleets.*
(W. Cooper, *A Voyage up the Mediterranean*)

89 bottom *Nelson pounced on the French ships some time after the troops had disembarked and was fortunate to find them at anchor. The French Admiral Brueys had not taken the advice of those who suggested he enter the port of Alexandria. The British bombardment almost completely destroyed the French fleet. This map depicts the events of the battles.*
(W. Cooper, *A Voyage up the Mediterranean*)

89

90 top *The French pushed south toward Upper Egypt, trying to engage the elusive Mamelukes. Depicted here is a French hussar, cut off from his companions, who puts up a desperate fight against four Mamelukes.*
(**Dominique Vivant Denon**, *Voyage dans la Basse et la Haute Egypte*, **Paris, 1802**)

91–94 *An episode from the Battle of the Pyramids, with the monuments silhouetted in the background. Precise fusillades and volleys of cannon fire from the French slaughtered the Mamelukes. The Mameluke tactics consisted of no more than a violent frontal charge, which proved suicidal against a disciplined and well-armed modern army. "The last cavalry charge of the Middle Age," as it was labeled by one military historian, ended in a massacre: over two thousand Mamelukes and several thousand fellahin lost their lives. Among the French, 29 men died and about 260 were wounded.*
(**D. V. Denon**, *Voyage dans la Basse et la Haute Egypte*)

95 *Napoleon, in the midst of a group of high-ranking officers, watches Muslim festivities in Ezbekiya Square from the balcony of the sumptuous palace of the Alfi Bey, which he had made his residence. "al-Sultan al-Kabir," as Napoleon was called by the Egyptians, tried to win over the people and, above all, their religious leaders with a policy of reconciliation and respect for the Muslim faith.*

Ibrahim Bey, had abandoned with his one hundred thousand men without putting up any resistance. This army was eventually reached and defeated on August 11 at Salaliya, with Ibrahim fleeing to Syria.

However, Napoleon's triumph was tempered by the disastrous news from Alexandria: Admiral Nelson had fallen upon the French fleet anchored in Abu Qir Bay and destroyed it. The master of Egypt, Bonaparte was now cut off from his homeland. The absolute control over the seas exercised by Britain inescapably changed the destiny of the expedition. The Egyptian population initially watched with bewildered approval as the new conquerors crushed the hated Mamelukes, and the oppressed fellahin applauded the French soldiers as they bent their bayonets into hooks with which to fish the cadavers of their enemies out of

the Nile before stripping them of their jewels, but this idyll was not to last.

The sultan of Constantinople, who according to the grand plan should have been convinced by Talleyrand's diplomatic attempts to persuade him that the elimination of the Mamelukes was to the advantage of the Ottoman Empire, listened to the British incitement rather than to the French blandishments and proclaimed a holy war. Cairo rebelled unexpectedly on October 21: inflamed by the imam against the infidels, the people lynched Frenchmen in the streets. There followed a bloody repression that left two thousand victims. An epidemic of bubonic plague then broke out and decimated the population while the Sublime Porte mobilized two armies that were to advance on Egypt in a pincer action, the forces from Damascus crossing the Sinai Desert and those from Rhodes

disembarking from British ships in the delta. Trusting in the proverbial Ottoman tardiness, Bonaparte decided to forestall the first threat by advancing into Syria.

Early in February 1799 the French troops began their march along the coast. They were blocked by unexpected resistance from the Turkish garrison at al-Arish, however, and did not reach the walls of the fortress of Acre, the strategic key to Palestine, until March 18. By that time the city's defenses had been organized by the combined efforts of the pasha Jazzar, the English commodore Sidney Smith, and a French emigrant Colonel Phélippeaux who, ironically, had attended the French military academy with Bonaparte. The siege lasted for over two months. On April 16, the 25,000 Turks of the Damascus army attacked the French at Mount Tabor, but they were beaten and dispersed. Acre, however, did

96-97 *Bonaparte had no difficulty in defeating the Turkish army, which, after landing, had unwisely remained idle at Abu Qir. This illustration shows a phase of the battle during which the British ships supported the Turks with cannon fire. In the center, the castle of Abu Qir can be seen burning in the background.*
(D. V. Denon, *Voyage dans la Basse et la Haute Egypte*)

97 top *The Turkish expeditionary force sent to fight the French was transported on British ships and landed at Abu Qir Bay. The waters of the anchorage still contained the wrecks of the French ships sunk by Nelson a year earlier.*
(W. Cooper, *A Voyage up the Meditteranean*)

98-99 *In front of the ruins of the Temple of Karnak, three stiff-backed grenadiers pay military honors to a group of French officers from the various forces. Acting as guide is a savant dressed in outlandish French-Egyptian apparel, who points out the monuments to the distinguished visitors.*

not fall in spite of all Napoleon's best efforts and the raging plague. On May 17, Bonaparte ordered his troops to retreat.

The return to Egypt was a torturous odyssey blighted by tragic episodes. The worst occurred at Jaffa where the wounded soldiers who could no longer be carried were given a coup de grâce. When they finally emerged from the Sinai the French army had lost a third of its forces but its general, who was well versed in the art of propaganda, staged a triumphant parade through the streets of Cairo, presenting himself as the conqueror of Syria while the Egyptians honored him with the name al-Sultan al-Kabir, the Great Sultan.

During the siege of Acre, Bonaparte had read in the German newspapers thrown onto the coast by Sidney Smith, another expert in psychological warfare, that France was in need of a savior. Its armies had been beaten on all fronts and the Austro-Russians had reconquered Italy. This was Bonaparte's great chance, and he decided to abandon Egypt, where the future held only an inevitable surrender, albeit after lengthy resistance. First, however, on July 25 he routed the 15,000 Turks of the Rhodes army at Abu Qir who had unwisely remained inactive for two weeks after disembarking. Then, on August 23, Napoleon abandoned Egypt along with a small group of trusted men, leaving the country and the remnants of his army to his furious and resentful colleague Kléber, who wrote to the Directory defining his former commander-in-chief as "that little scoundrel." Negotiations were set under way with the British regarding a French surrender, but no progress was made and the occupation dragged on for another eighteen months. During this period, on June 14, 1800, the honest, mild Kléber, known to the Egyptians as al-Sultan al-Adel, the Just Sultan, was assassinated in Cairo by a fanatic. Finally, in March 1801, an Anglo-Turkish expeditionary force landed near Alexandria, and the French, by then heartily sick of Egypt, surrendered after a token struggle. Their ephemeral domination left no lasting

traces on the torpid Islamic world. One analyst, in relating the events of 1798–1799, mentioned only that in "that year the pilgrimage to Mecca was discontinuous."

The Egyptian campaign was to have a far more significant effect on European culture, however. Bonaparte had had the bright idea of taking to war with him an entire academy—eminent savants, scientists, and academics chosen from among the various fields of human knowledge, from geology to medicine. Even the mathematician Monge and the balloonist Conté eagerly agreed to participate in the conquest of a country that would be available for them to study. Their talents had eminently practical purposes, but Bonaparte also invited a composer and a poet, perhaps to celebrate

100 top *Denon and other members of the French party approach the majestic columns of the Temple of Hermopolis. The soldiers are kitted out and armed, ready to respond to any Mamelukes who may be lying in wait.* (Dominique Vivant Denon, *Voyage dans la Basse et la Haute Egypte,* Paris, 1802)

100-101 *Denon is absorbed in sketching Egyptian ruins while his native servants sit on the ground nearby, waiting patiently. On the right are camels belonging to a caravan that has also made a stop here.* (D. V. Denon, *Voyage dans la Basse et la Haute Egypte*)

100 bottom *Using a long ladder, Denon has climbed up onto the head of the Sphinx with a fellow archaeologist and is measuring its height from the ground with a plumb line.* (D. V. Denon, *Voyage dans la Basse et la Haute Egypte*)

101 top *Smiling in this attractive self-portrait, Dominique Vivant Denon appears to be satisfied with the work he completed in Egypt.*

101 center *Printed on this page of* Voyage dans la Basse et la Haute Egypte *is Denon's dedication to Bonaparte, then First Consul, in which the name of the future emperor appears beside those of the great pharaohs, "conquerers and benefactors."*

in music and rhyme the triumphs forecast by the general, who during the voyage amused himself by organizing debates each evening in his cabin with that court of lofty minds. The troops were unhappy about the privileges enjoyed by the academics, however, and during the first phase of the campaign, when forming squares against Mameluke cavalry charges, the officers never failed to give the order "Asses and savants in the center!"

Following the conquest of Cairo their warrior-patron installed the savants in a Thousand and One Nights palace, which became the home of the Institute of Egypt, in the marvelous gardens of which they could philosophize like their predecessors in Athens. The general loved to visit them, leaving behind his

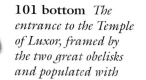

A BONAPARTE.

Joindre *l'éclat de votre nom à la splendeur des monuments d'Egypte, c'est rattacher les fastes glorieux de notre siecle aux temps fabuleux de l'histoire; c'est réchauffer les cendres des Sésostris et des Mendès, comme vous conquérants, comme vous bienfaiteurs.*

L'Europe, en apprenant que je vous accompagnois dans l'une de vos plus mémorables expéditions, recevra mon ouvrage avec un avide intérêt. Je n'ai rien négligé pour le rendre digne du héros à qui je voulois l'offrir.

VIVANT DENON.

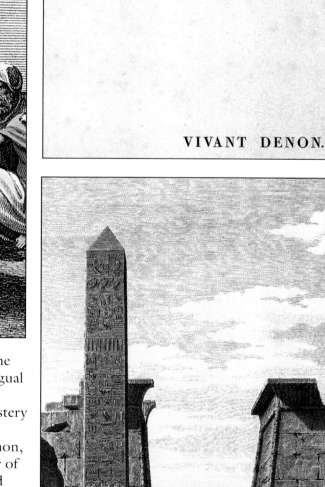

sword as a sign of deference and bringing to their learned attention practical questions regarding the purification of the waters of the Nile or the improvement of the local beer.

For three years savants and artists studied and documented everything they found in Egypt: plants, animals, men, temples, tombs, statues, and inscriptions. Among other endeavors they compiled a catalog of all the canals, indicating their state of maintenance, and drew up a land register of the arable terrain. Shortly before Bonaparte withdrew to return to France, taking with him only three of their number—the mathematician Monge, the chemist Berthollet, and the poet Grandmaison—the Rosetta Stone was discovered. Deciphering its bilingual inscription some decades later, Jean-François Champollion solved the mystery of hieroglyphics. The artist and archaeologist Dominique Vivant Denon, who was later to become the director of the museums of France, accompanied General Désaix to Upper Egypt and completed numerous drawings of the monuments, which were subsequently published in the splendid volume *Voyage dans la Basse et la Haute Egypte* (Paris, 1802).

When the savants were obliged to embark on British ships and abandon Egypt following the French surrender,

the British admiral ordered them to hand over all the material they had gathered and the reports they had compiled. One of the scientists, Étienne Geoffroy Saint-Hilaire, replied, "Rather than hand it over to you we will burn it. If it is fame you seek, you shall have it; you will go down in history as having been responsible for the burning of a second Alexandrian library." Those proud words saved the only lasting result of the bizarre Napoleonic campaign: the ten volumes of text and the fourteen volumes of plates of the *Description de l'Égypte*, the last of which saw the light of day after Bonaparte had died in exile and the Bourbons once again ruled France.

102-103 *At the top is the Temple of Luxor, in the center, the Temple of Edfu, and at the bottom, the façade of the temple of Esna. On the right is the so-called Zodiac of Dendera, with the constellations of the ancient Egyptians. Napoleon's conquest of Egypt was politically short-lived and strategically pointless. But its cultural consequences were enormous: it marked the birth of Egyptology, and the land of the pharaohs emerged from the mists of legend to become, at last, the subject of serious study. The scientists who accompanied the expedition at Napoleon's instigation collected masses of material that later appeared in numerous publications. Reproduced on these pages are some outstanding illustrations from Dominique Vivant Denon's book* Voyage dans la Basse et la Haute Egypte.

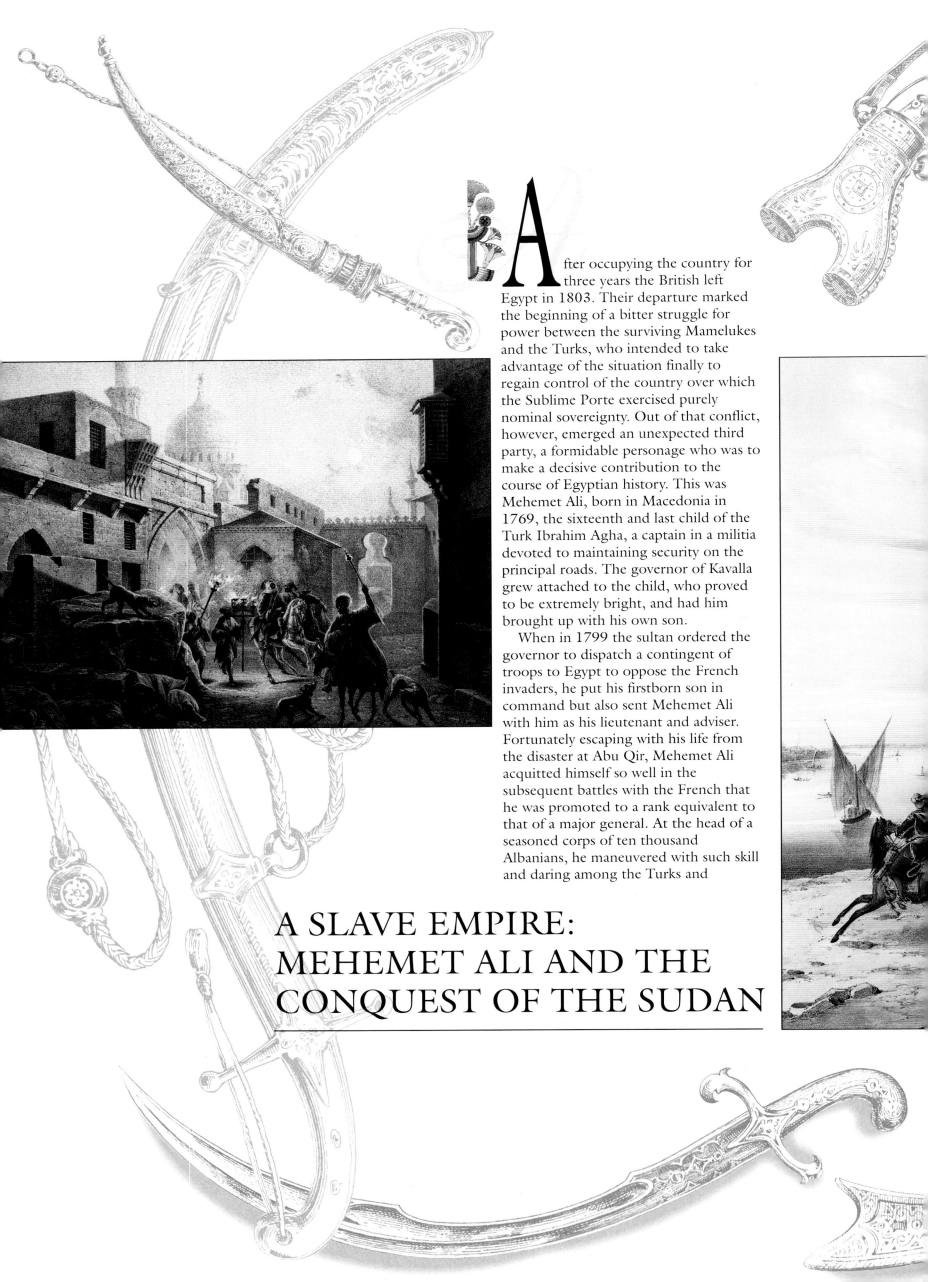

After occupying the country for three years the British left Egypt in 1803. Their departure marked the beginning of a bitter struggle for power between the surviving Mamelukes and the Turks, who intended to take advantage of the situation finally to regain control of the country over which the Sublime Porte exercised purely nominal sovereignty. Out of that conflict, however, emerged an unexpected third party, a formidable personage who was to make a decisive contribution to the course of Egyptian history. This was Mehemet Ali, born in Macedonia in 1769, the sixteenth and last child of the Turk Ibrahim Agha, a captain in a militia devoted to maintaining security on the principal roads. The governor of Kavalla grew attached to the child, who proved to be extremely bright, and had him brought up with his own son.

When in 1799 the sultan ordered the governor to dispatch a contingent of troops to Egypt to oppose the French invaders, he put his firstborn son in command but also sent Mehemet Ali with him as his lieutenant and adviser. Fortunately escaping with his life from the disaster at Abu Qir, Mehemet Ali acquitted himself so well in the subsequent battles with the French that he was promoted to a rank equivalent to that of a major general. At the head of a seasoned corps of ten thousand Albanians, he maneuvered with such skill and daring among the Turks and

A SLAVE EMPIRE: MEHEMET ALI AND THE CONQUEST OF THE SUDAN

104 *A torchlight procession winds its way through the moonlit streets of Cairo, accompanying a Mameluke leader on his way back to his palace.* (Maximilian in Bayern, *Bilder aus dem Oriente,* Stuttgart, 1846)

105 top left *An everyday scene in Middle Egypt: two veiled women ride on donkeys through the streets of Cairo, while a black eunuch stops passersby to let them through. Standing behind the two women is an Egyptian officer wearing the European-style uniform introduced by Mehemet Ali.* (Maximilian in Bayern, *Ansichten aus dem Oriente,* Munich, 1838)

105 top right *A soldier of fortune of Albanian origin, Mehemet Ali took advantage of the confusion that reigned in Egypt after the departure of the French to defeat the Mamelukes once and for all. He then founded his own dynasty.*

104-105 *The indefatigable Mehemet Ali loved traveling far and wide to visit every corner of his kingdom.* He customarily set out from Cairo down the Nile, sailing with a procession of feluccas, or else he rode on horseback along the river from one town to another. In this illustration his procession leaves the gates of a fortified town to descend to the riverbank, where boats are waiting. (Maximilian in Bayern, *Bilder aus dem Oriente*)

Mamelukes, pretending to favor first one and then the other but betraying both and proving to be their ruin, that in 1805 he was acclaimed as viceroy of Egypt by his faithful followers, a position subsequently confirmed by the sultan. Two years later he again proved his worth by forcing back to sea the British troops that had once again landed at Alexandria, capturing a thousand of them and obliging them to carry the heads of their dead companions to Cairo, where they were hoisted onto four 450 poles planted in Ezbekiyeh Square in a triumphant demonstration of the power and cruelty of the new pasha.

For some years Mehemet Ali appeared content to share the domination of Egypt with the last of the Mameluke beys. In actual fact, however, he was merely biding his time. His great opportunity came on March 1, 1811, when he invited the Mamelukes to participate in a ceremony in the Citadel at Cairo. At the end of the celebration the five hundred guests were invited to descend into the city by way of a narrow road carved into the hillside. The procession was preceded and followed by the pasha's Albanian troops who proceeded to close the gates at either end of the road and rapidly disperse to the higher ground from where they began to fire on the trapped Mamelukes. Those who were not killed immediately were decapitated later, and the massacre was completed with a merciless manhunt that lasted throughout the night and left thousands of victims among the followers of the Mamelukes. In the meantime Ibrahim, the eldest son of Mehemet Ali, ascended the Nile with a column of troops to eliminate the last survivors. Around three hundred managed to escape, fleeing with their wives and children beyond the cataracts into Nubia. Even there, however, as we shall see, they were not to be safe from the ruthless fury of their enemy.

Mehemet Ali was a man of vast ambition. Having wiped out all opposition in Egypt, he set about reorganizing the country and turned to the conquest of Hejaz, the province of Arabia in which the Islamic holy cities, Medina and Mecca, are located. The area had been torn from the grasp of the Ottoman Empire by the revolt of a strict Muslim sect, the Wahhabis, who now prevented the annual pilgrimage of the faithful to the tomb of Muhammad. The viceroy of Egypt was ordered by the sultan of Constantinople to regain control of the area. This task was finally completed by Mehemet Ali's son Ibrahim after eight years of bloody struggle. Ibrahim was rewarded by the sultan with sovereignty not only over Hejaz but also over the never conquered Christian Abyssinia. Mehemet Ali's Egypt thus became master of both sides of the Red Sea and was invited to expand its influence southward, at the expense of the infidels.

In 1819, a year after the conclusion of

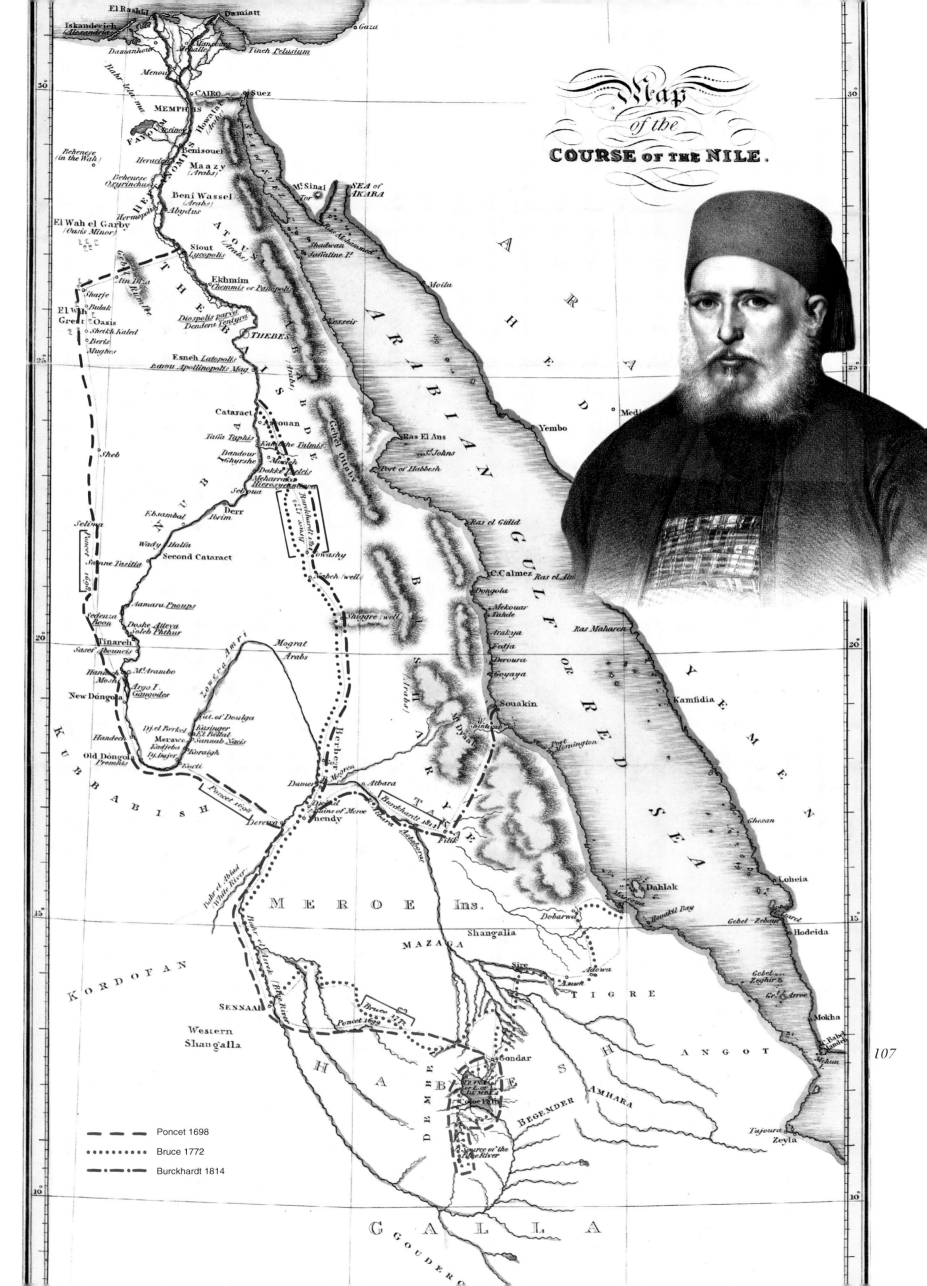

108-109 *Mehemet Ali watches with his counselors while in front of the walls of Cairo's Citadel the most dramatic episode of his long reign is being played out: the slaughter of the Mamelukes, which he himself had ordered on March 1, 1811. Invited to a celebration, around 500 Mamelukes assembled in Cairo. At the end of the ceremony they descended from the Citadel in a procession along a street winding through the rocks. At a certain point the pasha's Albanians opened fire on the Mamelukes. With no hope of defending themselves in a space crammed with men and horses, they were ruthlessly cut down. The very few survivors fled to Syria or into the Sudan, but even there a few years later the long arm of the pasha reached out to complete the extermination.* (L.N.P.A. Forbin, *Voyage dans le Levant,* Paris, 1819)

110 top *The camp of the larger part of the Egyptian expedition commanded by Ismail, the son of Mehemet Ali, near the city of Sennar, formerly the capital of a prosperous kingdom but now in decline and impoverished.* (Frédéric Cailliaud, *Voyage à Méroé*, Paris, 1826)

110-111 *The landing of the conquerors: the Egyptian soldiers disembark from their feluccas on the banks of the Nile, while in the foreground a squadron of irregular cavalry led by a menacing bearded figure heads toward the interior. The Egyptian conquest of the Sudan was a series of sackings and devastation rather than a military campaign.* (Maximilian in Bayern, *Bilder aus dem Oriente*, Stuttgart, 1846)

111 top left *A number of Europeans, determined not to abandon their top hats and frock coats, crossing the Upper Nile on a boat that is also carrying a camel.* (**G. A. Hoskins,** *Travels in Ethiopia,* **London, 1835**)

111 top right *Everyday life in a house in Dongola, the city in which the last Mamelukes sought refuge. On the appearance of the Egyptians, they chose to forgo useless resistance* and disperse into the desert. Just three hundred capable of fighting remained. (**G. A. Hoskins,** *Travels in Ethiopia*)

111 center *As in feudal Europe, the Sudan was divided into small sultanates and constellated by fortified castles. This engraving shows the walls of the fort at Koke set amid towering palms.* (**G. A. Hoskins,** *Travels in Ethiopia*)

111 bottom *Two typical Sudanese figures. On the left is Musa, the son of the* melek, *or king, of Berber, who surrendered to the Egyptians. On the right is an elegant Shendi woman.* (**G. A. Hoskins,** *Travels in Ethiopia*)

112 top *Over the centuries many monuments in ancient Egypt were adapted for use by the new religions that gained footholds in the country—first Christianity and then* Islam. *In this view of the Temple of Luxor at Thebes, note the minaret of a mosque built among the ruins.* (Jean-Jacques Rifaud, ***Voyage en Égypte, en Nubie***, *Paris, 1830*)

112-113 *With flags flying, and accompanied by drum rolls and cymbals, the holy men of the mosque of Said Tantawi begin to collect alms.*

113 top *Scenes of daily life in a Nubian village on the banks of the Nile: cooking, drawing water from the river, and mending nets.*

113 bottom *Sabers, pistols, muzzle loaders: the Bedouins of the desert traveled well armed, just like their rulers, the Mamelukes.*

(J.-J. Rifaud, *Voyage en Égypte, en Nubie*)

113

114 top *Cataracts like these presented a serious obstacle to navigation, forcing travelers to portage their boats overland.* (G. A. Hoskins, *Travels in Ethiopia*, London, 1835)

the long, exhausting Hejaz campaign, the viceroy's thoughts began to turn toward expansion into the Sudan. There were a number of potential advantages in such a conquest. First and foremost Mehemet Ali would finally be rid of the last remaining Mamelukes, who had sought refuge at Dongola, where they extorted and oppressed the locals, whom Ali's spies described as resentful and ready to rebel. However, his primary aim was to capture a vast number of slaves

with whom to restock his army, decimated after eight years of war in Arabia, and to lay his hands on the fabled gold mines of the area.

The third son of Mehemet Ali, Ismail, was appointed to command the expedition, and in the summer of 1820 a fleet composed of hundreds of boats of all kinds began to ascend the Nile toward Aswan. There were around four thousand combat troops, a good half of them Albanians and Turks, each

114 bottom *Two Shaiqiya warriors training for combat. The Shaiqiya were among the most determined opponents of the Egyptian conquest. They went into battle armed with just swords and spears and were massacred by the Egyptian guns and cannons.* (G. A. Hoskins, *Travels in Ethiopia*)

114

accompanied by a slave and an ass carrying his equipment. There was also a group of helmeted and armored Kurdish horsemen, Bedouins in chain mail, and poor half-clothed wretches armed with pikes, attracted by the hope of rich pickings and the promise of fifty piastres from the viceroy for every ear cut from an enemy head. In total, counting the servants, parasites, and prostitutes, the disorderly particolored horde numbered ten thousand. They camped each evening like a swarm of locusts around

Ismail's immense green tent, thirty meters wide and topped by a sparkling gilded globe. There were also a number of white men—the Americans, English, and British who were in command of the artillery; Greek and Italian doctors; the Englishman Waddington, and the Frenchman Cailliaud, about whom we will hear much more.

Having passed the First Cataract in August, the army reached Wadi Halfa in September and tackled the second; by the end of October all the boats were successfully beyond the obstacle. The army entered Dongola in a bloodless coup; the Mamelukes had retreated. Once the Egyptian forces penetrated the lands of the Shaiqiya tribe near Kurti, however, they were obliged to fight after a vain attempt at peaceful domination. On the morning of November 4 a screaming mob of Shaiqiyas armed with spears and sabers fell upon the Egyptian ranks. They were cut down by the invaders' gunfire. Three thousand ears were sent to Cairo, and Kurti was burned. A month later the Shaiqiyas made another attempt but were annihilated.

The daughter of one of the most important tribal chieftains fell into the

114-115 *Ismail's regal tent being approached by a group of horsemen bringing with them an important prisoner, Safia, the daughter of a Sudanese tribal leader. By handing her back to her father, Ismail won his trust and subsequently his surrender. This illustration is from* Voyage à Méroé, *by Frédéric Cailliaud, published in Paris in 1826.*

115 center *The ruins of the Pyramids of Meroë in a drawing by G. A. Hoskins, taken from his book* Travels in Ethiopia *(London, 1835).*

115 bottom *Hoskins, the British artist and traveler, drawing the ruins of a temple at Wadi Owataib, clothed in Oriental costume and assisted by a servant who is holding a parasol.* **(G. A. Hoskins, *Travels in Ethiopia*)**

hands of Ismail, who was astute enough to send her back to her father with great pomp and ceremony. Perhaps as a result of this unexpected move, perhaps out of pure terror of the "Turks," as the Sudanese natives called the invaders, the tribes surrendered one by one. In February 1821, Ismail once again began to advance deep into the Sudan, reaching Berber early in March. Here the great chief Mek Nimr of Shendi surrendered, together with the last of the Mamelukes who were then enrolled as members of the victor's bodyguard.

From then on the campaign resembled a massive roundup of slaves; the army marched on without meeting further opposition, devastating and sacking what lay in its path. Halfayat, at the confluence between the Blue and White Niles was reached on May 24 and a month later Ismail was in Sennar, the capital of the great kingdom, where the conqueror decided to celebrate his triumph in the ancient Roman manner with an interminable procession.

Up to this point the expedition had proceeded even better than expected; it had in fact been little more than a rather tiring route march. In July, however, when the rainy season set in, Ismail's forces began to experience serious problems. Malaria and dysentery decimated the Egyptians; by October only five hundred were capable of walking, but movement was out of the question anyway as the mud had made the roads impassable. Ismail's elder brother Ibrahim arrived with sufficient rations to prevent a mutiny of the starving troops, but he too was struck down by dysentery.

When the rains stopped in December, the brothers decided to continue their

116 top *The fortified residence of the ancient kings of Shendi. Shendi was the scene of Ismail's miserable death. He was returning to Egypt, having completed his conquest, when he offended the local chief with his exorbitant demands and his disdainful behavior. That night he was burned to death in his tent.* (Romolo Gessi Pasha, *Seven Years in the Sudan*, London, 1892)

116 center *Sennar was the capital of an ancient empire that included almost the entire Sudan. Because of tribal rebellions, Sennar had disappeared even before the coming of the Egyptians.* (R. Gessi Pasha, *Seven Years in the Sudan*)

advance, Ibrahim on the left bank of the river, Ismail on the right. They headed south in search of slaves and the elusive Sudanese gold. On January 1, 1822, they came within sight of the great Ethiopian mountains. A little farther on, the Blue Nile disappeared into an inaccessible gorge. There was not the slightest trace of gold, and the slaves died in droves; of a total of around thirty thousand, less than half reached Cairo. Extremely ill, Ibrahim promised ten thousand talers to his Italian doctor, Ricci, if he managed to get him home alive. The doctor succeeded and received his reward.

In mid-February Ismail also decided that he had had enough and returned to Sennar. From there he sent a message to his father asking for permission to bring the campaign to a close. Mehemet Ali's reply in the affirmative arrived in October, and Ismail departed immediately. By the end of the month he had reached Shendi and peremptorily asked Mek Nimr for a tribute of thirty thousand talers, six thousand slaves, and rations for his men within forty-eight hours. When the tribal chieftain replied that the requests were insane, Ismail struck him in the face with the long stem of his pipe. Mek Nimr furiously unsheathed his saber, but Ismail's guards forced him to his knees and obliged him to beg for pardon.

That night, while Ismail and his officers were sleeping off a sumptuous banquet, Mek Nimr had his warriors surround the tent before setting fire to it. Those "Turks" who managed to escape the flames were massacred; Ismail burned to death. The rebellion spread to all the other villages, but the Egyptians possessed

116 bottom
Ascending the course of the Nile with a large fleet, the Egyptian expeditionary force took lands in strategic areas. Here a number of feluccas are moored near Gebel al-Barkal. The soldiers' camp can be seen on the banks.
(George Waddington, Journal of Visits to Some Parts of Ethiopia, London, 1822)

117 *The sheikh Sayd, head of the Ababde tribe. The inhabitants of the Sudan were largely Arabicized over the centuries; they had been converted to Islam and lived like their fellow Muslims on the other side of the Red Sea. Only a few black tribes, especially in the south of the country, remained pagan. From these tribes and from among the Christian Abyssinians, black-skinned slaves were captured and were highly prized throughout the Islamic world.*
(G. A. Hoskins, Travels in Ethiopia, London, 1835)

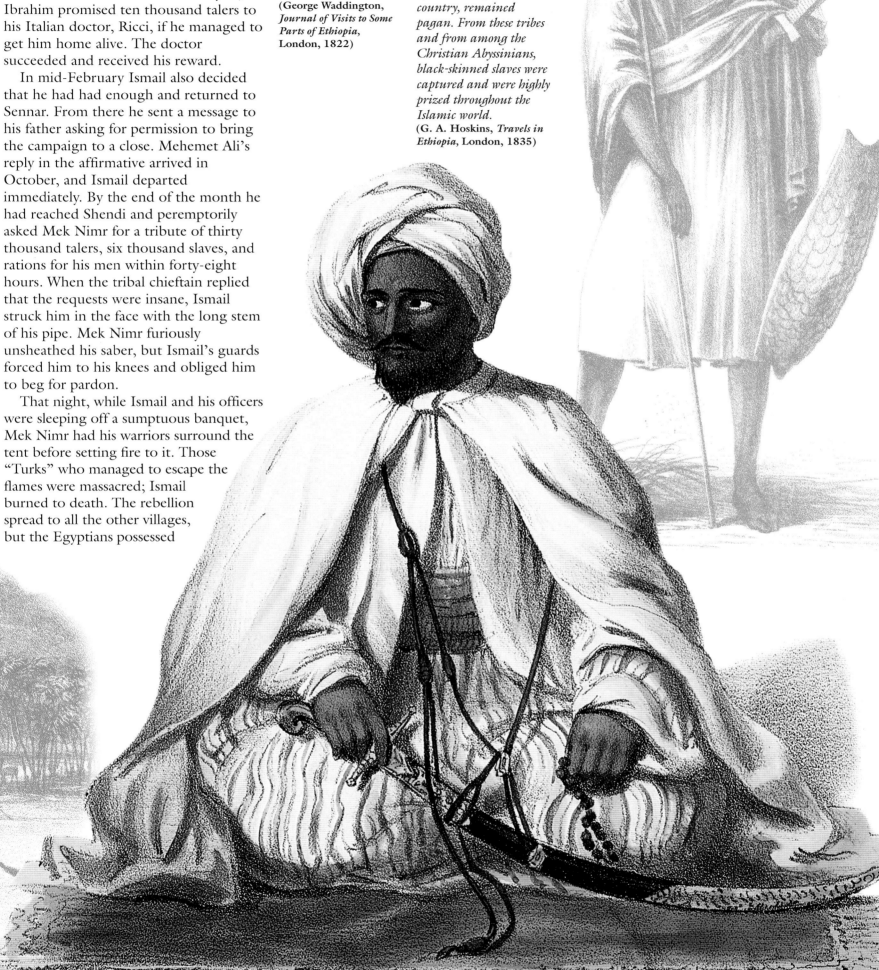

118 top *This intense profile belongs to an inhabitant of the Sudanese desert.* (Romolo Gessi Pasha, *Seven Years in the Sudan*, London, 1892)

118 center *A typical fortified house of a local chief. Like medieval Europe, the Sudan was dotted with castles made necessary by the continual wars and incessant sacking.* (R. Gessi Pasha, *Seven Years in the Sudan*)

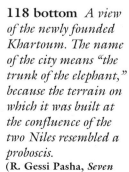

118 bottom *A view of the newly founded Khartoum. The name of the city means "the trunk of the elephant," because the terrain on which it was built at the confluence of the two Niles resembled a proboscis.* (R. Gessi Pasha, *Seven Years in the Sudan*)

the only firearms and soon crushed all resistance. Mohammed Bey, Ismail's lieutenant, returning from a raid into the Kordofan as far as Al-Ubayyid, put the entire region to the sword, trailing the fleeing Mek Nimr to the Ethiopian border. He failed to capture the chief but gave vent to his rage by having all the prisoners gutted and by cutting off the breasts of the women.

By the end of 1823, fifty thousand Sudanese had been killed, dozens of villages had been razed, the country was devastated, and the Egyptians were the masters of the Nile from its mouth to the mountains of Ethiopia.

In 1824, at the confluence of the two Niles, a small fishing village began its expansion into the city of Khartoum, which would soon boast a population of thirty thousand and would become the most important city in the Sudan. The Egyptians also established garrisons at Al-Ubayyid in the Kordofan, at Wad Medani on the Blue Nile and at Kassala on the Ethiopian border. These were the centers from which the slave and ivory hunters departed. In the meantime Mehemet Ali's expansionist ambitions turned in other directions. He sent Ibrahim to quell the Greek rebels and then to occupy Syria when the sultan refused to reward him. In the autumn of 1838, at the height of his power, Mehemet Ali decided to visit his Sudanese dominions, ascending the river as far as Khartoum and then following the Blue Nile to Fazogli. He was accompanied by European advisers and technicians who suggested or fostered grandiose projects: the elimination of the cataracts, a railway and a telegraph line from Alexandria to Khartoum, and cotton and indigo plantations on the Island of Meroë. The most important thing to come out of that journey, however, was the decision to organize an expedition to explore the upper reaches of the White Nile. In the spring of 1839 Mehemet Ali himself completed a kind of preliminary excursion, pushing on as far as the Shilluk Islands near al-Ais, which he considered the (temporary) southernmost tip of Egypt. There was one victim of the trip, a Swiss engineer named Baumgarten, who died of fever on his return to Khartoum.

The real expedition left from the city on November 9, led by three "Turks"—General Suleiman Kashef, Admiral Selim Bimbashi, and Vice Admiral Fayzallah—and two Europeans, the French adventurer Thibaut, who had taken the Islamic name Ibrahim Effendi, and the German Friedrich Werne, who had been a lawyer before dedicating himself to a military career in an East eager to bestow high ranks on European experts. They were equipped with ten large boats and fifteen smaller vessels, rations for eight months, cannons, a regiment of four hundred black riflemen, and a rowdy and rather unreliable crew of Dongola boatmen and Khartoum vagabonds. Fortune was on their side, keeping them in the main current and allowing them to reach comfortably a position at 6 degrees latitude north in the region inhabited by the Elliab tribe. Here the north winds, which had aided them thus far, faded and they were obliged to haul their boats—an exhausting task that did not please the crews. Bearing in mind the increasing difficulties, the leaders declared the expedition a success and celebrated their triumph with salvos of cannon fire and volleys of rifle shots. On January 26 they turned back toward Khartoum, reaching the city on March 30. Relatively brief as it was, this trip nevertheless produced some significant results: it proved that the White Nile was navigable for a long stretch, its immense length suggesting extremely distant sources, especially as no mountains had been seen, and that the famous swamp region known as the Sudd, which was dense with reeds and proclaimed as insuperable by Herodotus, could in fact be crossed by boats. Moreover, various tributaries and a number of black tribes

118-119 *A group of soldiers of the Egyptian army in the Sudan indulging themselves in frenetic gallop to demonstrate their skills as horsemen. A number of Sudanese prisoners observe the scene.* (Maximilian in Bayern, *Bilder aus dem Oriente*, Stuttgart, 1846)

119 top *The melek, Nasr al-Din, was the sovereign of one of the many Sudanese kingdoms whose terrain coincided more or less with the area inhabited by a tribe.*

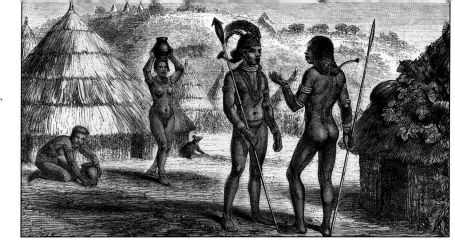

120 top *The illustrations on these pages depict a number of scenes of tribal life which the Egyptians saw during their ascent of the White Nile. In this engraving you can see a number of natives of Liza and Madi.* **(Samuel Baker,** *Albert Nyanza—Great Basin of the Nile,* **London, 1886)**

had been discovered.

Mehemet Ali had no intention of settling for such trifles, however, and ordered that a second expedition be organized. It departed exactly a year later, in November 1840, with the same leaders and a number of other white men, including two Frenchmen, the scientist d'Arnaud and the engineer Sabatier. As on the previous expedition, they ascended the river without encountering any problems. When they passed the point reached the year before, the landscape began to change. The Nile was wider and dotted with sandy islands. They then came across another area of swamps before the banks rose and began to be covered with forests alternating with cultivated fields and pastures. In this region there were numerous villages, and the natives were tall, well built, and friendly. The children welcomed the travelers with whistles and dancing.

One day a cry arose from the leading boat *Gabal* ("Mountain"). In the distance they caught sight of the long-sought highlands. Pressing on, they saw a ring of hills to the east, behind which rose a range of mountains; to the south and west isolated peaks broke the horizon. They reached the island of Chanker in the land of the Bari people, the king of whom proved to be extremely friendly. Like the conquistadores in America three centuries earlier, the Egyptians anxiously searched for any evidence of the presence of gold or other precious metals and were excited by the sight of the yellow copper and iron bracelets worn by the Bari people. They were disillusioned when they discovered the true nature of the metals, but the white engineers scented the possibility of mines in the interior. Questioned about the mountains and the river, the natives replied that the Tubiri, as they called the White Nile, originated in the south, a month's travel away in a distant country known as Angian. They continued for a few miles to a point at 4° 509 latitude north, where they were blocked by a cataract.

This expedition has been universally tainted with accusations of laziness and even cowardice; historians have questioned why at this point they decided to turn back rather than pressing on. In reality

disorganization was the order of the day: but there were abundant stores of food, but they were consumed indiscriminately with no thought to rationing, as were the munitions; the soldiers were intolerant of any form of discipline; and there were too many leaders, each of whom was looking after his own interests. The Circassian, Suleiman Kashef, for example, was concerned above all with his slaves, while the Cretan admiral Selim Bimbashi who aboard his ship had a minuscule harem composed of a slave woman and a eunuch, suspected betrayal by the natives and in the war dances executed in their honor saw premonitions of future massacres.

As for the Europeans, scientists or otherwise, it would appear that they dedicated themselves above all to the pleasures of the hunt rather than to the problems of Nile geography—all, that is, except the German Werne, the only one who would have preferred to go on. However, the excursion completed by that band of slave drivers, like the previous edition, was not altogether worthless, as it greatly amplified knowledge of the White Nile, the course

120 bottom *This warrior from the Commoro tribe, wearing a helmet decorated with beads and armed with a lance and a hippopotamus-skin shield, runs into battle with a number of companions who can be seen in the background.* **(S. Baker,** *Albert Nyanza—Great Basin of the Nile)*

120-121 *This Latuka funeral dance was executed to the sound of the great drums by the men in the center, wearing long ostrich feathers, and the women around them. The leaders of the Egyptian expedition, which included some Europeans, were accused of cowardice for having returned too soon, frightened by a world that they did not love, that they did not understand, and that they felt to be barbarous and hostile. In reality the scientific goals that were so important to the geographers were of no concern to them.* (S. Baker, *Albert Nyanza —Great Basin of the Nile*)

121 bottom *The Dari people, one of the tribes encountered by the Egyptian expedition along the Nile, were fearsome warriors and great rustlers of the livestock of others. Here we see them preying on the herd of an enemy tribe.* (S. Baker, *A Narative of the Expedition to Central Africa for the Suppression of the Slave Trade*, London, 1874)

122 These illustrations depict two different moments in the lives of the women of the era. At the top, an Egyptian lady is served by her maidservant while the view below is of the female baths at Cairo. (Maximilian in Bayern, *Bilder aus dem Oriente*, Stuttgart, 1846)

122-123 Dealt with harshly by European historians who have seen in him little more than a cruel despot, Mehemet Ali was in reality a figure of the caliber of Napoleon and Peter the Great. His ambition and his extreme farsightedness could have transformed Egypt into a thoroughly modern great power had his plans not been frustrated by the hostility of Great Britain, which was concerned about the prospect of the decadent Ottoman Empire being replaced by a vigorous, prosperous and militarily strong Egyptian empire. Under the reign of the Albanian, however, Egypt was opened up to the Europeans for whom it became a kind of oriental paradise. In this engraving taken from the book of G. Ebers Egypt: Description, Historical and Picturesque, *London*, 1884, Mehemet Ali is portrayed in his later years. A map of the course of the Nile is unfolded alongside the divan.

122

of which had now been followed for thousands of miles.

Mehemet Ali did not order further expeditions, perhaps because he had more pressing matters with which to deal. His dream of an Egyptian empire to replace the Ottoman rulers, from whom he planned to wrest Syria and Mesopotamia, aroused the opposition of the European powers, with the exception of France, which took little trouble to conceal its support. On July 15, 1840, a treaty was signed in London by Britain, Russia, Austria, and Prussia to save Turkey from dismemberment. Mehemet Ali received a suggestion—an order, to all intents and purposes—that he should content himself with being the hereditary viceroy of Egypt and the pasha of Acre for life. On his refusal, the fleets of the four great powers occupied the coastal cities of Syria, the Sublime Porte declared the decadence of the viceroy, and the Druse rebelled.

Ibrahim, the commander of the Egyptian army, felt it would be prudent to withdraw from Syria. Thanks in part to the good offices of France, an agreement was reached in February 1841 whereby Mehemet Ali obtained hereditary right to Egypt but was obliged to return Crete, Syria, and Hejaz to the sultan of Constantinople. This signified the collapse of all his grandiose projects, and the frustration of his ambitions might well have played a part in the viceroy's increasingly serious mental disturbances that, from 1847, placed power in the hands of Ibrahim.

The following year Ibrahim traveled to Constantinople to be officially invested as viceroy by the sultan. On his return, however, he fell ill with dysentery and preceded his father to the tomb by a few months. Ibrahim was succeeded by his nephew Abbas, the son of Tusun, Mehemet Ali's second son, described by dispassionate historians as lacking in spirit, fanatical, lazy, and sensual. While the favorite of his grandfather, Abbas was very different from him and, above all, lacked any expansionist ambitions whatsoever, so much so that among his first acts of power was the drastic reduction in size of the army and the navy. During his tyrannical reign, which lasted until 1854, the Sudan continued to be subjected to terrible slave-hunting raids while the governors starved the natives in the name of taxation. No further explorations were promoted and the most advanced Egyptian station was to be found two hundred miles upstream from Khartoum. On the death of Abbas his successor, Said, under the European influence that had become increasingly strong in Egypt, adopted less extreme policies. The country was reorganized and divided into the provinces of Dongola, Berber, Taka, Sennar, and Kordofan, which, under the name Egyptian Sudan, were assimilated into Egypt for administrative purposes.

123 bottom *The great-grandson of Mehemet Ali, Said, reorganized the administration of the Sudan.*

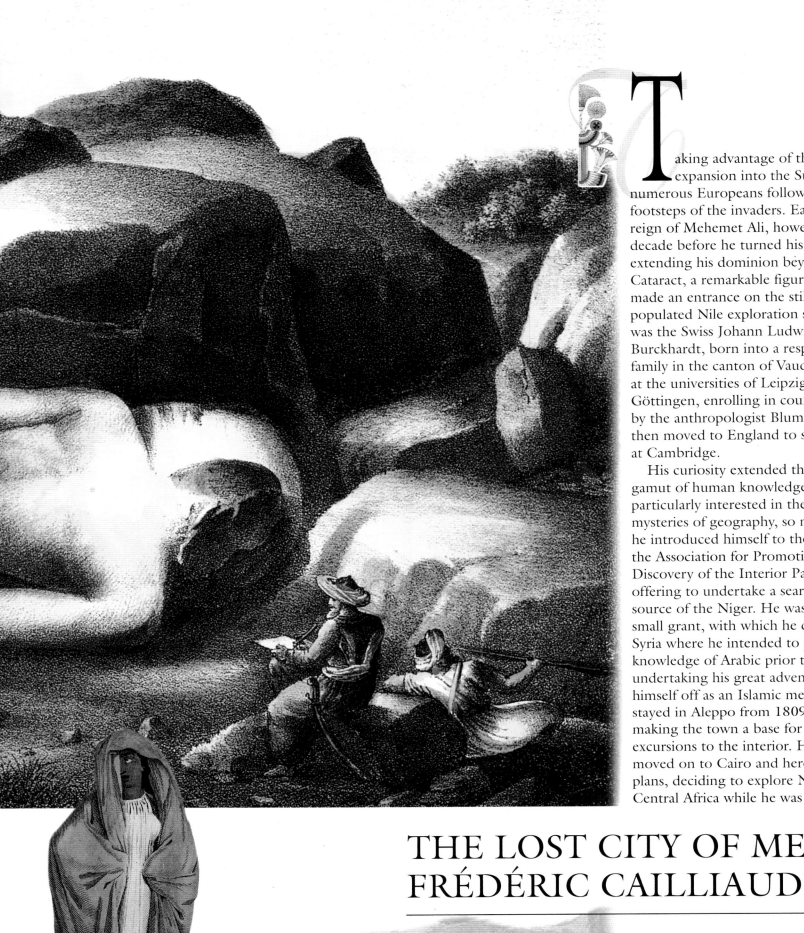

Taking advantage of the Egyptian expansion into the Sudan, numerous Europeans followed in the footsteps of the invaders. Early in the reign of Mehemet Ali, however, around a decade before he turned his thoughts to extending his dominion beyond the First Cataract, a remarkable figure had already made an entrance on the still sparsely populated Nile exploration stage. This was the Swiss Johann Ludwig Burckhardt, born into a respectable family in the canton of Vaud. He studied at the universities of Leipzig and Göttingen, enrolling in courses taught by the anthropologist Blumenbach. He then moved to England to study Arabic at Cambridge.

His curiosity extended throughout the gamut of human knowledge, but he was particularly interested in the many mysteries of geography, so much so that he introduced himself to the officials of the Association for Promoting the Discovery of the Interior Parts of Africa, offering to undertake a search for the source of the Niger. He was awarded a small grant, with which he departed for Syria where he intended to perfect his knowledge of Arabic prior to undertaking his great adventure. Passing himself off as an Islamic merchant, he stayed in Aleppo from 1809 to 1812, making the town a base for repeated excursions to the interior. He then moved on to Cairo and here changed his plans, deciding to explore Nubia before Central Africa while he was waiting for

THE LOST CITY OF MEROË: FRÉDÉRIC CAILLIAUD

124 top *The Frenchman Frédéric Cailliaud, dressed in Turkish costume, complete with scimitar, while drawing ruins, was granted permission to accompany the Egyptian expedition into the Sudan. He took advantage of the situation to visit the ancient city of Meroë. Initially treated harshly by Ismail, who had no love of foreigners, Cailliaud soon won his friendship and even became his favorite dining companion. However, the Frenchman subsequently became disgusted with the Egyptian* conquerors, who were more barbarous and ferocious than the "savages" they had supposedly come to "civilize." He abandoned the expedition to return to France, where his splendidly illustrated book on Meroë aroused great interest among devotees of Egyptology. (Frédéric Cailliaud, *Voyages à Méroé*, Paris, 1826)

124 center *As we can see in this illustration, the women of the Baraha tribe wore long dresses over trousers.* (Frédéric Cailliaud, *Voyages à Méroé*)

124 bottom *In that era the Temple of Abu Simbel was still largely buried in the sand.*

125 top *Prior to Cailliaud, the Sudan had been explored by the Swiss Johann Ludwig Burckhardt, here portrayed in eastern costume.*

125 center *Hauling the boats through the turbulent waters of the First Cataract was grueling work.* (Frédéric Cailliaud, *Voyages à Méroé*)

125 bottom *Faruglili, the sovereign of one of the states that composed the Sudan before the Egyptian conquest.* (Frédéric Cailliaud, *Voyages à Méroé*)

the annual caravan to Fezzan, which he meant to join.

Supporting himself on meager means, Burkhardt departed with a servant and two dromedaries and, in March 1883, became the first white man of modern times to admire the marvelous spectacle of the Temple of Abu Simbel. He then crossed the desert heading for Berber, rectifying with a scientific precision that was not lacking in a poetic dimension the terse description provided by Bruce, who had passed through the region in 1773: "The desert of Nubia is not a boundless expanse of sand in which nothing interrupts the desolate monotony. It is dotted with peaks, some of which reach no less than two or three hundred feet in height, and here and there they are shaded by dense, vigorous woods of palms and acacias. The weak canopy of the former is but a deceptive defense against the rays of the sun that

blaze down vertically. Thus the Arab proverb warns, 'Count on the protection of a potentate and on the shade of the acacia.' "

Burckhardt pushed on as far south as Darau, a land inhabited by a white population of "great beauty" that traded in slaves, rubber, gold, and ivory, communicating with Abyssinia through the valley of the Atbara, a tributary of the Blue Nile. He then crossed another desert that had never previously been visited by a European and eventually reached the Red Sea at Suakin. From there he traveled by boat to Arabia in order to visit Mecca disguised as a pilgrim. He also visited Medina, contracted plague, succeeded in recovering from the disease, and crossed the Red Sea once again to return to Cairo. There, however, he died in 1817, probably of malaria, still waiting for the Fezzan caravan he was never to join. The

126 top *The village of Agady in the country of Bertet, which was visited by the French traveler, lay at the bottom of a high rock in the Nile Valley.* (**Frédéric Cailliaud,** *Voyages à Méroé,* **Paris, 1826**)

126-127 *Among the most attractive regions of the Sudan are the islands of Tangouri, surrounded by the waters of the river.* (**Frédéric Cailliaud,** *Voyages à Méroé*)

126 bottom *The bellicose Shaiqiya lived in southern Nubia; this illustration depicts a warrior armed with a spear and a shield.* (**Frédéric Cailliaud,** *Voyages à Méroé*)

information he gathered on Nubia and its inhabitants' intolerance of the barbaric and violent dominion exercised by the Mamelukes was useful to Mehemet Ali in organizing his 1820 campaign of conquest, which was followed by the Frenchman Frédéric Cailliaud.

Born at Nantes in 1787, the son of a blacksmith, Cailliaud was a self-taught expert in mineralogy, a subject for which he had a true passion. After long journeys through various parts of Europe during which he collected mineral samples and traded in precious stones, he visited Turkey and reached Egypt in 1815 where he was warmly welcomed by Mehemet Ali. The ruler always paid great attention to European scientists, in particular those interested in mining. Ever eager to exploit new mineral deposits, the viceroy engaged Cailliaud to explore the deserts to the east and west of the Nile. Cailliaud left from Edfu in Upper Egypt and headed toward the Red Sea.

He first discovered a small Egyptian temple rich in paintings and hieroglyphics. Then, twenty-eight kilometers from the sea, he found the immense emerald mines of Mount Labarah, exploited in ancient times but abandoned and forgotten for many centuries. Penetrating into the deep galleries excavated in the mountains,

127 top *Dongola was one of the principal trading centers of the Sudan, famous for its boatmen who plied the river. In this engraving a warrior from the city can be seen.*

127 bottom *Cailliaud succeeded in reaching Meroë with his caravan, depicted here near the ruins of the great temple, before the country was occupied by the all-conquering Egyptian forces.*

Cailliaud found the tools of the miners: lamps, levers, and ropes dating back to the era of Ptolemy. Loaded with emerald samples that were intended to whet Mehemet's appetite, he continued on his journey and stumbled across traces of the ancient trading route from Coptos to Berenice along which in ancient times passed precious goods from India. The explorer then reached his final goal, the Great Oasis (Al-Kharga), where he discovered the remains of seven Greco-Egyptian temples.

In February 1819, Cailliaud landed in France with a precious collection of minerals and antiquities but departed again immediately for Egypt, this time to search the Western Desert as far as the oasis of Siwa. He subsequently presented himself at Aswan, where Ismail was organizing the expeditionary force that was to conquer the Sudan, and asked to accompany him. However, the son of Mehemet Ali, already overworked and insensitive to the appeals of science and archaeology, unceremoniously sent him packing. Cailliaud thus made recourse to the omnipotence of the father, and with Mehemet Ali he knew which strings to pull, describing not the Egyptian temples to be excavated but the gold mines to be discovered, or rather rediscovered: was it not said that the fabulous mines of King Solomon were to be found in some remote corner of the Sudan? The viceroy, who since he had seen the sacks of emeralds brought back

from Mount Labarah had found Cailliaud to be a fine fellow, gave way, and the Frenchman, together with two European companions, all dressed as Turks, joined the army on the march near Berber. The intolerant Ismail dared not oppose the will of his fearsome father and allowed Cailliaud to wander as he wished over lands already conquered and those still to be won.

(Frédéric Cailliaud, *Voyages à Méroé*)

127

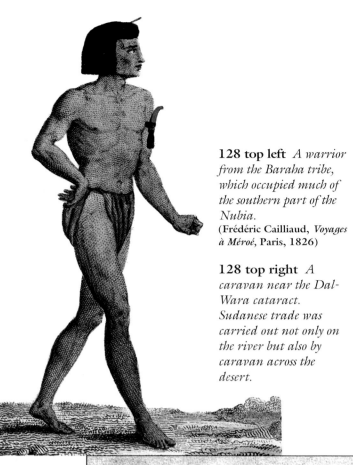

128 top left *A warrior from the Baraha tribe, which occupied much of the southern part of the Nubia.* (Frédéric Cailliaud, *Voyages à Méroé*, Paris, 1826)

128 top right *A caravan near the Dal-Wara cataract. Sudanese trade was carried out not only on the river but also by caravan across the desert.*

128

Cailliaud's true aim was not to discover the improbable mines of King Solomon but rather to locate the ruins of Meroë, the city that had once been the capital of the Sudan and for some time also that of Upper Egypt and that was already legendary at the time of Herodotus. Bruce and Burckhardt had made brief mention of it, but nobody had thoroughly explored the ruins, if there were any. Indeed, many doubted the ancient African city's very existence. However, Cailliaud was so anxious to see them that he departed with a companion named Leztorec ahead of Ismail's army.

At dawn on April 25, 1821, he wept with emotion at the sight of the first rays of the sun gilding the tips of the Pyramids of Meroë. They were certainly not as a grand as those of Egypt, and they were stepped and terribly damaged by the effects of time, but the Frenchman nevertheless felt as though he had fulfilled his life's dream. He climbed the highest pyramid to inscribe at the summit the name of the geographer d'Anville who in the eighteenth century had drawn a map of the Nile. For two weeks he searched through those remains of a lost civilization, copying the inscriptions and the drawings of the obese local pharaohs. He then rejoined the army to proceed toward Sennar.

Ismail had by now accepted Cailliaud,

and he was the only white man allowed to accompany the army raid from Sennar along the Blue Nile toward the Ethiopian border. He dined each evening with Ismail and spoke continuously of the gold he would discover in the fabled mines of Fazogli. However, when he reached the mines he found only insignificant quantities of the precious metal; either they were not the mines of King Solomon or they had been worked out in ancient times by the great sovereign of Israel. Cailliaud, who in reality had already achieved his goal by visiting Meroë, considered abandoning the expedition, disgusted by the indiscriminate massacres of the natives perpetrated by the "Turks." He eventually decided to remain because he hoped to ascend the White Nile, which he correctly believed to be the principal stream of the great river. He was not permitted to complete this exploration, however, and the events that followed the death of Ismail obliged him to return to Cairo and from there to France, where he died in 1869.

129 top *The extremely simple costume of a woman from Sennar.*

129 bottom *The Pyramids at Meroë formed a spectacular complex of imposing ruins.*

129

(Frédéric Cailliaud, *Voyages à Méroé*)

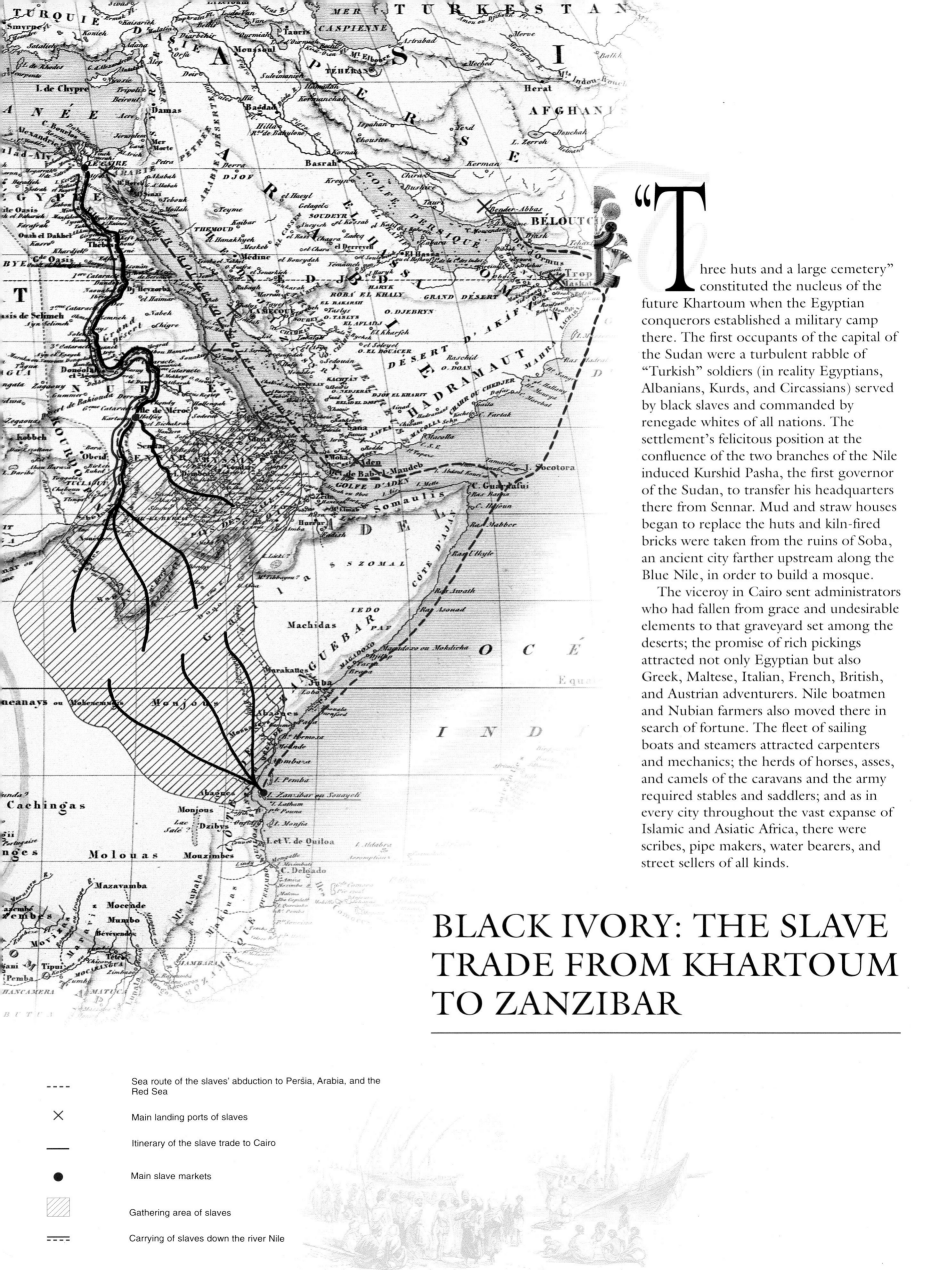

"Three huts and a large cemetery" constituted the nucleus of the future Khartoum when the Egyptian conquerors established a military camp there. The first occupants of the capital of the Sudan were a turbulent rabble of "Turkish" soldiers (in reality Egyptians, Albanians, Kurds, and Circassians) served by black slaves and commanded by renegade whites of all nations. The settlement's felicitous position at the confluence of the two branches of the Nile induced Kurshid Pasha, the first governor of the Sudan, to transfer his headquarters there from Sennar. Mud and straw houses began to replace the huts and kiln-fired bricks were taken from the ruins of Soba, an ancient city farther upstream along the Blue Nile, in order to build a mosque.

The viceroy in Cairo sent administrators who had fallen from grace and undesirable elements to that graveyard set among the deserts; the promise of rich pickings attracted not only Egyptian but also Greek, Maltese, Italian, French, British, and Austrian adventurers. Nile boatmen and Nubian farmers also moved there in search of fortune. The fleet of sailing boats and steamers attracted carpenters and mechanics; the herds of horses, asses, and camels of the caravans and the army required stables and saddlers; and as in every city throughout the vast expanse of Islamic and Asiatic Africa, there were scribes, pipe makers, water bearers, and street sellers of all kinds.

BLACK IVORY: THE SLAVE TRADE FROM KHARTOUM TO ZANZIBAR

----	Sea route of the slaves' abduction to Persia, Arabia, and the Red Sea
✕	Main landing ports of slaves
—	Itinerary of the slave trade to Cairo
●	Main slave markets
▨	Gathering area of slaves
-·-·-	Carrying of slaves down the river Nile

130 top *Midway through the last century there were two principal slave routes leading from East Africa to the territories of the Ottoman and Persian empires. The Egyptian and* Sudanese slavers *ascended the White Nile and the Abyssinian tributaries, channeling the slaves captured in those areas through to Khartoum. From there they were taken by river to the* *great market at Cairo. The island of Zanzibar performed a similar role, with the slaves captured in the great lakes region being transported from there to Arabia and Persia.*

130 bottom *The phases of the capture and transportation to the market were the hardest on the slaves and frequently proved fatal. Given the abundant supply of "goods," the slave traders did not hesitate to treat the unfortunate victims far worse than animals, and were unconcerned about those who died along the way. Once bought, however, the slaves would be treated humanely, almost as if they were members of their owners' families. Many grew so attached to their masters that they refused eventual opportunities for* liberty. This illustration shows slaves disembarking at Girga on the Nile. (Bartlett, *The Nile Boat*, London, 1858)

131 top *Arab slavers leading a caravan of black slaves with their necks chained to long poles across the desert.* (Thomas Archer, *The War in Egypt and the Sudan*, London)

131 bottom *The inspection of the "goods" at the slave market in Khartoum. A potential buyer is looking at the teeth of an Abyssinian woman.* (G. Ebers, *Egypt: Description, Historical, and Picturesque*, London, 1884)

Along the banks of the river, half-clothed natives ceaselessly loaded and unloaded the boats, and the merchants relaxed on couches in the shade of a rudimentary patio wheeling and dealing while smoking narghiles and sipping coffee. Rubber, ostrich feathers, ivory, and, above all, slaves were the goods that Khartoum sent down the river.

A French traveler described his encounter with the sad processions that convened in the Sudanese capital: "We saw a caravan approach composed of horsemen and pedestrians, or rather a column, as here and there sunlight glinted on bayonets. They were in fact cavalrymen wearing the uniform of the Egyptian army and conducting black slaves. Some rode camels, others horses or asses. The slaves on foot had their necks in a kind of fork to which their wrists were tightly bound while the two sticks of which it was composed converged behind the head and were kept open by a peg, leaving barely enough room to breathe. Moreover, a cord led from this kind of pillory to the saddle horn of the rider. The sweat that poured from the foreheads of the prisoners ran over faces that showed a degree of dejection verging on desperation. Still worse was the condition of those who were tied to the saddle not by a cord but by a long branch of the pillory itself. Their flesh was subjected to all the effects of the lurching animals and uneven terrain. But the riders appeared not to be concerned in the slightest about the deterioration of their goods and with complete indifference they dragged those poor souls through thickets of spiny bushes that lacerated their flanks terribly."

The slaves' only respite from suffering came when they reached Khartoum, where they were sold at the market and herded by their purchaser onto a felucca that would carry them on the long river trip to Cairo. There the wholesalers again put them up for sale, this time on the Egyptian capital's slave market, the most popular in the Near East. The elephant hunters and slave drivers pushed ever deeper into the country, ascending the White and Blue Niles and exploring unknown regions. The news of those incursions filtered through to European geographical circles and induced the true explorers to make Khartoum the point of departure for their expeditions in search of the sources of the Nile.

The Savoyard Antoine Brun-Rollet, having arrived in Egypt in 1831, ascended the Blue Nile as far as the Abyssinian border and then, having settled in Khartoum as a merchant with the Arab name Yaqub, established trading relations with the tribes living along the banks of the White Nile. He observed the customs, studied the country, ran terrible risks, and was subjected to repeated harassment by the governor of the Sudan, who was determined to maintain the Egyptian trading monopoly. Brun-Rollet thus appealed to the viceroy and

succeeded in persuading him to proclaim freedom of trade and navigation throughout eastern Sudan. He then decided to depart in search of the sources of the river, pushing as far as 4 degrees latitude north in 1845 and establishing a trading station at the farthest point reached by the Egyptian expedition of 1840. Once back in Europe he was appointed vice consul at Khartoum by the Sardinian government and returned to Egypt in 1855 to explore the marshy region to the west of the White Nile. He covered the 200 kilometers of lagoon between the main stream and the Bahr al-Ghazal, discovered the mouth of this tributary, mistook it for the true Nile, and ascended it for 100 kilometers before returning to the Sudanese capital where he died, exhausted by his efforts, in 1858.

The course of the White Nile had also been explored by the Austrian missionary Knoblecher. In 1849 he departed from Khartoum with a number of colleagues,

132 top *Giovanni Miani, shown here in Arab costume, was an extraordinary and little known solitary explorer, as audacious as he was unfortunate. He failed to discover the sources of the Nile only because he was misled by false information supplied by the natives. He advanced from Khartoum into the virtually impenetrable tropical forests.*

132 center *The dense tropical jungle inhabited by cannibalistic tribes. Miani always succeeded in gaining the respect and trust of the natives and, in many cases, their friendship too.*

132 bottom *These two warriors from the Mangbetu tribe, with their characteristic hairstyle, almost seem to be posing. The members of this tribe welcomed Miani with surprising hospitality.*

including the Italian Angelo Vinco, and conquered the rapids that had blocked Selim Bimbasci eight years earlier. He then pushed on as far as Mount Logwek, winning over the natives with the sound of his harmonica. In 1851 Knoblecher had founded the Gondokoro mission, a site that was to become celebrated in the annals of Nile exploration. Angelo Vinco died here in January 1853, but not before he had explored eastward into the kingdom of Robenga, where he hoped to find the elusive springs.

A few years later another Italian was to depart into the same regions, attracted by the hope of a solution to the problem that was obsessing geographers. His name was Giovanni Miani, born at Rovigo in 1810 and since 1849 resident in Cairo to which he fled after participating in the

vain defense of Venice against the Austrians. In Egypt Miani earned a living by teaching French and Italian, but his passion was for travel and exploration. He descended the Red Sea and from Suakin crossed the Nubian desert to reach the Nile at Berber. From there he followed the river to Khartoum, and it was there perhaps that he began to develop his idea for an expedition in search of the Nile springs. He began to study the languages of the Nilotic tribes and to compile a hydrographic map of the great river, which he presented at Paris. He was named an honorary member of the Geographical Society, attracted the attention of Napoleon III, and received financial backing from a Marseilles merchant, Revol. With Revol and four other Frenchmen, Miani departed from Cairo in January 1859. The expedition failed almost before it had started, however, and Miani reached Khartoum alone and penniless after his companions

withdrew because of illness and differences of opinion.

Fortunately, in the Sudanese capital Miani was helped by the Maltese merchant De Bono; the two came to an agreement relating to the exploitation of future discoveries and early in December began to ascend the White Nile with a small escort, traveling as far as Gondokoro. There they were informed that not far away a company of Egyptian soldiers had recently been massacred by the Liria tribe; Miani and De Bono felt obliged to seek revenge by burning the village and putting the natives to flight to avoid suffering the same fate.

They then recommenced their trip upstream, passing among protruding rocks and masses of floating vegetation that made navigation particularly difficult. When they reached the village of Machedo, the men refused to proceed, forcing Miani to return to Gondokoro, where he fell seriously ill with cerebral

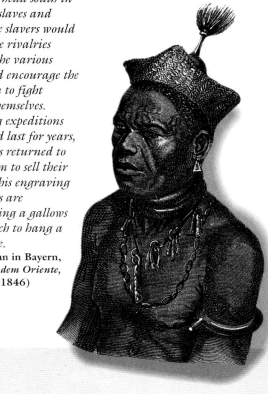

133 top *Ngaha, chief of the Mitoo tribe.*

133 bottom *Arab caravans head south in search of slaves and ivory. The slavers would exploit the rivalries between the various tribes and encourage the tribesmen to fight among themselves. Following expeditions that could last for years, the slavers returned to Khartoum to sell their prey. In this engraving the slavers are constructing a gallows from which to hang a rebel slave.* (**Maximilian in Bayern,** *Bilder aus dem Oriente,* **Stuttgart, 1846**)

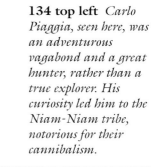

134 top left *Carlo Piaggia, seen here, was an adventurous vagabond and a great hunter, rather than a true explorer. His curiosity led him to the Niam-Niam tribe, notorious for their cannibalism.*

134 top right *The Niam-Niam, ferocious savages, took to Piaggia, and he remained among them for a year. This engraving depicts a Niam-Niam woman with an unusual headdress.*

fever. Healed by a providential witch doctor who incised his scalp and sucked his blood, Miani organized an elephant hunt in the territory of the Neambara and returned with a haul of ivory that permitted him to pay 100 troops and 150 Bari porters, with whom he departed southward once again in March of 1860, this time traveling overland. Because he had chosen to march in the rainy season, the terrain proved to be extremely difficult, and there were repeated skirmishes with the hostile natives. Nevertheless, the tenacious Miani pressed on as far as the confluence of the Aswa and the Nile and the cataracts of Meri, where the great river changed direction and flowed out of the west rather than the south. He reached Galuffi at 3° 329 latitude north in a feverish state due to an ulcer on his leg.

Here, in the shade of a large tamarind tree, he convoked the tribal elders, who replied to his anxious questions saying that it would take another full month's march to reach the springs. This was not true: Lake Albert, out of which the Nile flows and which was later discovered by Baker, was just sixty miles away. Miani was never to know how close he came to his objective. The fever was tormenting him, the season was unfavorable, his escort was threatening to abandon him, and he did not have the means to pay them for such a long trip. He therefore decided to turn back after having inscribed the letters MI on the trunk of the tamarind, which thereafter was known as Sped-der-el-Seuar, the Tree of the Traveler.

By the end of May Miani was back in Khartoum and reached Cairo in late August. By the beginning of December he was once again ready to depart on a new expedition with three Italian companions, arriving in Khartoum in February 1861. Here, however, an argument led to the dissolution of the group, and he also learned that De Bono had departed on his own account for the

134-135 *The center of the village of Diamvonoo. The villages of the Niam-Niam, hidden in the forest in hard-to-find* clearings, were *characterized by small granaries built on tall stilts to keep animals at bay. The tribe's dogs wandered all around.*

134 bottom *The Great Lakes region was the reservoir tapped by the slave traders of Zanzibar.*

The prisoners were forced to march to the coast tied one to another by their necks.

135 top *The village of Kurshook was protected by a palisade in front of which stood an imposing khaya tree.*

135 bottom *A caravan heading for Khartoum. The Kordofan, annexed for Egypt by the expeditionary force sent out by Mehemet Ali, was dominated by the slavers, the richest of whom lived like sultans in sumptuous palaces.*

Upper Nile and had in fact reached the village of Faloro at 3° 129 latitude north, beyond the point reached by Miani. Penniless, exhausted, and disillusioned, Miani returned to his homeland.

Another of his countrymen was also exploring the meanderings of the Nile in the same period, the miller from Lucca, Carlo Piaggia, born in 1827, whose travels were stimulated by a spirit of pure adventure rather than an interest in science or commerce. He left Italy in 1851 for Tunisia and then for Egypt; in 1856 he was in Khartoum. An enthusiastic hunter, he intended to kill as many marabou as possible in order to sell their valuable plumes. To this end he pressed on beyond Gondokoro as far as Rejaf at 4 degrees latitude north, preceding Miani by very little.

Piaggia then wandered, continuing to hunt, up and down various tributaries of the Nile and in 1860 at Khartoum, where sooner or later all African travelers congregated, he met another Tuscan hunter, Marchese Orazio Antinori. The pair ascended the Bahr al-Ghazal together with the intention of penetrating the unknown territory of the Niam-Niam, a tribe of infamous cannibals, but they fell ill, their supplies ran out, and they were obliged to turn back. An excursion into the territory of the cannibals remained a fixation for Piaggia, however, and in 1863, after numerous minor trips, he satisfied his curiosity at the head of a caravan composed of 90 armed men and 220 porters. The expedition was organized by the Sudanese ivory trader Ghattas at whose service the Italian had

placed himself.

As we have seen, all attempts to reach the mysterious Nile springs departing from Khartoum failed in spite of the fact that the expeditions reached points ever farther south. In those regions the difficulties appeared to be insurmountable, and all the information gathered from the natives suggested that the objective was still far from the most extreme positions reached on the White Nile and its tributaries up until then. In

136-137 *The capital of a sultanate that dominated the coast of Africa from Somalia to Mozambique in the nineteenth century, Zanzibar became a great center of trade with the Arabian Peninsula, Persia, and India while European* ships unloaded the cloth and glass beads the Arabs used for trading with the black tribes of the interior. (**Le Brick le Ducovëdic,** *Voyage a la côte orientale d'Afrique,* **Paris, 1846–48**)

136 bottom *The Sultan Seyyid Said, seen here, enjoyed excellent relations with the representatives of the white powers, so much so that he ceded to their pressure and* officially abolished the slave trade in 1845. In reality, however, the trade continued for a number of decades, occasionally harassed by British and French ships.

the meantime the first rumors from the east coast of Africa that spoke of a region of great lakes appeared to confirm the ancient traditions regarding the origins of the Nile in Ptolemy's Mountains of the Moon. Like Khartoum, the starting point for this as yet virgin southern route was a great slave market, the island of Zanzibar.

This was so because the slave drivers who ventured ever deeper into the interior of the dark continent with their caravans had the greatest firsthand knowledge of African geography. Zanzibar—or Zanguebar, as it was once written—had for centuries been the most important trading center on the long coastal strip of Africa known as Azania, which extended from Somalia to Mozambique. The Arabs settled in the area in the eighth century, founding a series of ports including Mogadishu, Malindi, Kilwa, and Sofala. When, eight centuries later, the Portuguese rounded the Cape of Good Hope and entered East African waters heading for India, Azania was divided into a series of small Muslim states they were easily able to dominate. The exception to the rule was Zanzibar, which remained under the control of an Arab sheikh.

The Portuguese domination was tyrannical and oppressive; the Moors, as the Arabs and mixed-race people were called, were treated with wretched, narrow-minded arrogance. If a Christian tripped over a rock and fell to the ground, an unfortunate Muslim passerby would be held responsible and forced to pay retribution. If chickens or goats belonging to a Moor strayed into the courtyard of a Portuguese, the owner who went to retrieve them would be told that his animals had converted to Christianity. It is no wonder that there were frequent revolts, all bloodily repressed until 1698, when the desperate Moors appealed to the sultan of Muscat, who arrived from Arabia with a fleet sufficiently powerful to sweep away the hated Europeans and push them back into Mozambique, beyond Cape Delgado. The coastal cities then returned to their traditional

137 top *Rubber, amber, and above all ivory, in addition to slaves, arrived at Zanzibar from central Africa. The elephant tusks seen in this contemporary photograph are being weighed. They were in great demand in Europe for the manufacture of billiard balls.*

137 bottom *The island of Zanzibar supplied the harems of the whole of the Islamic world with black and mixed-race slaves like these richly dressed women. (Le Brick le Ducovëdic, Voyage a la côte orientale d'Afrique)*

trading activities with the Arabian Peninsula and India. Ahmed ben-Said, who proclaimed himself sultan, or imam, of Muscat in 1741, reorganized the administration of the colonies with Zanzibar at the center and proclaimed there a governor and a garrison. A merchant himself, he had four ships transporting slaves, elephant tusks, and gold dust from Quiloa and Zanzibar to Muscat. His nephew Seyyid Said, who came to power in 1803, established a residence on the island in 1828, created a navy, and expanded the mercantile fleet to seventeen ships and around twenty smaller vessels; he drained the wealth of the hinterland, channeling it toward his ports and obliging the black chieftains to allow his caravans free passage. These caravans founded the trading station of Kazeh many miles inland, which was soon to become the principal market for black and white gold—ivory and slaves.

Bleak memories of Portuguese tyranny and religious intolerance made those ports inaccessible for European ships for the whole of the eighteenth century. The few that did dare to approach them out of necessity saw their boats sunk and sailors massacred and had to beat a hasty retreat. It was not until early in the nineteenth century that a few slave ships began to drop anchor at Quiloa or Zanzibar. Their captains' only concern was to procure a cargo of ebony while the products of Azania such as ivory, rubber, and amber, instead of being shipped directly to Europe, continued to be transported on Arab vessels to Muscat, Surat, and Bombay, from where they would be shipped to London or Paris as products of India. The true pillar of the Zanzibar economy was constituted, however, of the black slaves the island supplied to the entire Islamic world.

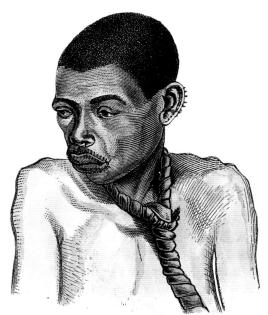

An eyewitness, Captain Thomas Smee, the commander of the English ship *Ternate*, who visited Zanzibar in 1811,

described the spectacle that could be seen every day in the streets of the market city:

"The show commences about four o'clock in the afternoon. The slaves, set off to the best advantage by having their skin cleaned and burnished with coconut oil, their faces painted with red and white stripes, which is here esteemed elegance, and the hands, noses, ears, and feet ornamented with a profusion of bracelets of gold and silver and jewels, are ranged in a line, commencing with the youngest and increasing to the rear according to their size and age. At the head of this file, which is composed of both sexes and all ages from six to sixty, walks the person who owns them; behind and at either side, two or three of his domestic slaves, armed with swords and spears, serve as a guard. Thus ordered, the procession begins and passes through the marketplace and the principal streets; the owner holding forth in a kind of song the good qualities of his slaves and the high prices that have been offered for them. When any of them strikes a spectator's

fancy, the line immediately stops, and a process of examination ensues, which, for minuteness, is unequaled in any cattle market in Europe. The intending purchaser having ascertained there is no defect in the faculties of speech, hearing, etc., that there is no disease present, and that the slave does not snore in sleeping, which is counted a very great fault, next proceeds to examine the person; the mouth and the teeth are first inspected and afterward every part of the body in succession, not even excepting the breasts etc. of the girls, many of whom I have seen handled in the most indecent manner in the public market by their purchaser; indeed there is every reason to believe that the slave-dealers almost universally force the young girls to submit to their lust previous to their being disposed of. The slave is then made to walk or run a little way, to show there is no defect about the feet; and after which, if the price be agreed to, they are stripped of their finery and delivered over to their future master. I observed they had in

138 bottom *As in the Sudan, in central Africa, the most successful and wealthiest slavers became veritable sovereigns over immense territories. The famous Tipoo Tib, seen in this photograph, lent his services to Stanley.*

139 bottom left *A procession of chained slaves about to be taken to the market at Zanzibar.*

139 bottom right *Abyssinian slaves were the most sought after for their beauty; this engraving shows one wearing a precious earring.* (Henry Salt, *Twenty Four Views Taken in St. Helena, The Cape, India, Ceylon, Abyssinia & Egypt*, London, 1809)

138 top *A slave still tied with a rope around his neck.*

138 center *An almost daily scene: the sale of slaves in the market at Zanzibar.*

138-139 *Arriving at Zanzibar after a long march during the course of which 10 percent of their number died, the slaves captured in the Great Lakes region were cleaned up and taken to the market, where the buyers made their selections. The chosen slaves were then forced to board ships and were taken to be sold again at the markets of Arabia or Persia. In this illustration a dhow loaded with slaves, is heading for the coast, fleeing from a British gunboat that has intercepted it.*

general a very dejected look; some groups appeared so ill fed that their bones seemed as if ready to penetrate the skin."

Twenty to thirty thousand of these unfortunate figures were captured in the African interior and dragged to the coast each year—forty thousand in the "best" years. A third of them were destined for work on the local plantations but the remaining two-thirds were loaded onto dhows, Arab sailing ships, and exported to Arabia, Persia, and Turkey.

The mortality rate was extremely high, both on the plantations and aboard the ships, where the slaves were treated worse than animals; therefore trade had to be continually renewed with more captures. On occasion, in order to complete a load, the owner of a dhow would not hesitate to lure free blacks aboard with the promise of liquor or women only to chain them and throw them into the hold.

Under pressure from the European powers, the sultan prohibited the export of slaves in 1845, but slavery continued to be legal in the Ottoman Empire. French and English ships patrolled the coast in order to block trade, with almost no success. The Arabs did not consider the trade in "ebony" immoral, and profits were so great as to justify all risks both during the "hunting trips" into the wild interior and while trying to elude the European blockade at sea.

In the mid-nineteenth century there were around five thousand Arabs living on the island of Zanzibar, many of whom possessed up to two thousand slaves who worked the clove and coconut palm plantations. The ivory trade, however, was in the hands of the Indian traders who settled in the area at the beginning of the century. The majority of the population, a total of half a million people, was composed of Swahilis, born

out of the union between Arabs and blacks; the same name was used for the lingua franca of the East African coast spoken from Mogadishu to Beheira.

The white traders involved in profitable business in the area were mostly Americans, Germans from Hamburg, Britons, and Frenchmen. They imported cotton, arms, colored beads, porcelain, and luxury goods. The sultan, who was well disposed toward them, enjoyed excellent relations with the consuls and frequently invited these useful infidels to his court. Life was sweet in the palaces of Zanzibar. The Arab plantation owners and slave traders had had grand residences built with courtyards shaded by luxuriant gardens and refreshed by fountains in which they passed the time in a pleasurable haze of sex, food, drugs such as opium and cannabis, and good conversation.

140

141

140 top *A view of the Nile at the frontier between Egypt and Nubia.* (William Henry Bartlett, *The Nile Boat*, London, 1858)

140 bottom *A number of Nubian slaves resting under the palms close to the Nile.* (David Roberts, *Egypt and Nubia*, London, 1846–1850)

140-141 *Nubian slaves executing a dance for their captors.* (Jean-Jacques Rifaud, *Voyage en Égypte, en Nubie*, Paris, 1830)

141 bottom *Ever since the time of the pharaohs Nubian slaves had been highly prized in Egypt. When the country was absorbed by the Ottoman Empire, the envoys of the sultan of Constantinople were sent to the market at Cairo each year to buy slaves for their master's immense harem.* (D. Roberts, *Egypt and Nubia*)

MAP OF THE ROUTES
between
ZANZIBAR AND THE GREAT
IN
EASTERN AFRIC
in 1857, 1858 & 1859.
by
R.F. Burton

I t was from the Arab merchants who penetrated more than a thousand miles inland from the African coast with their caravans that the few white men scattered through Azania first gained some confused information about the existence of a great inland lake. In 1848 two enterprising German Protestant missionaries, Krapf and Rebmann, in the service of a British Bible society whose sphere of action coincided more or less with what is today Kenya, departed from their mission at Rabai M'piu near Mombasa on a circular trip that was to take them within sight of the snowcapped peaks of Mounts Kenya and Kilimanjaro. The natives they encountered spoke of an immense stretch of water situated many days' travel away, a labyrinth of interconnected lakes collectively known as Ukerewe. Recalling the classical notions of African geography, the missionaries intuited that it was in that complex of lakes and snowy mountains that the sources of the Nile were to be found. Having gathered further information, Rebmann drew a somewhat hypothetical map with the help of his colleague Erhardt in which he depicted a sinuous inland sea at the heart of the continent. Published together with their report in the *Nouvelles Annales de Voyages* of 1856, the map aroused great

TOWARD THE MOUNTAINS OF THE MOON: BURTON AND SPEKE

142 *Richard Burton was thirty-six years old in 1857 when he departed in search of the sources of the Nile. He had come to fame as a result of two notable journeys that had taken him to two previously inviolate holy cities of the Middle East and*

Africa, Mecca and Harer in Ethiopia. He succeeded in entering the cities disguised as a Muslim, thanks to his perfect mastery of Arabic. (J. Ewin Ritchie, **The Pictorial Edition of the Life and Discoveries of David Livingstone**)

142-143 *This map, from* The Lake Regions of Central Africa *by Richard Burton, shows the itinerary of the explorers' expedition*

from Zanzibar to Lake Tanganyika and back, and the route followed by Speke to Lake Nyanza, which he renamed Lake Victoria.

LAKE NYANZA
3740 ft above the Sea level. Fresh water

Speke's route to
the Lake Nyanza
in 1858

Burton and Speke's
route to Lake
Tanganyika

AFRICA

*The Green line shows the
Fertile Regions*

143 center *A skilled draftsman, Speke produced a number of sketches of the places he visited; here we see the Wasegame hills, or Robeno chain, in Tanganyika.*

143 bottom *An officer in the British Indian Army, Speke had earned a reputation as a big game hunter on the slopes of the Himalayas and had accompanied Burton on an exploration of Somalia during which both were seriously injured.*

interest and persuaded the British Royal Geographical Society to organize an expedition that, it was hoped, would settle once and for all the age-old problem of the Nile.

The expedition was entrusted to one of the most remarkable figures of a Victorian Britain that was hardly lacking in bizarre characters: Sir Richard Burton. Born in 1821, the son of a British army colonel, Burton briefly considered entering the priesthood but then decided to follow in his father's footsteps by joining the British Indian Army in 1842. A brilliant linguist (he mastered around forty languages and dialects during his lifetime), he was a man of inexhaustible curiosity. He wrote books on the brothels of the Punjab and on Persian science. He also completed the first uncensored translation of *A Thousand and One Nights* to howls of disapproval from the puritanical elements in British society for having failed to omit the

143

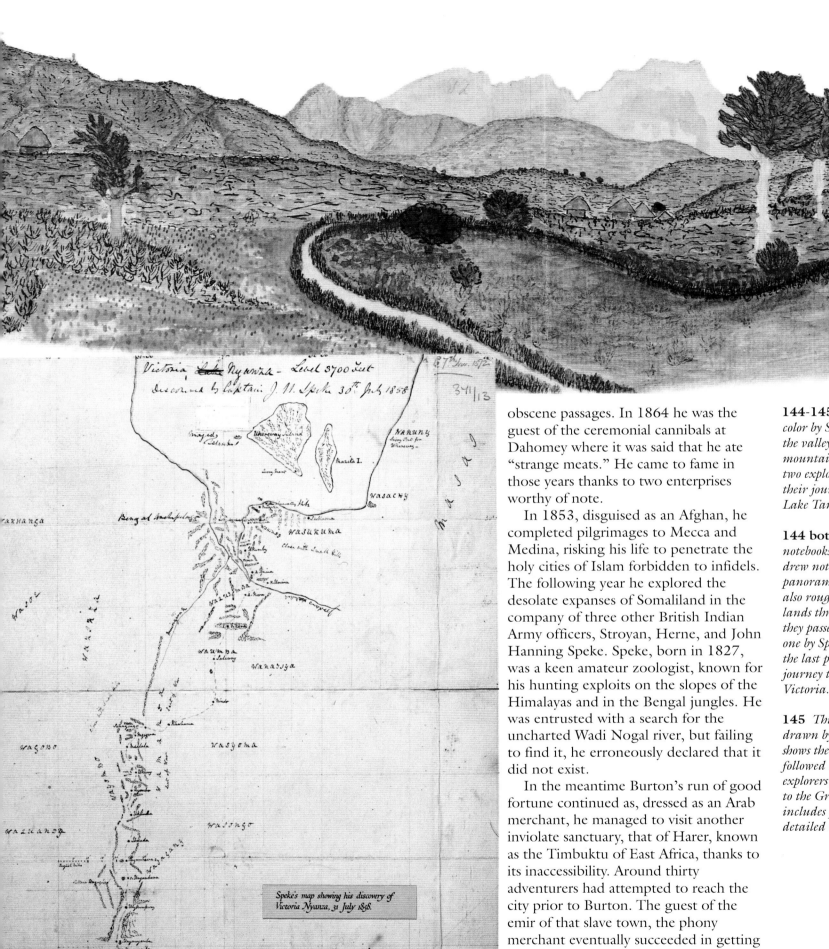

Speke's map showing his discovery of
Victoria Nyanza, 31 July 1858.

obscene passages. In 1864 he was the guest of the ceremonial cannibals at Dahomey where it was said that he ate "strange meats." He came to fame in those years thanks to two enterprises worthy of note.

In 1853, disguised as an Afghan, he completed pilgrimages to Mecca and Medina, risking his life to penetrate the holy cities of Islam forbidden to infidels. The following year he explored the desolate expanses of Somaliland in the company of three other British Indian Army officers, Stroyan, Herne, and John Hanning Speke. Speke, born in 1827, was a keen amateur zoologist, known for his hunting exploits on the slopes of the Himalayas and in the Bengal jungles. He was entrusted with a search for the uncharted Wadi Nogal river, but failing to find it, he erroneously declared that it did not exist.

In the meantime Burton's run of good fortune continued as, dressed as an Arab merchant, he managed to visit another inviolate sanctuary, that of Harer, known as the Timbuktu of East Africa, thanks to its inaccessibility. Around thirty adventurers had attempted to reach the city prior to Burton. The guest of the emir of that slave town, the phony merchant eventually succeeded in getting away in one piece and joining his three companions, together with whom he then departed on another expedition. Shortly after leaving Berbera, however, they were attacked by a band of Somalians who killed Stroyan and seriously injured Speke. Burton's cheek was pierced by a spear, and only Herne was unhurt. Deprived of all their belongings, hungry, and thirsty, the three survivors wandered along the coast for

144-145 *This water-color by Speke depicts the valleys and mountains seen by the two explorers during their journey toward Lake Tanganyika.*

144 bottom *In their notebooks the explorers drew not only panoramic views but also rough maps of the lands through which they passed, like this one by Speke showing the last part of his journey to Lake Victoria.*

145 *This map, drawn by Burton, shows the route followed by the explorers from the sea to the Great Lakes. It includes precise and detailed notes as well.*

12

days until they were spotted and saved by a group of British sailors belonging to a ship anchored off Berbera.

Burton wanted Speke with him on his search for the mysterious lake, and in January 1857 the pair completed a preliminary excursion in the region around Mombasa. There, however, they contracted the so-called coastal fever and returned in poor shape to Zanzibar to organize a proper expedition.

Burton's instructions from the Royal Geographical Society were to depart from the coastal city of Kilwa and head due west. Because of the hostility of the natives in that area of the hinterland, however, Burton decided to follow in the tracks of the Arab caravans that led to a place called Ujiji, said to lie on the shores of the lake. Accompanied by an escort of Beluch soldiers provided by the obliging sultan of Zanzibar, an Indo-Portuguese cook from Goa, a former slave called Sidi Bombay who acted as an interpreter, and numerous overloaded asses and black porters destined to take over from the animals in case of necessity, Burton and Speke marched slowly toward Kazeh. This town, later to be renamed Tabora, was situated in the Unyamwezi, or Land of the Moon, an auspicious name for those searching for Ptolemy's fabled Mountains of the Moon.

The five-hundred-mile route led through a series of small sultanates as they were called by the Arabs. Each of these territories of the various black African tribes extended for around fifty kilometers. The local despots lived on and occasionally grew wealthy extracting the *hongo*, a tribute payable by every passing caravan. At each passage there were lengthy negotiations as the tribes' practice was to demand an exorbitant toll before gradually allowing themselves to be beaten down.

The expedition was also delayed during the second half of the journey by a lack of water; at times the caravan had to wait in the villages for the rains.

146 top *Burton and Speke had many encounters with natives during their journey toward Lake Tanganyika. This engraving shows the large huts of the village of Msene, along with the explorers' tent.*

At last, on November 7, 1857, three months after leaving the coast, Burton and Speke arrived in Kazeh. The village boasted certain comforts, especially foodstuffs, as it was a kind of storehouse established by the Arabs for their caravans. The two explorers, both feverish, were able to take a welcome rest and regain their strength. Their host, the Sheikh Suai, provided detailed information about the lake, but it was very different from that published in Europe by the missionaries. There were, in fact, three lakes, Nyasa, Ujiji, and Ukerewe. The last of these was said to be the largest and was drained by a river known as the Juba in which Burton and

Speke saw the mirage of the sought-after source of the Nile, so much so that Speke was eager to head in that direction.

Burton, however, decided to continue on the same course toward Ujiji. He was very ill, suffering from temporary paralysis and partial blindness, and was obliged to hand over command of the expedition to Speke a month after setting out from Kazeh. They encountered fertile plantations of rice, increasingly dense forests, and rivers that flowed to the west rather than to the east. At last they reached Ujiji, but not before having been ruthlessly robbed by the chief of a shore-dwelling tribe.

146-147 *A caravan of porters can be seen in this view of the territory of the Unyamwezi, the Land of the Moon.*

146 bottom *Natives from the Usumbua tribe armed with bows and arrows and wearing helmets of palm fibers.*

147 top *A group of young women smoking pipes at the Arab station of Kazeh.*

The explorers were able to see little of the lake they had come so far to find: Speke had now also been struck by a disease of the eyes that blurred his sight and at times rendered him completely blind. They were again received hospitably at Ujiji, the principal Arab settlement on the lake that was later to be known as Lake Tanganyika. They set about surveying the lake, or at least mapping part of the shoreline, but the local tribes were at war and the canoes available in the area were unsuitable for such a task, being too fragile and unable to carry the necessary supplies. On the island of Kasenghe near the opposite shore lived a sheikh who possessed a

147 center *In order to penetrate the interior of Central Africa from the east coast, the explorers had to pass through the coastal mountain range illustrated here by Burton.*

147 bottom *The port of Bagamoyo was the point of departure for the caravans heading inland toward the Great Lakes.*
(R. Burton, *The Lake Regions of Central Africa*)

dhow. Speke left to search for him, crossing the great expanse of water in a dugout canoe propelled by twenty paddlers, whom he had to pay the exorbitant price of four American dhoti and four kitindi. Dhoti were strips of American cotton sheet measured from the elbow to the tip of the middle finger while kitindi were bracelets of brass wire.

No sooner had they set off than they were almost swamped by a violent storm. The worst however was still to come for Speke. When they camped for the night on an island close to the far shore he found his tent invaded by a horde of beetles. After a few vain attempts to drive them away, the exhausted explorer gave up and fell asleep in the middle of the seething black colony. Unfortunately one of the insects entered his ear, reaching the tympanum and causing unbearable pain, which he tried to relieve by probing with a penknife. Over the next few days the wound he caused in his attempts to extract the insect became infected and his face swelled up and prevented him from chewing. He was obliged to adopt a liquid diet, but in recompense he gradually recovered his sight.

The hospitable sheikh, once he got over the shock of seeing a white man at his door, willingly gave his permission for the expedition to use the dhow but could not provide a crew as he was about to leave on a trading expedition to the south. Speke therefore declined the offer, as the sailing vessel was useless without the men who knew how to handle it. He briefly considered accepting the sheikh's invitation to accompany him on his journey into regions that no European had yet visited but finally decided to return to Burton. A wise decision, as all members of the sheikh's caravan were subsequently massacred.

At this point the two explorers decided to turn back, and at the end of June, a year after having set out from Zanzibar, they were once again at Kazeh, where the sheikh was happy to feed them and revive their discussions about the immense lake Ukerewe and the kingdom of Uganda,

148 top *Numerous tribes of varying appearance inhabited the region between the Great Lakes and the coast that today forms the state of Tanzania. Burton enjoyed sketching their various hairstyles, as seen in these drawings.* (**Richard Burton,** *The Lake Regions of Central Africa*)

which extended beyond its shores. This time Burton acquiesced to Speke's desire to travel to see the fabled stretch of water but declined to accompany him as he was still too ill.

The caravan departed with twenty porters, ten armed Beluchs, the interpreter Bombay, and a rabble of native porters that decreased in number at every stop. The Beluchs, strict Muslims, cursed the porters who extended the rest periods to drink pombo, the local beer, and the hard stems of the plants curving over the ill-defined footpath that made them stumble. That frequently imperceptible track was in fact the main route for local trading: the explorers encountered caravans of ivory heading for the coast, livestock being driven to market, and herds of timid zebras and leaping antelopes.

One day, at a bend in the track, there

appeared a man leading a line of porters carrying elephant tusks. Under Speke's astonished gaze the first of his men and the newcomer stared sullenly at each other before running forward and head-butting each other like two furious rams until one of them gave way. The example was followed by the rest of the two caravans, and the Englishman found himself in the middle of what he believed to be an unusual form of native warfare to which he tried to put an end with a large stick; unfortunately he was unable to distinguish friend from foe. The head-butting battle ended as quickly as it had begun, and the natives laughed at the ingenuous white man who was unaware of the local custom for establishing the right of way on narrow tracks.

On another occasion Speke was invited—or rather ordered—to pay homage to the sovereign through whose territory he was traveling. Making the

148 bottom left *This engraving, taken from* The Lake Regions of Central Africa *by Burton, shows an imposing sycamore under whose branches the men of the expedition camped.*

148 bottom right *This drawing shows the unusual hairstyles worn by the members of the Unyamwezi an Ujiji tribes.* **(R. Burton, *The Lake Regions of Central Africa*)**

148-149 *After a grueling three-month march, Burton and Speke reached the Arab station of Kazeh, where they gained more precise information about the legendary Great Lakes. They began with an exploration of the closest of them, Ujiji, today known as Tanganyika, aboard long native canoes propelled by dozens of oarsmen. This engraving shows the two explorers setting out on a circumnavigation that proved to be beyond them, given the immensity of the lake and the violence of its storms. After having covered a number of kilometers in various directions, they gave up and returned to Kazeh.* **(R. Burton, *The Lake Regions of Central Africa*)**

149 bottom *Here Burton in his most famous disguise, that of a Muslim pilgrim. Similarly clothed, he had succeeded in entering Mecca some years earlier.*

150-151 *An elephant hunter with a magnificent tusk. The Arab slave and ivory traders dominated the Great Lakes region. Their headquarters was at Kazeh, later renamed Tabora, where the caravans that carried all that they had managed to procure peacefully or by force would congregate before heading to the coast.*

151 top left *Explorers' tents and a hut on the shore of Lake Tanganyika.*

151 top right *The defensive palisade surrounding a coastal village.*

151 center *A porter carrying a long ivory tusk to which he has tied a number of packets containing food and tobacco. Below, one of the fish traps used by the inhabitants of the shores of Lake Tanganyika.*

151 bottom right *This native armed with a kind of hatchet is carrying a child on his back.*

151 bottom left *Smoking was one of the few pleasures enjoyed by the natives. Here we see one squatting with a large clay pipe.*

150 bottom left *A native armed with a hatchet.*

150 bottom right *A view of the Maroro region.*

(R. Burton, *The Lake Regions of Central Africa*)

best of a potentially bad lot, he turned off the track and waited patiently for some days before Queen Ungagu, as she was called, deigned to receive him—a delay demanded by regal dignity. He was at last led into a maze of huts and pens full of livestock, seated on a stool in a small courtyard, and subjected to the examination of one of Ungagu's ladies-in-waiting, who presented him with milk and eggs before leaving to report to her queen.

The preliminary investigation must have been favorable, Queen Ungagu soon emerged from her hut. She was a sixty-year-old matron dressed in ancient Arab clothing, her legs and arms covered with gigantic bracelets of brass wire twisted around elephant tails and zebra manes. Settling on a ox skin close to the Englishman, she began to examine his clothes carefully, paying particular attention to his waistcoat, for which she manifested an anxious predilection. She obtained the waistcoat, together with other minor gifts, and in return decreed that a steer should be presented to the stranger. With that she dismissed the impatient Speke, but not without having praised his hair, similar to that of the mane of a lion, and emphasizing that the white man's gifts were not worthy of a person of her standing.

The expedition proceeded through a rich and fertile region dotted with villages in which supplies were abundant but hard to come by, as the local currency was colored beads and Speke had brought only white beads. The party then approached the lake only after taking a long detour to avoid the armed bands that infested the surrounding area. Finally, on July 30, 1858, from the top of a hill, Speke saw the waters of Ukerewe, the lake later to be named after Queen Victoria, glinting in the sunshine. In his diary scientific rigor appears to have the upper hand over emotion—true British phlegm. It was early morning when he got to the lake. According to his words

he had no idea of the size of the lake, which looked like an archipelago. His line of sight was in fact interrupted to the left because each island was composed of a single hill rising 600 to 1,000 meters above the water. To the right, the western horn of the island of Ukerewe hid from his eyes the distant waters to the east and the north. However, a branch of the lake, at the foot of the low range where he stood, extended far into the east where, in the hazy distance, a conical elevation of the lowlands marked what he understood to be the south east corner of the lake.

Because his supplies had run out, Speke roughly calculated the size of the stretch of water, gathered information from local chiefs on the basis of which he concluded that the lake must be the source of the principal stream of the Nile, and hurriedly departed, determined to return with a better organized expedition.

At Kazeh, the survivors of the discovery were welcomed in triumph during the last week of August. When Burton heard his companion's report, however, he was more prudent: the lake might well be the river's source—indeed it had to be, as Speke described—but there was no scientific proof. The lake had not been circumnavigated, and the claim that it was the true source of the Nile was for the moment pure, albeit well-grounded, hypothesis. There descended a palpable coolness between the two, but they returned to the coast together on reasonably friendly terms and embarked for Aden.

There Speke took advantage of a passing warship to return hurriedly to England, but Burton, still ill, preferred to convalesce in the warm, dry climate of the East. They agreed that nothing would be published regarding the alleged discovery before Burton, the formal leader of the expedition, returned to England.

ropelled by his own ambition and influenced by what the historians of exploration have regarded as bad advice, Speke failed to respect the agreement reached with Burton. By rights he should have waited for the leader of the expedition, but the chairman of the Royal Geographical Society, Sir Roderick Murchison, required heroes and triumphs, and when, on the very day he arrived back in London, Speke presented himself with maps of the two lakes he had "discovered" and the certainty of having found the Nile springs, Murchison convened a public conference to announce to the world that one of its age-old mysteries had been solved. Moreover, he immediately decided that a second expedition would be sent to comb the shores of Lake Victoria in search of the Nile outlet. Command of this expedition was to be entrusted to the hero of the day, John Hanning Speke. Murchison "could not help but present . . . in public his lion, whose roar was to thrill the ladies and show the institution in a good light," as the embittered Burton was later to write.

Burton himself did not return to London until the party was over at the end of May 1859. He then sparked off an unfortunate controversy by denying that Speke could prove his claims and putting forward as the more probable his own theory that the Nile had its origins

THE SOLVING OF THE ENIGMA: SPEKE AND GRANT

152 *Speke's claim to have identified Lake Victoria as the sole source of the Nile was contested by Burton who affirmed that his companion had no positive proof of the fact. In 1860* *Speke was thus commissioned to lead a second expedition to the Great Lakes to eliminate any lingering doubts. The complex hydrography of the area is traced in this map drawn by* *Speke and dated February 26, 1863. Below can be seen an engraving from Speke's book,* Journal of the Discovery of the Source of the Nile, *showing the expedition's camp.*

153 *Speke with another officer from the British Indian Army, James Augustus Grant, one of his old hunting companions. Here we see them portrayed by Henry Wyndham Phillips, together with Timbo, a native of the Upper Nile. Grant, on the left, is drawing while Speke is placing his compass on a map with a thoughtful air. On the right is a map drawn by Speke of a section of the shore of Lake Victoria from which the Nile issues (at the top).*

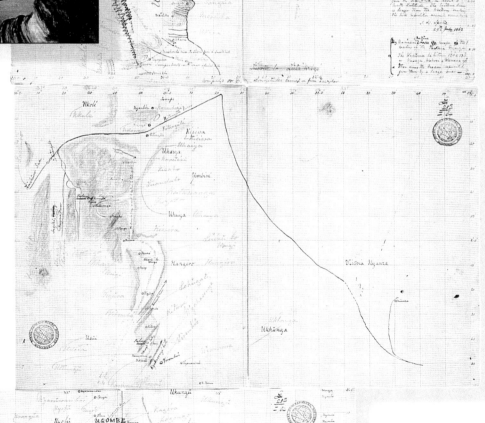

in a number of lakes rather than just one. Their dispute was destined to intensify. Speke was an Englishman of impeccable background, Burton an exuberant and rather undiplomatic Irishman, and the sympathies of the British public clearly lay with the former; moreover, casting doubt on Speke's "discovery" meant depriving England of glory, and the idea of stripping John Bull of his laurels appealed to no one.

Burton then left for America, in search of a less rancorous atmosphere among the Mormons of Utah and the gold miners of California, and Speke began organizing his trip. The first expedition had cost £2,500, almost all of it coming out of the explorers' own pockets. This time the British government provided the same sum, and the India Office put arms, scientific instruments, and gifts for the native chiefs at Speke's disposal. John Petherick, an ivory trader and the British consul at Khartoum, was instructed to send boats to the Upper Nile at Gondokoro to wait for the explorers, who planned to return by that route. Speke was accompanied by another officer of the British Indian Army, his former Himalayan hunting companion, the Scotsman James Augustus Grant, born in 1827. They set sail on April 27, 1860, and sailing by way of the Cape of Good Hope landed in mid-August at

Zanzibar, where they were greeted by rather disturbing news: the African interior was in a state of extreme agitation; there were continual skirmishes between the Arab slavers and the black tribes; and a German explorer named Roscher, who had reached Lake Nyasa, had been killed. The British consul had already sent fabrics and beads out to Kazeh for them to use as currency, however, and the new sultan of the island, Sayid Magid, was proud to be associated with the enterprise. He ordered thirty-four slaves to accompany the expedition, along with thirty-six freemen and around a hundred porters. Sidi Bombay and a number of other veterans of the first expedition were ready to follow Speke once again, and ten mounted Hottentot riflemen had been sent from Cape Town as a military escort.

The reader may well be wondering why the African expeditions used men rather than pack animals to carry their baggage. The answer is that in a region lacking roads and scattered with swamps and rivers, quadrupeds have a harder time of it than bipeds. Above all, however, there were vast areas teeming with deadly tsetse flies whose bite is fatal for horses, oxen, and mules, so that an expedition relying on pack animals would soon have risked being left with no means of transport whatsoever. Even asses were not resistant to any great extent, and Speke and Grant saw all those they had brought with them die within a short distance of the coast.

The caravan followed the old Arab track used by the previous expedition as far as Kazeh, and there were no incidents of note, apart from the usual extortion by the tribal chiefs and the usual desertions of the porters. The tribes were at war, however, and it was difficult to get hold of supplies, so the explorers had to rely on hunting to stock their kitchens. An encounter with a trader named Mamba (Crocodile), who reported going hungry to the point where he had had to boil the leather jerkins worn by his porters to make a broth, persuaded Speke and Grant to follow a route farther to the north than the one taken three years previously.

Early in June 1861 they penetrated the then unknown territory of the Uzingia, southwest of the great lake. But there too the wars between the natives, instigated by the Arabs in order to capture slaves, were incessant, and the frightened porters were reluctant to proceed further. Speke and Grant felt that it would be a good

154 top and center *Hunting, a passion shared by all the explorers, ensured a supply of fresh meat for the numerous members of the expedition. These two engravings show*

Speke killing buffalo with a sure aim and in the lower plate, saving a terrified porter. (John Hanning Speke, *Journal of the Discovery of the Source of the Nile*, London, 1863)

154 bottom *The proud bearing of a warrior of the Ugogo tribe.* (Speke, *Journal of the Discovery of the Source of the Nile*)

idea if they separated and followed different but roughly parallel routes. The only result, however, apart from an increase in the geographical knowledge, was that they were obliged to pay double tributes as the tribal chiefs seized the opportunity to treat them as two independent expeditions. Even an invitation to visit a chief such as that received from Suwarora, the sultan of Usui, did not provide exemption from payment of the *hongo*. Quite the contrary, throughout that country the payment for the right of passage was demanded and

their monarch and lived in a kind of African Arcadia rich in pasture, cultivated fields, and game and punctuated with ponds similar to those found in England.

On November 25, Grant and Speke entered Rumanika's palace, a residence that, while the usual agglomeration of huts and courtyards, had a touch of sophistication and elegance deriving from the king's Arab friends who had built him a large *baraza,* or reception hall. The king, his son, and his brother, all attractive men with Abyssinian

155 top *Beyond Kazeh, Speke and Grant followed a more northerly route than on the first expedition, passing through territories that no white man had ever visited and encountering tribes that were hospitable rather than avid for the traditional* hongo, *a kind of toll paid for right of passage. These engravings show some of the methods used by the natives for storing grain and other foodstuffs in Unyamwezi. The illustration on the right depicts a group of women grinding millet.*

155 center *A series of encircling palisades protected the villages of the Unyoro people. The town of Ukulima is seen here in an engraving worked up from a drawing by Speke.*

155 bottom *Captain Grant leaving Karague on a stretcher protected by mosquito netting, as a fever prevented him from walking.* (John Hanning Speke, *Journal of the Discovery of the Source of the Nile*)

obtained by each village they encountered until the explorers realized they had been invited deliberately so that they could be fleeced. Suwarora, whose subjects appeared to be permanently drunk on beer, delayed the meeting with Speke day after day. Finally, after having extracted all the possible gifts, he allowed Speke to depart without conceding him a hearing, as he was afraid of being enchanted by the white man.

Fortunately, the next king, Rumanika, the ruler of Karague, was a true gentleman. Not only did he waive any right to *hongo,* but he ordered his subordinates along the route followed by the caravan to welcome the explorers with all honors and supply them with free food. The people seemed worthy of

features, proved to be attentive, cordial, and intelligent. They were particularly interested in news concerning their equals among the royal families of Europe and curious as to how one communicated at a distance through signs drawn on paper. The royal wives, in a country in which obesity was considered the very essence of beauty, passed their time sipping bowls of milk and putting on weight to the point where their rolls of flesh reminded Speke of gigantic puddings and at least two slaves had to help them stand up.

The caravan was fed with great banquets of fowl and goatmeat. The explorers were unable to

156 top left and 156-157 *M'tesa, the king of Uganda (left), who called the explorers to his court, lived in the "palace" on the right, a vast agglomeration of huts occupying an entire hill.*
(**John Hanning Speke,** *Journal of the Discovery of the Source of the Nile,* London, 1863)

156 bottom *A group of Ugandans resting in the camp prepared for Speke and his men near the royal palace.*
(**John Hanning Speke,** *Journal of the Discovery of the Source of the Nile*)

buy milk because a local superstition forbade the sale to the white men of the products of the natives' cows, which would thereby become sterile. The good king got around this problem by presenting Speke with a cow, while to his great joy Speke in turn gave the king a pistol. This sent Rumanika into seventh heaven, because the prudent Arabs had always avoided distributing firearms among the blacks, but the white men were unable to satisfy the king's greatest desire—a spell that would kill his rebel brother who contested the throne. He refused to believe Speke's vigorous denial that he possessed such powers, but he continued to treat the explorers generously. On December 25, he honored them with the gift of an ox because he had heard from the Arabs that on that day the Christians performed "sacrifices of meat."

The time passed pleasantly thanks to a sequence of royal receptions, hunting parties, and much talk about

certain tiny men who lived in the trees in the kingdom of Rwanda and shot poisoned arrows at the monsters who hid in the forests waiting to strangle young girls, about the consumers of human flesh of Uliamwatu, and about another great lake, the Luta Nzighe, which another explorer would later name after Prince Albert.

On January 1, 1862, messengers arrived from Kamrasi, the king of Bunyoro, who sent word that he too would soon have the pleasure of the company of a group of white men ascending the Nile in boats. Speke had no doubt that it was Petherick and his men and sent messengers to meet them. Speke and Grant were then themselves met by the envoys of M'tesa, the king of Uganda, who had invited them to visit his court while they were at Suwarora and now insisted that they come.

Grant was suffering from fever and an ulcerated leg that prevented him from walking, and by Ugandan law no sick person was allowed to enter the kingdom, but to refuse the royal invitation would have been a grave breach of etiquette. Speke therefore departed alone and on February 19, 1862, he came within sight of M'tesa's *kabunga*, or palace, the imposing buildings of which occupied an entire hillside. Used to the affable, easygoing customs of Rumanika, Speke was not expecting the strict formality to which he was subjected.

The Ugandan court was run according to a protocol that was even more rigidly observed than in any European palace. First a salvo was fired to announce to the king the arrival of the strangers, who then had to retire to their lodgings and await the hearing arranged for the next day. The following morning Speke and his men dressed as well as they were able and marched toward the royal palace. The British flag preceded twelve men in scarlet uniforms, followed by the porters and the rest of the party, each carrying a gift, a spectacle that was greeted by the Ugandans with whispers of "*Irunghi! Irunghi!*" ("Good! Good!") Having reached the courtyard in front of the king's residence Speke was invited to sit on the floor and wait until the king was ready to receive him.

Intolerant of any loss of dignity by a representative of the United Kingdom, the explorer firmly demanded a chair, to the horror of the courtiers who had never heard of such audacity. As the negotiations dragged on, Speke turned on his heel and left with all his men, who fully expected to meet a hail of spears from one moment to the next. Instead M'tesa, convinced that the visitor would never have dared to behave with such arrogance had he not been endowed with magical powers, sent a messenger to beg him to return, bringing with him his folding metal chair. Thus Speke was able to sit on equal terms before the king.

157 *Relations that were almost cordial were soon established between the king of Uganda and Speke, partly because the Englishman won the favor of the Ugandan by curing the queen mother of an illness that was probably imaginary by prescribing abundant doses of palm wine. The king was also treated by the white "witch doctor," who on that occasion portrayed him naked on a page of his notebook.*

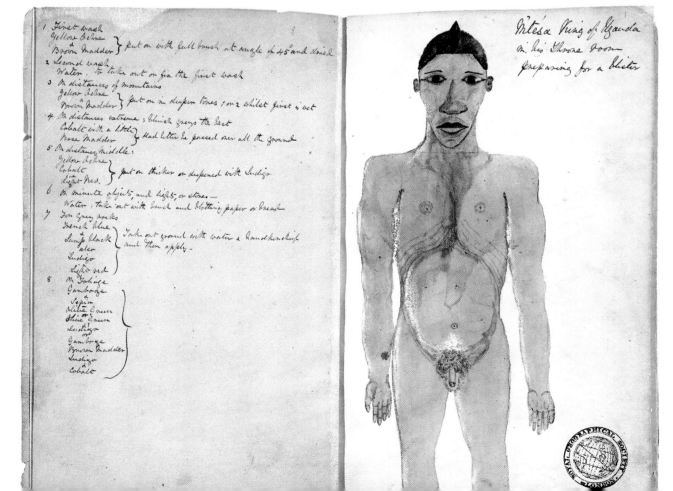

158 top *The cruelty of M'tesa horrified his British guests. On an almost daily basis the sovereign would condemn to death one or more of his concubines for some insignificant offense. In this engraving one of them is being pushed into a cage while another is being dragged off to be tortured.* (John Hanning Speke, *Journal of the Discovery of the Source of the Nile*, London, 1863)

They looked at each for a good half hour in virtual silence, partly because no interpreters were available. Every so often the king ordered a servant to ask Speke to remove his hat and put it on again and to open and close his umbrella. Finally an interpreter appeared, through whom M'tesa asked Speke if "he had seen him." When Speke replied in the affirmative the king left the hut imitating the movement of a lion, a gait whereby a monarch in Uganda expressed his regal dignity. M'tesa had vowed to fast from the moment the white man arrived until he "had seen him" and was now eager to satisfy his hunger.

Over the following days there were less formal encounters between the king and Speke, and a relationship that may be best described as amicable incomprehension

was established between the proud Englishman and the haughty Ugandan. Speke did, however, become close to the queen mother, whose favor he won by prescribing for her presumed afflictions doses of palm wine, a beverage of which she was particularly fond. Speke was horrified by the gratuitous cruelty of the king. One day when they were out walking together, one of the king's favorites picked a fruit and presented it to him. Furious that a woman had had the temerity to offer something to him, M'tesa gave orders that she should be strangled on the spot. It took the firm intervention of the explorer to save her life.

On another occasion Speke presented the king with a rifle. After having admired the gift, the king gave it to a young page to test, ordering him to "Go and kill a man." The page went out into

the courtyard, shot at the first man he saw, and returned triumphant. "The man is dead," he said. "The gun kills well!"

Concubines were killed almost every day, usually on a mere whim. Speke saw them pass by, a rope round their necks, dragged screaming toward their death by the palace guards. The harem was, however, abundantly restocked on a daily basis. Being part of the palace staff was a risky honor. Once when a meal had left something to be desired, M'tesa had around a hundred servants executed behind the scenes before Speke intervened.

The bloodthirsty tyrant willingly agreed to send his men to meet Grant, who had been convalescing with Rumanika and who was brought to Speke on a stretcher on May 27. M'tesa was reluctant to allow the two explorers to leave his kingdom, but finally, in a moment of good humor, he suddenly and unexpectedly gave them permission to depart.

The caravan left Uganda as hurriedly as possible before the unstable monarch could change his mind. Grant, however, fell ill again and turned to the east to enter the kingdom of Bunyoro while Speke pushed on alone toward the point at which his informants had placed the river issuing from the lake. On July 21, 1862, Speke finally set eyes on the river, and this time the entry in his diary was a little less phlegmatic. "It was the very perfection of the kind of effect aimed at in a highly kept park; with a magnificent stream from 600 to 700 yards wide, dotted with islets and rocks, the former occupied by fishermen's huts, the latter by terns and crocodiles basking in the sun,—flowing between fine high grassy banks, with rich trees and plants in the background, where herds of hartebeest could be seen grazing, while the hippopotamuses were snorting in the water, and florikan and guinea fowl rising at our feet."

159

159 top *It was by no means rare to see prisoners such as these two unfortunate souls being dragged from M'tesa's palace to be executed.* (J. A. Grant, *A Walk across Africa*)

159 center *Large and small drums, horns, and flutes composed the orchestra of the Ugandan court.* (Grant, *A Walk across Africa*)

159 bottom *Ugandan warriors paying homage to their king in front of the royal palace as a sign of their devotion.* (Grant, *A Walk across Africa*)

Speke ascended the river to the point where it issued from the lake, arriving on July 28. He baptized the falls there after Ripon, then the chairman of the Royal Geographical Society. The joy of discovery led him at this point to assume triumphant and then poetic tones: "I saw that old father Nile without any doubt rises in the Victoria N'yanza, and, as I had foretold, that lake is the great source of the holy river which cradled the first expounder of our religious belief. . . . This day also I spent watching the fish flying at the falls, and felt as if I only wanted a wife and family, garden and yacht, rifle and rod, to make me happy here for life, so charming was the place."

Downstream from the falls the party embarked to descend the river in the

hope of meeting Grant. However, when they entered Bunyoro they met with a hostile reception and in order to land they were obliged to clear the bank with a salvo of rifle shot. This welcome was unexpected, as King Kamrasi had previously been friendly, but it turned out that he had simply been disturbed by the news that white men were entering his country from two different directions, and he feared betrayal. Moreover, a rumor had spread that these explorers were cannibals and that in the chests they were carrying they concealed ferocious

161 The Ugandan court was governed by a strict etiquette. Almost every day ceremonies of diverse kinds and degrees of importance were held, to which the British guests were invited. One of these engravings shows the king watching a parade of his battle-hardened troops "lion-stepping" past and brandishing their lances while Speke, to one side, looks on rather unimpressed. In the plate below, the two explorers, who have been granted the very unusual privilege of sitting in the presence of the sovereign, are witnesses to a hearing before M'tesa in which his trembling, prostrate subjects are imploring him.
(John Hanning Speke, Journal of the Discovery of the Source of the Nile)

160-161 *Finally having obtained permission to leave Uganda, Speke reached the outlet of Lake Victoria—the yearned-for Nile— and pushed on as far as the waterfall he named after Ripon, the president of the Royal Geographical Society.*

160 bottom *Following his discovery, Speke continued along the river, the valley of which beyond the confluence with the Aswa River is depicted in this engraving.*

white dwarves ready to be taken out for who knew what evil purposes.

Crude, suspicious, and ruthless, Kamrasi was very different from M'tesa and Rumanika. He was also poorly advised by his brothers, who were intimidated by the "magical powers" of the white men. In order to placate his regal vexation, messengers were sent proffering friendship and gifts. As a penance, however, the sovereign kept the explorers waiting for many days and demanded significant tributes. He finally received his unwelcome guests in his palace, the filthiest and most fetid Grant and Speke had ever seen. The royal cattle were lying in a pool of dung in which the king waded up to his knees as he personally chose the beasts to be slaughtered to feed the foreigners, without exception the scrawniest of the animals. Kamrasi outdid his neighboring kings in only one area—the obesity of his wives; it took eight strong men to move one of them.

The explorers' stay in Bunyoro lasted four months; not until November 9 could Speke and Grant finally depart, having by then been obliged to give away almost all of their belongings. They sailed down the Kafue, a tributary of the Nile, expecting to meet Petherick's men at any moment. They were delighted to find ever more frequent traces of "civilization" in the villages in the form of junk produced in Europe and sold to the natives by the Egyptian slavers and ivory traders.

162 *From Uganda Speke and Grant passed through the territory of the Unyoro people whose king, Kamrasi, proved to be very different from both M'tesa and the courteous Rumanika, to whom in the lower engraving Grant is presenting the game he has killed. Kamrasi was an arrogant yet timid tyrant who was interested only in stripping the explorers of all their belongings. In the upper engraving we see them taking shelter in the king's village.*
(John Hanning Speke, *Journal of the Discovery of the Source of the Nile*)

162-163 and 163 bottom *Following the course of the Nile, on the bank of which a large herd of elephants can be seen in the lower engraving, Speke and Grant— seen here dancing with a native woman during a lively celebration—headed toward the Sudan, where they should have found help and supplies.*
(John Hanning Speke, *Journal of the Discovery of the Source of the Nile*)

163

Finally, on December 3, they spotted the outposts of a large camp where they were greeted with extraordinary fervor by a black man in Egyptian uniform. He was the leader of a band of ivory hunters composed of around two hundred "Turks"—that is, Egyptians, Nubians, and men of various African tribes. His name was Mohammed, and he was the *wakil*, or agent, of Andrea De Bono, a Maltese merchant from Khartoum who had sent them there three years earlier in search of tusks. The hunters had settled in so well at Faloro, as the place was

called, that the huts were already teeming with the children of native girls they had taken as temporary wives.

Mohammed knew nothing of Petherick—he had been told only to look after his friends—so Speke and Grant impatiently recommenced their journey toward the Nile in January 1863, but stopped at Apuddo to allow Mohammed's men to complete their task —that of stripping the country bare. At Apuddo they found on the trunk of a tamarind an inscription of which they had heard rumors: the partially canceled letters MI. It was said that the inscription was the work of a long-bearded white man and they immediately thought of Petherick. In reality the letters had been carved two years earlier by Giovanni Miani. Mohammed's "Turks" descended upon Apuddo like a swarm of locusts: they stripped the roofs from the huts to make tents and requisitioned all the pots and the reserves of grain, leaving the natives to eat grubs. They then recruited three hundred locals to carry

their haul of ivory and headed with all speed to Gondokoro, arriving on February 15.

It was a return to civilization, symbolized by the white chapel of the Austrian missionaries who for years had vainly attempted to convert the natives. Where was Petherick? Descending the river to check whether the boats he could see were his, Speke had a quite remarkable encounter. He was embraced and almost suffocated by a bearded giant whom he eventually recognized as his friend and hunting partner Samuel Baker. Baker had

ascended the Nile in the company of his wife with three boats and a large escort in the hope, he said cheerfully, of sharing in their glory by finding them in dire straits in the equatorial regions and coming to their rescue.

Baker's was not the only rescue expedition funded through private generosity. In July 1861 three Dutch ladies had departed from the Hague: Madame Tinné, the widow of a British merchant; her daughter Alexandrine; and her sister, Baroness von Capellan. They had spent the winter at Cairo and ascended the Nile in September 1862 as far as Gondokoro, where they hoped to receive news of Speke and Grant. They were too early, however, and so in November they returned to Cairo. They set out once again in February of the

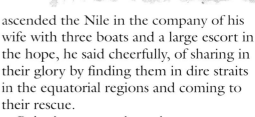

164 top left *A group of Wagani with various hairstyles and examples of body painting in their village Koki. The freshness of the naïve drawings in Grant's notebooks helps to impart the flavor of a world that white men were seeing for the first time.* (James Augustus Grant, *A Walk across Africa*, London, 1864)

164 top right *Kamrasi, the king of Unyoro, sitting on his raised throne with a Bible in his hands, a gift from the explorers who attempted to explain the basis of Christianity to him.* (J. A. Grant, *A Walk across Africa*)

164 bottom *This drawing shows the arms and costume of a Ugandan warrior.*

164-165 *This water-color by Grant depicts an enchanting sunset in the Isumburu Mountains.* (J. A. Grant, *A Walk across Africa*)

165 bottom *A group of natives and members of the expedition portrayed in an Unyoro village in September 1862.* (J. A. Grant, *A Walk across Africa*)

following year, while the two Englishmen were meeting Baker, to explore the Bahr al-Ghazal accompanied by Baron d'Ablaing, Dr. Steudner, and Baron von Heuglin. This was perhaps the most extravagant expedition ever seen in Africa and also quite the most unsuitable: maids in white caps and crinolines and luxury furniture in the cabins, all of which was burned to feed the boilers in the infinite maze of streams and reed beds of the Nile swamps. All of the Europeans contracted malaria while in that morass; Steudner died in April, Madame Tinné in June. The survivors struggled back to Khartoum in July 1864 where Baroness von Capellan also succumbed to the disease. Miss Tinné, who enjoyed a reputation as being the richest heiress in Holland, settled at Cairo, where she lived

165

166 top *Following the course of the White Nile, the British explorers and their escort, seen posing in this engraving with their weapons proudly displayed, finally encountered not the hoped rescuers but a* caravan of ivory hunters from Khartoum with whom they descended the river toward civilization. (John Hanning Speke, Journal of the Discovery of the Source of the Nile, London, 1863)

in Oriental splendor until 1869 when she decided to cross the Sahara, departing from Tripoli, to reach Lake Chad. She was assassinated by a band of Tuaregs attracted by the excessive luxury in which the adventurous lady was once again traveling.

While Speke and Grant rested at Gondokoro, catching up on events in the civilized world, among which were the death of Prince Albert, the husband of Queen Victoria, and the outbreak of the American Civil War, Petherick finally arrived, accompanied by his wife and the naturalist Murie. He apologized for his lateness, explaining that he had made the mistake of deciding to build a new boat and had therefore missed the north winds necessary to ascend the river against the current. He also candidly admitted that he had held out no hope of ever seeing them again alive.

On February 26, Speke and Grant began their long trip home, finally setting foot in England after an absence of three years and fifty-one days. They were welcomed in triumph, but the "Hero of the Nile," as the press called Speke, was to meet with a sad and mysterious end at just thirty-seven years of age. The British Association called a public debate on September 16, 1864, at Bath, Speke's hometown, to discuss the problem of the Nile sources. Livingstone and Burton were also to be present, the latter claiming that the Nile must originate in Lake Tanganyika rather than Lake Victoria and possibly also from the snows of Kilimanjaro and Mount Kenya, Ptolemy's Mountains of the Moon.

Wrote Burton, "Early in the afternoon fixed for what silly tongues called the Nile Duel I found a large assembly in the rooms of Section E. A note was handed round in silence.

Presently my friend Mr. Findlay broke the tidings to me: Captain Speke had lost his life yesterday, at 4:00 P.M., whilst shooting over a cousin's grounds. He had been missed in the field, and his kinsman found him lying upon the earth, shot through the body close to the heart." The circumstances of the accident remain unclear. According to the official version, Speke caught the trigger of his gun on a protruding stone or branch while climbing over a drystone wall. Many, however, and Burton among them, believed that he had committed suicide because he could not bear for his reputation as the discoverer of the true source of the Nile to be questioned.

Ivory hunters on the march in Madi
Feb 1863.

no 2 View of same hills from the W.

no 3 View from the N.W. 20 march 1863.

167 top *This drawing by Grant shows a group of Madi ivory hunters on the march.*

167 bottom *James Augustus Grant carefully recorded even the most banal scenes of everyday life. This watercolor depicts a group of men carrying the roof of a hut.*

166-167 *This unusual study by the British explorer shows views of a number of sections of the banks of the White Nile.*

166 center *Porters at rest in the village with their precious load of ivory.*
(John Hanning Speke, *Journal of the Discovery of the Source of the Nile*)

166 bottom *Wageni warriors with their characteristic decorations.*

Courtyard.   Scenes in Madi. 1863.   Flitting.

The man who had embraced the dumbfounded Speke with such brotherly fervor at Gondokoro was himself to have a significant role in the exploration of the Nile basin. In 1863 Samuel White Baker was no longer a young man, having been born in London in 1821. He had come to know the Dark Continent and its hazards as a mature man after tempering himself in mind and body in various parts of the world. He was born into a very wealthy family. His father was a ship owner and directed a bank and a railway company. Samuel and his brother had founded an agricultural colony in Ceylon. Then he had taken part in the Crimean War and directed the construction of the first Ottoman railway, which went from the Danube to the Black Sea, crossing the desolate plain of Dobruja. His great passion, however, was for big game hunting. He had killed elephants in Ceylon, tigers in Bengal, and bears in the Balkans and was first attracted to Africa as a game reserve. After the death of his first wife, the daughter of a Protestant minister, he had married Florence Ninian von Sass, a beautiful fair-haired Hungarian woman fifteen years younger than he was. He then settled the three children from his first marriage with relations in England and set off with his new wife for the Sudan. Because Baker was interested not only in hunting but also in geography, he thought to mix business with pleasure by traveling up the White Nile to its source while hunting along its banks.

A VERY VICTORIAN COUPLE: THE BAKERS AND THE DISCOVERY OF LAKE ALBERT

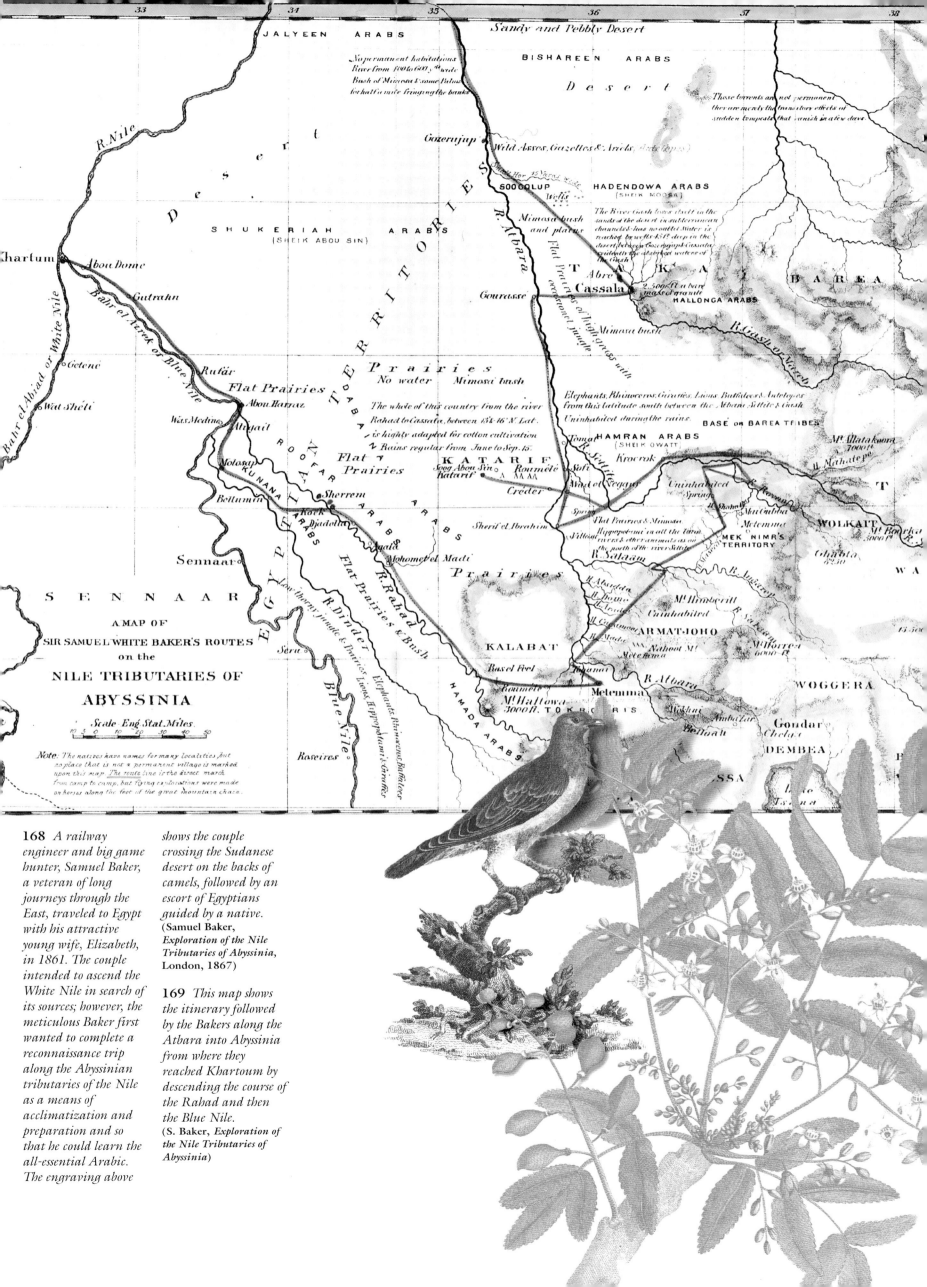

A MAP OF

SIR SAMUEL WHITE BAKER'S ROUTES

on the

NILE TRIBUTARIES OF

ABYSSINIA

Scale Eng. Stat. Miles.

Note: The natives have names for many localities, but no place that is not a permanent village is marked upon this map. The route line is the direct march from camp to camp, but flying explorations were made on horses along the foot of the great mountain chain.

168 *A railway engineer and big game hunter, Samuel Baker, a veteran of long journeys through the East, traveled to Egypt with his attractive young wife, Elizabeth, in 1861. The couple intended to ascend the White Nile in search of its sources; however, the meticulous Baker first wanted to complete a reconnaissance trip along the Abyssinian tributaries of the Nile as a means of acclimatization and preparation and so that he could learn the all-essential Arabic. The engraving above* shows the couple crossing the Sudanese desert on the backs of camels, followed by an escort of Egyptians guided by a native. *(Samuel Baker, **Exploration of the Nile Tributaries of Abyssinia**, London, 1867)*

169 *This map shows the itinerary followed by the Bakers along the Atbara into Abyssinia from where they reached Khartoum by descending the course of the Rahad and then the Blue Nile. (S. Baker, Exploration of the Nile Tributaries of Abyssinia)*

Baker was an engineer, and as such he had a practical, rational mind. Whatever he did he prepared meticulously. He was wary of interpreters, ready as they were to take advantage of travelers and line their own pockets, so he decided that he absolutely had to learn Arabic in order to deal with the natives directly. He thus decided on a year's stay in the Sudan, during which time he would study the language and explore the Abyssinian tributaries of the Nile.

The couple left Cairo in the middle of April 1861 and reached Korosko in less than a month. They crossed the Nubian Desert to avoid having to follow the great curve of the Nile and arrived at Berber at the height of summer, when the temperature was 45°C in the shade. They then traveled to the confluence with the Atbara to await the annual floods. They camped within sight of the riverbed, which was dry but studded with immense ponds, some up to a kilometer long. Crocodiles, hippopotamuses, hyenas, and gazelles crowded their banks. On the night of June 23 a deafening roar announced the arrival of the waters, and the next morning the Bakers found before them a 500-meter-wide course of water whose tumultuous currents carried great floating islands of vegetation

170 *Big game hunting was Baker's great passion. He had already killed elephants in Ceylon, tigers in Bengal, and bears in the Balkan forests. These illustrations, sketched by him from life, show four natives armed with* swords attacking an elephant and a furious rhinoceros charging a terrified horse tied to a tree. **(S. Baker, Exploration of the Nile Tributaries of Abyssinia, London, 1867)**

downstream. The trees growing on the banks that had seemed dry and dead turned green with leaves as soon as the water touched their roots.

The Bakers ascended the Atbara for about 350 kilometers, reaching Kassala, the remotest Egyptian outpost on the border with Ethiopia, where the "Turkish" garrison was constantly assailed by guerrilla attacks from the local black tribes who were ill-disposed to the foreign presence. Everywhere they traveled they came across nomads moving northward away from the mud and the tsetse fly, the two scourges of the rainy season. The Bakers, on the other hand, were heading southwards to the Atbara again, to the village of Sofi

where an Austrian bricklayer named Florian had built himself the only stone house within hundreds of kilometers. Florian had come to the Sudan with the Austrian missionaries who had settled in Khartoum but then he had decided to leave the mission. He had bought a rifle and lived a Robinson Crusoe life among thousands of Man Fridays, hunting and making objects to sell. The Bakers wanted to meet him because he was undoubtedly the white man who knew the most about the topography of the region.

As there was now almost daily heavy rain, they decided to settle there until the arrival of the dry season. "I succeeded in

purchasing [a house] from the owner for the sum of ten piastres," wrote Baker. "In that happy and practical land, the simple form of conveyance is the transportation of the house [the roof] upon the shoulders of about thirty men, and thus it is conveyed to any spot that the purchaser may consider desirable. Accordingly, our mansion was at once seized by a crowd of Arabs, and carried off in triumph, while the sticks that formed the wall were quickly arranged upon the sites I had chose for our camp. In the short space of about three hours I found myself the proprietor of an eligible freehold residence, situated upon an eminence in parklike grounds, commanding extensive and

170-171 bottom *Baker's original drawings were used as the basis of the engravings that illustrated his book about the expedition along the Abyssinian tributaries of the Nile. In this plate the explorer takes aim at a rhinoceros.* **(S. Baker,** *Exploration of the Nile Tributaries of Abyssinia)*

171 top *In this wild gallop behind two rhinoceroses, Baker is preceded and followed by natives brandishing great swords.* **(S. Baker,** *Exploration of the Nile Tributaries of Abyssinia)*

172-173 *In this engraving Baker, on the right, is admiring the spectacle of the eddies at the* confluence of the Royan and Satit rivers. (S. Baker, *Exploration of the Nile Tributaries of Abyssinia*, London, 1867)

172 bottom *The hunting techniques of the natives, who were accustomed to tackling fearsome beasts armed only with lances, swords, and harpoons, aroused the admiration of the hunter Baker. In his book he devoted more space to hunting stories than to the hydrography of the Nile tributaries. In this plate two natives are stalking a crocodile with their harpoons.* (S. Baker, **Exploration of the Nile Tributaries of Abyssinia**)

romantic views of the beautiful wooded valley of the Atbara, within a minute's walk of the neighboring village of Sofi, with perfect immunity from all poor-rates, tithes, taxes, and other public burdens."

They waited three months while they studied Arabic, went hunting, and observed the local customs. Baker was particularly struck by a very special form of Turkish bath practiced by the women in the desert areas. Each woman would dig a hole inside her tent, fill it with red hot embers, and scattering a variety of spices and perfumes over it: cloves, ginger, incense, cinnamon, sandalwood oil, and myrrh. Then she would crouch over the embers naked beneath her ample dress, which was fixed to the ground around the hole like a tent so that none of the aromatic smoke would escape. "She nows begins to perspire freely in the hot-air-bath," Baker wrote, "and the pores of the skin being thus opened and moist, the volatile oil from the smoke of the burning perfumes is immediately absorbed." The last part of the operation, however, probably ruined the aromatic effect somewhat. It consisted of spreading the skin and hair with great quantities of grease. Baker maintained that a woman could be smelled at a distance of a hundred meters, even in the forest.

The rains ceased at the end of October, and the Bakers set off again eastward for the Satit River and followed its still unexplored course upstream as far as the border, where an inaccessible gorge compelled them to turn back and cross the territory lorded over by the son of the Nimr, who had burned Ismail alive and who continued to fight against the hated "Turks," making devastating incursions into Sudanese territory every dry season. "The area," wrote Baker, "was a refuge for all the local scoundrels who were attracted by the anarchy caused by the continuing border warfare."

173 **top** *Among Baker's favorite prey were lions. Here the explorer has drawn the final moments in the hunt when he is about to shoot the wounded animal in the head.*

173

173 **bottom** *This plate depicts the attempts of a group of natives to move a hippopotamus.* (S. Baker, **Exploration of the Nile Tributaries of Abyssinia**)

THE DISCOVERY OF LAKE ALBERT

At the end of April the Bakers reached the Ethiopian town of Gallabat and then made a wide detour, touching on the White Nile at Wad Medani and entering Khartoum on June 11, 1862. The city appeared to them "dirty and squalid," as in fact it was. There Baker and his wife received a welcome assignment based on false information. Word had spread in the city that Petherick, who had been commissioned to go to meet Speke and Grant, had died during an expedition to the south. The Royal Geographical Society asked Baker to take his place and go to the aid of the two explorers, if they were still alive. Baker and his wife, who had secretly planned to go in search of the source of the Nile on their own account, accepted with enthusiasm.

It took six months' patience and persistence, however, to overcome the various obstacles slyly put in their way by Governor Musa Pasha, who did not want any interfering white men, probably inspired by humanitarian ambitions, in the lands that were the richest source of slaves. Finally, however, Baker managed to buy three boats and hire about 100 men, with whom he left for Gondokoro on December 18, 1862, in the company of a German explorer, Johann Schmidt, who had asked to travel with them. On February 15 of the following year Baker had the joy of finding his friend Speke, whom he had thought lost forever, alive together with his companion.

Perhaps there was a touch of disappointment in the happiness with which Baker welcomed the reappearance of Speke and the fact that he had solved the mystery of the Nile. A short while later he ventured to ask his friend whether some laurel branch remained for him in the region of the sources. At this Speke and Grant told him about Luta Nzighe, which they had not been able to explore. They had heard, however, that the Nile, on leaving Lake Victoria, entered it and exited again almost immediately and at that point became navigable.

Delighted that the two explorers had involuntarily left him something to discover in the intricate hydrographic network of the Nile basin, Baker eagerly started to organize his expedition. Not much more than a month later, on March 23, 1863, the husband and wife team set off toward Bunyoro. The enterprise, however, was to be far more difficult than anticipated. The seasonal

174 *Anxious to earn "some laurels," as he put it, Baker was happy to learn from Speke and Grant, whom he met at Gondokoro, that there was still a great lake that no white man had ever seen: the Luta Nzighe, through which the Nile perhaps flowed. The explorer and his wife, portrayed in the ovals above, departed in March 1863 in the direction of the lake they renamed for Prince Albert.* (Samuel Baker, ***Albert Nyanza—Great Basin of the Nile***, London, 1886)

174-175 *This map shows the route followed by Samuel Baker's expedition in 1863.*

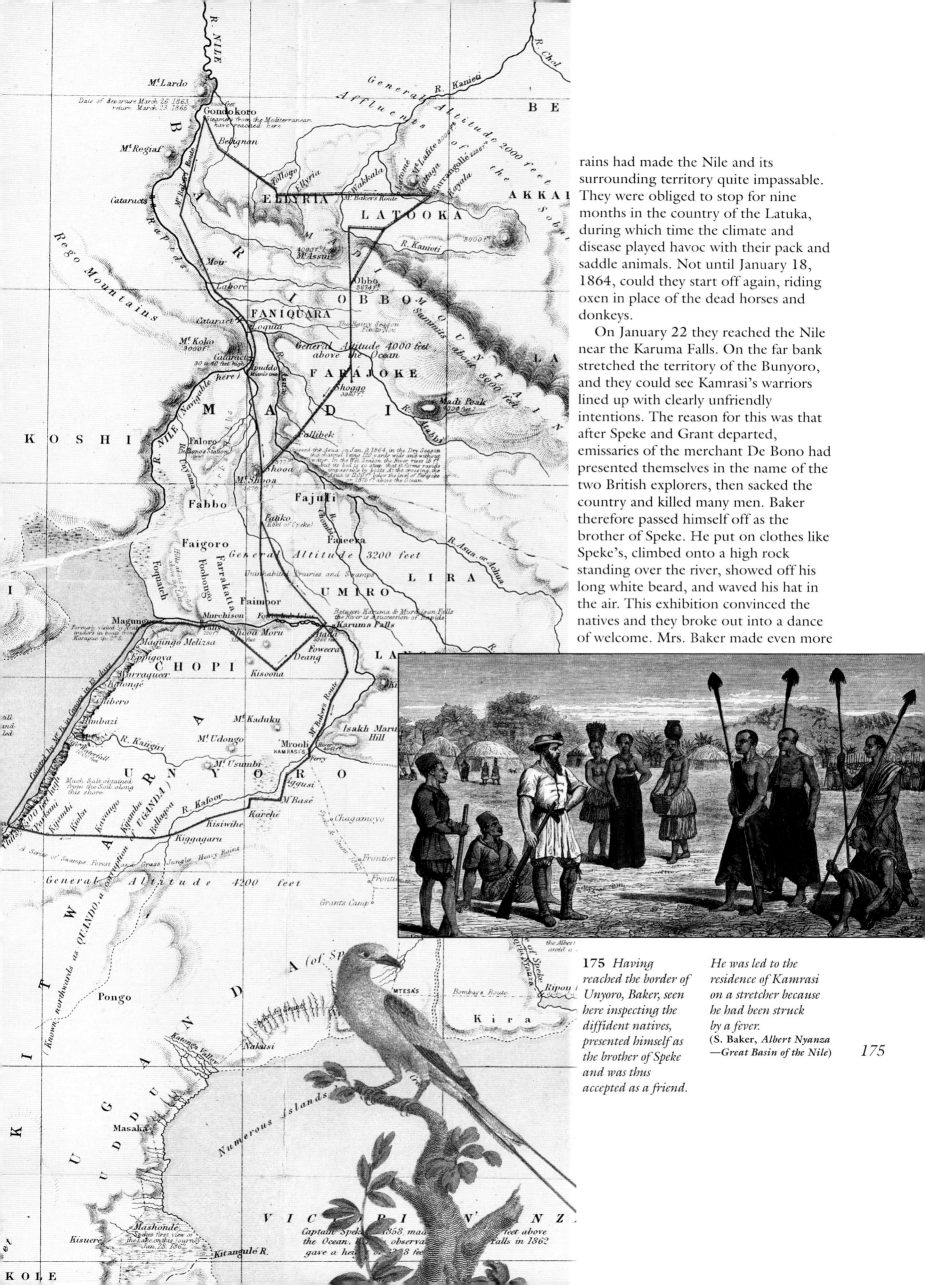

rains had made the Nile and its surrounding territory quite impassable. They were obliged to stop for nine months in the country of the Latuka, during which time the climate and disease played havoc with their pack and saddle animals. Not until January 18, 1864, could they start off again, riding oxen in place of the dead horses and donkeys.

On January 22 they reached the Nile near the Karuma Falls. On the far bank stretched the territory of the Bunyoro, and they could see Kamrasi's warriors lined up with clearly unfriendly intentions. The reason for this was that after Speke and Grant departed, emissaries of the merchant De Bono had presented themselves in the name of the two British explorers, then sacked the country and killed many men. Baker therefore passed himself off as the brother of Speke. He put on clothes like Speke's, climbed onto a high rock standing over the river, showed off his long white beard, and waved his hat in the air. This exhibition convinced the natives and they broke out into a dance of welcome. Mrs. Baker made even more

175 *Having reached the border of Unyoro, Baker, seen here inspecting the diffident natives, presented himself as the brother of Speke and was thus accepted as a friend.*

He was led to the residence of Kamrasi on a stretcher because he had been struck by a fever.
(S. Baker, *Albert Nyanza —Great Basin of the Nile*)

of a sensation when they saw her wash her waist-length fair hair.

The Bakers were accompanied to the court of Kamrasi ten days' march away. Baker was much weakened by malaria at this point and had to be carried on a litter and laid down at the feet of the king, who received them while sitting on a stool set on top of a pile of leopard skins. He immediately made out an exaggerated list of gifts he expected to receive, which ranged from colored beads to rifles. The sick Baker asked his regal host to help him reach Luta Nzighe, about which he had been gathering information. The fantastic tales he had heard excited him a great deal: the natives said that it was far larger than Lake Victoria (in actual fact it is only one-tenth its size).

The wily Kamrasi, determined to keep the two white guests at his court to despoil them of all they had, just as he had done with Speke and Grant, explained that the lake was very distant, a six months' march away, and the white man could never attempt such a journey in his condition. He should rest and recuperate, and then the king would supply him with the necessary guides and bearers. Much against his better judgment, Baker was then obliged to undergo the ceremony of the "brotherhood of blood" with the king. He managed on a pretext to have himself replaced by a proxy, and one of his men and the sovereign cut their arms, and licked each other's blood.

Baker had run out of supplies, especially of quinine with which to treat his malaria. He was being despoiled by the king, and his men, on hearing that their goal was so far away, were beginning to desert him. He was about to give up in despair, but at that point one of Kamrasi's courtiers came to his help. Perhaps touched by the white man's condition, he secretly revealed to

176-177 *Reaching Lake Albert on March 14, Baker and his wife boarded a fragile canoe to circumnavigate it in search of the influent and to ascertain whether in fact this inlet did lead from another great lake that Speke had baptized Victoria. On more than one occasion the couple risked drowning during the furious storms that tormented those waters.* (S. Baker, *Albert Nyanza—Great Basin of the Nile*, London, 1886)

176 bottom *This drawing by Baker depicts the war dance of the Obo tribe.*

177 *Baker and his wife ascended the Victoria Nile as far as this great waterfall, which Baker named after Murchison, then the president of the Royal Geographical Society. Before beginning their return journey, they were detained at length in Unyoro because the country was ravaged by tribal warfare, of which the Egyptian slavers took advantage. The engraving below shows a group of slavers fighting against the natives.*
(**S. Baker**, *Albert Nyanza —Great Basin of the Nile*)

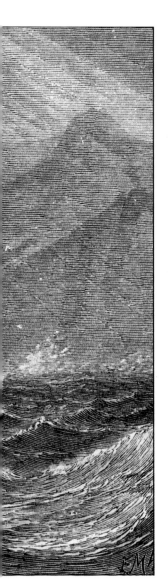

him that the lake was no more than ten days' march away, fifteen at the most if the party was heavily loaded. The king, seeing there was nothing more to extract from his guests, accepted the last gifts Baker had to give him—a sword and a double-barreled shotgun—and gave his permission for the departure.

At the very last minute, when the column was about to start, he made a last and decidedly unexpected request: he proposed exchanging wives with Baker, as was usual between "blood brothers." Baker was furious. He pointed his pistol at the king's chest, and his wife rained abuse on Kamrasi in German, English, and Hungarian.

Kamrasi, stunned by such a violation of the local custom and even more by the fact that Baker had refused the graces of a young black girl in favor of his more careworn wife, let them leave.

The caravan was finally able to depart but almost immediately came up against a treacherous swamp and an inextricable tangle of vegetation where it was impossible to pass either riding on oxen or carried on the litter. Baker went ahead on foot, telling his wife to walk in his footsteps. But when he looked back to see if everything was all right he saw her "standing in one spot, and sinking gradually through the weeds, while her face was distorted and perfectly purple. Almost as soon as I perceived her, she fell, as though shot dead." He rushed to her aid, and with the help of his men, dragged her out of the water. She was suffering from sunstroke. They carried her for two days on a makeshift stretcher, but on the morning of the third day she woke up delirious and the raving lasted a week. Baker desperately tried to treat her, but all he had at his disposal was a little wild honey and a few guinea hens.

All this was happening while the rain poured down incessantly. Finally the exhausted Baker himself collapsed, but when he came to his senses several hours later, his wife was well enough to recognize him. They rested for two days and then started off again on their exhausting march, and on the morning of March 14 they sighted the lake. "There, like a sea of quicksilver, lay far beneath [us] the grand expanse of water, a boundless sea horizon on the south and southwest, glittering in the noonday sun; and on the west, at fifty or sixty miles' distance, blue mountains rose from the bosom of the lake to a height of about 7,000 feet above its level."

The couple dismounted from their oxen and walked down the slope to the edge of the lake near a small fishing village called Vacovia. "I led the way, grasping a stout bamboo," Baker wrote.

178-179 *In effect the Bakers explored only a small part of Lake Albert, the east shore from the extreme northern tip. The trip by native canoe was dangerous, as only rarely were the waters as calm as in this drawing by Baker in which the only threat is posed by the disturbing presence of a crocodile.* (S. Baker, *Albert Nyanza—Great Basin of the Nile,* London, 1886)

"My wife in extreme weakness tottered down the pass, supporting herself upon my shoulder, and stopping to rest every twenty paces. After a toilsome descent of about two hours, weak with years of fever, but for the moment strengthened by success, we gained the level plain below the cliff. A walk of about a mile through flat sandy meadows of fine turf interspersed with trees and bush brought us to the water's edge. The waves were rolling upon a white pebbly beach: I rushed into the lake, and thirsty with heat and fatigue, with a heart full of gratitude, I drank deeply from the sources of the Nile. . . . No European foot had ever trod upon its sand, nor had the eyes of a white man ever scanned its vast expanse of water. . . . Here was the great basin of the Nile that received every drop of water, even from the passing shower to the roaring mountain torrent that drained from Central Africa toward the north. This was the great reservoir of the Nile."

Baker named the lake after Albert, the prince consort who had recently died. It was still necessary, however, to find proof that it was connected to the Nile system. The two explorers embarked on fragile canoes and sailed along the northeast shore, risking their lives at one point in a terrible storm, until thirteen days later they reached the point at which the Nile entered the lake, coming from Lake Victoria. They sailed up the

Nile for a stretch until they came across the stirring sight of a waterfall, which they named after Murchison. The raging waters were channeled into a narrow gorge from which they burst out in a boiling explosion of foam. While the Bakers were admiring this natural wonder, a hippopotamus attacked them and upturned their boat, tipping them into the crocodile-infested water. Luckily the violent current soon tossed them onto the bank.

They returned to Lake Albert and headed northward until they found the point at which the White Nile issued from the lake, at the village of Magungu. The exploration could now be considered complete and the mystery of the great river solved. The Bakers started on the long journey back. It took them two months just to get back to the court of Kamrasi, where a surprise awaited them. The person they had thought was the king was found to be a younger brother called M'Gambi. Kamrasi had made his brother take his place, being afraid that the white men were dangerous. Now, having ascertained that they were harmless, he agreed to meet them in person. Baker dressed for the occasion in his kilt, sporran, and tam-o'-shanter. It seems that Kamrasi was rather impressed.

The Bakers stayed in Bunyoro for six months, trying to regain their health, while the country was prey to interminable intertribal wars. King M'tesa of Uganda attacked his neighbor;

179 top *While awaiting a suitable moment to begin his return journey, Baker indulged his passion for hunting, not always with great success. Here we see him being pursued by a menacing elephant.*

179 bottom *In this illustration by Baker himself, we can see his triumphant entrance into Gondokoro, followed by his escort and acclaimed by celebrating natives.*

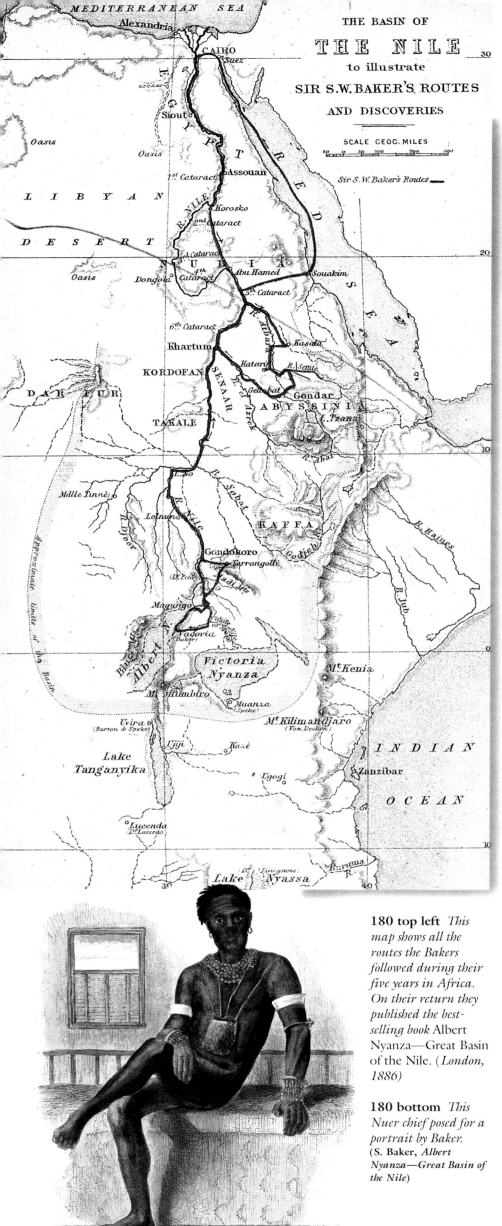

THE BASIN OF
THE NILE
to illustrate
SIR S.W. BAKER'S ROUTES
AND DISCOVERIES

SCALE GEOG. MILES

Sir S.W. Baker's Routes _____

180 top left *This map shows all the routes the Bakers followed during their five years in Africa. On their return they published the best-selling book* Albert Nyanza—Great Basin of the Nile. (*London, 1886*)

180 bottom *This Nuer chief posed for a portrait by Baker.* (S. Baker, *Albert Nyanza—Great Basin of the Nile*)

and it seems that one of his aims was to make the European couple his prisoners and take them to his court. But the Bakers followed Kamrasi in flight to the north. On the way they came across a threatening column of 150 men from Gondokoro, slave traders in the pay of the Maltese De Bono, armed with rifles and determined to seize everything they could. The inept Kamrasi fled, but Baker raised the Union Jack over his hut and warned the leader of the slavers that Bunyoro was under British protection and any hostile act would be punished by hanging the offenders in Khartoum.

The attackers were cowed and withdrew, making up for their losses on the return route by sacking their allies. Kamrasi was increasingly terrified by M'tesa's advance and sought refuge as far away as he could, abandoning the Bakers at the Karuma Falls. From there the couple managed to send a message to a caravan of ivory traders whom they had met on the outward journey and who were still in the area. The message said that Kamrasi had a large collection of tusks to sell. The traders duly arrived and the two explorers could finally join them and start on their journey back. As they said they would take their leave, Kamrasi asked them to give him the most powerful talisman they had, the Union Jack, at the sight of which the slavers had withdrawn. Baker refused, saying that the magical power of the flag did not work unless it was in the hands of a British subject.

In February 1865, after an absence of two years, they finally reached Gondokoro, where they made a triumphant entrance riding on oxen, flags to the wind, and joyfully firing volleys of rifle shots. They had run grave risks, even on the last stretch of their journey, in the territory of the Bari people, where slavers and ivory hunters had been particularly aggressive for many years. Their caravan had been attacked and many of the men had died in a hail of poisoned arrows.

At Gondokoro the Bakers learned that they had been given up as lost in Europe

180 top right *Baker drew numerous scenes of African daily life that were subsequently used to illustrate his book. Here we see a discussion between Kamrasi, the king of Unyoro, dressed in a leopard-skin cloak and a feathered headdress, with one of his subjects.* (S. Baker, *Albert Nyanza—Great Basin of the Nile*)

181 top *The king of Unyoro carried on the shoulders of a robust subject and followed by a slave carrying a jug of water to quench the royal thirst.*

181 bottom left *A number of Unyoro craftsmen intent on forging spear tips.*

181 bottom right *A group of natives marching across the savanna, including a young woman with an elegant hairstyle carrying two cones that appear to be about to fall to the ground. Baker described with a great sense of humor the costumes of the natives for whom he demonstrated a degree of comprehension unusual for his times.* (S. Baker, *Albert Nyanza—Great Basin of the Nile*)

180-181 *This engraving shows a village of the Madi tribe on the Upper Nile with large huts that were entered on all fours, granaries raised on stilts to protect them from insects, and a warrior followed by his wife adorned with tattoos on her belly. Both are holding long pipes.* (S. Baker, *Albert Nyanza—Great Basin of the Nile*)

182-183 *The notebooks of Samuel Baker are rich in tinted drawings of great spontaneity that reveal, even more than his prose, his sense of humor. Here Baker is aiming his gun at a* herd of giraffes in the savanna. One of the animals is grazing on the grass while the others seem to be stiffly walking on. In its simplicity the scene has a balletic grace.

183 *Comfortably sitting in the background on the left, near their hut, the Bakers watch a welcoming dance in their honor in the* village of Shoa on November 21, 1864, during their return journey toward the Sudan. This is another of Baker's own drawings.

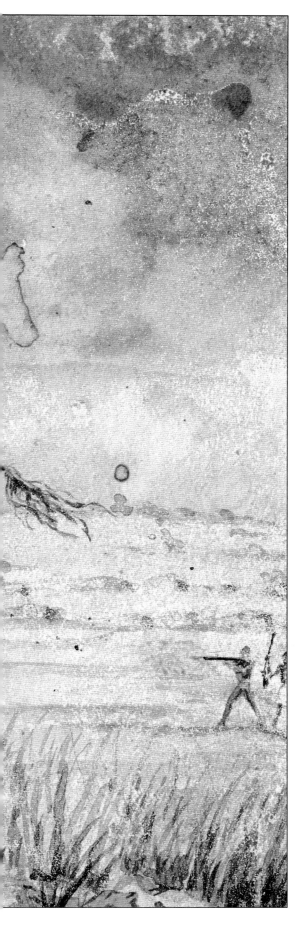

after word spread that they were killed while trying to reach Zanzibar. They hired a boat and sailed down the White Nile toward Khartoum but they were blocked in the morass of the Sudd for several weeks. As they waited for favorable winds, many of the men who had been with them on all their travels contracted fevers and died in that terrible swamp, a desolate stretch of infinite reedbeds where the Nile deposits all the plant material it carries down from the mountains, which then decomposes and gives off a foul stench.

By October 1865, they were in Suez where Baker could satisfy a desire he had had for five years, ever since he entered the untamed regions of Africa—to drink a tankard of Allsopp's beer.

Eventually they embarked for England. On board ship the explorer, who was perhaps feeling rather dazed with fatigue, wondered if the whole

adventures recounted in pleasant prose in Baker's book. His story read like a novel compared with the less gripping texts by Speke and Burton, who had been subjected to just as many perils and adventures. The presence of a woman in Baker's tale, however, together with his sense of humor, turned his book into a best-seller. Queen Victoria knighted him, and London society opened its doors to the couple.

In geographical circles, however, there was less enthusiasm. The discovery of Lake Albert had not really solved the mystery of the Nile, and it was realized later that Baker had vastly overestimated the size of the lake, which he did not circumnavigate. In particular he could not prove that the river that left the lake to the north was the Nile because he had not followed its course. And even if it was the Nile, which was the real source, Lake Victoria or Lake Albert? If Lake

adventure had not been a dream. He found his own answer: "A witness sat before me; a face still young, but bronzed like an Arab by years of exposure to a burning sun; haggard and worn with toil and sickness, and shaded with cares happily now past; the devoted companion of my pilgrimage, to whom I owed success and life—my wife."

The British public was also fascinated by that heroic lady, especially after reading about the couple's incredible

Albert really was as large as Baker claimed, then it was probably the main basin and was fed by a large river farther south. Greater proof was needed. Sir Roderick Murchison announced that the Royal Geographical Society would commission a new exploration to the area south of Lake Tanganyika, led by a man who was not new to African prizes and who was convinced the real source was to be found there. His name was David Livingstone.

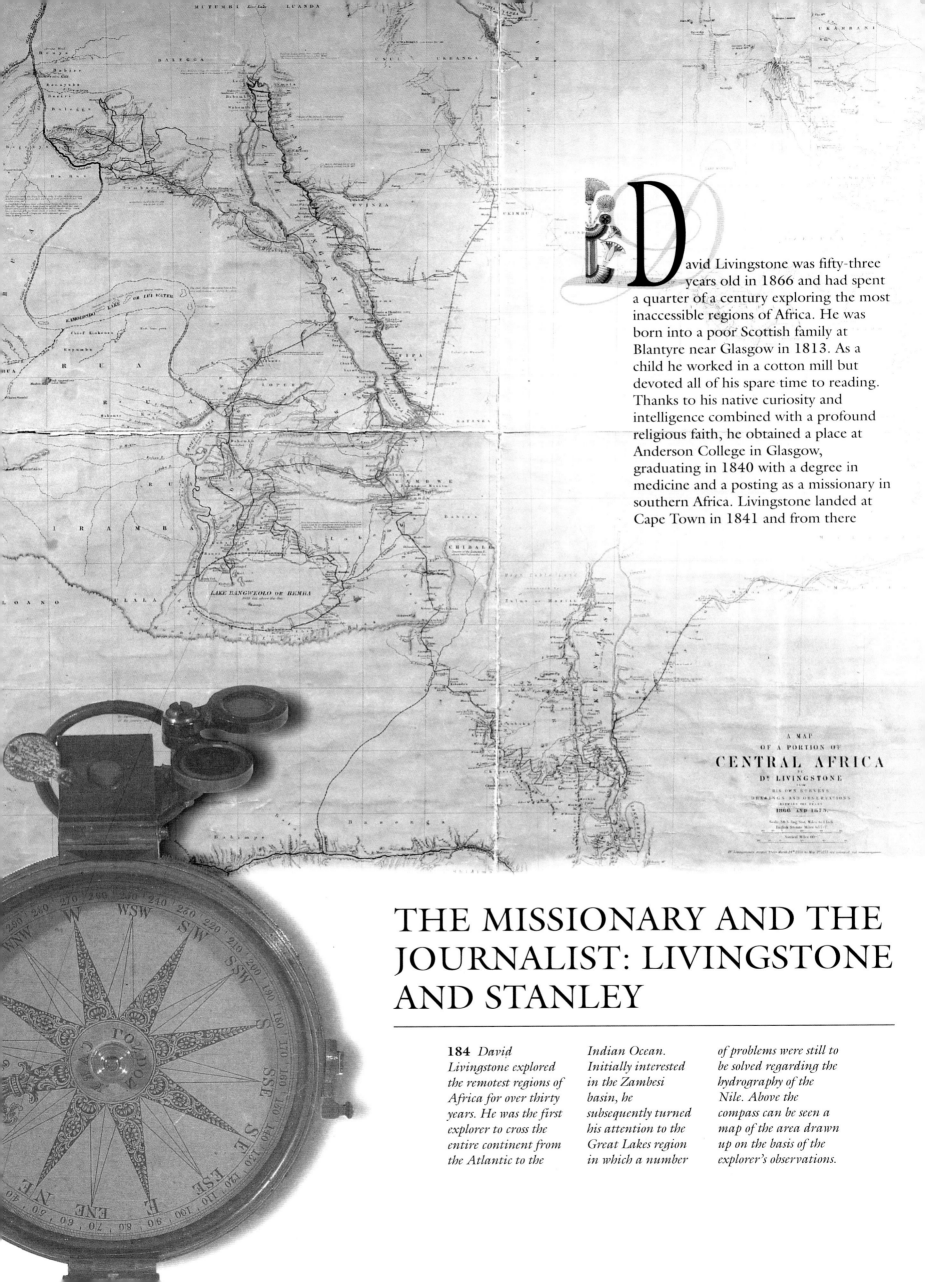

D avid Livingstone was fifty-three years old in 1866 and had spent a quarter of a century exploring the most inaccessible regions of Africa. He was born into a poor Scottish family at Blantyre near Glasgow in 1813. As a child he worked in a cotton mill but devoted all of his spare time to reading. Thanks to his native curiosity and intelligence combined with a profound religious faith, he obtained a place at Anderson College in Glasgow, graduating in 1840 with a degree in medicine and a posting as a missionary in southern Africa. Livingstone landed at Cape Town in 1841 and from there

A MAP
OF A PORTION OF
CENTRAL AFRICA
BY
Dr LIVINGSTONE
FROM
HIS OWN SURVEYS
DRAWINGS AND OBSERVATIONS
BETWEEN THE YEARS
1866 AND 1873

THE MISSIONARY AND THE JOURNALIST: LIVINGSTONE AND STANLEY

184 *David Livingstone explored the remotest regions of Africa for over thirty years. He was the first explorer to cross the entire continent from the Atlantic to the* *Indian Ocean. Initially interested in the Zambesi basin, he subsequently turned his attention to the Great Lakes region in which a number* *of problems were still to be solved regarding the hydrography of the Nile. Above the compass can be seen a map of the area drawn up on the basis of the explorer's observations.*

traveled to Port Elizabeth before heading inland to the mission at Kuruman in Bechuanaland, an area not yet part of the British-ruled Cape Colony.

Livingstone intended to live for six months with no contact with other whites so as to learn the natives' language, customs, and way of thinking. Then, early in 1843, he founded his own mission at Mabotsa, where he was seriously injured by a lion while out hunting: one arm was partially disabled for the rest of his life. The following year he married Mary, the daughter of Dr. Robert Moffat, the head of a mission. Mary was "a resolute woman, a small, sturdy black-haired girl, energetic, just as I needed," wrote her husband, adding that her greatest virtue was a lack of that "mental constriction" typical of the daughters of missionaries. With Mary at his side, Livingstone settled farther north in the village of the chief Setscele whom he converted after three years of religious instruction. The husband-wife team, together with two English hunters, Oswell and Murray, departed in June 1849 to cross the Kalahari Desert, or rather to skirt around its northern borders to reach Lake Ngami, for the discovery of which they were rewarded by the Royal Geographical Society with the sum of twenty-five guineas.

On two other occasions Livingstone traveled north of the Kalahari: in 1850

186 *The explorers shooting an elephant from Livingstone's boat* Ma Robert *while navigating the Shire, a tributary of the Zambesi. The animal*

is raising its trunk in fury. The painting was executed in 1859 by Thomas Baines, an artist who took part in the expedition.

187 top left *The feverish Livingstone is riding an ox; he was escorted to the Zambesi by the chief Sekeletu's warriors.*
(The Life and Explorations of Dr Livingstone the Great Missionary Traveller, London)

187 *This map depicts Lake Shirwa or Chilwa, explored by Livingstone and Kirk in April 1859. The course of the Shire can also be seen.*

187 bottom *Livingstone's freehand sketch showing Victoria Falls. The explorer drew it during his second visit there in August 1860.*

he was forced to turn back after the tsetse fly killed his caravan animals, but on the second expedition, in 1851, he reached the territory of the Makololo people, where he was offered a cordial welcome by the benevolent chief Sebituane. The chief offered Livingstone as much land as he wanted to settle with his family in that rich, fertile area. However, the explorer left his wife and children in the village of Linyanti and pressed on with Oswell until in June they reached the Zambesi at Sesheke. The great river flowing into the Mozambique Channel was around six hundred meters wide at that point during the dry season.

The missionary-explorer's third child, William Oswell Livingstone, was born in September, an event that prompted him to return to the civilized world. On reaching Cape Town, Livingstone packed his family off to Britain while he himself headed north in 1853, returning to Linyanti in triumph on a cart pulled by oxen. The entire population of six or seven thousand people joyfully

welcomed him back, and he was regally received by Chief Sekeletu, the successor to Sebituane, while the court herald loudly declaimed the white man's virtues. Livingstone had brought with him as gifts pedigree goats and poultry as well as two cats that were much appreciated.

Having overcome an attack of fever, the Scotsman completed a nine-week excursion along the Zambesi accompanied by the chief, who intended to inspect those parts of his kingdom that he had not yet visited.

The royal procession was a cheerfully picturesque gaggle of servants with lions' manes or ostrich feathers on their heads, notables carrying clubs equipped with rhinoceros horns while their servants carried shields, bearers loaded with supplies, and warriors armed with hatchets. The king, astride an old horse given to him by Livingstone, was surrounded by his guard mounted on haggard oxen that collapsed every few steps. Jars of beer and bowls of milk circulated freely, and the welcome

offered by the king's subjects was always enthusiastic.

When they reached the river, they headed upstream for a good stretch in a flotilla of thirty-six canoes. This pleasant trip finally concluded with a return to Linyanti, where Livingstone began to organize the great journey he had at heart: to ascend the Zambesi to its source and then head on to the coast of Angola. A general assembly was called, and in spite of the old witch doctors' prophesies of doom, the majority were convinced by the arguments of the white man who spoke of the advantages of opening a trade route between an Atlantic port and that remote realm at the heart of the continent. Twenty-seven volunteers were selected to accompany him. They left Linyanti on November 11, 1853 and ten days later reached Sesheke as the rainy season began. From there they began to ascend the Zambesi as far as the confluence of the Liba. On the basis of the hypotheses formulated up until then by geographers who thought the African

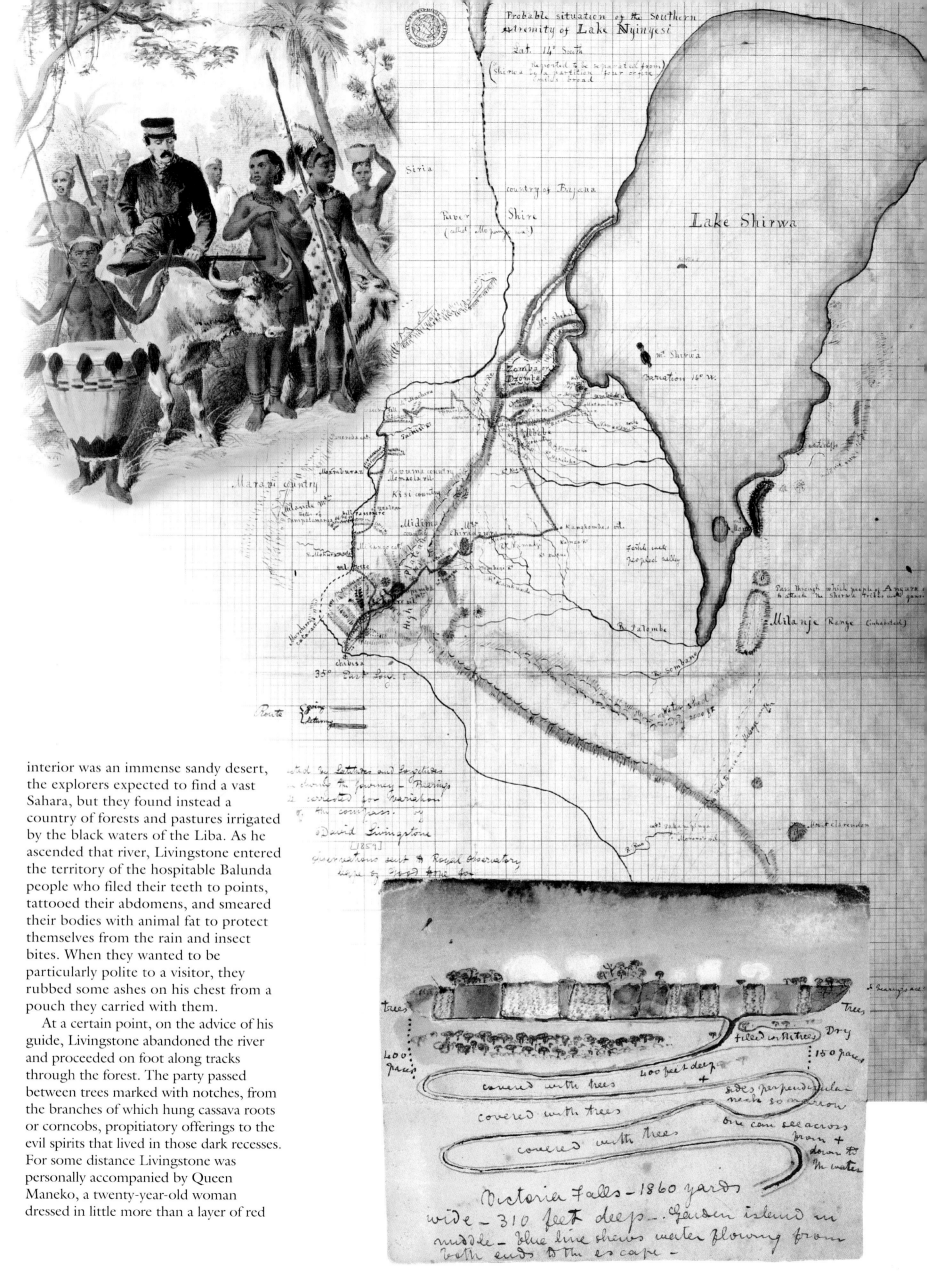

interior was an immense sandy desert, the explorers expected to find a vast Sahara, but they found instead a country of forests and pastures irrigated by the black waters of the Liba. As he ascended that river, Livingstone entered the territory of the hospitable Balunda people who filed their teeth to points, tattooed their abdomens, and smeared their bodies with animal fat to protect themselves from the rain and insect bites. When they wanted to be particularly polite to a visitor, they rubbed some ashes on his chest from a pouch they carried with them.

At a certain point, on the advice of his guide, Livingstone abandoned the river and proceeded on foot along tracks through the forest. The party passed between trees marked with notches, from the branches of which hung cassava roots or corncobs, propitiatory offerings to the evil spirits that lived in those dark recesses. For some distance Livingstone was personally accompanied by Queen Maneko, a twenty-year-old woman dressed in little more than a layer of red

ochre, who escorted him to her uncle, the powerful chieftain Scinte. In his village the party encountered two Portuguese slave traders from Angola, with a column of chained victims. A rumor had spread through the area regarding the arrival of a strange white man who lived in the sea like a mermaid, the Scot's straight hair being thought by an imaginative native to be the result of the action of salt water. Scinte held a great reception to which natives came from all around to admire the guest of honor.

When the party set out again they had to cross a swamp region. The tribal chieftains now proved to be increasingly less welcoming and more rapacious. The explores had arrived in Angolan territory, where the slave trade ruled and where white men understandably aroused distrust rather than curiosity. When they reached the territory of the Chiboque people, Livingstone's camp

188 top *The Makololo people called the Victoria Falls "smoking thunder." Livingstone saw the falls for the first time in November 1859.* (*The Life and Explorations of Dr Livingstone the Great Missionary Traveller*, London)

188 center *The miserable death of a woman who accompanied the expedition and was devoured by crocodiles after falling overboard.* (*The Life and Explorations of Dr Livingstone the Great Missionary Traveller*, London)

188 bottom *Livingstone, like all the African explorers, was an expert shot. Here we see him taking aim at a crocodile from a canoe paddled by a native.* (*The Life and Explorations of Dr Livingstone the Great Missionary Traveller*, London)

was surrounded by warriors with leveled guns who demanded the payment of a tribute for the right of passage. Fortunately the episode was concluded without bloodshed, the local chief having allowed himself inadvertently to be surrounded in turn by Livingstone's men. From then on, however, the demands for tolls multiplied while the explorer felt ever weaker due to repeated attacks of fever. His supplies were also running very low. Now discouraged, his faithful followers began to manifest a desire to turn back, but they changed their minds when Livingstone declared that he would continue on alone. He had only four oxen left with which to placate the greed of the natives, but these were needed for riding and in, case of extreme necessity, as food. The Chiboque had refused one with a piece of its tail missing, fearing that it might have been poisoned, so Livingstone cut the tails of the other three, and there were no more demands for oxen.

Reaching the banks of the Kwango River, the explorer and his team attempted to pay a toll to be ferried across with the last of their copper rings, but the natives attacked them, firmly convinced that they were a slave convoy. Fortunately a Portuguese sergeant from a nearby militia post, Cypriano, came to their aid, helped them to cross the river, and provided them with supplies. They finally arrived at Xassengue, the remotest Portuguese inland station, where Livingstone found a change of clothes to replace the rags he had been wearing. On May 31, 1854, escorted by a corporal of the native troops, who exploited his rank by being carried in a hammock by two slaves every time he entered or left a village, the explorer set foot in São Paulo de Loanda, the capital of Angola, where he was cordially received by the British consul Gabriel. His Makololo tribesmen, who were enterprising as well as daring, began trading in firewood and unloading ships in the port, using the profits to purchase a satisfactory quantity of goods to take home with them.

Together with Livingstone, they set off again on September 20. This time the explorer intended to follow the course of the Zambesi to its mouth to establish whether a trade route to the Indian Ocean rather than the Atlantic would be more convenient. He carried letters of introduction from the

189 *While following the course of the Zambesi toward its source and while heading for Angola, Livingstone suffered recurrent attacks of malaria. In those periods his porters carried him through the jungle on a stretcher, protecting him from insects with mosquito netting.* (**The Life and Explorations of Dr Livingstone the Great Missionary Traveller,** London)

Portuguese authorities in Mozambique, was accompanied by twenty porters supplied by the bishop of Loanda, and was equipped with plenty of supplies, beads and cloth for trading, and a new tent presented to him by the officers of the British ships anchored in the port of Angola. The Makololo people had new rifles. The party followed a different route from the outward journey, first a little farther to the south and then to the north. Having met up with their friend Cypriano in February 1855, they entered the area of exorbitant tributes. This time, however, the caravan was well armed and commanded greater respect. Nevertheless, while passing through a forest they were ambushed and fired upon by the Chiboque. Livingstone persuaded the chief to desist by presenting him with a revolver.

The party entered the Zambesi basin in June and were in Makololo territory by July. There they were received with extravagant demonstrations of joy, being regarded as spirits returned from the kingdom of the dead, as the soothsayers had declared they were lost. Chief Sekeletu organized a great feast at Linyanti; Livingstone was particularly proud of not having lost a single man during that arduous trek, and his Makololo followers were so devoted to him that they offered to accompany him on the next stage of his journey eastward.

The caravan set out again on November 3, 1855, with asses, oxen, and goods provided by Sekeletu and an expert Matabele guide, Sekuebu, who had ascended and descended the Zambesi on a number of occasions. The party was

190 top *One of the great dangers of African exploration is shown in this engraving in which a lion is attacking a horseman, perhaps Livingstone himself.* (**The Life and Explorations of Dr Livingstone the Great Missionary Traveller,** London)

190 bottom *The British explorer's caravan reached the shore of Lake Ngami after crossing the Kalahari Desert. Livingstone is seen here in the foreground holding his son by the hand.*

191 top *A vehement opponent of slavery, on a number of occasions during his explorations Livingstone encountered the sad caravans of "black ivory" heading toward the coast. This caravan is guided by a half-caste Portuguese.* (*The Life and Explorations of Dr Livingstone the Great Missionary Traveller,* London)

191 bottom *This engraving depicts a rhinoceros hunt during which a pack of dogs was used to attack and disorient the animal.* (*The Life and Explorations of Dr Livingstone the Great Missionary Traveller*)

accompanied by the king and two hundred warriors as far as Sesheke. From there they took to canoes and headed towards the "smoke that sounds" as the Makololo called the immense waterfall that Livingstone named after Queen Victoria, the columns of spray rising from which could be seen from a distance of twenty miles. Sekeletu then turned back while Livingstone proceeded with 114 men, leaving the river and heading northeast to avoid an area infested with the tsetse fly. He then entered the land of the Batoka people, great fruit growers and smokers of cannabis, who had their incisors out once they had reached puberty. They had once owned large herds of livestock, but had been impoverished by the continual raids of neighboring tribes. The explorer was struck by their way of greeting: they threw themselves onto their backs and rolled around slapping their thighs. He earned their gratitude by treating their sick.

After passing the confluence of the Kafue, they entered the territory of the elephant-hunting Batonga people, and then that of the Mburuma people, who

took up arms at the sight of the caravan. They had recently been attacked by an Italian with an armed band, who had captured slaves and appropriated ivory; he had, however, paid for the episode with his life. Once again Livingstone's diplomatic skills won over the distrustful natives and he was able to proceed to Zomba, an abandoned and ruined Portuguese station. The first Portuguese were encountered at Tete, which the explorer reached on March 3, 1856. The commander of the station, Major Sicard, sent a sedan chair and a European-style breakfast to meet him. The Makololo were assigned a piece of land on which to build a temporary village and raise a crop while they waited for the cutting of firewood and hunting to provide them with funds to return to Linyanti. Some of them were to accompany Livingstone as far as Quelimane, and the Matabele guide Sekuebu followed him to the island of Mauritius. There, however, Sekuebu fell victim to a bout of depression, slipped into the sea, and drowned.

Livingstone remained at Tete for around twenty days, hoping to avoid the unhealthiest season at Quelimane. He left on March 22 by boat and descended the river to the delta. From there he sailed up the coast and arrived at Quelimane on May 20, suffering from fever. He had left Cape Town four years earlier and had covered a distance of 11,000 miles. Before him, the African continent had been crossed from coast to coast only by the half-Portuguese Pombeiro brothers, who between 1806

192 top *Between 1858 and 1864 Livingstone dedicated himself to an exploration of the vast Zambesi Basin. This was carried out in a number of stages both by land and along the rivers in steamboats. During one of the expeditions Livingstone's wife, who had traveled out to Africa to meet him in January 1862, died of a tropical disease in the April of that year. This illustration shows Ripon Falls, considered the source of the Nile, at the point at which the White Nile issues from Lake Victoria.*

and 1811 had traveled from Benguela in Angola to Tete. They were traders, however, not explorers, and they left no record of their journey.

At Quelimane, Livingstone waited six weeks for a ship that was to take him to Mauritius and from there to England, where he landed on December 9, 1856, to a hero's welcome. He was decorated with medals and sundry honors. The enthusiasm aroused by his feat induced the government to send him back to Africa on another trip, this time under its auspices, the aim of which was to be the exploration of the entire Zambesi Basin and the lake that was thought to be the source of one of its tributaries.

The expedition left Britain on March 10, 1858, and reached the mouth of the Zambesi a little over a month later. Invested with the title of consul of the United Kingdom for that region, Livingstone was accompanied by his brother, Charles, and a number of other compatriots including the botanist John Kirk, the artist Thomas Baines, the geologist Richard Thornton, and the engineer Rae. They were very well equipped, but their steam launch proved to be very slow—Livingstone referred to it as "the asthmatic"—and another was ordered from England. The Makololo people he had left at Tete warmly welcomed him back. Unfortunately around thirty of them had died during an outbreak of smallpox, and six had been assassinated by a Portuguese half-caste.

In January 1859, while waiting for the new boat, the explorers ascended the Shire, a tributary on the left bank of Zambesi. Their passage was eventually barred by rapids, which they named after

192 bottom *Making progress through the swamp regions was particularly arduous. In this engraving one of Livingstone's carts struggles to open a path through the reeds, preceded by two dogs to provide advance warning of the presence of wild animals.*

193 *In this plate Livingstone is being carried by his men during one of his many bouts of fever.*

(*The Life and Explorations of Dr Livingstone the Great Missionary Traveller,* London)

Murchison, the president of the Royal Geographical Society. Skirting the rapids on foot, they continued their search for the great lake, the existence of which had been known since the days of the Portuguese but which no white man had ever reached. They first came across Lake Shirwa, an expanse of bitter fish-filled water populated by hippopotamuses and crocodiles. Then, moving farther north, they passed through the territory of the Manganja people, where they were struck by the use of an extremely unusual female ornament, the lip plate that grossly deformed the mouths of the native women. On September 16 the party reached the southern tip of the immense Lake Nyasa.

On their return the explorers dedicated themselves to the exploration of the Zambesi Basin for the whole of 1860, ascending the river to take the faithful Makololo people home, as Livingstone had promised. Many of them, however, had married women from Tete and found life in that semi-civilized area to be better than in their home villages, and they refused to leave; others turned back after the first day's march. When, in August 1860, Livingstone set foot in the town of Sesheke, after having visited Victoria Falls for the second time, he found his friend Sekeletu much changed: he was afflicted with leprosy, which he attributed to the curse of a witch doctor. He had put to death many suspects and now lived alone far from his people. He was to die within four years, and his great kingdom collapsed.

Back in Tete in January 1861, the expedition finally took delivery of its new boat. The *Pioneer* was an excellent vessel, but its draft was excessive, causing it to run aground frequently in shallow water. A group from the Oxford and Cambridge Mission arrived with the boat. They intended to evangelize the area around Lake Nyasa.

In the meantime, however, the Portuguese, irritated by the strong protests Livingstone in his role as British consul had sent to the government in Lisbon about the slavery practiced by its subjects in the region, had closed the Zambesi to foreign navigation. The Scotsman therefore decided to explore the river Ruvuma, which descends from the Lake Nyasa region to the sea. He ascended its course for some distance, but was back at the great lake in August, intent on completing a circumnavigation. Interrupted by

frequent bad storms, the exploration of the lake shore lasted from September 2 to October 27.

By late January 1862, Livingstone was back on the coast of Mozambique to meet his wife, Mary, who was traveling from England to join him, together with a number of other women who were to settle at the new mission. Another new boat, the *Lady Nyasa,* was delivered to the explorer in sections ready to be assembled. This vessel had been ordered and paid for by Livingstone himself. While he was guiding the newcomers inland, the explorer received the news that two of the missionaries had died of fever. Then, on April 3, Livingstone suffered the appalling pain of losing his wife to a tropical disease.

After completing further explorations of the Ruvuma and the Shire, he decided to return home, and he was in England by the end of July 1864. During the years spent in Africa he had become

convinced that the watershed between the basins of the Zambesi and the Nile was to be found in the region of Lake Tanganyika. He also suspected that the true source of the Nile was the lake itself. His next expedition set out to settle this question.

Livingstone landed in Africa once again on March 24, 1866, at Mikindani, north of the mouth of the Ruvuma. On April 5 he departed for Lake Nyasa accompanied by thirty Indian soldiers recruited at Bombay, thirty natives, and a good number of camels, asses, mules, and buffalo. This expedition, however, proved to be a disaster. Livingstone was the classic solitary explorer in whom leadership qualities were conspicuous by their absence. He preferred to push on ahead of the group while his undisciplined and lazy men followed some distance behind, stealing and mistreating the natives and animals. Disgusted by the behavior of this rabble, whom he considered worse than the "savages" they encountered, Livingstone reached an agreement with a group of Arab slave traders whereby they would accompany most of his men back to the coast. In the end, as a result of death, abandonment, and desertion, he was left with just five young blacks.

Having reached Lake Nyasa, the now much reduced group headed very slowly northwest, reaching the southern shore of Lake Tanganyika on March 31, 1867, a year after leaving the coast. From there, with the aid of Swahili merchants, Livingstone was able to send letters to Zanzibar asking that supplies and goods be sent to him at Ujiji on the east coast of the lake. He was aided and assisted by the famous Arab slaver Hamidi bin Muhammad, nicknamed Tipoo Tib in imitation of the sound of the discharging

194 top *Fishermen preparing traps among the reedbeds of Lake Nyasa. Following a two-year spell in the United Kingdom, Livingstone departed once again in March 1866 for his last trip to Africa, heading* *for the Great Lakes region and hoping to resolve the last doubts regarding the sources of the Nile. He went first to Lake Nyasa where he encountered the inhabitants of the shores of the lake.*

194 bottom left *At the center of a Nyasa village Livingstone observed the so-called Tree of War with the heads of slain enemies impaled on the trunk.*

194 bottom right *An everyday scene of two women milling grain with a stone.* (**The Life and Explorations of Dr Livingstone the Great Missionary Traveller**)

195 top *The* falhi *were the most respected craftsmen in the villages of the Great Lakes region.*

195 center *Indian millet or sorghum, here being thrashed by the men of a tribe, was a staple of the diet in that area.*

195 bottom right *The native music used percussion instruments almost exclusively.*

195 bottom left *The women were responsible for brewing an alcoholic drink similar to beer and known as* pombe.

guns that accompanied his raids. Tipoo Tib and other traders treated Livingstone with generous hospitality and made it possible for him to reach Lake Mweru, one of the reservoirs of the Congo, in November—although Livingstone was convinced that all those waterways were related to the Nilotic basin—and subsequently to reach the court of Cazembe who in earlier times had been a great sovereign to whom the Portuguese sent important diplomatic missions but who was now just a minor tribal chieftain. The only trace remaining of his former power appeared to be the royal executioner who was always at the king's side with his great sword and a kind of guillotine for slicing off ears or hands; considering the number of people without ears or hands, Livingstone deduced that justice in that country could be very harsh.

After a second visit to Lake Mweru, Livingstone headed south toward Lake Bemba, or Bangweulu, the principal reservoir of the Congo. He reached the lake on July 18, 1868, to the wonder of the natives, who had never before seen a white man. Convinced that he was about to resolve definitively the mystery of the sources of the Nile, he headed north once again to Lake Tanganyika, which he felt to be the only weak link in this intricate (and erroneous) hydrographical network.

On March 14, 1869, carried on a makeshift litter made of intertwined branches by his Arab rescuers, Livingstone entered Ujiji exhausted, feverish, having lost almost all of his teeth, and reduced to a heap of bones. He then discovered that the supplies he had requested, and which had been dispatched from the coast, had almost all been stolen en route. Ujiji at that time

195

(**The Life and Explorations of Dr Livingstone the Great Missionary Traveller**, London)

196 top *While Livingstone wandered among the lakes and rivers of Central Africa, rumors of his death had begun to spread in Europe. Rescue missions were organized to ascertain what had happened to him. They were all beaten to the tape by the improvisations of a journalist, Henry Morton Stanley, who had been instructed by his editor to find the lost explorer and had been provided with all the necessary resources to do so. This engraving is perhaps the most famous image of African exploration: the meeting between Stanley and Livingstone that took place on November 10, 1871, at Ujiji on Lake Tanganyika.* (**The Life and Explorations of Dr Livingstone the Great Missionary Traveller,** London)

196 bottom *All explorers, including Livingstone, a trained doctor, carried with them a medicine chest with remedies for malaria and snake bites. A number of these bottles carry labels from Bombay and were purchased by Livingstone during his brief stay in India in 1864.*

was the headquarters of the Arabs who traded in ivory and slaves in the region, and this meant a return to a relative degree of civilization. The Arab reputation for hospitality proved to be well founded, and the affable slavers put themselves out seeing to the well-being of the run-down explorer. They were not willing to carry his letters to the coast, however, because they knew the messages contained graphic descriptions of the horrors they had perpetrated at the expense of the black population. Livingstone thus found himself cut off from all contact with Europe, and rumors began to spread that he was dead.

Once he recovered somewhat, the tenacious explorer gathered what little remained of the supplies that had been sent to him at Ujiji and, now obsessed by the problem of the sources of the Nile, departed in July 1869, heading west toward a great river, the Lualaba, which he presumed to be the Nile. He did not reach the river, which was in fact the upper course of the Congo, until March of the following year, after an extremely arduous trek through harsh terrain that was made all the worse by the hostility of the natives, who had been provoked by the activities of the slavers. So great were the difficulties Livingstone faced that ironically he was obliged to join one of the slave caravans in order to make any progress. At Nyangwe, a village on the banks of the Lualaba, Livingstone witnessed the massacre of defenseless natives by the Arabs on the pretext of having been cheated over the price of a chicken. Between three and four hundred died under a rain of bullets or drowned in the river trying to escape, and the massacre continued over the next few days as the villages were burned. This was but one example of the horrors to which the slave trade exposed black Africa.

Sickened by what he had seen, his health seriously compromised, and with only his profound religious faith on which to lean, Livingstone returned slowly to Ujiji, where he was obliged to rely on the charity of the Arabs to survive. A month later, on November 10, 1871, the settlement was thrown into an uproar by news of the approach of a caravan led by a white man, a flag bearing the Stars and Stripes to the fore. They ran to inform Livingstone, who came out to meet the unexpected visitor. The white man in question described the scene that was to be turned into the most famous print in the annals of African exploration in the following terms:

"My heart beats fast, but I must not let my face betray my emotions, lest it shall detract from the dignity of a white man appearing under such extraordinary circumstances. So I did that which I

thought was most dignified. I pushed back the crowds and, passing from the rear, walked down a living avenue of people, until I came in front of the semicircle of Arabs, in front of which stood a white man with a gray beard. As I advanced slowly toward him, I noticed he was pale, looked wearied, had a gray beard, wore a bluish cap with a faded gold band around it, had on a red-sleeved waistcoat, and a pair of gray tweed trousers. I would have run to him, only I was a coward in the presence of such a mob—would have embraced him, only, he being an Englishman, I did not know how he would receive me; so I did what cowardice and false pride suggested was the best thing—walked deliberately to him, took off my hat, and said: 'Dr. Livingstone, I presume?'

" 'Yes,' said he, with a kind smile, lifting his cap slightly.

"I replace my hat on my head, and he puts on his cap, and we both grasp

197 top *A canvas-covered pith helmet (top) was standard wear for the nineteenth-century African explorer. This photo shows the one worn by Stanley during the famous encounter with Livingstone. In his role as British consul, on the other hand, Livingstone wore the blue cap, below, in which he is depicted in most contemporary illustrations.*

197 bottom *By this magic lantern (top) the explorer showed the natives biblical scenes in order to convert them to the Christian faith and tried to impress them with European technological marvels. Livingstone always carried with him a carabine (center) and a case containing his surgical instruments (bottom) to be prepared for any situation.*

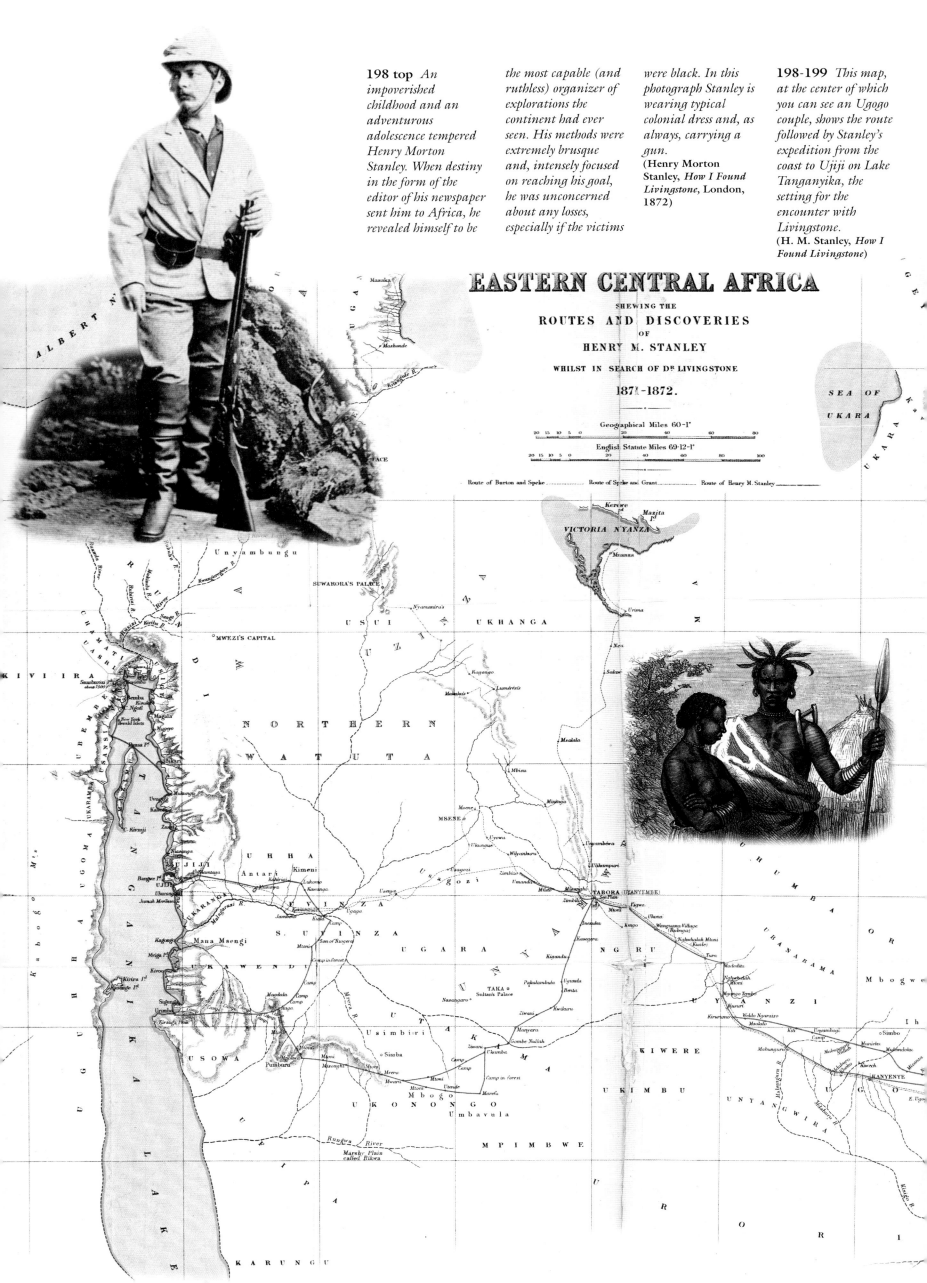

198 top *An impoverished childhood and an adventurous adolescence tempered Henry Morton Stanley. When destiny in the form of the editor of his newspaper sent him to Africa, he revealed himself to be the most capable (and ruthless) organizer of explorations the continent had ever seen. His methods were extremely brusque and, intensely focused on reaching his goal, he was unconcerned about any losses, especially if the victims were black. In this photograph Stanley is wearing typical colonial dress and, as always, carrying a gun.*
(Henry Morton Stanley, *How I Found Livingstone*, London, 1872)

198-199 *This map, at the center of which you can see an Ugogo couple, shows the route followed by Stanley's expedition from the coast to Ujiji on Lake Tanganyika, the setting for the encounter with Livingstone.*
(H. M. Stanley, *How I Found Livingstone*)

EASTERN CENTRAL AFRICA

SHEWING THE

ROUTES AND DISCOVERIES

OF

HENRY M. STANLEY

WHILST IN SEARCH OF Dʳ LIVINGSTONE

1871-1872.

Geographical Miles 60-1"

English Statute Miles 69-12-1"

Route of Burton and Speke .... Route of Speke and Grant .... Route of Henry M. Stanley ....

199 top *Zanzibar, of which the port crowded with Arab and European ships and defended by the old Portuguese fortress is seen here, was the point of departure for all the expeditions to the interior. Porters could be recruited here, and the necessary goods for trading with the natives could be purchased.*

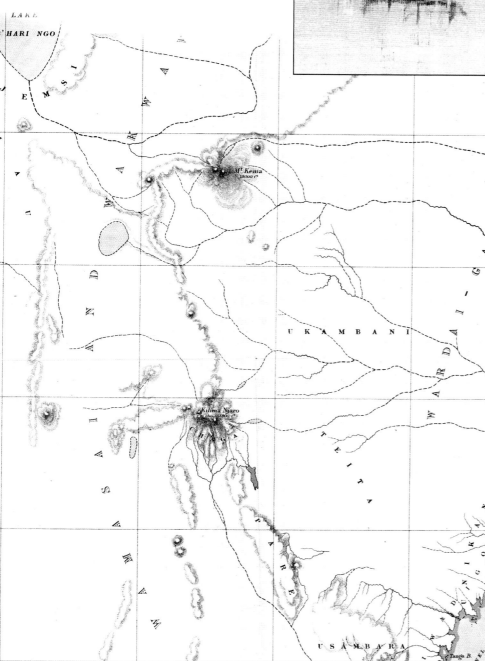

hands, and I then say aloud: 'I thank God, Doctor, I have been permitted to see you.'

"He answered, 'I feel thankful that I am here to welcome you.'"

That white man who seemed to have appeared out of nowhere with his well-equipped caravan and his American flag was one Henry Morton Stanley, or rather John Rowlands, to give him his original name. He was actually Welsh, not American, having been born at Denbigh in 1841. His life story reads like a novel by Dickens. After a childhood of crushing poverty he emigrated to the United States, embarking as a cabin boy on a sailing ship. He landed at New Orleans, took the name of the generous American who adopted him, took part in the American Civil War, fighting in the front line for the Confederates and then the Union, fought against the Indians, and finally became a reporter for the *New York Herald*. In this guise he followed the British expeditions to Abyssinia and against the Ashanti in West Africa and covered the Carlist Wars in Spain.

In 1869 his editor, James Gordon Bennett, while passing through Paris, called Stanley to the French capital's Grand Hotel to present to him a concise but intensive program of work for the next few months and years. Stanley was required to travel first to Egypt to report on the opening of the Suez Canal, then to ascend the Nile, describing all that might be of interest to American tourists. He was then to go to Jerusalem, Constantinople, the Crimea, and the Caucasus before crossing the Caspian Sea and reaching India by way of Persia. Having completed this tour, he was to travel to Zanzibar from Bombay and organize an expedition to find Livingstone, if he was still alive, or else proof of his death.

This was not the first time an expedition had set out to look for Livingstone, all trace of whom had been lost for some years in the shadows of Africa. A number of the men who had deserted him shortly after the start of his

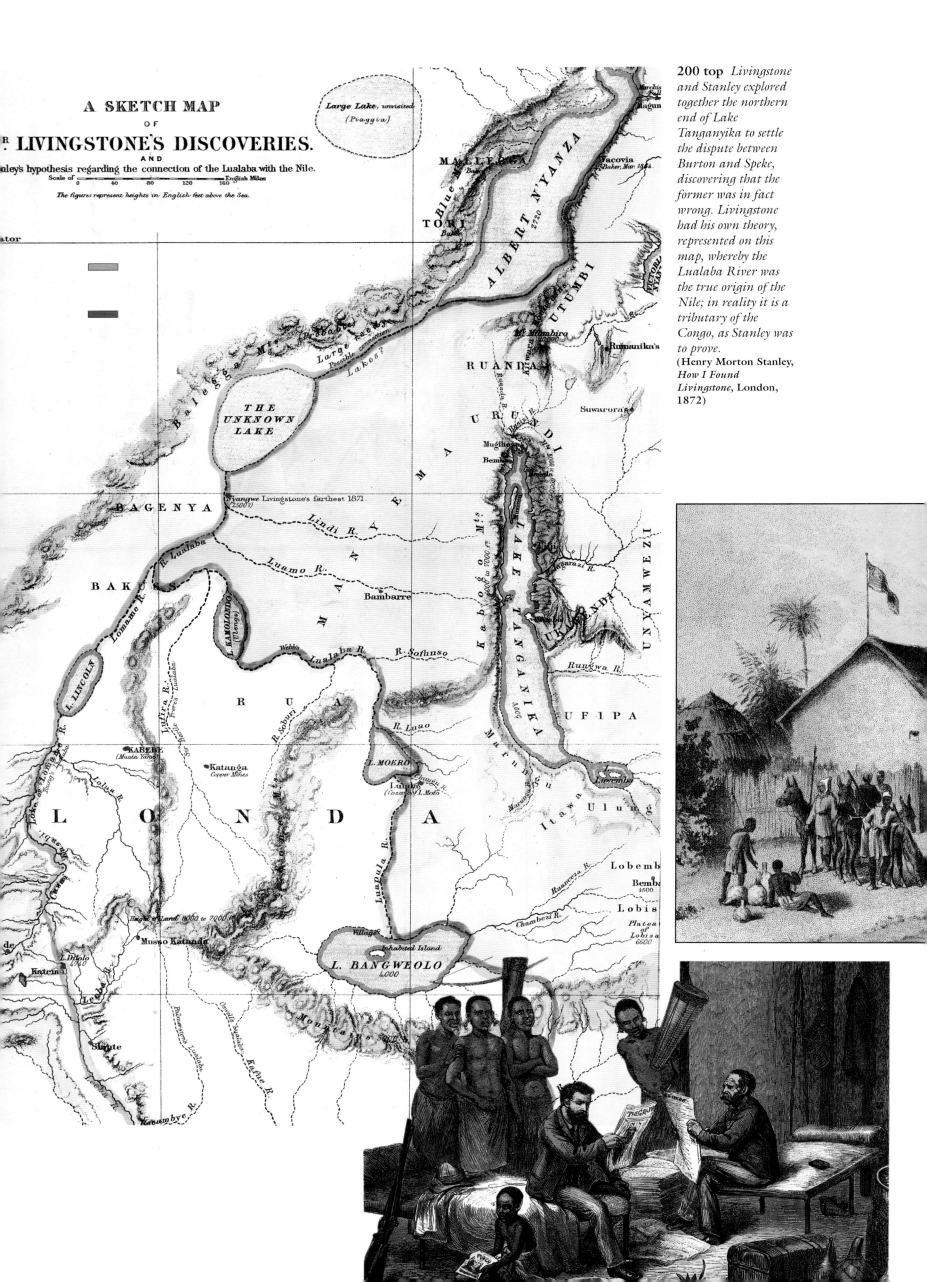

A SKETCH MAP
OF
ᴰͬ LIVINGSTONE'S DISCOVERIES.

AND
...ley's hypothesis regarding the connection of the Lualaba with the Nile.

Scale of
0   40   80   120   160   English Miles

The figures represent heights in English feet above the Sea.

Large Lake, unvisited
(Piaggia)

MALLEGGA

Blue

ALBERT N'YANZA

Vacovia
Baker, Mar 1864

TORI

UTUMBI

2720

VICTORIA N'YANZA

Mᵗ Mfumbiro
10000

Rumanika's

RUANDA

Large Lakes

Possible connection
Lakes?

THE
UNKNOWN
LAKE

Suwarorass

U R U N D I

Mugihewa

Bemba

5000

BAGENYA

Nyangwe Livingstone's farthest 1871
(2500?)

Lindi R.

K a b o g o   M ᵗˢ

6000 to 7000 ft

LAKE TANGANIKA

Luamo R.

R. Lualaba

Bambarre

3000

BAKUSS

Lomame R.

KAMOLONDO
(Ulenge)

Webb's Lualaba R.

R. Sofunso

Lufira R.

Sir Bartle Frere's Lualaba

L. LINCOLN

M A N Y U E M A

UKARANDA

Rungwa R.

UNYAMWEZI

R U A

R. Sobwri

R. Lugo

UFIPA

KABEBE
(Muata Yanvo)

Katanga
Copper Mines

L. MOERO

Lunda
(Cazembe) L. Molo

Innan R.

Loweimba

Marungu

Itawa Uluns

L O N D A

Lolua R.

Luapula R.

Lobemb

Bemba
4500

Musso Katanda

Lobis

Chambezi R.

Plateu
of
Lobisa
6600

Village

Inhabited Island

L. Dilolo
4760

Katema

L. BANGWEOLO
4,000

Leeba R.

Slante

Monkey Is.

Moma's Is.

Quelle Lualaba

Rafine R.

Kasumbye R.

Manchis Fall

Magun

200 top *Livingstone and Stanley explored together the northern end of Lake Tanganyika to settle the dispute between Burton and Speke, discovering that the former was in fact wrong. Livingstone had his own theory, represented on this map, whereby the Lualaba River was the true origin of the Nile; in reality it is a tributary of the Congo, as Stanley was to prove.* (Henry Morton Stanley, *How I Found Livingstone*, London, 1872)

200-201 *The courteous Arab slavers who dominated the Lake Tanganyika region were frequently willing to collaborate with the white explorers and maintained good relations with them. Here Stanley and Livingstone receive a visit from a group of Muslim traders in the village of Kwirara.* (H. M. Stanley, How I Found Livingstone)

201 top *The expeditions from Zanzibar landed on the mainland at the frankly uninviting port of Bagamoyo, seen in this illustration.* (H. M. Stanley, How I Found Livingstone)

last expedition had returned to the coast and attempted to justify their actions by claiming that the explorer had been killed in an ambush by Zulu raiders. While that story was plausible, it did contain some inconsistencies, and Sir Roderick Murchison decided that it would be worthwhile seeking out the truth. He sent to the area Edward Young, formerly the gunner on Livingstone's boat, *Pioneer*. Departing in mid-May 1867, Young completed his mission and returned eight months later with ample proof of the falsity of the deserters' story. Moreover, a number of letters from Livingstone, which had found their way to Zanzibar, had reassured those who were concerned for his safety. However, after the supplies he asked for were sent to Ujiji, nothing more had been heard from him.

In preparing for his expedition, Stanley naturally considered Ujiji his first objective. It took him eight months to get there, and the two white men who

200 bottom *Stanley had packs of newspapers and magazines sent from the coast to Tabora so he could keep up with events. In this engraving he can be seen reading them avidly together with Livingstone, to the astonishment of the natives, for whom writing was a kind of magic.* (Pictorial Africa, Its Heroes, Missionaries and Martyrs)

had departed with him died along the way; the two English seamen, Shaw and Farquhar, were both victims of fever. Stanley had to make a long detour around Kazeh, now known as Tabora, because the area was the theater of a war between the Arabs and the blacks. Despite this precaution he was caught up in the conflict, but his iron will eventually overcame every obstacle.

After a few days' rest Stanley accompanied Livingstone on a trip to clarify another mystery regarding the hydrography of the Nile by exploring the northern tip of Lake Tanganyika. They discovered that Burton had been

201 center *The numerous swamps that barred the routes inland made any journey toward the interior exhausting and dangerous.* (H. M. Stanley, How I Found Livingstone)

201 bottom *The shores of the lakes housed numerous native settlements. Here we can see a village on the shore of the Ugonto, overlooked by the peak of the same name.* (H. M. Stanley, How I Found Livingstone)

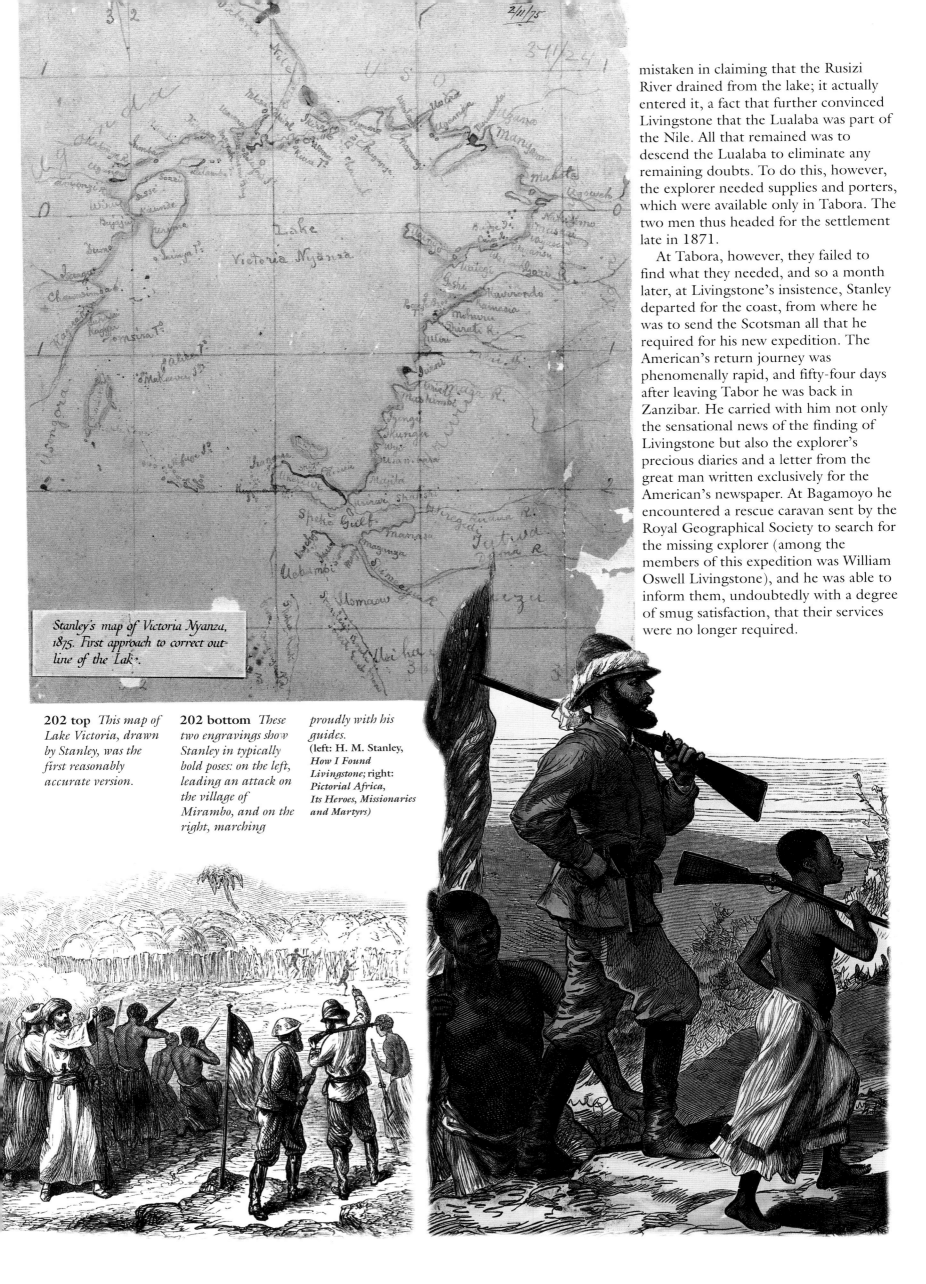

mistaken in claiming that the Rusizi River drained from the lake; it actually entered it, a fact that further convinced Livingstone that the Lualaba was part of the Nile. All that remained was to descend the Lualaba to eliminate any remaining doubts. To do this, however, the explorer needed supplies and porters, which were available only in Tabora. The two men thus headed for the settlement late in 1871.

At Tabora, however, they failed to find what they needed, and so a month later, at Livingstone's insistence, Stanley departed for the coast, from where he was to send the Scotsman all that he required for his new expedition. The American's return journey was phenomenally rapid, and fifty-four days after leaving Tabor he was back in Zanzibar. He carried with him not only the sensational news of the finding of Livingstone but also the explorer's precious diaries and a letter from the great man written exclusively for the American's newspaper. At Bagamoyo he encountered a rescue caravan sent by the Royal Geographical Society to search for the missing explorer (among the members of this expedition was William Oswell Livingstone), and he was able to inform them, undoubtedly with a degree of smug satisfaction, that their services were no longer required.

Stanley's map of Victoria Nyanza, 1875. First approach to correct outline of the Lake.

202 top *This map of Lake Victoria, drawn by Stanley, was the first reasonably accurate version.*

202 bottom *These two engravings show Stanley in typically bold poses: on the left, leading an attack on the village of Mirambo, and on the right, marching* *proudly with his guides.*
(left: H. M. Stanley, How I Found Livingstone; right: Pictorial Africa, Its Heroes, Missionaries and Martyrs)

203 top left *By exploring Lake Tanganyika in two canoes flying the British and American flags, Livingstone and Stanley were able definitively to disprove the theory that the great lake was part of the Nile Basin, as claimed by Burton, who had believed that the Ruzisi River issued from the lake, whereas in reality it entered it.* (H. M. Stanley, *How I Found Livingstone*)

203 bottom left *A group of armed warriors. During the expedition in search of Livingstone, Stanley allowed himself to be caught up in the wars between the Arabs and the black tribes in the Unyamwezi region.* (H. M. Stanley, *How I Found Livingstone*)

In May 1872, the world was informed of the news, and Stanley, having arrived in England, was the man of the moment, though many Britons took exception to the fact that one of their own had been found by a man who had renounced his British citizenship to become an American. Irritated by the great scoop, a number of rival newspapers even implied that Stanley was a fraud. Behind this reaction perhaps lay a guilty conscience; Britain had in effect abandoned its greatest explorer to his own devices for a number of years, and the fact that a

simple journalist—part of what was felt to be a rather ignoble profession at the time—had ventured where professional explorers had not even attempted to go was a stinging blow.

In the meantime Livingstone was still waiting for the caravan of porters Stanley had promised to send to Tabora. The American had, however, left him with sufficient supplies for four years. He waited for five months, preaching to the natives, reading the Bakers' book about Lake Albert, which the American had left with him, and pondering the Lualaba-Nile question. He was fifty-nine years old and by now worn out by illness; perhaps realizing that he did not have long to live, he was gripped by a

203 top right *Livingstone explaining to Stanley his theories about the source of the Nile during their halt on Lake Tanganyka while the curious natives and the paddlers observe the two explorers.* (H. M. Stanley, *How I Found Livingstone*)

203 bottom right *Wagogo warriors marching to war. The Arab merchants in the area instigated wars between the tribes in order to buy prisoners as slaves.* (H. M. Stanley, *How I Found Livingstone*)

204 top *Following the death of Livingstone, Stanley, portrayed here, organized an expedition to resolve the remaining enigmas regarding the hydrography of the Great Lakes region.* (Henry Morton Stanley, *Through the Dark Continent*, London, 1878)

204-205 *This map shows the route followed by Stanley from the coast to Lakes Victoria and Albert, then south to Lake Tanganyika, which he circumnavigated for the first time, and* *finally west toward the Lualaba-Congo. Financed by two newspapers, Stanley's expedition was the richest ever seen; the procession of porters was over a kilometer long.*

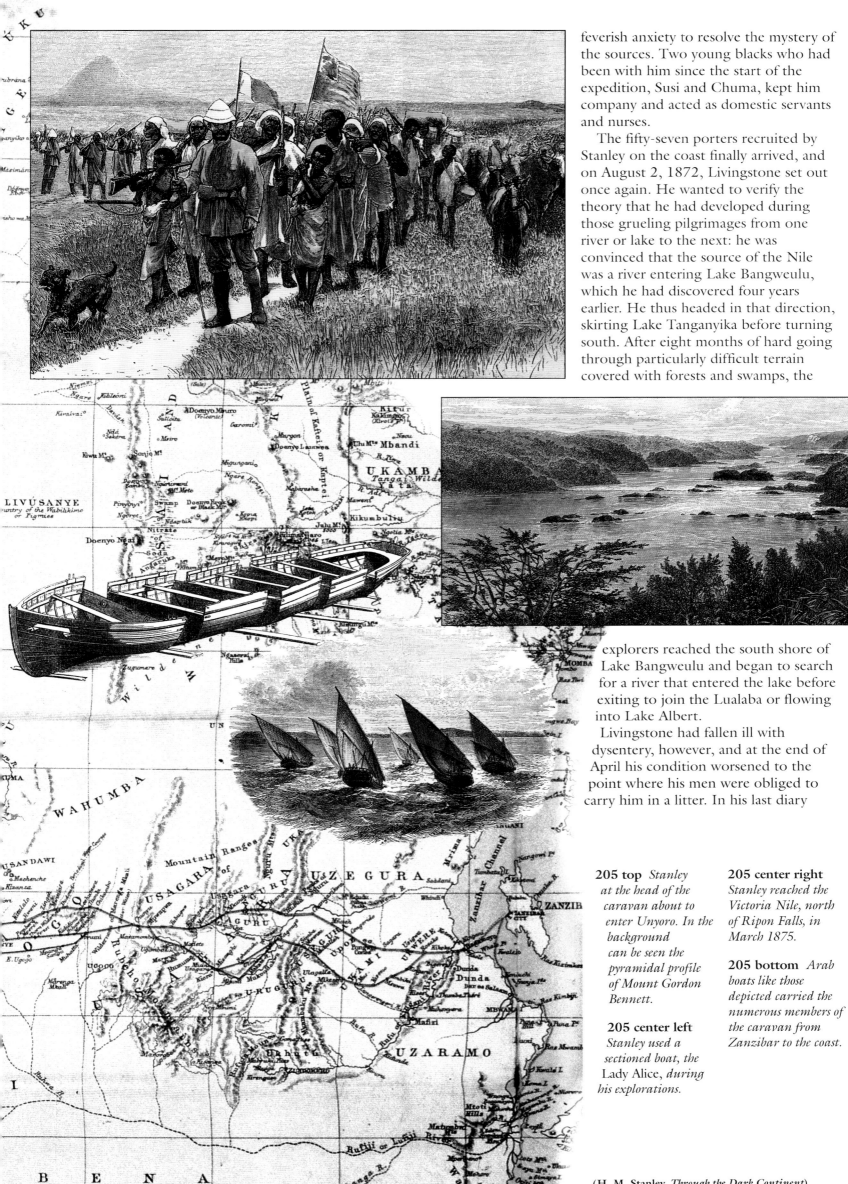

feverish anxiety to resolve the mystery of the sources. Two young blacks who had been with him since the start of the expedition, Susi and Chuma, kept him company and acted as domestic servants and nurses.

The fifty-seven porters recruited by Stanley on the coast finally arrived, and on August 2, 1872, Livingstone set out once again. He wanted to verify the theory that he had developed during those grueling pilgrimages from one river or lake to the next: he was convinced that the source of the Nile was a river entering Lake Bangweulu, which he had discovered four years earlier. He thus headed in that direction, skirting Lake Tanganyika before turning south. After eight months of hard going through particularly difficult terrain covered with forests and swamps, the

explorers reached the south shore of Lake Bangweulu and began to search for a river that entered the lake before exiting to join the Lualaba or flowing into Lake Albert.

Livingstone had fallen ill with dysentery, however, and at the end of April his condition worsened to the point where his men were obliged to carry him in a litter. In his last diary

205 top *Stanley at the head of the caravan about to enter Unyoro. In the background can be seen the pyramidal profile of Mount Gordon Bennett.*

205 center left *Stanley used a sectioned boat, the* Lady Alice, *during his explorations.*

205 center right *Stanley reached the Victoria Nile, north of Ripon Falls, in March 1875.*

205 bottom *Arab boats like those depicted carried the numerous members of the caravan from Zanzibar to the coast.*

205

(H. M. Stanley, *Through the Dark Continent*)

entry, dated April 27, he noted that he was going to stop because he was very tired; he was then on the banks of the river Molilamo. He was laid in a hut in the village of a chief named Chitambo. On the morning of May 1 his men found him dead, on his knees beside the bed. He had died praying.

Livingstone's heart and internal organs were buried below a great cedar in the bark of which an epitaph was inscribed. The body was exposed to the

206 center right *Lake Victoria was frequently the scene of battles between fleets of the lakeshore kingdoms. Here, canoes and rafts of the Waganda and Wavuma tribes engage in a bloody struggle in the channel between the island of Ingira and Cape Nakaranga.*

206 bottom *Now around forty years old, M'tesa had developed into the wise monarch of a flourishing kingdom, defended by a well-armed and well-trained army. This illustration depicts the king's bodyguards parading European-style to welcome Stanley on the beach at Usavara.*

206 top *Having entered Uganda, Stanley was received by King M'tesa, whose flotilla of war canoes is seen here crossing the Napoleon Channel near Lake Victoria.* (Henry Morton Stanley, *Through the Dark Continent*, London, 1878)

206 center left *This picturesque avenue led to Rubega, M'tesa's new capital whose palace, surrounded by a palisade, can be seen at the top of the hill.* (H. M. Stanley, *Through the Dark Continent*)

206

sun for fifteen days until it dried and was then wrapped in canvas and packed into a cylinder of bark. The bundle was then sewn into a large canvas sail, slung on a pole, and carried by two men in shifts. The now leaderless caravan composed of around sixty men, including the faithful Chuma and Susi, set off in the middle of May heading for the coast 1,600 kilometers away, a journey that took eleven months. When, in October 1873, they arrived at Tabora, they met another belated British rescue expedition led by the Royal Navy officer Verney Lovett Cameron, who proceeded to Ujiji to recover other writings by Livingstone.

On February 15, 1874, Susi and Chuma entered Bagamoyo with the body of their beloved leader. The ship *Vulture* was waiting to carry the corpse to Zanzibar. From there, after having lain for some time in the British consulate, it was taken to Southampton and then by special train to Westminster Abbey, where it was buried on April 18, 1874, Queen Victoria having proclaimed a period of national mourning.

Four months later Stanley left England on a new expedition that was intended both to complete Livingstone's work and to demonstrate that he had been wrong. Early in November the feet-equipped and best-organized caravan ever seen in Africa set out from Bagamoyo: 356 men, 8 tons of provisions, and a 12-meter sectioned boat, the *Lady Alice*. In single file the column stretched out for a kilometer. The enterprise was financed by two newspapers, the *New York Herald* and the *Daily Telegraph*. There were three other white men besides Stanley—the brothers John and Edward Pocock and Frederick Barker, selected for their steadfastness and discipline. Edward Pocock died almost immediately of typhus, Barker died a few months later, and John Pocock drowned in the Congo

207 top *Assembled and disassembled for transportation overland, the 12-meter long* Lady Alice *was a boon to Stanley. This engraving shows the vessel being severely tested by a difficult passage through rapids.*

207 bottom *This engraving was made from a photograph taken by Stanley of M'tesa and his court of dignitaries. The natives were no longer naked but richly dressed in Arab-style clothing, thanks to the profitable trading links established with Zanzibar.*

(H. M. Stanley, *Through the Dark Continent*)

208 top *The flotilla of porters' canoes preceded by the* Lady Alice, *whose gunmen are firing on a hostile tribe trying to bar Stanley's way at the confluence between the Congo and the Aruwimi. After having circumnavigated Lake Tanganyika, Stanley headed west to ascend the river Lualaba, which according to* Livingstone, *should have been the upper and principal course of the Nile. In reality it was the Congo and its current carried the expedition not into Egypt but to the Atlantic coast after an interminable odyssey marked by tragic episodes.*
(Henry Morton Stanley, *Through the Dark Continent*, London, 1878)

208 center *Stanley and his men repelling with gunfire the attack of 63 Bangala canoes. The navigation of the Congo was characterized by a continual series of conflicts.*
(Henry Morton Stanley, *Through the Dark Continent*, London, 1878)

208 bottom left *The son of the king of Chumbri (top) and a Watuta warrior (bottom). No white man had ever before set foot in the Congolese territories crossed by Stanley.*

208 bottom right *The* Lady Alice *sailing in front of the Mtombwa Urungu headland, the home of a river spirit, according to the natives.*

208-209 *Stanley wanted to rename the great waterfall he discovered on the lower section of the Congo after Livingstone.*

toward the end of a trip that was to last three years.

On March 8, 1875, having reached Lake Victoria, Stanley had his boat assembled and, leaving behind the bulk of the equipment, sailed as far as the Ripon Falls before entering the kingdom of M'tesa, who received him hospitably. In that forty-year-old and considerably wiser sovereign, now a mature, affable, and intelligent man, it was difficult to recognize the capricious despot encountered by Speke. Since trading relationships had been established with Zanzibar, M'tesa's kingdom was now much wealthier, and his warriors were all armed with guns. Out of the Sudan the previous year had come an envoy, Charles Chaillé–Long, an American. The Frenchman Linant de Bellefonds, who arrived while Stanley

was there, treated the sovereign and the explorer to pâté, salami, and sardines.

Stanley returned to Lake Victoria in May. His survey proved that Speke was correct: it was a single lake drained by just one major river to the north. He now needed to explore Lake Tanganyika to discover what links it had with the other great lakes. He therefore headed south where he met another old acquaintance, the now elderly chief Rumanika, who received him proudly displaying the gun he had been given by Speke.

In June 1876, Stanley departed from Ujiji and completed a circumnavigation of Tanganyika, definitively proving that it had no outlet that could be the source of the Nile. Two months later he tackled the last of the problems he had set out to solve: the Lualaba, on which

he embarked to trace the whole of its immense length, discovering in the process that it was in fact the Congo. This was an epic enterprise not lacking in dramatic episodes: storms and shipwrecks, attacks by native tribes and wild animals, the loss of supplies, and death through disease and accidents. The survivors, 114 men out of 356, reached the mouth of the interminable river exactly 999 days after their departure from Zanzibar. They were met and revived by a group of European traders who could hardly believe their eyes and ears: the journey described by Stanley seemed impossible. With this remarkable achievement, the American journalist had solved the principal questions regarding the Great Lakes region, and the hydrography of the Nile was now clearly defined.

(H. M. Stanley, *Through the Dark Continent*)

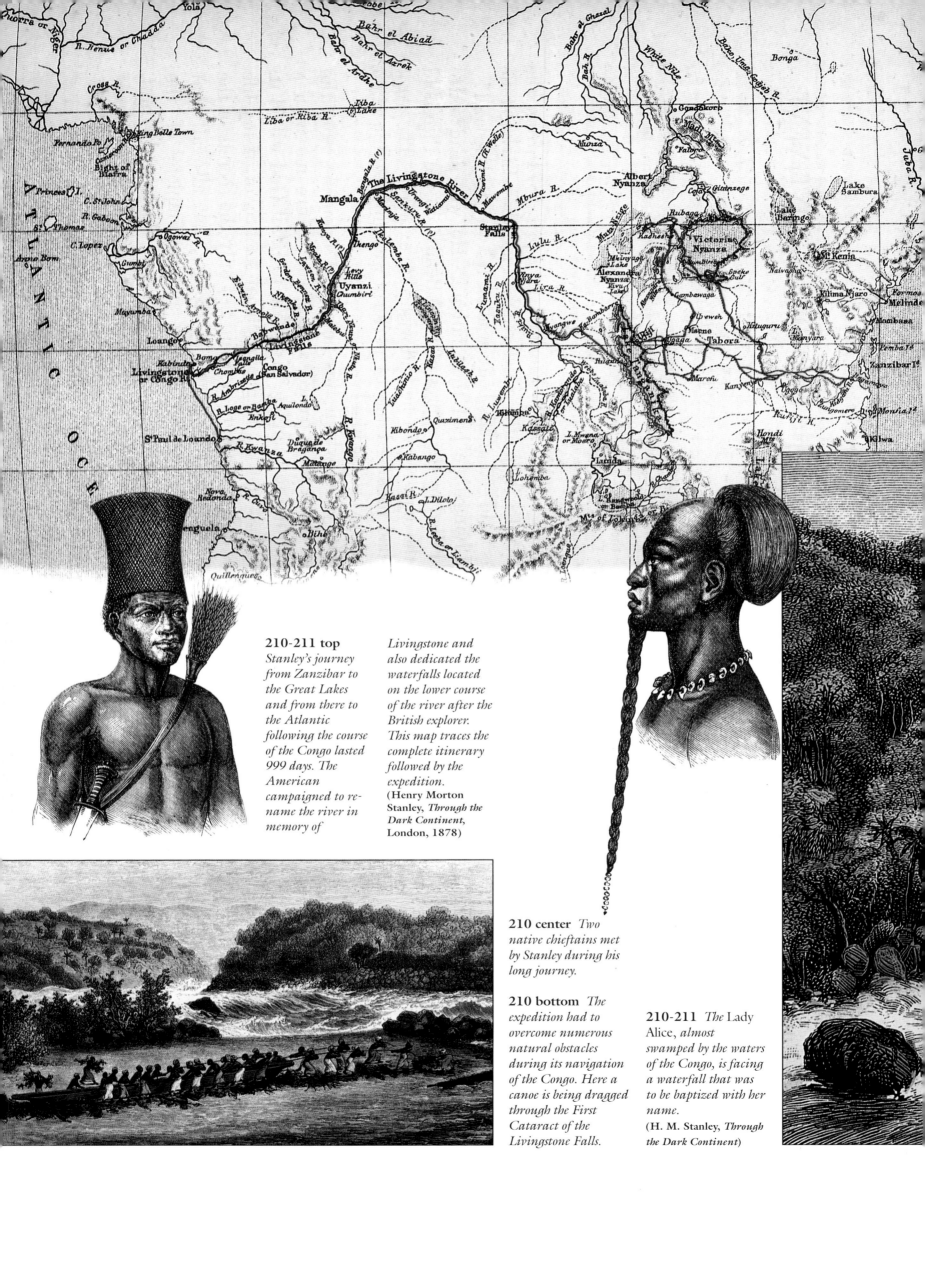

210-211 top
Stanley's journey from Zanzibar to the Great Lakes and from there to the Atlantic following the course of the Congo lasted 999 days. The American campaigned to re-name the river in memory of *Livingstone and also dedicated the waterfalls located on the lower course of the river after the British explorer. This map traces the complete itinerary followed by the expedition.* (Henry Morton Stanley, *Through the Dark Continent*, London, 1878)

210 center *Two native chieftains met by Stanley during his long journey.*

210 bottom *The expedition had to overcome numerous natural obstacles during its navigation of the Congo. Here a canoe is being dragged through the First Cataract of the Livingstone Falls.*

210-211 *The* Lady Alice, *almost swamped by the waters of the Congo, is facing a waterfall that was to be baptized with her name.*
(H. M. Stanley, *Through the Dark Continent*)

211 top *Of the 356 men who left Zanzibar with Stanley (standing, dressed in white), only 114 reached the mouth of the Congo alive; the expedition was decimated by disease, hunger, boating accidents, and hostile natives. When the Europeans living on the Atlantic coast saw the survivors appear out the jungle they could hardly believe their eyes: what Stanley had done seemed impossible.*

While Livingstone was exploring the Great Lakes of Africa in search of the sources of the White Nile, an entire army of his compatriots was invading the Blue Nile region, the Christian country of Abyssinia that had long been one of the expansionist objectives of Mehemet Ali and his successors.

In the first half of the nineteenth century, the venerable Ethiopian Empire, the sovereigns of which proudly claimed descent from Solomon, was going through one of the periodic phases of disintegration that had blighted its long history like a biblical scourge. The power of the great feudal chieftains, the rasers, absolute masters of their provinces, obscured that of the puppet emperors who were installed on the throne through

212 This view of the village of Asceriah shows the typical rocky-sloped Abyssinian hills known as ambas. (Henry Salt, *Twenty Four Views taken in St. Helena, the Cape, India, Ceylon, Abyssinia and Egypt*, London, 1809)

A BRIGAND ON THE THRONE OF SOLOMON: THE BRITISH EXPEDITION TO ABYSSINIA

212-213 In the mid-nineteenth century the ancient Christian kingdom of Abyssinia, shown on this map drawn by Henry Salt in 1809-1810, extended over a territory

corresponding to about a quarter of present-day Ethiopia. Set among Muslim countries, Abyssinia represented something of a challenge for the Ottoman Empire and Egypt; for centuries they

had dreamed of and attempted in vain to conquer the country and convert its population to Islam. (Henry Salt, *Twenty Four Views taken in St. Helena, the Cape, India, Ceylon, Abyssinia and Egypt*)

213 bottom left
The royal palace at Gonder, the capital of Abyssinia, revealed in all its majesty. (Henry Salt, *Twenty Four Views taken in St. Helena, the Cape, India, Ceylon, Abyssinia and Egypt*)

213 bottom right
An Abyssinian warrior displaying the splendor of his richly decorated costume. (Henry Salt, *Twenty Four Views . . .*)

214

214 *A woman from Serae and some of the jewelery worn by the local women: from the top a necklace of ivory and glass beads, a diadem in gold and silver, a hairpin in gilded silver, a brooch, and two silver bracelets.*

214-215 *A wealthy noblewoman from Tigre attended by an equally attractive servant. The beauty of the Abyssinian women, celebrated throughout Africa and the Middle East, made them sought-after prey for the slave traders who raided the country from the Sudan.*

(Théophile Lefebvre, *Voyage en Abyssinie*)

216 top *This intense portrait by Théophile Lefèbvre, published in his* Voyage en Abyssinie (*Paris, 1845), depicts a Sciré peasant.*

216 bottom *The violence of the Davernt waterfall during the wet season was one of the most spectacular sights in Ethiopia.*

216-217 *A typical panorama with the church of Hannas on the road to Aksum and a ring of ambas in the background. It was not only the urge to win over new recruits to Islam that spurred the repeated attempts to conquer Abyssinia by the Turks and the Egyptians, but also the wealth and fertility of the Ethiopian highlands.* (War Office, *Views in Abyssinia,* London, 1867)

216

the caprice of one or another of the antagonists. The emperors lacked not only power but also the means of exercising it, and on their death the royal treasury was frequently unable even to pay for their funeral. That anarchical situation of incessant internecine warfare appeared to favor the Egyptian aims: in 1818 the Sublime Porte had conferred theoretical governorship of the "province of Abyssinia" upon Ibrahim, the son of Mehemet Ali, and following the conquest of the Sudan, a raid by the "Turks" in 1838 had reached and sacked Gonder, the ancient imperial residence. Two years later the Egyptians established a fortified outpost at Kassala, and it appeared that they intended to advance from there toward the Red Sea to link their Sudanese possessions with the port of Massawa, which they had already occupied in the name of the Ottoman Empire.

The hostility of Britain to this potential conquest or dismemberment of Ethiopia

eventually induced Mehemet Ali to lower his sights; but while military expansion had been halted, the religious penetration of Islam, the prelude to a hoped-for colonization, continued apace. Ethiopian Christianity was on the retreat on all fronts. The nomadic tribes of the valleys and the deserts that fringed the Abyssinian highlands were the most vulnerable to the preaching of the Sudanese emissaries and of those unwitting missionaries who were the Arab merchants. Meanwhile, the raids launched on Kassala by the slavers were converting the more stubborn through brute force. In 1843 the French explorer Antoine d'Abbadie noted that in many regions the Christian communities had lacked priests for a number of generations and the people inevitably lapsed; with no priests to say mass, the faithful could do no more than congregate around the church each Sunday.

In the heart of the Ethiopian state the ecclesiastical hierarchy was still strong and

217 top *On the Tacarré River, set amid the mountains, a group of Abyssinians stalk a hippopotamus.* (Henry Salt, *Twenty Four Views taken in St. Helena, the Cape, India, Ceylon, Abyssinia and Egypt*, London, 1809)

217 center *The oxen of the Galla people were characterized by very long horns.* (Henry Salt, *Twenty Four Views taken in St. Helena, the Cape, India, Ceylon, Abyssinia and Egypt*, London, 1809)

well respected, however. In fact, in that atmosphere of extreme feudal breakdown it represented the only centralized power in which the continuity of the national traditions was concentrated and to which the population threatened by the invasion of Islam could turn. And it was the Church that made a decisive contribution to the restoration of imperial power with the elevation to the throne of a highly individual and tragic figure, Tewodros (Theodore) II.

His real name was Kasa Hayla, and he was born around 1818 in the Quara region, traditionally an area of brigandage, west of Lake Tana. His father was a peasant farmer, his mother a seller of *cusso*, a tapeworm remedy of which the Abyssinians, great consumers of raw meat, made constant use. (According to other sources he was the son of the governor of Quara and one of his concubines, and it does appear likely that he was related to the family of the

governor.) He nevertheless grew up in poverty until he was taken in by a charitable tanner who taught him his trade. His enemies later mocked him with the nickname Tewodros the Tanner when, having taken the throne, he claimed to be descended from Solomon and Alexander the Great. His mother subsequently found him a place in a monastery as a clerk. He learned by heart the Psalms of David and absorbed those ecclesiastical notions that formed the cultural baggage of the Abyssinian elite. He also developed a love of books, which led him, as emperor, to put together a collection of illuminated manuscripts that is today one of the great treasures of the British Museum.

One fine day the tranquil life of the monastery was disrupted by an attack by brigands, who sacked and burned it. The young Kasa Hayla was forced or persuaded to join them and become a *shifta*, or brigand, himself. Brigandage at that time

217 bottom *The attractive plumage of an Abyssinian eagle* (Helotarsus ecaudatus). (T. Lefebvre, *Voyage en Abyssinie*, Paris, 1845)

in Ethiopia was actually quite an honorable—and profitable—profession, and the new recruit proved to be strong and audacious and covered himself in glory in skirmishes with the Egyptians preying on the plains of Sennar. He was soon at the head of his own band and fought against the "Turks," against the Galla tribes that had converted to Islam, and against anyone else who came within firing range. As his fame grew throughout western Abyssinia, the governor of Gojam attempted to bring him into his fold. D'Abbadie, who visited the court in 1843, was so impressed by the effervescent warrior that he predicted with admirable farsightedness that one day he would become the master of Ethiopia.

At this point it becomes difficult to separate history from legend, which says that a powerful Egyptian expedition heavily armed with artillery was turned against the ragged troops of the reigning empress Menen and routed the Ethiopians. The daughter of the sovereign, the princess Tauabac, sent to oversee the tactics of her worthless generals, was taken prisoner by the "Turks." The Egyptian commander,

218 top *This priest or* abba, *which means father, is playing a kind of harp.* (Théophile Lefebvre, *Voyage en Abyssinie,* Paris, 1845)

218 bottom *The city of Aksum, which boasted ancient monuments including the famous obelisks,* *was the religious capital of Abyssinia. These illustrations show two of the city's buildings.*

(Henry Salt, Twenty Four Views taken in St. Helena, the Cape, India, Ceylon, Abyssinia and Egypt, *London, 1809)*

218-219 *This accurate engraving depicts the solemn celebration of Palm Sunday in a church at Gonder.*

Musa Pasha, fell for the beautiful Ethiopian and assigned her to his harem. Fortune had it that Kasa Hayla was in the area with his band. Hearing of the imperial disaster, he launched a surprise attack on the invaders and liberated the princess. However, on the point of being raped by her guards, she had stabbed herself with a poisoned blade. Her savior was undaunted and sucked the poison from the wound before sending her back to her mother in triumph. In recompense the infamous Ras Ali, the son and black sheep of the empress's family as well as the true master of the empire, sent an army against Kasa Hayla. The brigand's feat had aroused such enthusiasm, however, that thousands of young men had hurried to enroll under his flag. He cast aside his adversaries, marched directly to Gonder with fifteen thousand men, and asked for the hand of Tauabac.

The history books tell a less romantic story: Ras Ali had decided to avail himself of the services of the talented brigand, and in order to create a bond between himself and Kasa Hayla in 1847 he offered him the hand of his daughter, none other than Tauabac.

In any case, this marriage allowed the son of the laxative seller to enter the family of the most powerful chieftain in the country and the inner circle of the imperial court. Kasa Hayla, however, was not one for the niceties of imperial etiquette and the aristocrats despised his wife for having married beneath herself. Suborned by her resentment and urged by his awareness of his own worth, he fled from the palace, which was populated by impotent phantoms interminably discussing obscure points of ceremonial procedure while the country was falling into ruins. He returned to the crags and forests of his native Quara, gathered his faithful followers about him, and raised the flag of rebellion.

Ras Ali sent his most reliable and valorous officer, Wend Irad, with four thousand men, infantry and cavalry, against Kasa Hayla. The rebel, who could count on just three hundred men, courageously awaited his fate on the plain of Ciacio. Engaging in hand-to-hand combat with the commander of the opposing forces as if in a swashbuckling adventure story, Casa struck him down and took him prisoner. Then, with that derisive sense of humor that appeared to be a characteristic of many Eastern princes, he made him drink a large dose of *cusso*, a laxative, "in the name of my sainted mother."

Ras Ali barely had time to receive news of the disaster when the victors, inebriated with their success, were upon him and he was forced to flee. Then, with a series of skillful guerrilla maneuvers, Kasa Hayla defeated the scattered imperial forces battalion by battalion, thus succeeding in arming his troops with the precious guns of the dead and his prisoners. Empress Menen, who was under no illusions as to the outcome of the struggle, made a last-ditch defense on the Dembia plain with 20,000 infantrymen and 3,000 mounted troops. On an open battlefield the numerically far inferior rebel forces would have been overwhelmed, but Kasa Hayla shrewdly positioned his men behind a slight crest

220-221 *As in medieval feudal Europe, the Abyssinian Church was a great power and the owner of extensive lands throughout the country. Ritual ceremonies like the procession of the ark preceded by dancing monks, depicted here, dated back to primitive Christianity and still contained elements derived from Judaism.* (Théophile Lefebvre, **Voyage en Abyssinie**, Paris, 1845)

220 bottom *A careful study of the costume of a carpenter at Gonder.*

220

221 *Diverse Abyssinian costumes. From top to bottom: Chalaka Thaime, who was sent as an ambassador to the King of France; the costume of an army officer; the Arab-style costume of an* engueda, *or lawyer.*

221

and waited. It was the rainy season and the plain was a mud bath. Menen ordered her cavalry to attack but the men refused; they knew that once their horses were bogged down, they would be sitting ducks for the enemy rifles. The empress treated them like cowards, and to set an example she spurred her mule into the bog, advancing as far as the enemy lines where, dazzled by such boldness, no one had the heart to shoot her. Eventually wounded in the thigh, she was unhorsed and led as a prisoner to Kasa Hayla's tent, where she was received with as much refined courtesy as he could muster. The imperial army disbanded, convinced that the gods were against it.

Ras Ali gathered a coalition of feudal chieftains against his rival and enjoyed a degree of initial success; but Kasa Hayla then won one decisive battle after another, obtained the support of the metropolitan bishop of Ethiopia, Abuna Salama, who recognized him as the champion of the Church and lent credit to the rumor that he had been sent by God to save the empire. In exchange, Kasa Hayla proclaimed Coptic Christianity to be the

state religion and outlawed all others, including Catholicism.

On February 3, 1855, near the village of Deraghie in the province of Simen, the old and the new Ethiopia clashed for the last time. On the one hand there was the old feudal aristocracy under the flag of Ras Ubie while on the other were brigands, adventurers, and peasant farmers all lined up behind one of their own, the tanner, the son of a *cusso* seller. The battle lasted for hours. At dusk, the most famous chiefs having fallen and the most illustrious aristocratic families having been decimated, Kasa Hayla was proclaimed Negus Neghesti, King of Kings, by his followers on the corpse-strewn battlefield. Abuna Salama crowned him three days later in the little church at Deraghie.

With the last of his adversaries dispersed, the new emperor attempted to establish effective control over the vast country. He had taken the name Tewodros, or Theodore, II, reviving an ancient prophecy whereby an Ethiopian sovereign of this name would eliminate Islam, reconquer Jerusalem, and reign over the entire Christian world. He moved the capital from the hated Gonder, cradle of the aristocracy, to the natural fortress of Magdala between Tigray and Wolo. Tewodros was astute and intelligent but preferred force to political finesse: he cut through every knot with the sword; any resistance exasperated him and sparked the most violent and cruel reprisals. Moreover, he was increasingly consumed by religious fanaticism. Egypt attempted to ingratiate itself with him by sending the Coptic patriarch of Alexandria, Cyril IV, as an ambassador. Furious that a Christian prelate should put himself at the service of the Muslims, Tewodros imprisoned him for a year, from December 1856 to November 1857, before allowing him to return to Cairo. Tewodros would not tolerate followers of Islam in his country. Even the most pacific of Ethiopian

Muslims had to leave the country, and as most of them were shopkeepers and craftsmen, their departure marked the decline of many towns and villages.

Tewodros also raged against the Christians, however. He attempted to impose morality through brute force, forbidding the widespread practice of concubinage. He eliminated his erstwhile colleagues and thus for the first time managing to rid the country of brigandage, passed extremely civilized laws, such as the abolition of slavery and the prohibition of the traditional practice of castrating dead and wounded enemy soldiers in battle, which were then ignored. In order to demonstrate the superiority of the cross over the crescent moon, he dreamed of invading the Sudan where, in the meantime, in 1862, Egypt

had concentrated an army ready to conquer Ethiopia. War was avoided only because an epidemic struck the "Turks." Tewodros also considered diverting the Blue Nile to lower the level of the Nile proper so as to starve Egypt.

If he had reigned for longer, this black, wilder but no less genial version of Peter the Great might have succeeded in whipping Ethiopia into a civilized state, much as his northern counterpart had done in Russia. However, his maniacal susceptibility transformed an insignificant episode of European diplomatic stupidity into an infernal chain reaction of reprisals that was to be his undoing. In 1862 Tewodros entrusted the British consul Cameron, a recent arrival in Ethiopia, with a letter for Queen Victoria in which he proposed a close alliance with Britain

against the "Turks" occupying the Sudan and the Red Sea ports. With typical disdain for such an initiative on the part of a "barbarian" king, Cameron—who had promised to deliver the letter personally—sent it via Aden and then went into the Sudan. Having reached London, the letter disappeared into some Foreign Office pigeonhole, probably after having raised a smile or two among the civil servants. Tewodros, who was anxiously awaiting a response to what he considered a serious proposal from one Christian power to another, heard that Cameron had not in fact taken the letter to his queen but was touring the Sudan negotiating with the hated "Turks."

For a man such as the negus, who had lived since childhood in a world of infidelity and betrayal, it would have taken

222 center *After studying in a monastery and then becoming a brigand, Kasa Hayla, the son of a laxative seller, led one of the many bands that roamed Abyssinia. He grew in power to the point at which he was able to defeat all his rivals and proclaim himself emperor in 1855 with the name Tewodros. Genial, bizarre, and perhaps more than a little insane, he was accustomed to giving hearings surrounded by his tamed lions, the*

roars of which terrified his subjects and European visitors.

222 bottom
Emperor Tewodros established his residence at the top of Magdala hill. (**Coomassie and Magdala; The Story of the British Campaigns in Africa,** London, 1874)

222-223 *A group of warriors on foot and on horseback heading toward the camp of Tewodros's army.* (**T. Lefebvre,** *Voyage en Abyssinie,* **Paris, 1845**)

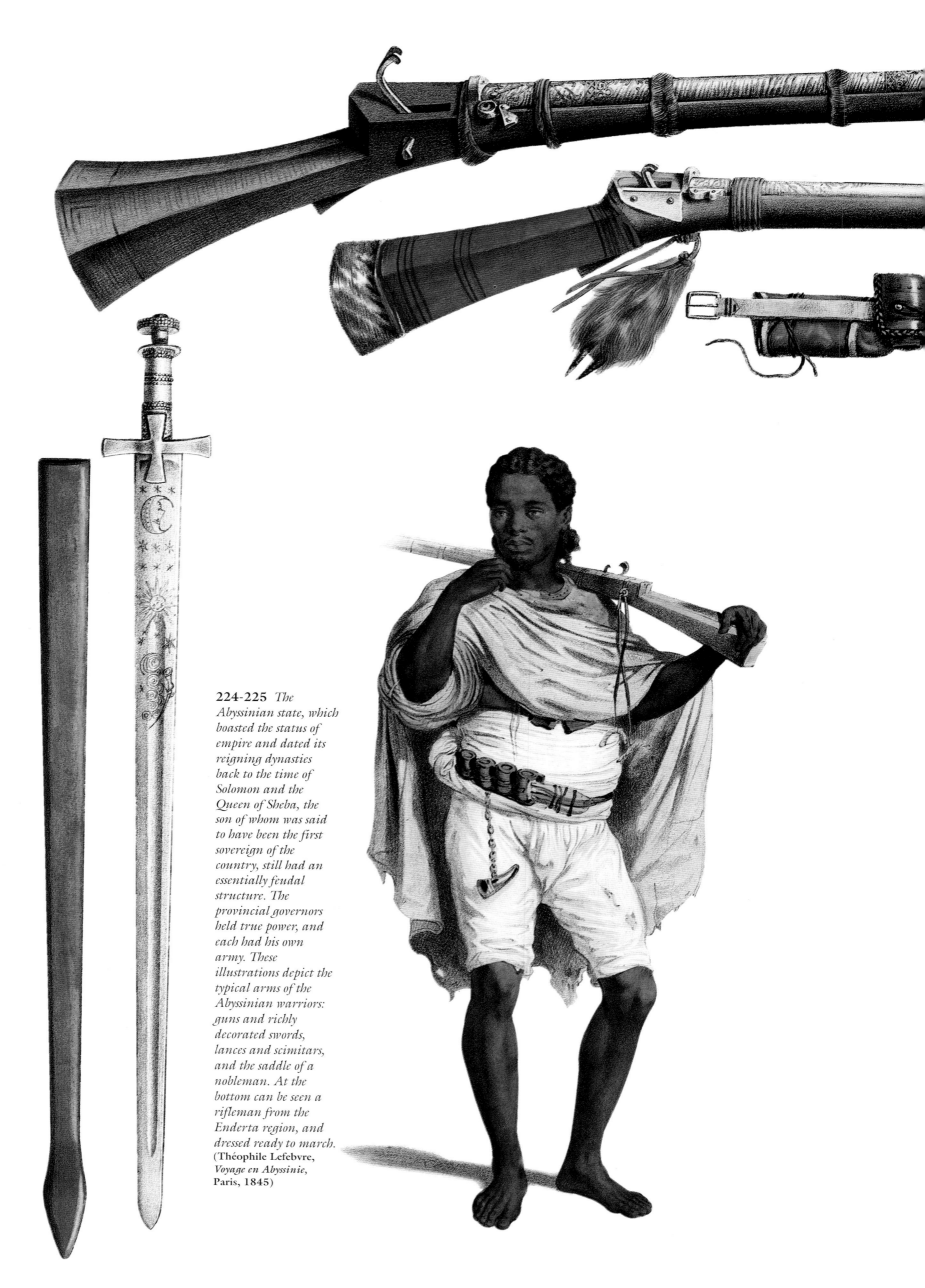

224-225 *The Abyssinian state, which boasted the status of empire and dated its reigning dynasties back to the time of Solomon and the Queen of Sheba, the son of whom was said to have been the first sovereign of the country, still had an essentially feudal structure. The provincial governors held true power, and each had his own army. These illustrations depict the typical arms of the Abyssinian warriors: guns and richly decorated swords, lances and scimitars, and the saddle of a nobleman. At the bottom can be seen a rifleman from the Enderta region, and dressed ready to march.* (Théophile Lefebvre, *Voyage en Abyssinie*, Paris, 1845)

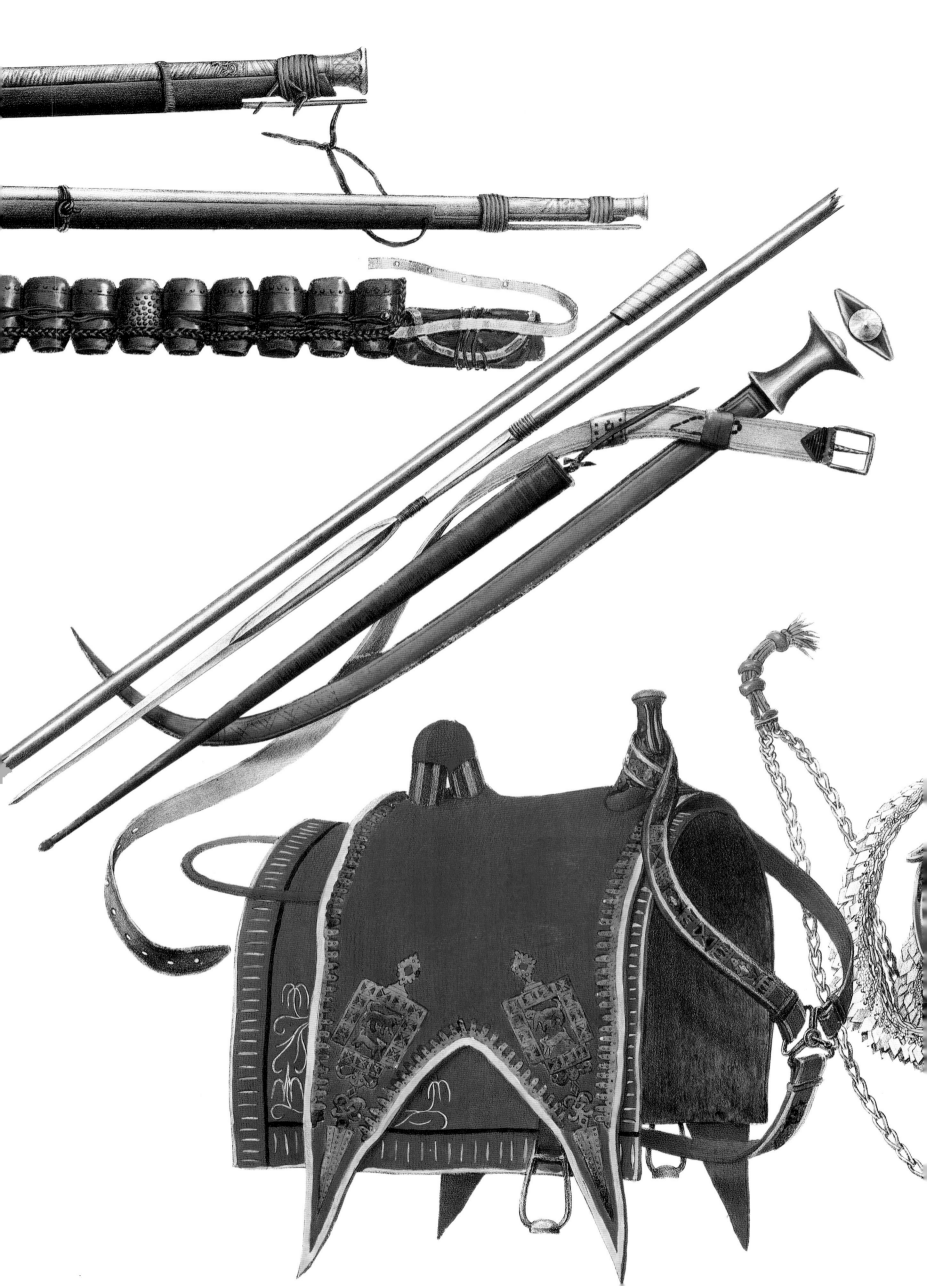

226 *These two Abyssinian warriors in battle dress decorated with a lion skin are lancers from Tigre.*

226-227 *These two maces, faithfully reproduced by the draftsman, belonged to Tigre warriors.*

226 center left *The elephant-hide shield on the left was used by the Adal people. The one on the right in buffalo hide decorated with the mane and tail of a lion was carried by Tigre noblemen.*

226

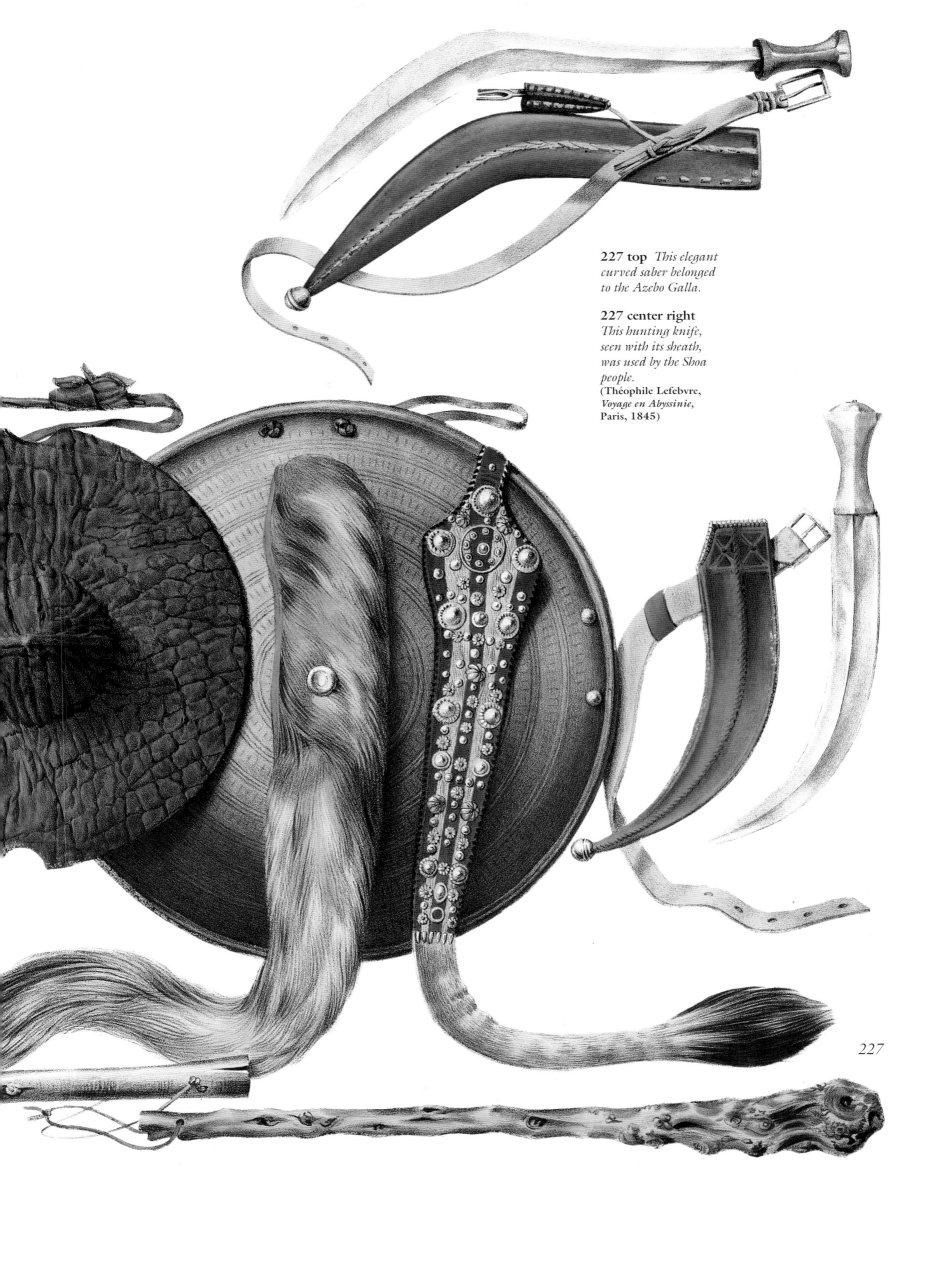

227 top *This elegant curved saber belonged to the Azebo Galla.*

227 center right
This hunting knife, seen with its sheath, was used by the Shoa people.
(Théophile Lefebvre, *Voyage en Abyssinie,* **Paris, 1845)**

227

far less to arouse the suspicion that the Briton was plotting behind his back. The lack of a reply, moreover, profoundly wounded his delicate pride. Tewodros had a number of white men on whom to extract revenge: two Frenchmen and the German missionaries of Gonder, one of whom, the increasingly furious emperor was informed, had dared to mention in a book published the previous year in Europe his derogatory nickname Ligg Cusso, the Son of the Laxative. They were all arrested and imprisoned at Magdala; some of them, like the incautious missionary, were also beaten. Returning from his ill-considered trip to the Sudan in 1864,

MAP
OF THE PORTION OF
ABYSSINIA
Traversed by
THE BRITISH EXPEDITION in 1868
from Annesley Bay to Magdala
to accompany
H. M. STANLEY'S
'COOMASSIE & MAGDALA'.

SCALE OF ENGLISH MILES.

Cameron himself was imprisoned, as was, shortly afterward, an aide sent to him from Britain carrying messages from the Foreign Office, but not the coveted reply from the queen. Slowly but surely, the number of missionaries, technicians, and diplomats imprisoned at Magdala grew to over sixty and the town was wittily nicknamed the Hôtel des Ambassadeurs. An Iraqi in the service of Great Britain, Hormuzd Rassam, blessed with the admirable virtue of Oriental subtlety, was charged with the task of solving the awkward problem. In spite of his praiseworthy efforts, the matter was complicated still further by a belated letter from Queen Victoria of Great Britain to the emperor of Ethiopia in which no mention was made of the proposed alliance. Rassam negotiated for two years from 1864 to 1866, first corresponding from Massawa and then dealing with Tewodros in person. He finally obtained

228 top left
Cameron, the British consul whose stupid neglect sparked the war.

228 bottom left
The huts of Magdala in which Cameron was held prisoner with other Europeans.
(Coomassie and Magdala;
The Story of the British Campaigns in Africa,
London, 1874)

228 right *This map of Abyssinia shows the route followed by the British expedition from the port of Zeila (Zulla on the map) on the Red Sea to the amba of Magdala.*
(Coomassie and Magdala;
The Story of the British Campaigns in Africa,
London, 1874)

229 top *British forces disembarking at Zulla. Rassam's attempts at mediation having failed, force was the only remaining alternative.*

229 center left
Hormuzd Rassam, an Iraqi in the service of Great Britain, was instructed to negotiate with Tewodros for the release of the prisoners but was himself imprisoned by the irascible negus.

229 center right
After the landing, a huge tented city was established at Zulla with the neatly arranged stores of the expeditionary force.

229 bottom *This drinking trough was constructed for the British forces' animals during the march inland toward Magdala.*

the release of the hostages, but the following day, when they all gathered in his tent to be set free, the fickle negus changed his mind and had them all imprisoned again, adding Rassam to the list for good measure. Tewodros then sent one of them, the German missionary, Flad, to Britain, asking to be sent workers skilled in the manufacture of arms in exchange for the prisoners, whose conditions varied. While some were free to roam the town, others—including Cameron, perhaps the only guilty party—were locked up in chains.

Patience was once more the order of the day in London. The workers and machine tools were sent to Massawa, accompanied by Flad, who carried with him a letter from the queen accepting the exchange but threatening war if the white men were not released. As soon as the prisoners reached the coast the workers would depart for the interior. Tewodros waffled, however, proposing that the encounter between those leaving and those

arriving should take place in his residence at Debre Tabor in the Quara region near Lake Tana. At this point the British lion roared, and in July 1867 war was declared.

In need of money and supplies for the troops he was mustering, Tewodros, who was now completely insane, according to certain sources, decided to strip the wealthy monasteries of their treasures and grain stores. The first to be seized was that of Deck on an island in Lake Tana. After having stripped the monastery, he locked the monks in their huts and burned them alive. He then entered Gonder like the wrath of God and abandoned himself to a frenzy of looting. Having destroyed the city and transported to Magdala all that he could lay his hands on, from bells to manuscripts, he devastated Begemdir, mutilating and slitting the throats of thousands of peasants to force them to reveal where they had hidden their grain. Finally, certain that he had squeezed that unfortunate country dry, he torched the entrenched camp of Debra Tabor and set off for the impregnable Magdala. Five thousand armed men and sixty thousand porters, women, elderly people, and children marched through the harshest areas of Ethiopia, all rugged mountains and precipitous gorges infested with hostile peoples who refused the migrants even a day's respite. When the animals died of hunger and exhaustion, the men dragged the cannons through the bush. When they reached the towering Mount

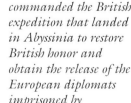

230 top *General Robert Napier commanded the British expedition that landed in Abyssinia to restore British honor and obtain the release of the European diplomats imprisoned by Tewodros.*

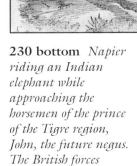

230 center *Napier was efficiently backed up by Major General Staveley, who was entrusted with the most important aspect of an African campaign: logistics.*

230 bottom *Napier riding an Indian elephant while approaching the horsemen of the prince of the Tigre region, John, the future negus. The British forces* *encountered few problems on their march toward Magdala, partly because they were able to recruit the support of many of the Abyssinian rases, who* *recognized an opportunity to depose Tewodros who had attempted to curtail their feudal power.*

230-231 *The British infantry engaging Tewodros's army on the Arroge plain near Magdala.*

231 bottom *A discussion between General Robert Napier and Prince John, in the presence of dignitaries and officers.*

on October 21, 1867, and immediately began transforming the makeshift landing place into a port with two jetties.

In April a road heading inland was constructed and was flanked by a Decauville railway—one hundred kilometers of track from the sea to Senafe on the plateau. Zulla, in the meantime, was invaded by the remaining troops, 50,000 pack animals were acquired in markets throughout the Levant and the Mediterranean, and 40 Indian elephants were trained to carry artillery pieces in the mountains. At last, on January 3, 1868, the commander in chief disembarked, and the following month the army began its slow march inland over incredibly difficult terrain. Slow progress was made, partly because the road was being built as they went along and also to acclimatize the men. In the meantime treaties were established with rebel Ethiopian chiefs, who were showered with generous quantities of silver talers.

Meanwhile, the negus, who perhaps in the past would have hurled himself upon the British forces, tormenting them with his masterful guerrilla tactics, sat and waited on the amba of Magdala in a mood of dark resignation. He knew that he had by now lost the support of the Ethiopian population, having tried their patience once too often, and that his empire had been reduced to that one fortress. He was counting on its impregnability, the only card he had left to play, but as he said to

Sciascio, they found the route barred by a sheer basalt wall. The indomitable Tewodros had a passage cut through the rock and hoisted the cannons and carts up to the plateau where they could finally find food. Having at last negotiated the last of the rivers flowing between 2,000-foot-high cliffs, the horde camped near the fort of Magdala, celebrating their arrival around a hundred human torches.

Britain had entrusted the organization and command of the difficult expedition to one of its best officers, General Robert Cornelius Napier, who had been born in Ceylon and spent his life in India. An engineer, Napier had built roads and bridges and had fought in the Sikh Wars in 1857 and in a subsequent campaign in China. He had 4,000 British and 8,000 Indian troops at his disposal as well as no fewer than 26,000 auxiliaries, as this was not so much a military campaign as an exercise in logistics. Zulla, in Somalia, to the south of Jibuti, was chosen as the place where the expeditionary force would disembark. The first brigade came ashore

Rassam, he would "allow the will of God to be done."

Two months after their departure, the leading British troops, reduced to half their original number by disease and the climate, came within two days' march of the fortified hilltop. On April 3, Napier sent a letter ordering the negus to free the prisoners. Tewodros did not reply but recognized that the end was near. On April 7, in his dress uniform, he freed his 175 servants and had his Abyssinian prisoners assembled, the enemies he had dragged with him to the Magdala amba. To mark his own death, he sentenced the most hardened and dangerous of them to be burned alive on the day the fortress fell, and he ordered the others to be thrown from the walls of the fortress. Two monks who had approached "to watch" were also pushed over the edge of the precipice—"so they can see better,"

commented the caustic Tewodros. At dawn on April 10 the British troops began to climb the low Arroge plateau from which the amba rose. The cannons of the negus had them within their sights, but the largest, which carried his name, burst: an omen. "God is telling me my reign is over," said the sovereign.

In the afternoon the Abyssinian warriors fell like an avalanche against the attackers advancing slowly through the rocky cliffs. It was a grave error: the British forces, well entrenched behind the rocks, slaughtered them, thanks to their superior firepower. Three hours later a thousand Ethiopians lay dead and as many were wounded. The British counted two dead and eighteen wounded and the following morning continued their advance, moved up their mountain batteries, and began to bombard the amba. When Tewodros sent an envoy to inquire as to the conditions for peace,

Napier demanded surrender and the release of the hostages. The negus, who above all else valued his dignity, decided to take his own life, but his followers grabbed the pistol from his mouth. Blood for blood, demanded his lieutenants, who suggested that he execute all the European hostages. However, his wife, Tauabac, persuaded him to spare them and set them free. On April 12 they were sent to the British camp with a gift of livestock and a letter.

The inflexible Napier refused both and the following day moved his artillery still closer to the fortress. Tewodros withdrew to the summit of the amba with his last surviving followers, who fell one by one under the British fire. The negus embraced the few left alive, dismissed them, and shot himself in the head. His corpse, wrapped in silk and gold brocade sheets, was buried in the church of the

Savior of the World at the top of the hill.

The fortifications having been destroyed and the imperial treasure that Tewodros had accumulated by despoiling the churches and monasteries having been seized, Napier decided to return hurriedly to the coast. Now that the hated emperor was dead, the Ethiopian chiefs whom the British forces had previously bribed did nothing to conceal their distrust. Fearing that the victors intended to remain in Ethiopia, they called their men to arms. Covering the 400 miles from Magdala to Zulla while fighting against tens of thousands of Abyssinians would have been impossible. Distributing gifts, which the hostile rases ostentatiously refused, the expeditionary force departed on June 18 and embarked for India. Napier was already on his way to England where he was to receive an ecstatic welcome, promotion, and a barony.

233 top right
Following the death of the negus, his widow also killed herself; her funeral is shown in this plate.

233 center right
The prisoners were at last released and headed to the British camp with a tumultuous retinue of servants.

233 bottom right
On his return home Napier was given a hero's welcome at Dover.

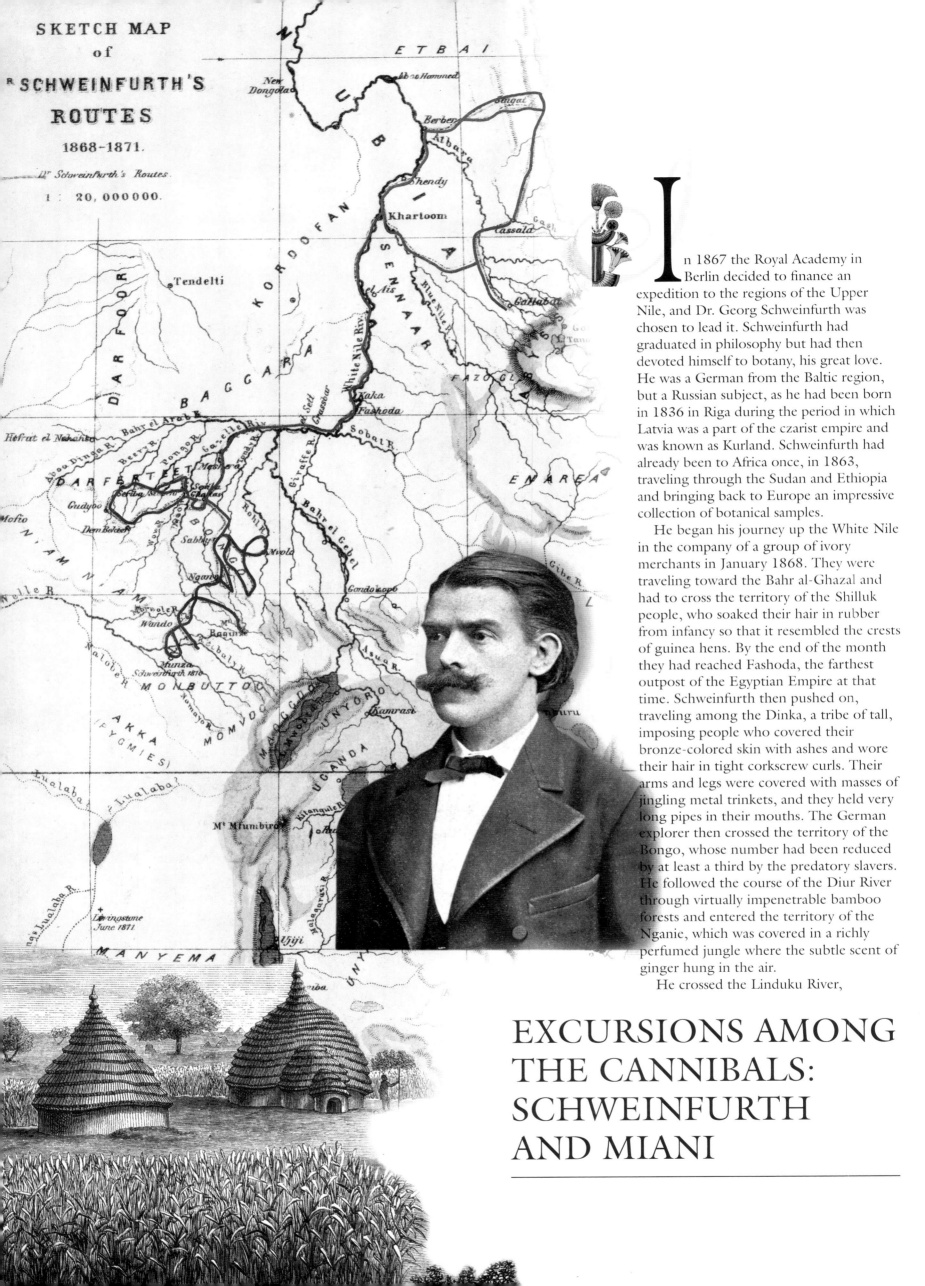

SKETCH MAP
of
Dʀ SCHWEINFURTH'S
ROUTES
1868-1871.

Dr Schweinfurth's Routes.

1 : 20,000000.

In 1867 the Royal Academy in Berlin decided to finance an expedition to the regions of the Upper Nile, and Dr. Georg Schweinfurth was chosen to lead it. Schweinfurth had graduated in philosophy but had then devoted himself to botany, his great love. He was a German from the Baltic region, but a Russian subject, as he had been born in 1836 in Riga during the period in which Latvia was a part of the czarist empire and was known as Kurland. Schweinfurth had already been to Africa once, in 1863, traveling through the Sudan and Ethiopia and bringing back to Europe an impressive collection of botanical samples.

He began his journey up the White Nile in the company of a group of ivory merchants in January 1868. They were traveling toward the Bahr al-Ghazal and had to cross the territory of the Shilluk people, who soaked their hair in rubber from infancy so that it resembled the crests of guinea hens. By the end of the month they had reached Fashoda, the farthest outpost of the Egyptian Empire at that time. Schweinfurth then pushed on, traveling among the Dinka, a tribe of tall, imposing people who covered their bronze-colored skin with ashes and wore their hair in tight corkscrew curls. Their arms and legs were covered with masses of jingling metal trinkets, and they held very long pipes in their mouths. The German explorer then crossed the territory of the Bongo, whose number had been reduced by at least a third by the predatory slavers. He followed the course of the Diur River through virtually impenetrable bamboo forests and entered the territory of the Nganie, which was covered in a richly perfumed jungle where the subtle scent of ginger hung in the air.

He crossed the Linduku River,

EXCURSIONS AMONG THE CANNIBALS: SCHWEINFURTH AND MIANI

235 top
Schweinfurth joined a party of Sudanese ivory traders whose flotilla we can see here. The ships are flying the Egyptian flag while anchored in a bight of the White Nile known as Port Rek.
(G. Schweinfurth, *The Heart of Africa*, London, 1873)

235 center *The boat on which the explorer embarked was chased by a host of canoes manned by the Shilluk people, one of the most bellicose tribes of the Bahr al-Ghazal.*
(G. Schweinfurth, *The Heart of Africa*)

235 bottom *The Dinka people were great livestock farmers; here we see a group of them camped with a large herd of long-horned oxen.*
(G. Schweinfurth, *The Heart of Africa*)

234 top *This map shows the routes followed by Schweinfurth over four years, from 1868 to 1871.*
(Georg Schweinfurth, *The Heart of Africa*)

234 center *A Russian subject but of German nationality, the botanist Georg Schweinfurth was commissioned to explore the Bahr al-Ghazal region by the Royal Academy of Science in Berlin.*
(*The Nile Quest*, London, 1903)

234 bottom *The first wild region into which Schweinfurth ventured was inhabited by the Dinka tribe. This engraving depicts their large huts topped with spired roofs.*
(G. Schweinfurth, *The Heart of Africa*)

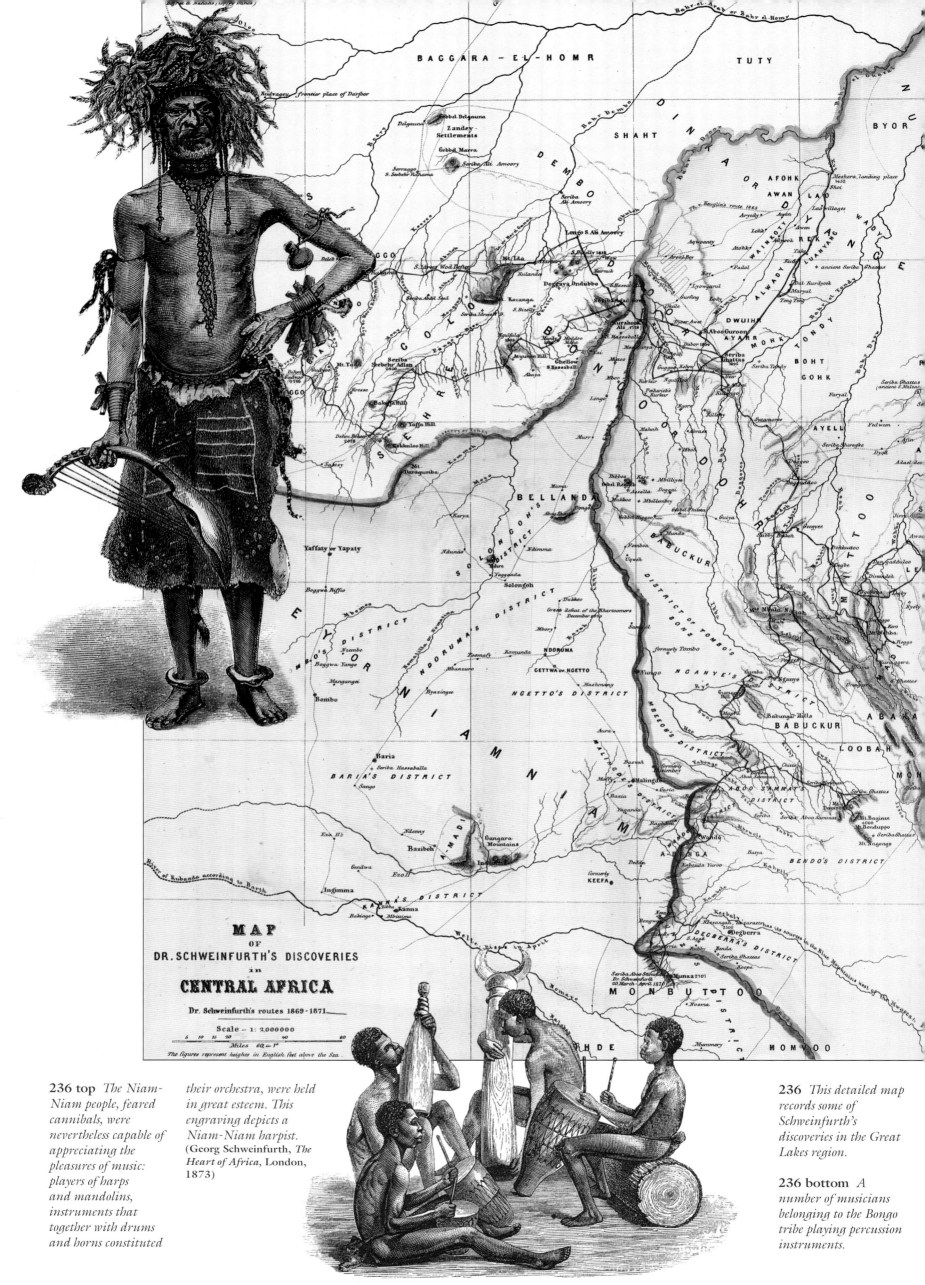

MAP
OF
DR. SCHWEINFURTH'S DISCOVERIES
in
CENTRAL AFRICA

Dr. Schweinfurth's routes 1869-1871 _____

Scale - 1: 2,000000

Miles 60 = 1°

The figures represent heights in English feet above the Sea.

236 top *The Niam-Niam people, feared cannibals, were nevertheless capable of appreciating the pleasures of music: players of harps and mandolins, instruments that together with drums and horns constituted their orchestra, were held in great esteem. This engraving depicts a Niam-Niam harpist. (Georg Schweinfurth,* The Heart of Africa, *London, 1873)*

236 *This detailed map records some of Schweinfurth's discoveries in the Great Lakes region.*

236 bottom *A number of musicians belonging to the Bongo tribe playing percussion instruments.*

becoming the first European to cross the watershed between the Congolese and Nilotic basins from the north. Here he found himself in that botanical paradise that Piaggia had imaginatively called the "gallery-forests." Like Piaggia, Schweinfurth wanted to visit the land of the "great man-eaters," the Niam-Niam, whose true name was Zande. He entered their territory at the end of January 1869 and was welcomed by the cannibal tribe, who filed their teeth to points, arranged their hair in spirals or crests, dressed in civet skins, and were armed with spears and scimitars. Although they were ferocious warriors, they loved music and were enchanted by harp and mandolin concerts. The roads and huts of their villages were decorated with great numbers of human skulls and bones, and pieces of meat hung from the timber frames.

South of the Niam-Niam territory was the home of the Mangbetu, who were also cannibals. On March 19 the explorer crossed the Uele, which he mistakenly thought belonged to the Lake Chad rather than the Congo Basin. Three days later he was received at the court of King Munza in a huge hall 150 feet long and 50 feet high. A trumpet fanfare was followed by a solo played on an ivory horn. The king's hair was gathered into a cap surmounted by three rows of parrot feathers, and on his forehead was a half-moon made of copper. He beat time to the music with a basketful of pebbles.

Munza had never seen a European before and was amazed by Schweinfurth's weapons, his matches, and, above all, his boots, which he thought were an integral part of the visitor's body, rather like the hooves of a horse. The white man was no less impressed by the sovereign's appearance, especially his metal ornaments, which he ironically compared to saucepans: "He was a man of about thirty years of age, of a fair height, of a slim but powerful build, and, like the rest of his countrymen, stiff and erect in figure. Although belonging to a type by no means uncomely, his features were far from prepossessing, but had a Nero-like expression that told of ennui and

237 top *The vigorous Munza, king of the Mangbetu people, struck Schweinfurth with his appearance and especially his cruel expression. This engraving portrays him on his throne, holding a rather elaborate hook that serves as a scepter. He is wearing a* complicated ceremonial headdress. (Georg Schweinfurth, *The Heart of Africa*, London, 1873)

237 bottom *In this plate King Munza is dancing for his wives, sitting around the walls of a very large vaulted hut.*

237

(G. Schweinfurth, *The Heart of Africa*)

238 top *This illustration shows the unusual plaited hairstyle of a young Niam-Niam girl.* (Georg Schweinfurth, *The Heart of Africa*, London, 1873)

239 top *A village near the sources of the Diur River, which were Schweinfurth's most important discoveries.*

239 bottom left *In the course of his journey Schweinfurth came across the fabled Pygmies, the Akka people, one of whom named Bomby, portrayed here, was persuaded to accompany the explorer to Europe. Having reached the Sudan, however, Bomby fell ill and died.*

238-239 *A view of the Kibali River with three natives in the foreground launching a very long dugout canoe. The complicated hydrography of the Nilotic region around the Bahr al-Ghazal, with its numerous affluents, was carefully studied by Schweinfurth, whose scientific mind set him apart from his predecessors, who were adventurers rather than academics.*

238 bottom *King Munza's almost Arcadian residence. The sovereign, seated on a stone near the conical hut on the far right, is being attended to by a valet.*

satiety. . . . Around his mouth lurked an expression that I never saw in any other Mangbetu, a combination of avarice, violence, and love of cruelty."

Schweinfurth stayed with the Mangbetu for about five weeks, and there he was the first to discover the Akha Pygmies. He announced his intention to visit their country, which was about four days' journey from Munza's capital, but the king forbade him to go. Schweinfurth then persuaded one of the small men to accompany him to Europe but unfortunately the Pygmy died on the journey at Berber.

In May 1870, having taken up his journey to Sudan again, Schweinfurth found the source of the Diur, a major tributary of the White Nile. After enjoying triumphant receptions in Europe, Schweinfurth returned to Egypt in 1872 to found and become the first president of the Khedivial Geographical Society in Cairo at the request of the viceroy Ismail.

Niam-Niam warriors with elegantly decorated shields featuring geometric motifs, and the unusual female hairstyles of the same tribe.

(Georg Schweinfurth, *The Heart of Africa*)

In 1888 he settled in Germany where he lived to a great age and died in 1925.

Giovanni Miani, whose early explorations we have already mentioned, had returned to Egypt to organize an expedition to look for the source of the Nile refuting Speke and Grant's claims. However, on hearing of Baker's feats he had given up the idea and had accepted the viceroy Ismail's nomination as director of the Zoological Gardens in Khartoum in 1869. While there he heard of Schweinfurth's discoveries and was gripped by the desire to depart and out-do the German explorer by pushing on beyond the latitude reached by Schweinfurth in the direction of the equator.

He was unable to obtain sufficient funds from the Egyptian government, however, so he turned to the Ghattas trading company in Khartoum, which was about to send an expedition in search of ivory in the regions he wanted to visit. The company offered him support and protection.

240 top left
Having been appointed director of the zoo at Khartoum, Giovanni Miani, portrayed here a few years before his death, heard of the discoveries of Schweinfurth, a good friend of his, and was bitten by the exploring bug.
(Georg Schweinfurth, *The Heart of Africa*, London, 1873)

240 top right *Even though Miani was over sixty years old, he wanted to depart for Bahr al-Ghazal. He too joined an ivory-trading caravan of which here we can see the zareba, or permanent camp.*
(Georg Schweinfurth, *The Heart of Africa*, London, 1873)

240-241 *The expedition's boats navigating the marshes of the Nile, dangerous obstacles to navigation which were infested with malaria-carrying insects.*

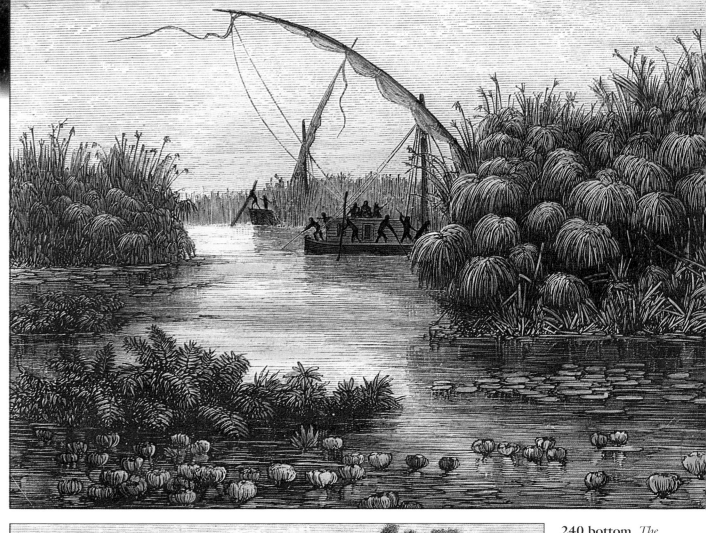

240 bottom *The expedition's porters crossing a liana bridge slung across the Tondy River by the natives.*

Miani left with the expedition on March 15, 1871, traveling up the White Nile toward the Bahr al-Ghazal. The explorer was sixty-one years of age and was already weak and infirm; the worst of his afflictions was the incurable *mal d'Afrique*. The journey, of course, proceeded according to the requirements of the traders, with prolonged stops sometimes lasting months to buy up stocks of ivory, and secure provisions and supplies for the caravan, which was composed of five hundred armed men and the slaves who were acquired along the way. Miani took advantage of these pauses in the journey to make excursions to the sources of the smaller tributaries and to collect skulls and craft work.

Gradually, however, the caravan proceeded south, following a wide curve in the basin of the right-bank tributaries of the Bahr al-Ghazal until, having crossed the watershed, the waters began to flow in the opposite direction. Miani was old and tired by now and was no longer the White Lion, as the natives had called him during his first African venture. He was also unlucky: his mule drowned and he had to ride a bull, a fire destroyed many of his papers and collections, and fevers tormented him more than ever. He eventually found some respite in the territory of the Mangbetu, which had recently been visited by Schweinfurth. Munza received him hospitably and he was able to rest in the king's huts. Miani too encountered the Akhas and

attempted, without success, to take one home with him.

On May 25, 1872, Miani left with part of the Ghattas caravan to go westward to follow the course of the Uele. They entered the territory of the Niam-Niam tribe, where the forest was so thick that they had to cut their way through with hatchets. The only way through was on foot and by now Miani was very weak.

He picked up some strength after a long halt in a village inhabited by the Bacangoi and managed to make some excursions along the right bank of the Uele, collecting seeds, plants, skulls, and other objects. He then turned back and reentered the capital of King Munza in October. Here he had the joy of receiving a letter from Schweinfurth.

241 right *Miani also reached the territories of the Mangbetu and Niam-Niam peoples; but subsequently, having returned to the court of King Munza, he died of exhaustion. The bellicose Mangbetu people, two of whom are depicted in this engraving armed with lances and bows and arrows, honored him with great funerary tributes.*

241 bottom *During his exploration Miani followed the meandering course of the Tondy River, depicted in this engraving.*

(Georg Schweinfurth, *The Heart of Africa*)

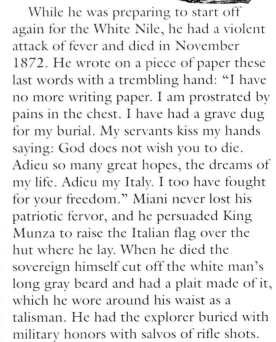

While he was preparing to start off again for the White Nile, he had a violent attack of fever and died in November 1872. He wrote on a piece of paper these last words with a trembling hand: "I have no more writing paper. I am prostrated by pains in the chest. I have had a grave dug for my burial. My servants kiss my hands saying: God does not wish you to die. Adieu so many great hopes, the dreams of my life. Adieu my Italy. I too have fought for your freedom." Miani never lost his patriotic fervor, and he persuaded King Munza to raise the Italian flag over the hut where he lay. When he died the sovereign himself cut off the white man's long gray beard and had a plait made of it, which he wore around his waist as a talisman. He had the explorer buried with military honors with salvos of rifle shots.

242 top *To ensure a successful outcome to his mission, Baker was impressively equipped and benefited from* steamboats, which were carried in sections by camels across the desert.

242 center *The Suez Canal was inaugurated in 1861, and Egypt began to see itself as a great civilizing power.*

Since 1863 the khedive, or viceroy Ismail reigned over Egypt and its territories in the Sudan. At the beginning of his reign Egypt went through a very favorable economic phase because the American Civil War had sent the price of cotton soaring and the Egyptian crop brought in five times its previous figure. Ismail, a determined advocate of modernization, took advantage of the economic situation to start an imposing program of public works that ranged from slum rebuilding in Cairo to new railways, telegraph networks, and irrigation canals. It was an ambitious investment policy that attracted swarms of businessmen, both honest and dishonest, and soon brought the kingdom to bankruptcy—partly because Ismail was even more lavish in his

ISMAILIA: BAKER CONQUERS EQUATORIA

242 bottom *Having returned to Egypt as an interpreter in the retinue of the Prince of Wales, Samuel Baker was commissioned by* the khedive Ismail to lead an expedition to conquer and annex for Egypt the Central African region of Equatoria, surrounding the *upper course of the White Nile.* (Samuel Baker, *Ismailia: A Narrative of the Expedition to Central Africa for the Suppression of the Slave Trade,* London, 1874)

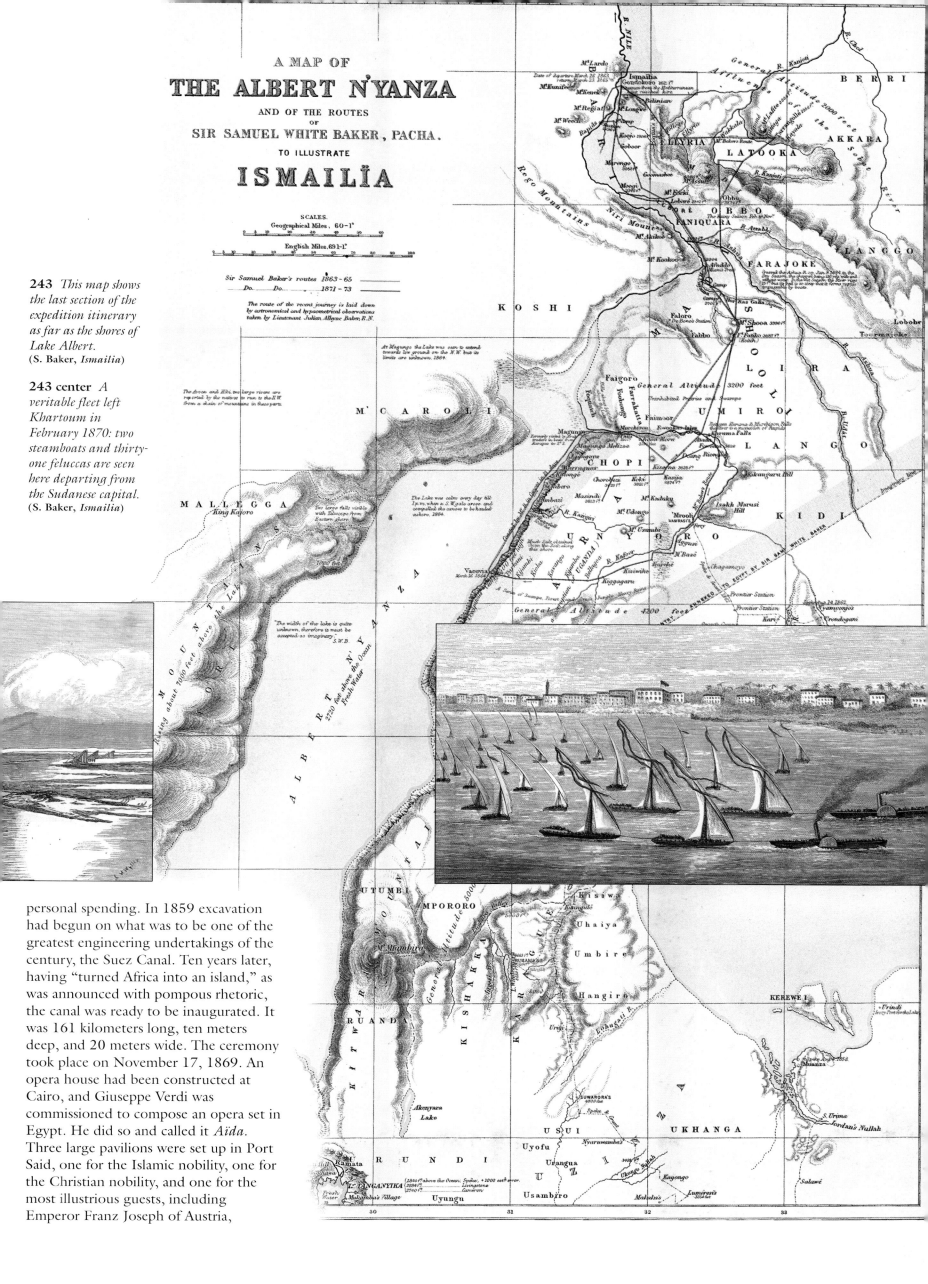

A MAP OF
THE ALBERT N'YANZA
AND OF THE ROUTES
OF
SIR SAMUEL WHITE BAKER, PACHA.
TO ILLUSTRATE
ISMAILIA

SCALES.
Geographical Miles, 60-1°
English Miles, 69 1-1°

Sir Samuel Baker's routes 1863-65
Do. Do. 1871-73

The route of the recent journey is laid down
by astronomical and hypsometrical observations
taken by Lieutenant Julian Alleyne Baker, R.N.

243 *This map shows
the last section of the
expedition itinerary
as far as the shores of
Lake Albert.*
(S. Baker, *Ismailia*)

243 center *A
veritable fleet left
Khartoum in
February 1870: two
steamboats and thirty-
one feluccas are seen
here departing from
the Sudanese capital.*
(S. Baker, *Ismailia*)

personal spending. In 1859 excavation
had begun on what was to be one of the
greatest engineering undertakings of the
century, the Suez Canal. Ten years later,
having "turned Africa into an island," as
was announced with pompous rhetoric,
the canal was ready to be inaugurated. It
was 161 kilometers long, ten meters
deep, and 20 meters wide. The ceremony
took place on November 17, 1869. An
opera house had been constructed at
Cairo, and Giuseppe Verdi was
commissioned to compose an opera set in
Egypt. He did so and called it *Aïda*.
Three large pavilions were set up in Port
Said, one for the Islamic nobility, one for
the Christian nobility, and one for the
most illustrious guests, including
Emperor Franz Joseph of Austria,

Empress Eugénie of France, Russian grand dukes, and sovereigns of the small German principalities.

On the morning of the great day priests and ministers of every faith blessed the waters, flags fluttered, cannons thundered, bands played military marches, and a fleet of sailing vessels and steamships set out from Port Said to meet another such fleet coming from Suez. They met at the newly founded city of Ismailia. That evening, after the banquet, there were interminable fireworks displays and a ball was held in the light of ten thousand lanterns. The only guests missing were the British royal family; Great Britain had opposed the construction of the canal, as it was a French enterprise, and chose to show its opposition by snubbing the inauguration. Some months previously, however, the Prince of Wales, Victoria's heir, had made

244 bottom left *Samuel Baker in his eye-catching Egyptian uniform constellated with decorations.* (S. Baker, *Ismailia,* London, 1874)

244 top *Baker formed a bodyguard of sharpshooters ironically nicknamed the Forty Thieves: among the troops recruited by the Egyptian government for the enterprise there were in fact numerous former convicts.*

244 center *Baker's flotilla was trapped for no less than seven months in the Sudd swamps where masses of floating vegetation prevented the boats' passage. This plate shows a* Baleniceps rex *in the reed beds near the stranded boats.*

a journey along the Nile with his wife, Princess Alexandra.

Samuel Baker had traveled in the prince's retinue as an interpreter. During a masked ball at Cairo he had met with Ismail, who made him a handsome proposal. The khedive had issued a decree abolishing the slave trade in the Sudan several years earlier, but it had been ignored. Now, to win the favor of the European powers, he was determined to abolish slavery altogether. The only way to do so was to put under effective Egyptian control the regions from which human beings were being

exported throughout the Islamic world. The number of slaves reached 40,000 to 50,000 a year, not counting those who died on the journey. In the name of progress and civilization, Ismail intended to extend the Egyptian Empire as far as the equator and Abyssinia. In return for his anti-slavery policy, he would obtain from Europe the credit and financial support necessary for his modernization program. He offered Baker the title of pasha, the rank of general, the sum of £40,000 for four years, an army of 1,700 men, and carte blanche in the choice of equipment and staff.

245 top *The smaller boats in Baker's flotilla were frequently attacked and reduced to matchsticks by hippopotamuses.*

245 bottom *The navigability of the river was a real problem. This illustration shows a vain attempt to free one of the steamboats by having it dragged through the swamp grasses. Baker was finally obliged to block the river with a rudimentary dam to raise the level of the water and allow his boats to float free.*

(S. Baker, *Ismailia*)

Baker accepted and began to organize the expedition corps, which was composed of two regiments, one of Sudanese and the other of Egyptians, most of whom, he discovered when it was too late, were erstwhile prisoners. There were also two artillery batteries, one cavalry squadron, and a bodyguard composed of forty snipers, whom he nicknamed the Forty Thieves. He chose ten Europeans as his closest collaborators, one of whom was his nephew Julian, a navy lieutenant; there were also two engineers, a doctor, a storekeeper, and five carpenters. The expedition was equipped with sheet zinc huts, designed to be dismantled, and a fleet of boats, the largest of which was a paddle steamer over thirty meters long. These vessels had to be dismantled into manageable sections, transported by camel, and then reassembled when the expedition passed the cataracts. As Baker himself said, nothing was lacking, "from needles to iron levers, from handkerchiefs to sails." Ninety steamboats and fifty-five sailing vessels were required to carry all the men, beasts, and materials that in February 1870 inundated—as may well be said—the sandy plain around Khartoum with bales, crates, tents, and quadrupeds, after having overcome obstacles of all kinds, including the traditional Egyptian slothfulness and the none too subtle sabotage attempts of those in whose interests it was to keep the slave trade alive.

Khartoum, the capital of the slave trade, observed this invasion with hostility and fear. The city was in the hands of Egyptian functionaries, the dregs of a corrupt and inefficient state who had been exiled there in punishment, all of them ready to do anything for gain. These people had so despoiled the local inhabitants that nearly half of them had departed. The natives living along the banks of the river had given up cultivating the land because their harvests were inevitably confiscated by the Egyptian tax gatherers. Everyone was involved in the slave trade, even though it had been officially abolished. At least 15,000 Arabs were slave traders, some of whom ruled over thousands of square kilometers of territory like feudal lords.

The khedive had given full power to Baker, but he could act only after he reached the Upper Nile regions, not while he was in Khartoum. He therefore left the hostile city, accompanied by the curses of the slavers, and began to ascend the White Nile with a thousand armed men and his ever-faithful wife.

The Englishman's forces should have

been sufficient to earn the respect of any enemy, but Baker had not foreseen the natural difficulties that were to block his passage for many months. When his boats reached the Sudd swamps, he discovered that there were no open channels. The immense river was no longer navigable, as it had been transformed into an interminable mass of vegetation. The soldiers, up to their waists in the water, attempted to open the passage with bill-hooks, but their efforts were fruitless. After two months of struggle they had managed to advance only a few miles while the level of the water continued to fall, as it was the dry season.

Sadly but wisely the commander decided to turn back and wait near Malakal for the periodic flood that was due at the end of the year. He stayed there for seven months, making good use of the time by pursuing the boats carrying slaves to Khartoum. Then, early in December, the floods arrived, and they set off again, 1,600 men and women in 59 boats. They started on another odyssey, with the soldiers cutting down the reeds and pulling the boats through the swamps with ropes. Many died of fever and sunstroke. There was no land in sight, only reedbeds and masses of floating vegetation as far as the eye could see.

They were still bogged down at the beginning of March 1871, and Baker was

beginning to lose hope of ever getting out of that trap as the water began to subside again. He decided to make one last attempt and pushed on ahead in a dinghy. To his enormous relief he found that the water ran free at the confluence of the Bahr al-Jebel and Bahr al-Zaraf. He ordered his carpenters to construct a sort of dam behind the boats to raise the level of the water. The soldiers were ordered to fill sacks with sand and prepare bundles of canes. After a few days when all was ready, Baker's unprecedented scheme to dam the Nile

waters was put to the test. This is how he described the event:

"I stood on one of the stranded boats only a few yards from the row of piles. The men were all in their places. The buglers and drummers stood upon another vessel ready to give the signal. At the first bugle, every two men lifted the sacks of sand and clay. At once all the drums and bugles then sounded the advance, and 500 heavy sacks were dropped into the row of piles, and firmly stamped down by the men. The troops now worked with intense energy. It was a

race between the Sudanis and the Egyptians; this was a work to which the latter were accustomed in their own country. The sailors worked as vigorously as the troops; piles of fascines and clay balls were laid with extraordinary rapidity, while some stamped frantically and danced upon the entangled mass, all screaming and shouting in great excitement, and the bugles and drums kept up an incessant din. A long double line of men formed a transport corps, and passed a never-failing supply of fascines to the workers who stood in the water and kneaded firmly the adhesive mass. At 2:15 P.M. the river was completely shut in, and the people with increased energy worked at the superstructure of the dam, which now rose like a causeway for about 110 yards from shore to shore. At 3:30 the water had risen to an extent that obliged the men in some places to swim. The steamer that had been hopelessly stranded, and the entire fleet, were floating merrily in the pond."

Thus was the expedition finally able to proceed. A month later it reached the ruins of the Austrian mission at Gondokoro, which had been abandoned for years. Baker ordered the boats to be unloaded and a fort to be built together with a village of huts. He had the land plowed and sown with wheat and vegetables. When this distant outpost had

246 left *Having finally reached open water, Baker could once again proceed upstream, and the steamboats majestically ascended the river as far as Gondokoro, where Austrian missionaries had established a subsequently abandoned village.* (Samuel Baker, *Ismailia*, London, 1874)

246-247 *Baker constructed fortifications around his camp, and on May 26, 1871, he proclaimed the annexation of the new province of Equatoria on behalf of Egypt.*

246 bottom *This engraving depicts the flag-raising ceremony at Gondokoro, subsequently rebaptized Ismailia in honor of the khedive Ismail.*

247 top *At Ismailia Baker accepted the submission of numerous tribes of the area; in this illustration he is ordering the liberation of slaves. In the foreground one of Baker's officers is removing a slave's shackles.*

(S. Baker, *Ismailia*)

248 top left *Baker organized a number of expeditions from Gondokoro-Ismailia to all parts of the surrounding territory in search of slavers. He then headed into Unyoro, where the king, Kabba Rega, welcomed him into his capital, Masindi, feigning submission. He then tried to kill the explorer by sending him poisoned wine, but fortunately Baker did not drink it. The Englishman*

organized his defenses and massacred the natives. In this illustration Kabba Rega has granted Baker a hearing. (Samuel Baker, *Ismailia*, London, 1874)

248 top right *Flames rise from the huts during the destruction of Masindi ordered by Baker.*

248 bottom *The Egyptian army marching across the fertile Mongi Valley.*

finally acquired an almost civilized appearance, he decided to mark the conquest officially with a solemn ceremony on May 26th, 1871. He drew up his 1,200 men who for the occasion had washed their uniforms—or what remained of them. The Egyptian flag was raised to the top of a 25-meter pole to the accompaniment of blaring trumpets. Baker proclaimed the region a province of Egypt and named it Equatoria, or Hatalastiva in Arabian. He declared the capital of the region to be Gondokoro, renamed Ismailia in honor of the khedive who had sent them there. That evening the officers dined on roast meat and an incongruous Christmas pudding and drank toasts with glasses of rum.

Despite having been proclaimed with

such solemnity, the khedive's sovereignty over that remote area was still rather theoretical. In the first place they were cut off from the rest of the country. The Nile was still obstructed, and the new subjects of Egypt, who still did not know they were such, seemed none too pleased at being annexed by a civilized country, partly because all the "Turks" they had come across till then had been slave traders or raiders. The local Bari people frequently assaulted the palisade around the new town of Ismailia, shooting poisoned arrows and receiving volleys of rifle shots in return. To procure food and cattle for themselves the liberators had to plunder the very people they had "liberated." On returning from one of these outings, Baker discovered that a thousand of his men had had enough and had fled downstream, taking thirty boats with them.

Fortunately the Forty Thieves resisted all the instigations to mutiny to which the desperate slavers now made recourse. Together with the Sudanese soldiers, Baker's bodyguard formed a nucleus of faithful followers on whom he could always count. He therefore left a garrison at Ismailia and took two hundred men plus porters to Fatiko where the slave traders submitted to him and obeyed his orders to return to Khartoum. Baker then penetrated Bunyoro, the kingdom of Kamrasi, whom he had visited in 1864.

Kamrasi was dead and his son Kabba Rega now reigned in the capital Masindi following a war of succession that had enriched the slave trade immensely, as the pretenders exchanged their enemies for weapons and ammunition.

Baker entered Masindi with the arrogance of a conqueror and immediately arrested twenty-two slavers, but Kabba Rega made a formal act of submission to Egyptian sovereignty by allowing the red flag with the half-moon to be raised in his city. In reality he had realized that if he wanted to remain king of Bunyoro he would have to get rid of the white man, so

he plotted an astute scheme, which failed only by chance. On June 17, 1872, the king graciously sent to the Egyptians a present of seven large earthenware jars of palm wine. The grateful troops drank the wine, and a few minutes later forty of them were writhing on the ground in agony. Baker and the other officers, who had fortunately not touched the poisoned wine, gave emetics to the intoxicated soldiers and prepared to face Kabba Rega's warriors.

The attack came the following morning. The Egyptians' discipline got the better of the natives, who were routed despite their furious attacks. Masindi was burned down, and its eight thousand inhabitants fled to the forest. But although Baker had won the battle, he risked being trapped in a

hostile country without guides or supplies. He decided the only way out was to make a rapid withdrawal. He destroyed the newly built governor's residence—which was no more than a reed hut with portraits of Queen Victoria, hunting prints, and fashion plates pinned to the walls—and then commenced a week-long march through the jungle, tormented by snipers hidden among the trees and high grass, who picked off his men with rifles and poisoned arrows.

When he reached the Victoria Nile, Baker made an alliance with the chief of the Rionga tribe, an enemy of Kabba Rega, beguiling him with the idea that he might become king of Bunyoro in place of the would-be poisoner. Baker had a fort built on a nearby island and left sixty men

249 top *Abandoning the ruins of Masindi, Baker withdrew toward the Nile, in continuous combat with the natives who tried to ambush him, and seeking out alliances with the enemies of Kabba Rega, here portrayed with his retinue of courtiers.*

249 bottom *Baker admiring the course of the Victoria Nile beyond the last cataract. On the far bank gleam the white tents of his troops, neatly arranged in three camps.*

249

(S. Baker, *Ismailia*)

in charge of it. He then hastened to Fatiko in search of reinforcements. However, the country was in turmoil because word had been spread that the white man was dead and the slave hunters had happily resumed their raids again, even hoping to make up for the lost trade. Baker returned just in time to engage in a battle with the arrogant slavers and defeat them with a bayonet assault. One of their leaders, Mohammed Uat-el-Mek, surrendered and swore allegiance to Baker with his hand on the Koran. He then helped recruit soldiers from among the prisoners. After news of the battle had spread throughout the country, other raiders either surrendered or withdrew, and the Englishman and his recruits could devote their attention to Kabba Rega who, having been abandoned by most of his followers, fled to Lake Albert.

Between August 1872 and March 1873 Baker camped at Fatiko and concentrated on reorganizing the kingdom he had conquered, only half of which had been explored. He was rather satisfied with himself and wrote: "In the end, every opposition was overcome: hatred and insubordination yielded to discipline and order. A paternal government extended its protection through lands hitherto a field for anarchy and slavery. The territory within my rule was purged from the slave trade. The natives of the great Shooli tribe, relieved from their oppressors, clung to the protecting government. The White Nile, for a distance of 1,600 miles from Khartoum to Central Africa, was cleansed from the abomination of a traffic which had hitherto sullied its waters. Every cloud had passed away, and the term of my office expired in peace and sunshine. In this result, I humbly traced God's blessing."

This was at least partly an illusion: the slave trade had been hampered and disrupted but not destroyed. It resumed cautiously at first, then with increasing audacity, thanks to the same old Egyptian functionaries at Khartoum and the new stations established in Equatoria. Egypt's reputation abroad was saved, however, and the khedive could hold his head high when he asked the Europeans for the loans that were to bring his country to ruin.

Leaving Fatiko with a garrison commanded by an Egyptian officer, Baker and his wife descended the Nile to Cairo in August 1873. Even the lavish Ismail was rather dismayed when he was presented with the bill for the expedition—half a million piastres—but he paid the £40,000 he owed to the civilizer of Equatoria without batting an eyelash.

250 top *Having reached Fatiko, Baker continued to fight the slavers and managed to force the surrender of one of their leaders, Mohammed Uat-el-Mec, whom we see here shaking Baker's hand in a sign of peace.* (Samuel Baker, *Ismailia*, London, 1874)

250 center *Baker left Unyoro and tried to rejoin the larger part of his forces at Fatiko, seen here in a drawing by the explorer himself.*

250 bottom *Egyptian soldiers repelling an attack by natives who, during the night, had set fire to the camp.*

250-251 *Baker heads with a flotilla of canoes toward the island of Rionga, where he hopes to establish a pact with the ruler, an enemy of Kabba Rega. For almost a year Baker scoured the region attempting to eliminate as many slavers as he could until he was finally able to delude himself that he had established "the protection of a paternal government." His victory would prove to be ephemeral, however.*

251 bottom left
*Samuel Baker leading
an attack by the
Egyptian troops
against a slavers'
camp during the final
phase of the
campaign.*

251 bottom right
*One of Baker's
detachments was cut
off and then
massacred in a
surprise attack by a
Bari tribe.*

251

(S. Baker, *Ismailia*)

A similarly strong character was required as a worthy replacement for Baker. It was Nubar Pasha, an intelligent Armenian minister of the khedive and perhaps the only true Egyptian statesman of his era, who thought of a British officer he had met at Constantinople and who had provided irrefutable evidence of his abilities in the Crimea and, above all, in China.

Charles George Gordon, born at Woolwich on January 28, 1833, had in fact earned the nickname "Chinese Gordon" while fighting in the Celestial Empire against the Taiping rebels threatening to overthrow the Manchu dynasty. Captain Gordon had arrived in China in September 1860, "too late to

252 top *Arab slavers in a drawing showing the typical vegetation of southern Sudan.*

252 center *A panoramic view of Khautoum.*

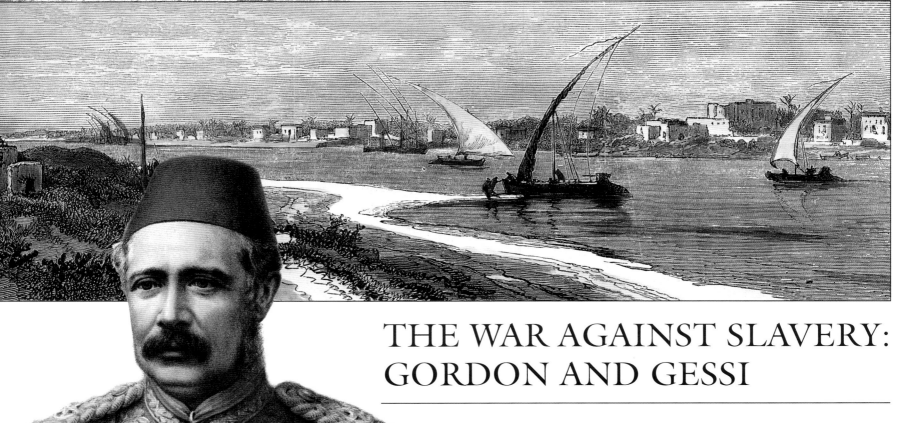

THE WAR AGAINST SLAVERY: GORDON AND GESSI

252 bottom *Charles George Gordon in his dazzling governor's uniform. Gordon was a British officer who had come to fame in China, leading the troops of the Celestial Empire against the Taiping rebels. In 1874 he was called to organize the region of* Equatoria *conquered by Baker. His principal task was to wipe out the slave trade. With this gesture the khedive Ismail hoped to ingratiate himself with the European powers whose support was indispensable to his plans for modernizing Egypt.*

253 *This map of Africa, from the* Hand Atlas *printed at Gotha in 1850, shows the Nile basin.*

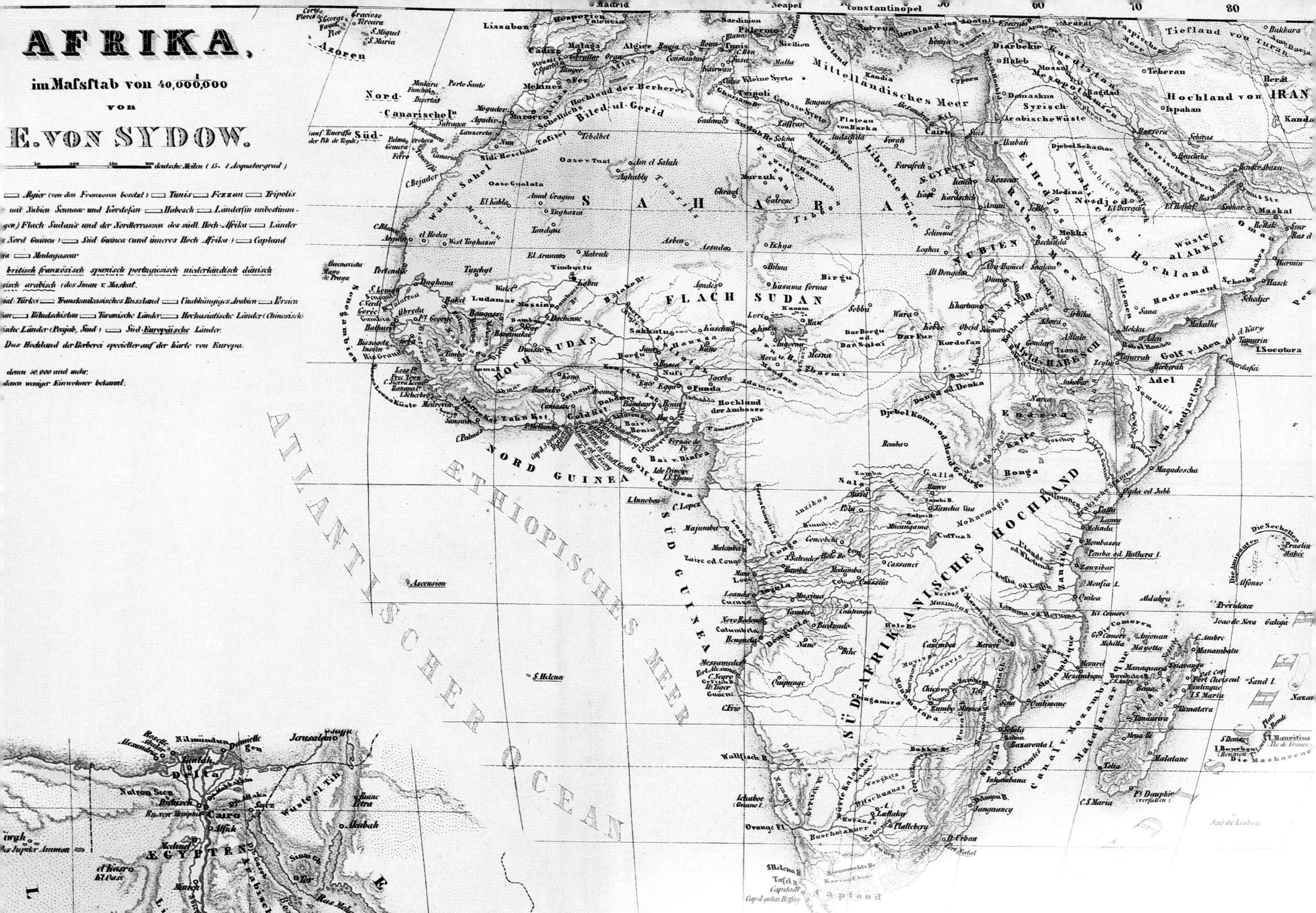

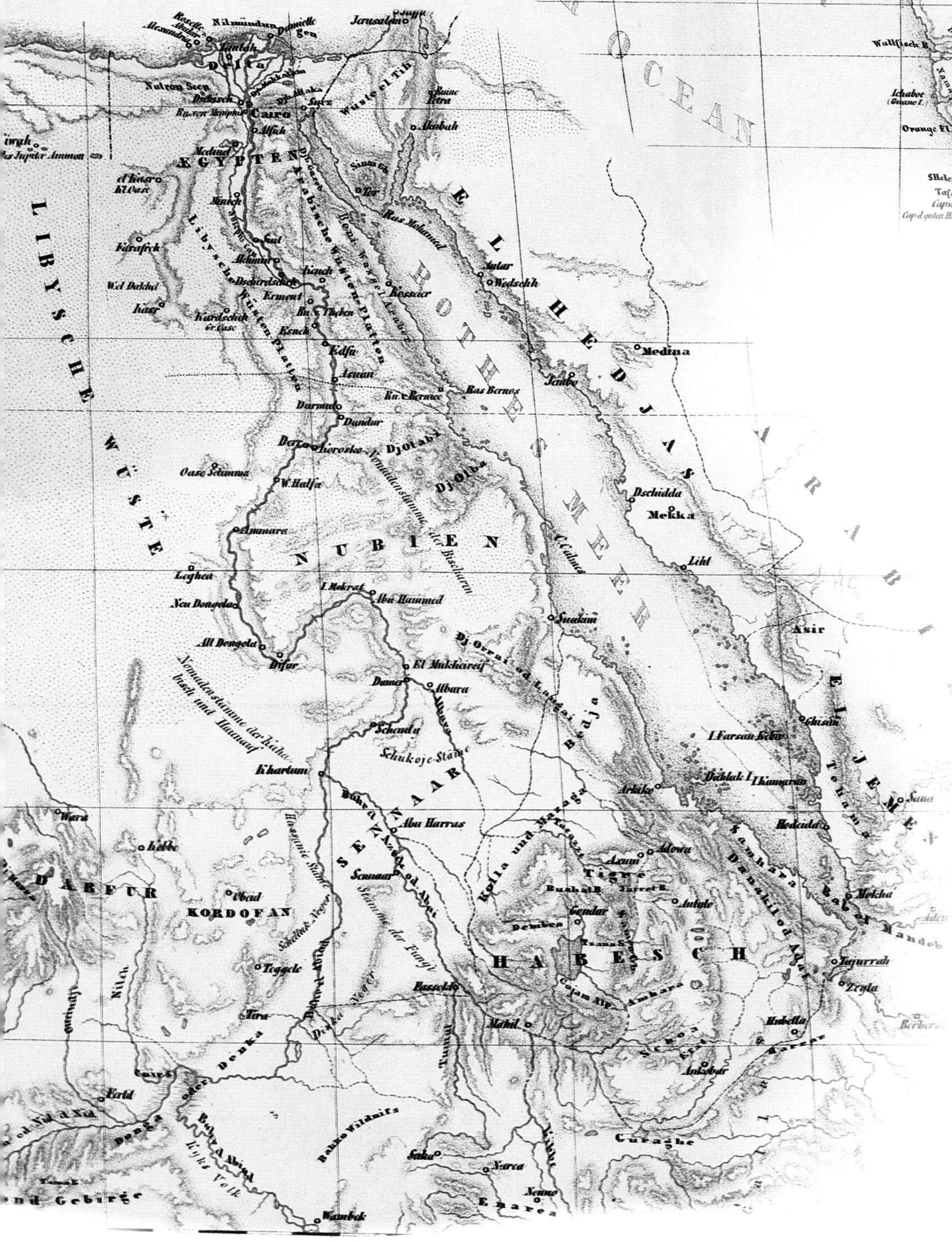

AFRIKA,

im Maſsſtab von 40,000,000

von

E. VON SYDOW.

"enjoy himself"—too late, that is, to participate in the Anglo-French campaign that concluded with the occupation of Beijing and the sacking of the Summer Palace. He remained in the country with the British troops left there to ensure that the recently signed treaty guaranteeing free trade for the Europeans was respected.

His great opportunity came around two years later. Having defeated the imperial forces on a number of occasions, the Taiping rebels—the champions of radical agricultural reform that struck at the very roots of the Chinese social structure—had reached the gates of the cosmopolitan city of Shanghai. A British contingent was ordered to break the siege and the Chinese authorities were so impressed by Gordon's performance that they asked for the young officer to be entrusted with the command of their troops. "The ever-victorious army" as it was known in imperial rhetoric was a rabble of reasonably well armed but absolutely undisciplined Chinese soldiers led by the worst of European adventurers.

On taking command, the twenty-nine-year-old Gordon reorganized and

253

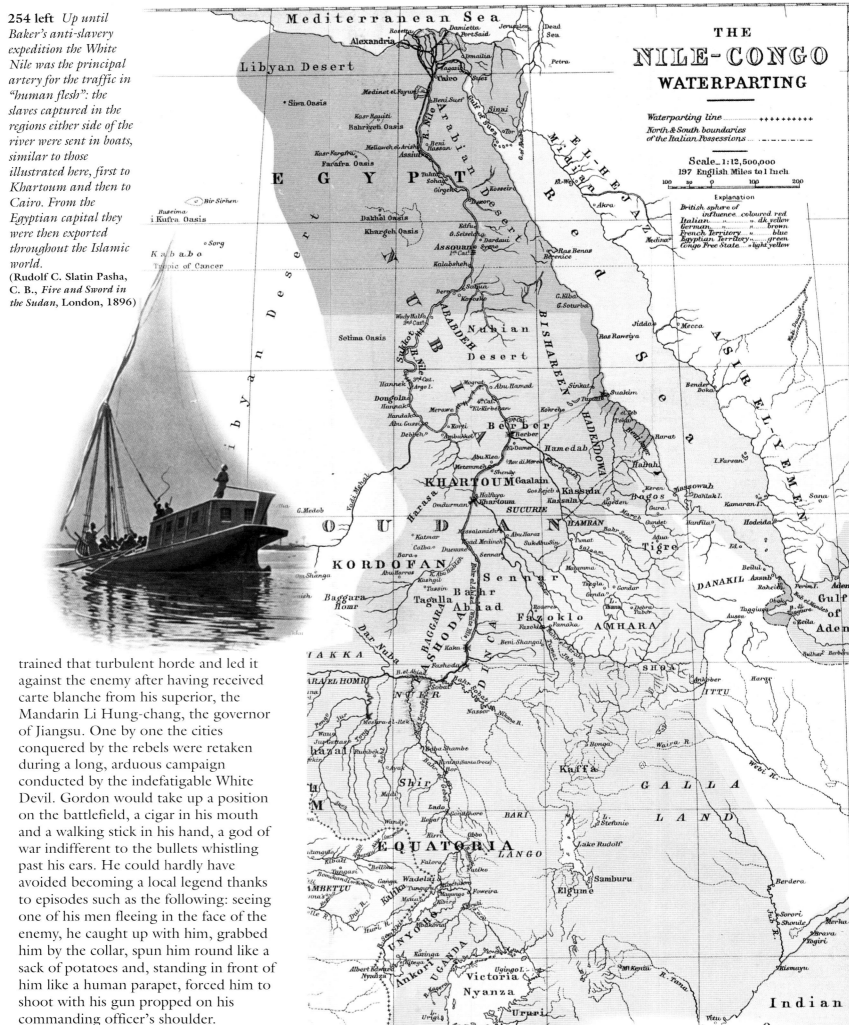

254 left *Up until Baker's anti-slavery expedition the White Nile was the principal artery for the traffic in "human flesh": the slaves captured in the regions either side of the river were sent in boats, similar to those illustrated here, first to Khartoum and then to Cairo. From the Egyptian capital they were then exported throughout the Islamic world.*
(Rudolf C. Slatin Pasha, C. B., *Fire and Sword in the Sudan*, London, 1896)

THE NILE-CONGO WATERPARTING

Waterparting line .... +++++++++
North & South boundaries
of the Italian Possessions

Scale 1:12,500,000
197 English Miles to 1 Inch
100 50 0 100 200

Explanation
British sphere of
influence ..coloured red
Italian   „   „ dk yellow
German   „   „ brown
French Territory „ „ blue
Egyptian Territory „ green
Congo Free State „ light yellow

trained that turbulent horde and led it against the enemy after having received carte blanche from his superior, the Mandarin Li Hung-chang, the governor of Jiangsu. One by one the cities conquered by the rebels were retaken during a long, arduous campaign conducted by the indefatigable White Devil. Gordon would take up a position on the battlefield, a cigar in his mouth and a walking stick in his hand, a god of war indifferent to the bullets whistling past his ears. He could hardly have avoided becoming a local legend thanks to episodes such as the following: seeing one of his men fleeing in the face of the enemy, he caught up with him, grabbed him by the collar, spun him round like a sack of potatoes and, standing in front of him like a human parapet, forced him to shoot with his gun propped on his commanding officer's shoulder.

Only two things undermined his reputation among the Chinese: he would not tolerate looting by his victorious troops, and he spared the lives of the defeated. A serious diplomatic incident occurred when a number of Taiping leaders, who had been arrested and to whom Gordon had promised a pardon, were treacherously assassinated when

254 right
Obstructed by the governors of the other Sudanese provinces, which were occupied by Egyptians who secretly favored the slave trade, the source of prosperity for the whole of that vast area, Gordon set about reconquering the region, shown in this map.
(Gaetano Casati, *Ten Years in Equatoria and the Return with Emin Pasha*, London, 1891)

255 top *Gordon orders his men to attack a slave traders' camp.*
(Walter Scott, *Life of General Gordon*)

they went aboard the governor's junk for a reconciliation banquet. The highly indignant Briton even threatened to change sides and join the rebels. It took all the blandishments of the persuasive East to calm him down.

The war ended in March 1864, with the complete collapse of the rebel forces, and Gordon returned home after having refused honors and monetary rewards, content with glory and the rank of lieutenant colonel. He was bored in Britain, however, and was profoundly disillusioned when the War Office turned down his request to take part in the 1868 expedition to Abyssinia. Three years later he was sent to Galați on the Black Sea as the British member of a commission that was to regulate traffic on the Danube. It was in that bleak river port that the proposal from the Egyptian minister reached him. He was immediately enthusiastic, but had to wait on tenterhooks for authorization from his own government.

At last, in February 1874, Gordon arrived in Cairo where he received from Ismail the title of governor general of Equatoria and "deliciously vague" instructions. He was to be independent of the governor of the Sudan and was to report directly to the khedive. In practice his was a dual mission of vast breadth: he was to guarantee communications between the Sudan and the Great Lakes and to combat and finally eradicate slavery, the true scourge of the region.

Baker's success in this field had, in fact, been somewhat illusory. According to numerous witnesses and participants, the effects of the crusade against the slave trade were worse than the evil it was intended to abolish. Because the right to possess slaves was condoned in the Koran, Muslims regarded the abolition of slavery as tantamount to heresy, and they refused

to recognize the Egyptian government's right to suppress a law of the Prophet. Moreover, the economic prosperity of the Sudan was based on the slave trade—at the expense, of course, of the regions of the upper Nile that were devastated and depopulated. No slave trader was willing to forgo his wealth simply to please the European protectors of the khedive in the name of an abstract principle contradicting the most profound Islamic dogma. The trade could not simply disappear, and in fact it did not disappear; it merely abandoned the water routes it had used until then with the conniving participation of the Egyptian authorities. Instead of being conducted openly, it became clandestine and followed new routes. The European consuls at Khartoum no longer saw boats loaded with human flesh arriving in the city and could report to their governments that the disgraceful business had been eliminated, but the blacks being captured by the slave traders were suffering even greater privations than previously.

For the slaves the worst part of the experience occurred while they were being transported to the market, as they were treated no better than livestock. Once they were bought, they became somewhat second-degree members of their owners' families and were not generally mistreated. They were denied their liberty, but their standard of living was incomparably higher than in their home villages. When slavery was abolished, many slaves refused their newfound freedom and stayed with their masters.

Now that transport via the rivers was

255 center *A mirage appears before a caravan on the march. Obliged to abandon the waterways controlled by the government, the Sudanese trade created* new routes across the deserts. **(J. Ewin Ritchie, The Pictorial Edition of the Life and Discoveries of David Livingstone)**

255 bottom *Dead slaves and camels in the desert. The struggle against the slave trade had the reverse effect of increasing its horrors: the mortality rate among the slaves, now forced to complete* interminable treks through areas lacking water and food, increased enormously. **(J. E. Ritchie, The Pictorial Edition of the Life and Discoveries of David Livingstone)**

256 top *Ascending the Nile with his steamboats, Gordon swooped down on the slavers' camps and burned them.* (Charles Chaillé-Long, *Central Africa: Naked Truths of Naked People*, London, 1876)

256 *This map shows the route followed by Chaillé-Long during his mission.*

256 center *Supplies for Gordon and his men were sent out from Khartoum, depicted here.*

256 bottom *The indefatigable Gordon also nurtured a dream of annexing the kingdom of Uganda on behalf of the Egyptian Empire. He*

therefore sent one of his lieutenants, the American Chaillé-Long (portrayed here alongside a map depicting his itinerary) to the court of M'tesa, who welcomed him with all honors and declared himself willing to accept the sovereignty of the khedive of Egypt.

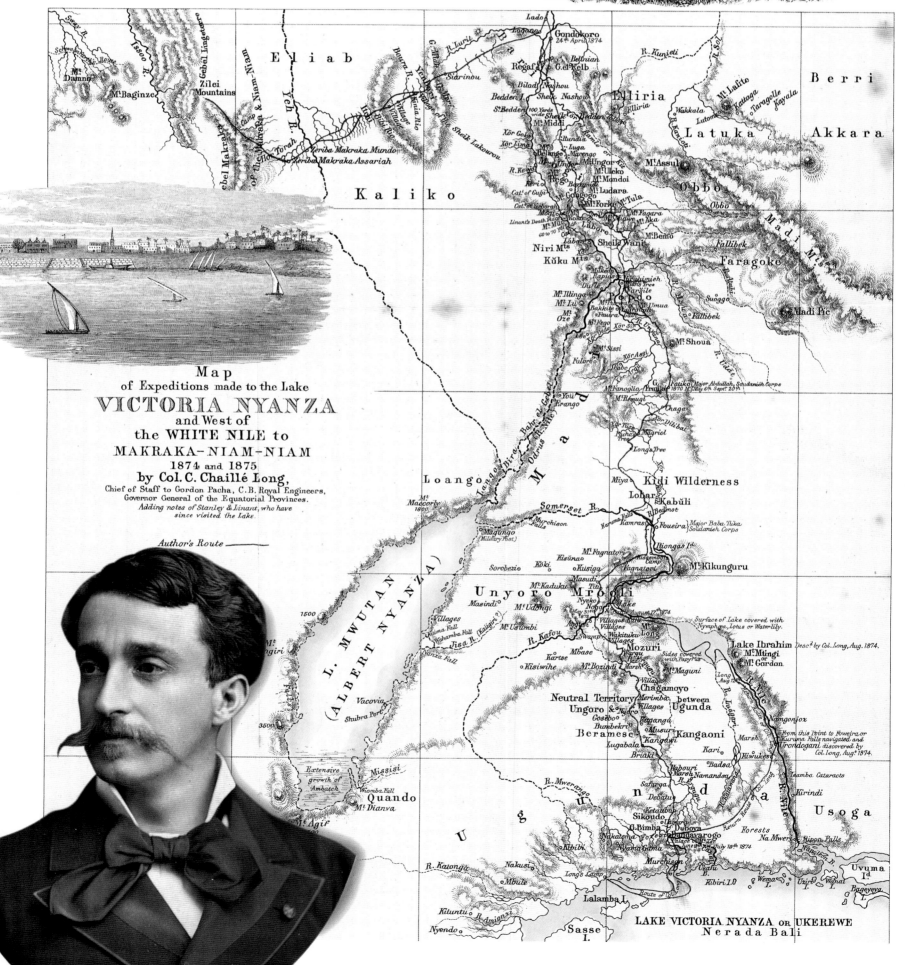

Map
of Expeditions made to the Lake
VICTORIA NYANZA
and West of
the WHITE NILE to
MAKRAKA–NIAM–NIAM
1874 and 1875
by Col. C. Chaillé Long,
Chief of Staff to Gordon Pacha, C.B. Royal Engineers,
Governor General of the Equatorial Provinces.
Adding notes of Stanley & Linant, who have
since visited the Lake.

Author's Route ———

LAKE VICTORIA NYANZA or UKEREWE
Nerada Bali

prohibited, the mortality rate among the blacks increased enormously. Previously they had been packed into boats like sardines, and when they were unloaded around 10 percent of them were found to have died of suffocation or dehydration. Now they were forced to march for hundreds of kilometers, staying away from the Nile, to the Kordofan region. There they were sent to the various markets via Tripoli or Cairo. During those interminable, grueling marches across mainly desert regions, 30 and frequently 50 percent of those poor souls would die. It made no difference to the slavers, who could easily absorb the losses, as once the trade became illegal, the price of a slave increased more than tenfold.

With his usual promptness, Gordon set about his thankless task by surrounding himself with a general staff composed of two Americans, Chaillé-Long and Campbell; an Italian, Romolo Gessi; a Frenchman, Auguste Linant de Bellefonds; two Englishmen, Anson and Russell; and three Germans, Witt, Menges, and Bohndorff. Within six months the African climate and diseases had claimed four victims from among them.

At Khartoum Gordon and his men

257 top *To guarantee the security of his lines of communication, Gordon established fortified villages along the White Nile and its principal tributaries. Like the one illustrated here, each had a small garrison and stocks of rations and ammunition.*

257 bottom *Gondokoro, the provincial capital that Baker had renamed Ismailia. Gordon ascended the White Nile as quickly as possible as far as Gondoko, but he wanted to move the administrative residence farther South to Ladò.*

(Charles Chaillé-Long, *Central Africa: Naked Truths of Naked People*)

were affably received by the governor general of the Sudan, Ayub Pasha, "a pleasant Circassian" who was extremely skilled in extracting maximum gain, legitimate or otherwise, from his position. After three more weeks of difficult navigation, the new pasha of Equatoria finally reached his capital on the Upper Nile, the miserable village of huts that Baker had renamed Ismailia but which everyone continued to call Gondokoro. Seven-eighths of the people in his jurisdiction were slaves, and the avid district governors, the mudirs, helped and encouraged the slavers who swarmed through the country heedless of the fact that they had been officially outlawed.

The indefatigable Gordon set in motion a frenetic program of activities

257

(and in spite of his superhuman energy, he wrote that he felt "almost dead"): he impatiently returned to Khartoum and from there to Berber to track down some baggage that had not been sent on quickly enough; he ascended the White Nile once again and transferred the administrative residence to Lado; he created a chain of fortified outposts along the river and its principal tributaries; and he repressed the cruelty and thieving of the mudira with an implacable sense of justice. He also harbored grandiose plans, which were certainly shared and perhaps suggested by the khedive Ismail. He wanted to extend the Egyptian dominion into Uganda and perhaps even as far as the coast. He therefore sent one of his lieutenants, Colonel Chaillé-Long, to the court of M'tesa. (A by no means secondary objective of this expedition was to confirm the existence of a link between Lakes Albert and Victoria, a problem that Baker had left unresolved.)

On May 3, 1874, Chaillé-Long reached Miani's tree, and on June 10 he entered Uganda, where his horse greatly impressed a population that had never before seen one. M'tesa received him, had him sit at his side, and in his honor sacrificed thirty human lives. The king of Uganda accepted the protectorate of Egypt, perhaps without really understanding what that meant. At any rate, the remoteness of his realm made this annexation by Ismail's empire a purely platonic affair. Chaillé-Long then asked for the sovereign's aid in completing the scientific part of his mission; he intended to cross Lake Victoria to its outlet and descend the Nile to Gondokoro.

He embarked on July 14, but had to abandon the overly ambitious plan to cross the lake: what he had taken to be the opposite shore was just an archipelago, the Sese Islands, while the true distance to be covered was much greater. He therefore sailed north in an

259 top *One of the tribal leaders, Parafio, with his wife. The American explorer, together with the Austrian Marno, also annexed the cannibal kingdom of Mangbetu on behalf of Egypt.*

259 center *A group of hunters presenting a notably large boa constrictor to Chaillé-Long and Marno, both dressed in their white Egyptian uniforms.*

259 bottom *The explorers, their escort, and their native allies dealing with an attack from the Yanbari tribe.*

(Charles Chaillé-Long, *Central Africa: Naked Truths of Naked People*)

attempt to discover the presumed link with Lake Albert. While descending the outlet, the Victoria Nile, on August 11 he discovered Lake Kyoga, which he renamed Lake Ibrahim. It was, however, so densely covered with lilies that it was impossible to navigate. He then descended the Albert Nile as far as the Karuma Falls and confirmed that the two lakes were linked.

Following this successful enterprise, the American decided to venture into Mangbetu, accompanied by the Austrian Marno, to annex this country for Egypt as well. Given its excellent climate and sanitary conditions, it appeared to be perfectly suited to colonization. Once a reasonably secure communications route was established, that remote land of cannibals was the next country to see the Egyptian flag raised and a small garrison of "Turks" installed.

Gordon entrusted another of his lieutenants, Major Romolo Gessi, with the task of ascending the Nile as far as Lake Albert. The Italian departed in October 1875, after a preliminary expedition along the White Nile during which he had freed numerous caravans of slaves. He had also organized navigation on the river so that the

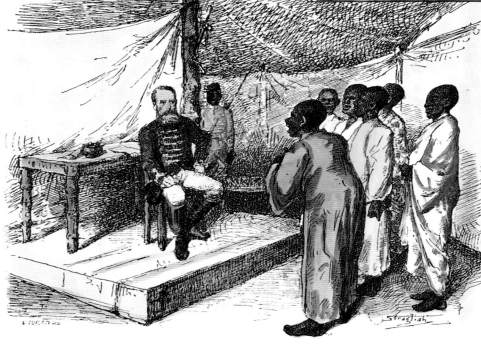

journey from Khartoum to Gondokoro took just fifteen days rather than the previous thirty-five. His second trip, however, ended at Fashoda, a station downstream of the confluence with the Sobat that was to become famous a few decades later after the small Egyptian garrison there was besieged by thousands of Shilluk and had to flee together with the people of the surrounding villages.

Gessi was finally able to get under way in March 1876, together with another figure we have met before, Carlo

Piaggia, who had returned to the Sudan following a trip into Abyssinia. They used two iron boats left by Baker at Dufli, a short distance upstream from Gondokoro, that performed very well in the water but proved to be a liability at the points where they had to be transported by land as they required a thousand porters. The two Italians were accompanied by eighteen boatmen and twelve soldiers. They ascended the river amid tremendous storms, extremely hostile natives, and floating islands that made navigation hazardous. At last,

however, they reached Lake Albert, and on March 22 they landed on the eastern shore near Magungo, where they raised the red Egyptian flag. They then ascended the upper course of the Nile until they found their way barred by the grandiose foam-capped rock wall of the Murchison Falls. Piaggia proceeded up the river while Gessi returned to the lake and began to circumnavigate it despite daily torrential rain, winds that raised huge waves, bellicose natives who prevented him from landing, and attempted mutinies by the boatmen who

260-261 *During his journey through Uganda and southern Sudan, Gessi stopped in numerous villages. This engraving depicts a number of boats neatly moored at the village of Meshra el-Rek.*

261 bottom *The Agar tribes built their huts on stilts to keep them free of insects and harmful animals. On the right can be seen the unusual hair-style of the Agar chief.*

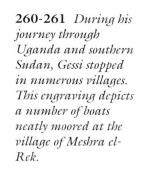

260 top *Another of Gordon's lieutenant, the Italian Romolo Gessi, seen here, was instructed by the governor of Equatoria to ascend the White Nile as far as Lake Albert and to circumnavigate the huge stretch of water for the first time. This he did in March 1876 with another Italian explorer, Carlo Piaggia.* (Romolo Gessi Pasha, *Seven Years in the Soudan*, London, 1892)

260 bottom left *In the Bahr al-Ghazal region the villages were built on higher land, as in Fadasi, seen in this engraving.*

260 bottom right *Gessi won over the natives of the region with his daring and his essential good-heartedness. Here he is giving a hearing to the chiefs of Gaba-Shambe.*

(R. Gessi Pasha, *Seven Years in the Soudan*)

were accustomed to the placid waters of the Nile, not to these lacustrine hurricanes. The survey was completed in nine days, however, and Gessi, having rejoined Piaggia, return to Khartoum where Gordon received him warmly. The governor, however, paid Gessi a backhanded compliment that aroused the ire of the touchy Italian, a great patriot and a former officer under Garibaldi: Gordon told him that it was a pity that he was not an Englishman. Gessi threw his fez to the floor and resigned on the spot, returning to Italy shortly afterward.

If the Italian was irritated with his superior for his infelicitous turn of phrase and also because he felt that he had not been adequately rewarded for his achievements, Gordon felt much the same way about the khedival government that had entrusted him with an extremely difficult task while denying him the means with which to complete it. In fact, the governorship of Equatoria and all the extensive local power that it entailed were useless if at Khartoum and in Kordofan and Darfur there were other equally independent pashas with equally wide-ranging powers who continued quite openly to favor the slavery with which the functionaries of all Egypt, from the mudirs to the last askaris in the remotest of villages, lined their pockets.

Early in September 1876 the righteously furious Gordon headed for Cairo, having decided to abandon the service of the khedive, whose moral support, he said, was no longer adequate and was insufficient to convince the Egyptians to abandon the slave trade. Ismail, who said of Gordon, "When this man enters my cabinet I feel as though as I am in the presence of a superior," swore that all the irregularities would be eliminated and that he would make his authority felt; and he would not let Gordon depart for England before he obtained a promise that he would return.

At that time Ismail had greater need than ever for the support or at least the indulgence of Europe as he was nurturing expansionist ambitions even greater than those of his predecessor, Mehemet Ali.

The negus Tewodros had been very shrewd when he

proposed an alliance with Queen Victoria against Egyptian expansionism; Egypt was yet again attempting to swallow Ethiopia after having claimed, in 1866, the best Red Sea ports by obtaining full sovereignty over Massawa and Suakin from the Ottoman Empire. Following the breaching of the Suez isthmus, Ismail, considering himself the great sovereign of an imperial power, intended to extend Egyptian control over the whole course of the White and Blue Niles as well as the coasts of Somalia and Azania, thus making his country the focus of the greatest African empire, stretching from the Mediterranean to the Indian Ocean.

The Egyptian attempt at expansion in East Africa is inseparable from the name of Werner Munzinger, a Swiss scientist and adventurer, who transformed himself from a pedantic professor of philology into an ambitious conqueror of empires, a kind of Lawrence of the nineteenth century. Having settled at Alexandria in the service of a trading company, he had traveled in 1854 to Massawa, then a squalid nest of slave traders and pearl fishermen, and from there he had made a number of excursions into Ethiopia. Married to an Abyssinian and boasting a perfect command of the local languages and customs, he had joined Napier's expedition as head of the political service responsible for relations with the various rases. Then, in 1871, the khedive

appointed Munzinger as the governor of Massawa and East Sudan. He fortified the town, constructed a causeway that linked the island of Massawa with the mainland, and made the port the largest and most comfortable on the Red Sea. He housed a large garrison there and began to prepare for the conquest of Ethiopia, the detailed plan for which he personally presented to Ismail. It appeared to both of them to be an easy task: hadn't the English reached Magdala almost without firing a shot?

In 1872 Munzinger, at the head of a column of fifteen hundred "Turks," took his first steps by occupying Cheren and the territory of the Bogo people in the Eritrean highlands. For this he was

262 top *The khedive Ismail, seen in this contemporary engraving, had expansionist ambitions. He dreamed not only of Egypt being included among the great powers but also of transforming it into a great African empire extending to the Indian Ocean.*

262 bottom *The bucolic Samayat Valley in Abyssinia, flanked by mountain peaks.* (Henry Salt, *Twenty Four Views taken in St. Helena, the Cape, India, Ceylon, Abyssinia and Egypt,* London, 1809)

262-263 *The port of Massawa on the coast of what was to become the Italian colony of Eritrea.* (George Viscount Valencia, *Voyages and Travels to India, Ceylon, the Red Sea, Abyssinia and Egypt,* London, 1811)

263 bottom left *The governor of Massawa, Werner Munzinger, pleaded and plotted for a military campaign in Ethiopia, which he felt to be ready for the taking. In 1875 he set out at the head of an Egyptian army with the aim of conquering Harer; however, he and almost all his men were massacred by the Dankali people.* (George Viscount Valencia, *Voyages and Travels to India, Ceylon, the Red Sea, Abyssinia and Egypt*)

263 bottom right *An Ethiopian warrior.* (George Viscount Valencia, *Voyages and Travels to India, Ceylon, the Red Sea, Abyssinia and Egypt*)

rewarded with the title of pasha. Negus Johannes, the successor to Tewodros, was involved in an ongoing struggle with the turbulent ras and could do nothing. The Swiss then attempted to establish an alliance with the emperor's principal enemy, Menelik, king of the Shoa people, and also received orders from the khedive to take possession of the Somalian coast from Zulla to Cape Guarafui. Munzinger complied with these instructions, establishing himself at Zulla from where he took the opportunity provided by the death of the emir of Marrar and the outbreak of a providential war of succession to occupy that city, too, in October 1875. Corresponding with Menelik, he devised a plan to lure the negus and his forces into southern Tigre. There two Egyptian armies, one from Massawa and the other from Tagiura, would catch him in their crossfire and the imperial crown would fall into the hands of the Shoan chief.

The army from Tagiura departed under the command of Munzinger himself: eight well armed companies with a number of cannons. They had to cross the Hausa to reach the Shoa. Trusting in the agreements reached with the local tribal leaders, the commander neglected to take any precautions and during the night of November 15–16 a horde of Dankalis fell upon the sleeping Egyptian camp. Munzinger, who slept in the center with his wife, found himself surrounded. He felled three attackers, but a fourth caught him with a sword thrust and another wounded him in the shoulder. He was finished off with spears.

264 top *Sheer cliffs crowned the gentle slopes of the Kalmati Valley in Abyssinia.* (Henry Salt, *Twenty Four Views taken in St. Helena, the Cape, India, Ceylon, Abyssinia and Egypt,* London, 1809)

264 bottom *In December 1875, Ismail organized a new expedition to Abyssinia to take revenge for the defeat suffered a few months earlier, putting his son Hassan in command. This second enterprise also ended tragically with a shameful defeat.*

The few survivors attempted to return to Tagiura but they were overtaken and massacred. Another twenty-two hundred men with six cannons had left from Massawa under the command of Arakel Bey, the nephew of Nubar Pasha, who was assisted by the Danish colonel Arendrup Bey. With imprudence similar to that of Munzinger they ventured into unknown territory without taking any precautions. Having passed Asmera they reached the Mereb Wenz and there encountered the entire Abyssinian army: 50,000 men and six cannons led by the negus. With well-orchestrated flanking movements, Negus Johannes herded the Egyptians into the Gudda Guddi Valley

and surrounded them. It was November 17, two days after Munzinger's debacle. The slaughter lasted from nine o'clock in the morning to three in the afternoon. There were very few Egyptian survivors. The prisoners were castrated and some of them, roughly doctored, were sent back to Massawa as a warning of what future conquerors could expect.

Ismail was incensed by the news of the disaster. The mirage of his African empire was not all that was at stake; it was now also a question of dynastic prestige. A new expedition of twenty-five battalions and forty-six cannons was rapidly prepared for departure by the khedive's son Massan, who had studied in the

German military academies. Effective command of the troops was, however, entrusted to Ratib Pasha.

The Egyptians landed at Massawa in December 1875 and headed inland, this time with extreme caution. They decided to occupy a strong position at the center of the Eritrean Plateau and wait there for an Abyssinian attack that would inevitably be crushed by their superior firepower. Egyptian morale was rather low, however, because rumors had spread among the soldiers of the khedive that the savages castrated their prisoners.

The negus, thanks to popular support that transformed the war into a veritable crusade against the Muslims, had assembled 70,000 men, but only 10,000 of them were armed with guns. The wave of indignation directed against the "Turks" was so overwhelming that even Menelik had been obliged to send reinforcements to the hated negus.

Well provisioned and entrenched in a fortified camp that was impregnable, the Egyptians had only to follow the plan conceived by General Ratib: sit and wait until the lack of supplies caused the great Abyssinian army to begin to self-destruct, then finish off what remained. Prince Massan, however, was in search of glory and despised that horde of poorly armed savages; and he had, after all, been sent there to avenge the earlier Egyptian humiliation.

On the morning of March 7, he led his men out of the fort and attacked. The Abyssinians could hardly have hoped for such great good fortune. Their enemies fought with desperate energy, preferring to be killed rather than captured, knowing as they did the fate that awaited those who fell into Ethiopian hands. Sheer weight of numbers won the day. At the end of the battle 50,000 men lay dead, a third of them Egyptians. His ammunition exhausted, Massan gave orders to withdraw to the camp. The Egyptians and the Abyssinians were tightly bunched, however, and the commander of the fort did not have the courage to shoot into the melee, and the Abyssinians penetrated the trenches along with the retreating Egyptians. Only an internal stronghold was secured, and the survivors were equipped with cannons, ammunition, and supplies of food but no water. There followed a terrible night with the screams of the castrated Egyptian troops echoing around the fort.

Massan made an offer of peace and ceded the territory of the Bogos, but Negus Johannes demanded unconditional surrender. The Egyptians were eventually saved by a betrayal: in exchange for the expedition treasury containing £ 20,000 sterling, and 30,000 talers, one of the Abyssinian chiefs, Ras Bariu, who was guarding the road to Massawa,

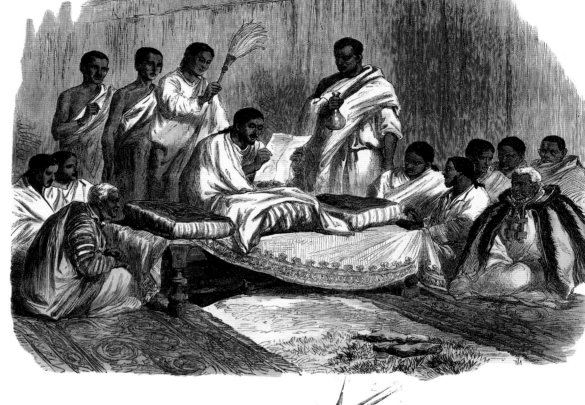

265 top *Negus Johannes reading a message while surrounded by members of his court.*

265 center *Abyssinian soldiers armed with lances, sabers, and muzzle loaders.*

265 bottom right *The French Colonel de Sèves placed himself at the service of Egypt under the name Suleiman Pasha and reorganized the khedive's army.*

265 bottom left *Menelik, later to become emperor of Ethiopia, was victorious over the Italians at Adwa.*

allowed the besieged invaders to escape. Prince Massan arrived at the port alone, fleeing on horseback during the night of March 9. He was joined the following day by the few exhausted and terrified survivors of the massacre. Ras Bariu, suspected of corruption, was blinded and imprisoned at the top of an amba.

Gordon returned to Egypt in January 1877. There had been talk of entrusting him with the governorship of Bulgaria on behalf of the European powers or with the command of a new expedition from the Indian Ocean to the Great Lakes, but the khedive had written to remind him of his promise and Gordon kept his word. He nevertheless imposed conditions he felt would be

266 top *Having resigned in 1876 due to the sabotage of his efforts by the other Egyptian functionaries, Gordon (seen here in dress uniform while leading a camel regiment) was convinced by the Khedive to return to the service of Egypt in 1877. This time he was granted the governorship of the entire Sudan and set about eliminating the slave trade thanks to the full powers at his disposal; he displayed a degree of realism, recognising that he could not abolish slavery with the stroke of a pen and so avoided outlawing it altogether but impeded the capture and trade in new slaves.* (Walter Scott, *Life of General Gordon*)

266 bottom *This print records the horrors of slavery: an armed Arab is guarding a group of laboring slaves.* (**Pictorial Africa, Its Heroes, Missionaries and Martyrs**, London, 1890)

unacceptable: he demanded the governorship of the entire Sudan with full powers. To his great surprise Ismail agreed without batting an eyelash, and Gordon found himself the absolute master of 1.5 million square kilometers of terrain extending from the Tropic of Cancer to the Equator and from the Red Sea to Darfur. By May he was in Khartoum, where he proved to have a realistic understanding of the situation. He issued a decree that maintained the legality of slavery for the time being but forbade Europeans from owning slaves. He justified this action, saying that slaves are actually the property of their possessors until the owners receive compensation or until a certain period of time has passed. In this way he was

decreeing liberation after a certain number of years.

He nevertheless intended to deal ruthlessly with the slave trade so as to interrupt the continual supply of new slaves; he rightly thought that once "production" had been halted, the problem would resolve itself over time. One of the most powerful slave traders, Ziber, who had been the virtual sovereign of Darfur, was dethroned by the Egyptian government with typical Levantine guile: he was called to Cairo on the pretext of conferring honors and rewards upon him; he was then obliged to remain under house arrest. In the Darfur, however, his son Suleiman with a few thousand well-armed men rebelled and threatened to sweep away the

"Turks." He had yet to discover that he was dealing with that master of war Gordon, who left Khartoum at the head of 300 men, crossed the desert at the height of summer "with the rapidity of the telegraph," as a stupefied Arab in his service was to report, and plunged into Darfur. He freed the besieged garrisons, and at Gara on September 2, 1877, he found himself confronting Suleiman, whose men, the terror of Central Africa, outnumbered the Egyptians ten to one. Gordon put on the gold-embroidered uniform he kept for the most solemn occasions and, with an escort of fifty light cavalrymen, presented himself at the camp of the rebel, who was petrified with surprise. Gordon asked Suleiman for a glass of water and ordered him to

repay the visit the following day at Dara. The tamed beast obeyed, and the governor general sent him to cool off in the swamps of the Bahr al-Ghazal.

There, however, having recovered from his shock and having received secret instructions from his father, Suleiman renewed his attacks, destroying the small government outposts scattered throughout the vast region, capturing the principal station, Dem Idris, and seizing supplies, arms, quantities of ammunition, and a steamboat. He then proclaimed himself an independent sultan.

Informed of this catastrophe, Gordon was fortunate in finding at Khartoum the right man to entrust with the reconquest of the Bahr al-Ghazal: Romolo Gessi, who was back in the Sudanese capital to organize an expedition to explore the Sobat Basin. Convinced by the Englishman's rhetoric, Gessi accepted the post of governor of the lost province, and on July 15, 1878, he set out to reconquer it aboard a steamboat towing two barges containing 500 troops. He ascended the river as far as Lado, the capital of Equatoria, the governorship of which Gordon had recently entrusted to a man of whom we shall hear much more, Emin Pasha. During the long trip Gessi collected more troops from the local garrisons and captured many boats loaded with "black ivory," frequently belonging to government functionaries who supplemented their meager salaries with the profits of slavery. He liberated and fed the unfortunate captives while developing an intense hatred for the entire khedival bureaucracy. From Lado,

267 top *Governor General Gordon passing through the streets of the capital, being saluted with bows and curtsies. Having established himself at Khartoum as governor general of the Sudan, Gordon rapidly won the affection and respect of his administrators with his simple, reliable ways that were very different from the petty arrogance of the Egyptian functionaries, who* *treated the country like a land of conquest.* (Thomas Archer, *The War in Egypt and the Soudan*, London)

267 bottom *Vast colonies of birds inhabited the marshy banks of the White Nile. This plate shows a number of flamingos among the reed beds of Meshra el-Rek.* (Gaetano Casati, *Ten Years in Equatoria nd the Return with Emin Pasha*, London, 1891)

268 top *Gordon entrusted Romolo Gessi with the reconquest of the Bahr al-Ghazal region in which the slaver Suleiman had taken refuge, proclaiming himself an independent sultan. Gessi succeeded in driving Suleiman out of the fort of Dem Idris, which he in turn occupied and defended from the furious attacks of the slaver. Thanks to such feats,* Gessi became known as the Garibaldi of Africa. (**Romolo Gessi Pasha**, *Seven Years in the Soudan*, **London, 1892**)

268 bottom *A typical Bahr al-Ghazal landscape sketched by Gessi: an imposing baobab* (Adansonia digitata), *a tree "whose branches look like roots," behind which can be seen the village of Roseres.* (**R. Gessi Pasha**, *Seven Years in the Soudan*)

Gessi headed west through the swamps of the Bahr al-Ghazal. He had 2,500 poorly armed men; Suleiman, firmly entrenched at Dem Idris, could count on 15,000 and waited for him like a spider waiting at the center of its web for a fly.

Gessi, however, who was to become known in Italy as the Garibaldi of Africa, was a very crafty fly: once he reached Dem Idris, he ensured that the rebel received the false information that he was surrounded by superior forces. The impressionable Suleiman hurriedly struck his camp and disappeared into the meandering swamps while Gessi settled in the occupied town without firing a shot in anger. He was then able to resist the subsequent return and repeated attacks of the slave trader, who suffered heavy losses.

However, while Suleiman was unable to retake Dem Idris, Gessi was not in a position to defeat the rebel: he had too few men to venture into the open, and those he had had begun to fall ill due to the hundreds of rotting corpses that lay unburied around the trenches. Supplies of food and ammunition were also beginning to run short. The impasse was broken by the Italian on March 16, 1879, with another clever strategy: a sortie by his men, divided into four companies and attacking from different directions, cut off the enemy's only sources of water, and Suleiman was obliged to flee to the north while his men dispersed.

Restocked with ammunition from Lado and food from Khartoum (they had eaten nothing but boiled rice without salt for three months), Gessi sent out flying columns in all directions, destroying the remnants of the rebel forces and freeing slaves until, on July 15, 1879, after an exhausting chase lasting over a year, Suleiman was overtaken near Gara, southwest of Darfur, and was persuaded to surrender, even though his forces far outnumbered those of his adversary. "I had Suleiman and nine principal rebel leaders shot as they had tried to escape after a failed attempt to convince my troops to rise up against me," said Gessi with suspect brevity; he had probably decided in any case that a draconian example was needed in order to strike at the very roots of slavery.

On his return to the Bahr al-Ghazal, having eradicated all the remaining nuclei of slave traders on the way, the Italian set about reorganizing the province. However, his energetic program was interrupted by the political changes that had taken place in Cairo. The khedive Ismail had been deposed and succeeded by his son Tewfik, whose intentions were very different from those of his father. He had decided, above all, to replace the high-ranking European functionaries with Arabs or assimilated Arabs. In the Sudan this meant replacing Gordon and his most trusted lieutenant, Gessi. The Englishman, who was in any case tired of the situation, presented his resignation to the khedive, who entrusted him with a diplomatic mission at the court of Negus Johannes of Abyssinia; Gordon was finally able to embark for England in January 1880.

The return of Gessi, who left his governorship to Emin, was transformed into a tragic odyssey by an unusual and enormous increase in the islands of floating vegetation in the Sudd region.

269 center right
When the khedive Ismail was deposed and replaced by Tewfik, Gordon resigned and left the Sudan. Gessi did likewise but had to undergo a traumatic odyssey during his return journey. His boat, depicted in this engraving, remained trapped in the Sudd swamps for four months during which time 430 of the 600 people aboard died of hunger and disease.

269 bottom
Miraculously saved by the arrival of a rescue boat captained by the Austrian explorer Marno, Gessi continued his journey to Khartoum and from there across the desert to the Red Sea and Suez. Unfortunately, the Italian's health had been destroyed by the terrible privations suffered during his enforced stay in the swamps, and he died a few months later in a hospital at Suez.

Partly as a result of the captain's inexperience, his steamboat—which was towing three barges as well as other smaller boats with a total of around 600 passengers, including women and children—was imprisoned in the masses of vegetation that extended from bank to bank for up to two kilometers. The floating islands rose ten or fifteen meters above the level of the water and left no free channel. The drama of the unfortunate victims trapped on the river —Gessi had vainly reminded the authorities at Khartoum to maintain a free passage through the Sudd—lasted from September 16, 1880, to January 4 the following year and became worse with each passing day. The wood for the boilers ran out, the food supplies ran out, the undernourished men were increasingly exhausted by their efforts to cut a path through the vegetation, and they began to succumb to disease. Every piece of leather on board the vessels was eaten, including belts, bags, and shoes; some even ate the flesh of the dead. The cadavers, which were thrown overboard, rotted alongside the immobilized boat, giving off a foul stench.

All hope of finding a way through That deadly barrier appeared lost when, one morning, the skeletal survivors heard gunshot. It was a steamboat under the command of the Austrian explorer Marno, sent out from Khartoum to search for the missing party. Of the 600 people who had departed, 430 had died, and many of the survivors died after their arrival in Khartoum. Among the victims was Gessi himself. He never recovered from the experience and died on April 30, 1881, in a Suez hospital.

269 top left and top right *On the occasion of this sortie from Dem Idris Gessi routed Suleiman's forces, which dispersed into the marshes. The Italian followed in the slaver sultan's footsteps and captured him more than a year later near Gara in the Darfur region. In these drawings Gessi depicted the final phase of the last battle (top left) and the subsequent execution of Suleiman and nine of his officers (right) after "they had tried to escape"—a rather suspect justification.* (R. Gessi Pasha, *Seven Years in the Soudan*, London, 1892)

269

(R. Gessi Pasha, *Seven Years in the Soudan*).

Under Ismail, Egypt had become a "paradise on earth for all those who had money to lend at usurious interest, or inferior wares to get rid of by selling them at the prices of superior quality merchandise." Seventeen foreign consulates in 1870 represented about 100,000 foreign citizens, most of whom were concentrated in Alexandria and Cairo, and until 1876 they were exempt from paying taxes to the Egyptian government. This policy was very unpopular with the heavily exploited subjects of the khedive. Also unpopular was the fact that many high-ranking government posts were held by infidels. Hatred of the domineering Europeans was becoming more and more widespread.

After sixteen years of extravagant and wasteful spending, Ismail was on the verge of bankruptcy. By 1875 the poverty of the fellahs, from whom the taxes were extracted with a ruthless use of the whip, had reached such a point that the increasingly meager resources gathered were not sufficient even to pay for the day-to-day administration of the state. The khedive had no choice but to sell the 176,602 shares he owned in the Suez Canal Company. They were bought by the British government. No one could have imagined it at the time, but what seemed a normal, albeit large, financial transaction was to mark a decisive turning point not only in the history of the canal, which until then had been under French control, but also in the history of Egypt and of the British Empire.

THE BANKRUPTCY OF THE KHEDIVE: BRITISH OCCUPATION OF EGYPT

271 top left *The Cairo prisons were crammed with unfortunate debtors arrested for insolvency.* (T. Archer, *The War in Egypt and the Soudan*)

271 top right *General Wolseley, seen here, commanded the British expeditionary force that occupied Egypt following the bombardment of the Alexandrian forts.* (T. Archer, *The War in Egypt and the Soudan*)

271 bottom *Tax collectors going about their business with whips. In an attempt to find a way out of the country's desperate economic situation, Ismail had increased the fiscal burden to an unbearable degree, taxing the already poverty-stricken peasants to the hilt.* (Maximilian in Bayern, *Bilder aus dem Oriente*, Stuttgart, 1846)

270 top *The khedive Ismail attempted to modernize Egypt by making huge investments; he was, however, overcome by the vast debts he incurred and was obliged to abdicate by the European powers, who induced the sultan of Constantinople, the nominal sovereign of the country, to replace him with his son Tewfik.* (Thomas Archer, *The War in Egypt and the Soudan*, London)

270 bottom left *The hatred of the domineering foreigners provoked a xenophobic revolt at Alexandria. This illustration shows the terrorized Europeans seeking refuge on the French and British ships anchored in the port.* (T. Archer, *The War in Egypt and the Soudan*)

270 bottom right *The bloody rebellion that swept through the streets of Alexandria.* (T. Archer, *The War in Egypt and the Soudan*)

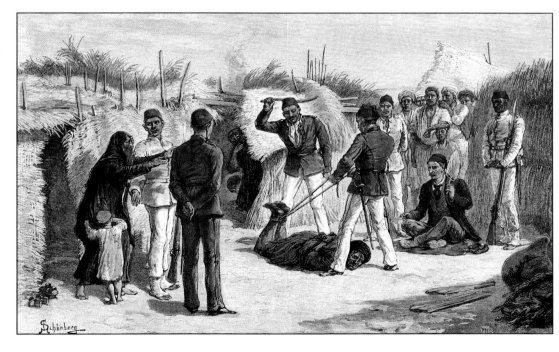

The sale of the shares was not sufficient to save the situation, and the public debt continued to grow. A special bank was set up with international control over the country's revenues. Then, in May 1878, a committee of inquiry was established (on which General Gordon was invited to sit, although he eventually quarreled with all the other European members). The committee extended international control over all the immense territories of the khedive. Ismail, on the verge of desperation, was forced to concede constitutional order and nominated Nubar Pasha as head of the government, with the Englishman Rivers Wilson as finance minister and the Frenchman Blignières as minister of public works. The khedive could thus pompously announce that from now on Egypt was no longer part of Africa, as it had become part of civilized Europe. After only six months, however, he was champing at the bit to regain absolute power and secretly organized a military revolt in Cairo to overthrow the government he had been obliged to appoint. France and Britain, suddenly remembering that Ismail was, after all, but a representative of the sultan of Turkey, obliged his nominal master to remind him of the fact. On June 26, 1879, Ismail received an unexpected telegram from Constantinople addressed with caustic irony to "The Former Khedive of Egypt." It informed him that he had been deposed and had been succeeded by his son Tewfik. Resigned to his fate, he embarked on his yacht, the *Marousa*, without protest but not without emptying the Treasury coffers of

272-273 *Following the Alexandrian revolt and the massacre of the Europeans, the British government bowed to the weight of public opinion and intervened to "restore order." This illustration records one of the first skirmishes between the British and the Egyptians at Kindji Osman on August 5, 1882.*

272 bottom *A battery of cannons is placed in position during the march inland.*

273 top and bottom *Following the bombardment of the forts of the great port, seen in these engravings, the British forces disembarked and began to march toward the Suez Canal to prevent Egyptian sabotage.* (**T. Archer,** *The War in Egypt and the Soudan*)

273 center *An armored train of the Royal Navy at rest near Lake Mareotis.*

all they held. He took his nest egg of £9,000,000 with him and left to pass the rest of his days in a palace on the Bosporus.

Now that Ismail had been exiled, France and England might have conceded some respite to the exploited country, but instead, they continued to turn the screw, provoking a wave of xenophobia against not only the Europeans but also the "Turks," compatriots of the foreign dynasty that had reigned over the country since the beginning of the century. Tewfik was hated because he refused to oppose the Franco-British interference, and when on September 8, 1881, he ordered a turbulent and undisciplined group of young officers to leave Cairo, they responded by marching on his palace with their soldiers and imposing the

274 top *Tell el-Kebir, a village located around a hundred kilometers from Cairo, was the setting for a dramatic battle. Here we see an initial tactical reconnaissance by the British forces on August 5.*

274 bottom *The bayonet charge by the Scottish troops was one*

of the culminating episodes of the battle of Tell el-Kebir on September 13.

275-278 The battle of Tell el-Kebir was the only significant battle of the brief campaign. Even though the Egyptians were entrenched behind well-constructed fortifications, they were defeated in two hours.

nomination of their commanding officer Ahmed Arabi as minister of defense in a nationalist government. The French and the British protested vehemently, but the whole of Egypt acclaimed the event and the hated Europeans were spat upon and insulted in the streets of Alexandria and Cairo.

Britain decided to react decisively. The Mediterranean fleet was ordered to leave Malta and set sail for Alexandria, and a Franco-British message demanded the resignation of the new government and the removal of Arabi. The members of the government resigned, but the people of Cairo rebelled and forced them to remain at their posts at the head of the country. Arabi began to prepare for the

now inevitable war. Gripped by panic, the European residents fled to Alexandria where an international fleet was waiting to take them on board. On June 11, when 14,000 people had already been taken to safety and a further 6,000 were awaiting their turn to embark, a riot broke out in the city. Hundreds of people lost their lives, fifty of whom were whites. Houses and shops were sacked and burned.

Chaille-Long, who was there by chance, organized the defense of the American consulate in the consul's absence and saved dozens of lives. He also notified the British admiral of what was happening. Assault troops occupied the European quarter and gathered up

the survivors. Prime Minister Gladstone had no intention of getting caught up in the Egyptian hornets' nest, but the enormous pressure of public opinion following the death of British subjects forced him to act. After consulting France and Italy, who refused to intervene, Britain reluctantly decided to move alone in the name of the whole civilized world. On July 10, Admiral Seymour sent an ultimatum to the Egyptian garrison ordering the coastal batteries to be dismantled. The Egyptians proposed a compromise, but it was too late. At seven o'clock the next morning the bombardment began. It lasted until five o'clock in the afternoon as the inhabitants fled terrified into the desert.

275 *The flight of Ahmed Arabi, an officer who had assumed leadership of the Egyptian nationalist movement; he was captured at Cairo a few days after the battle, condemned to death, pardoned, and exiled.*

Only the looters remained to raid the empty houses and set fires everywhere. Order was not established until three days later when the landing troops occupied the smoking ruins of the city.

Arabi withdrew toward Cairo threatening to destroy the canal, but the only effect of his bravado was to make the British hasten their operations. General Wolseley occupied the canal area in the middle of August with 20,000 men. He then marched from Ismailia toward the interior. The Egyptian army confronted the British on September 13 outside the village of Tell el-Kebir about 100 kilometers from Cairo. It was a formidable position, well fortified according to the military rule book.

There were 22,000 Egyptians entrenched behind the crest of a hill on which they had positioned their batteries—and there were 17,000 British with sixty-seven cannons.

Wolseley attacked at dawn after a march across the sand on a particularly dark night. Less than two hours later the Egyptians had been routed and were dispersed in the desert. Arabi, who had not commanded his men personally, escaped on horseback to Cairo. On the evening of the next day the British cavalry, after a forced march of sixty-five kilometers in the desert under a burning sun, entered the Egyptian capital just in time to prevent it being destroyed by rebels exasperated by the defeat. Arabi

was captured, condemned to death, reprieved, and exiled to Ceylon. On September 25, Tewfik, who had taken refuge during the troubles in one of his residences near Alexandria, returned to Cairo to pretend to reign over Egypt again, this time under a new master. Great Britain, which had once strongly opposed the construction of the Suez Canal, now controlled it in both military and financial terms. Britain also imposed a puppet government but seemed to have no intention of remaining in Egypt indefinitely. Early in 1882 most of the British troops were preparing to embark once again when alarming news began to arrive from the Sudan.

In July 1880, Captain Gaetano Casati, an Italian, was progressing slowly up the White Nile to join Romolo Gessi on the Bahr al-Ghazal. Four days out of Khartoum, passing the island of Aba, he was surprised to see all the Muslims on board—crew, passengers, and soldiers—turn toward this apparently silent and deserted strip of land and pray. They explained to him that a saint lived there, a great saint who had returned to earth (having already lived seven centuries earlier) as the son of a camel driver from Dongola. He prayed, meditated, performed penance, and worked miracles. It was already being said that perhaps he was the true heir to the Prophet, the descendant of Ali, the messenger of Allah, al-Mahdi, "the Guided One." His name was Mohammed Ahmed, and he was thirty-two years old.

Early in 1881, the Rauf Pasha, who had replaced Gordon as the governor of Sudan, also learned from a venerable sheikh that in the mosques and bazaars of Khartoum, people were speaking about nothing but the coming of al-Mahdi, who, according to a very ancient prophecy, had been charged with the definitive subjugation of the world to Islam prior to the Universal Judgment. Mohammed Ahmed, the hermit of Aba, not only qualified through his preaching and miracle working but also bore the signs that were supposed to identify the chosen one, a mole on his left

GOD'S ENVOY IN THE SUDAN: THE REVOLT OF AL-MAHDI

cheek and a space between his upper incisors. Carrying only a pilgrim's cane and a begging bowl, he had set out across the Sudan, smiling, affable, and convincing, distributing to the poor all the donations he received and announcing the imminence of a new era. He was greeted everywhere as the Guided One. Among other feats, he won over Abdullahi al-Tashi of the Baggara tribe, a community of Kordofan shepherds and slave traders famous for their skills in war. Abdullahi al-Tashi became his disciple and lieutenant and was the first to recognize him publicly as al-Mahdi.

The preacher gathered around him all those races of the Sudan oppressed by the hated "Turks." To the corruption of the Egyptian clerks, the overwhelming taxes collected by force, and the expulsion of all the Sudanese administration imposed

282 top *Khartoum, the nerve center for negotiations and treaties in those years.*

282-283 *The British forces achieved some success in minor skirmishes such as the one illustrated here.*

283 top and center left *Shortly after the British occupation of Egypt, the Sudan was swept by rebellion. An Egyptian army under the command of the British General Hicks (top) ventured into Kordofan to face the Madhists but was murdered following the grueling march represented in this engraving.*
(Thomas Archer, *The War in Egypt and the Soudan*, London)

by Rauf after Gordon's departure, was added the economic collapse caused by the suppression of the slave trade, the primary source of the country's wealth. One spark was enough to light a blaze: the converted, who clothed themselves in the costume of holy poverty, a white tunic decorated with multicolored patches, were trembling with impatience, waiting only for the redeemer to give the signal for the jihad, or holy war.

The perspicacious Rauf read the threat of imminent misfortune in this news and immediately sent his deputy Abu Saud to the island of Aba to bring Mohammed Ahmed to Khartoum for an interview. Abu Saud duly departed but returned alone; the saint disdained any contact with the authorities. Increasingly worried, Rauf

decided to take drastic steps before it was too late: Abu Saud embarked once again on the steamer *Ismailia*, this time with two companies of soldiers and orders to capture the agitator dead or alive. Through prudence—or betrayal, according to the more suspicious historians—Abu Saud remained aboard his vessel, while during the moonless night his men disembarked among the reedbeds of the island, convinced they would surprise al-Mahdi and his followers in their sleep. Instead, before firing a single shot, the Egyptians were attacked in the darkness by a screaming mob armed with lances and clubs. Most were slaughtered instantly; those who were taken prisoner, faced with a choice of death or desertion, committed themselves to the new prophet; very few managed to escape and swim back to the *Ismailia*,

which turned tail and headed back to Khartoum at full steam.

This first spilled blood signaled the beginning of the revolt. It was May 1881. A few days later, al-Mahdi, who in imitation of Mohammed wanted his own hegira, crossed to the left bank of the Nile and entered Kordofan, escorted by his faithful followers, to a roll of drums announcing the holy war. Nobody dared resist him; and when he pitched his tent at the foot of Mount Ghedir, a holy spot in which, according to legend, the Prophet once rested, believers from throughout the Sudan arrived to assemble around him.

From here he sent out messengers in all directions, asking for the aid of all good Muslims in the completion of his mission: the slaughter of the

283 center right *The energetic Abd-el-Kader was sent in vain to be governor of Khartoum. He was a former leader of* Baker's Forty Thieves.
(Gaetano Casati, *Ten Years in Equatoria and the Return with Emin Pasha*, London, 1891)

283 bottom *A dervish wearing the characteristic patched costume.*
(Rudolf C. Slatin Pasha, C. B., *Fire and the Sword in the Sudan*, London, 1896)

infidels; the liberation of Egypt, Mecca, and Constantinople; and the conversion of the world. Again like Mohammed, he appointed four caliphs. The first was Abdullahi, who marched with his Baggara people behind a black banner. The second was Mohammed al-Sharif leader of the people of Dongola, with a green insignia. The fourth, with the white flag, was Ali Uad Melu, from Gezira. The third post, that of the yellow banner, was offered to a powerful sheikh of the Senussi Confederation residing in the distant oasis of Cufra, in the middle of the Libyan Desert; he refused the offer, out of either caution or disaccord.

Two expeditions departed tardily from Khartoum, the first composed of 1,500 soldiers, the second of 6,000; both were routed. Cairo recalled Rauf in June 1882 and replaced him with the more dynamic Abd-el-Kader, formerly the leader of Baker's Forty Thieves. Egypt, however, was in the grip of the crisis that was to lead to the British landing, and could do little; in fact, Ahmed Arabi recalled the available troops from the Sudan in order to face the British, and the insurrection spread as irresistibly as the flooding Nile.

Al-Mahdi suffered only one setback, when his 30,000 men, with virtually no firearms, marched on Al-Ubayyid, the capital of Kordofan. This small garrison put up a desperate defense, and a third of

the attackers were left dead on the ground. Reinforcements failed to arrive, however, and the besieging rebels cut all lines of communication. The heavens then sent an auspicious sign to the Guided One: a comet appeared from the direction of Mecca, and the year 1300 of the Muslim era began, the year in which, as all Muslims knew, the true Mahdi would manifest himself. Deprived of provisions, Al-Ubayyid fell on January 17, 1883. The city's rifles, cannons, and ammunition fell into the hands of the besiegers.

Consternation now reigned in Cairo. The khedive, Tewfik, asked the British government, which had become the guardian of Egypt, for advice. In London, Prime Minister Gladstone was reluctant to engage in any African adventure and refused to offer any help, declaring his complete disinterest in Sudanese affairs. He would have preferred that the Egyptians left Darfur and Kordofan to the rebels, but, faithful to his proclamation of neutrality, he made no official announcement of such a preference. Left to its own devices, the Egyptian government again chose to use force against those whom the European press had begun to call the dervishes, a term that at one time denoted the ascetic beggars of Islam and subsequently came to include all who belonged to any religious brotherhood. Abd-el-Kader was replaced

by a new governor, Alaa al-Din, and Lieutenant William Hicks, a former officer in the British army in the service of the khedive, was sent to Khartoum with orders to reconquer Al-Ubayyid.

Having ascended the White Nile as far as Ad Duwaym, Hicks headed west, into the desolate Kordofan at the head of 10,000 men. These troops were well armed but poorly trained and even less well disciplined, and included the fugitives of Tell el-Kebir, who had been incorporated by force, in chains. The officer corps was composed of European adventurers who, for the most part, were ignorant and incapable. For two months, the column dragged itself, short of rations and dying of thirst, through the thorny bush, spied upon night and day by an invisible and elusive enemy and betrayed by guides who led them far from the wells.

Having passed Rahad, the troops were lured into forested gorges, attacked by surprise on November 15, 1883, and massacred. The few bleeding and naked prisoners were driven into the camp of al-Mahdi, who awaited them, smiling, perched on the back of a magnificent white camel. His dervish tunic was studded with scarlet patches, pieces of British uniforms that had been gathered on the battlefields, and red brocade torn from the sacred vestments of the Catholic mission in Al-Ubayyid. A few days earlier,

at the other end of the Sudan, near Suakin, an Egyptian division of 500 men had been exterminated; among the dead was the English consul. The whole country was aflame. Al-Mahdi covered the terrain from one end to the other, subjecting his camp to interminable marches like a true nomadic city in the center of which was pitched his tent and those of his ever more numerous women, captives of war or the daughters of sheikhs looking for marital alliances with the victors.

Each caliph occupied a separate quarter with his warriors. At one end was a market, where the strict Islamic law was enforced by the *qadi*. Drinkers, smokers, and unveiled or bejeweled women were punished with lashes; adulterers were stoned to death; and thieves had their hands cut off. The faithful were required to bring all personal goods and spoils of war to the communal treasury. Five times a day al-Mahdi called them to prayer. He preached and received the delegations of his increasingly numerous followers, messengers, and the "Turks" who hurriedly shifted their allegiance to his side. He took pleasure in spending his free moments discussing theology with the imprisoned Christian missionaries, dumbfounding them with the depth of his religious culture. The camp often rang to the deep bellow of the caliph Abdullahi's ivory horn,

284-285 *The fanatical assault of the Mahdists, armed only with lances, sabers, and shields against the ordered ranks of the Redcoats. By no means inclined to become involved in a colonial campaign,* the British government under Gladstone advised Egypt to abandon the Sudan, guaranteeing in exchange help with the defense of the Egyptian border and the Red Sea ports threatened by the *incursions of the dervishes. The rebels were faced and defeated by a British detachment near al-Tab, not far from Suakin in February 1884.*

285 bottom *A British detachment sent to protect the southern border of Egypt watering on the Nile near Wadi Halfa.*

285

calling his men to prepare for war. The caravans would depart, their lances and rifle barrels glinting in the sun, behind an immense black banner embroidered with a verse from the Koran. Now strong with the 10,000 modern Remington rifles taken from Hicks's soldiers, the dervishes met with no further obstacles. The provinces of Equatoria and Bahr al-Ghazal, entrusted to the German Emin and the Englishman Lupton respectively, were isolated. Following an able and tenacious defense, the Austrian governor of Darfur, Slatin Bey, was abandoned by his soldiers, who deserted him to join al-Mahdi. To save his life, he entered the prophet's camp, embraced the Muslim faith, and became the servant of Caliph Abdullahi. His enslavement lasted twelve years.

Hicks's disaster also upset the plans of Gladstone, who was about to pull the

English forces out of Egypt. Obliged to make a clear statement of its position, the London government came out in favor of abandoning all lands south of Aswan, or at least of Wadi Halfa, guaranteeing in exchange to defend the remaining Egyptian territories and the Red Sea ports. This meant the evacuation of Khartoum, a move that was warmly recommended. This was in theory a simple solution, but one that was difficult to put into practice: how could the thousands of Egyptians and Europeans, widely scattered in distant, isolated stations, be gathered in the Sudanese capital and then accompanied across the desert without falling into the hands of the dervishes? There was a risk of slaughter on a vast scale, noted Gordon, interviewed in the *Pall Mall Gazette* in his role as the leading English authority on Sudanese affairs. While the governments of London and Cairo lost themselves in discussion of the insoluble problem, the English press was unanimous in imposing its solution: send Gordon, the hero. He was the man for the job.

Gladstone gave way to the pressure of public opinion and in turn obliged Egypt to give way. Gordon, who had peremptorily declared in his interview the need to defend Khartoum "at whatever cost," in turn gave way, and agreed to direct the evacuation. Like al-Mahdi, he considered himself a man of God; each had a boundless faith in his own destiny. Assigning the parts like an able playwright, destiny brought them together, the protagonists of a grand tragedy. In the company of Colonel Stewart, a skilled officer who knew the Sudan well, Gordon left for Egypt. At Cairo he was cordially received by the khedive and the English resident Sir Evelyn Baring, the future Lord Cromer, who was to be an omnipotent imperial proconsul and the real master of the country for nearly a quarter of a century.

Gordon was instructed to guarantee not only the evacuation but also a degree of order following it, leaving behind him a Sudanese government based on a confederation of minor local sultans. Gordon, who had his own ideas, thought

286 center left *The governor of Darfur, the Austrian Slatin, portrayed here in dervish costume, was captured and feigned conversion to Islam to save his life.* (Rudolf C. Slatin Pasha, C. B., *Fire and the Sword in the Sudan*, London, 1896)

286 center right *An Australian contingent disembarking at Suakin in March 1885.* (T. Archer, *The War in Egypt and the Soudan*)

286-287 and 287 top *The pressure of public opinion forced the British government to send troops to the rescue of Gordon, cut off in the besieged Khartoum. The British forces slowly ascended the course of the Nile, far too slowly. The dervishes were defeated at Abu Klea (top) on January 17, 1885, and at Kerbekan (bottom) on February 10, when Khartoum had already fallen.* (T. Archer, *The War in Egypt and the Soudan*)

to ask for the help of the old slave trader Ziber, now banished to Cairo, whose son Suleiman had been shot by Gessi on his orders. Gordon considered Ziber the sole Sudanese who could oppose al-Mahdi with as much influence. But Ziber refused to help, and Gordon left for Khartoum on January 26, 1884, as the general governor of Sudan, certain that he would resolve the all-consuming problem within six months.

When he arrived in Berber, on February 11, the disappointments began. He received notice that just a few days before, Sir Valentine Baker, brother of the explorer and commander of the Egyptian gendarmerie, who had been sent with 3,000 men to liberate two garrisons on the Red Sea, had been defeated by a far outnumbered group of dervishes: by now the Egyptians were overwhelmed by fear

at the rebels' very appearance. Gordon attempted a move toward peace: he sent al-Mahdi a cloak of honor and the offer to leave him Kordofan and the title of sultan. But after reflection during a sleepless night, he convoked the sheikhs of the area and announced the government's intention to evacuate Sudan. He was hoping that the tribal chiefs, faced with the prospect of inheriting the country, would turn against al-Mahdi. Instead, the Sudanese, among whom the news spread like wildfire, felt they were being abandoned by those who were supposed to defend them and consequently joined forces with the enemy. At Berber Gordon also read a proclamation stating that when Sudan became independent, the Anglo-Egyptian convention of 1877, on the basis of which the slave trade was due to cease in

1889, would become worthless. The anti-slavery organizations in England and the rest of the world were outraged; but Gordon's only concern was with separating the slave traders from al-Mahdi by any means, and he felt in any case that his proclamation simply reflected reality and that there was nothing wrong in saying so.

When the revived governor general disembarked at Khartoum from the steamer *Tewfikieh* to a delirious welcome from the entire population on the morning of February 18, he immediately performed a typically theatrical gesture, building a bonfire in front of his palace, into which he cast the lists of unpaid taxes as well as the whips that the tax collectors had used to encourage reluctant contributors. "In this way both the signs of debt and the emblems of oppression disappeared," a *Times* correspondent telegraphed to London.

Gordon himself said that he had come without soldiers, only God at his side, in order to heal the ills of Sudan with the arms of justice. In the meantime, good army engineering officer that he was, he

288 top *A column of rescuers commanded by General Wilson was sent on ahead in an attempt to reach Khartoum before it was too late. The drawing shows a boat being hauled past the Second Cataract.*

288-289 *Wilson's men embarking at Gubat. The general came within sight of Khartoum aboard his steamboats shortly after the fall of the city.*

289 *During the return journey from Khartoum Wilson's boat was wrecked near the island of Meruat. In the engraving at the left he is scrutinizing the Nile while waiting for rescuers. The plate at the top depicts the boat sent to pick up Wilson and his men subjected to intense gunfire from the dervishes on either side of the river.*

fortified the city, reorganized the garrisons, and stockpiled foodstuffs. Al-Mahdi, also convinced that God was on his side, responded to the governor's offer with the command to repent and convert to the true faith and, in the meantime, advanced upon the city. On March 12 a group of dervishes cut the telegraph line at Halfaya, a few miles downstream from Khartoum, and dug in on both banks of the Nile. Thus the siege began.

Trapped in the city, Gordon could not attempt an evacuation without outside help. In the last telegraphs he was able to transmit, he asked for a diversionary maneuver at Berber, a small British expeditionary force that would occupy the key Nile city and revive the vacillating faith of the surrounding tribes. The British government, ever reluctant to intervene in Sudan, and convinced that all Gordon had to do was carry out the orders to evacuate the city, procrastinated and wasted precious time while public opinion called for the besieged hero's rescue.

The governor armored the ten small steamships at his disposal and had them cruise up and down the river to keep the dervishes at a distance and plunder crops

and livestock. But far from Khartoum, the situation was worsening. In May Berber fell into the hands of al-Mahdi; 5,000 inhabitants were killed and the rest enslaved. The climax was drawing near. The press finally succeeded in pressuring the British government into sending an expeditionary force under the command of General Wolseley. That army all too slowly gathered in Egypt and began combat training in that unaccustomed climate. Gordon sent a flotilla down the Nile, under the command of Colonel Stewart, who after bombarding Berber was for head to Egypt, to bring news of the besieged city and beg for assistance. Leaving the others behind, Stewart proceeded from Berber with just one steamer, only to be wrecked against a rock. On landing, he was treacherously killed along with all his crew by the followers of al-Mahdi. If he had only been able to continue along the river, he would have encountered an advance party from the English expedition at Merani, captained by an officer destined for a grand future, Major Herbert Kitchener.

While Wolseley lingered, the huge army of al-Mahdi was marching from Kordofan in the direction of Khartoum, to gather about the city. Late in October

the Guided One pitched his tent near the outskirts of Omdurman, but he was in no hurry. With the aid of his prisoner, Slatin, al-Mahdi began sending messages exhorting Gordon to surrender, and in November his forces began their bombardment.

In the meantime, the message that Gordon received from Kitchener, announcing the arrival of assistance, provoked a vain hope in the city. Wolseley was still far away, however, at Kurti, where on December 30, 1884, a messenger from the governor arrived with the news that the city was in grave danger. At last the general realized that there was no more time to be lost and began to move, sending 1,600 men of the Camel Corps ahead across the desert in order to meet up with the Nile again at al-Matamma, after having fought 25,000 dervishes at Abu Klea. On January 21, the rescuers commanded by Colonel Wilson saw four small boats traveling down the river flying the Egyptian flag: Gordon's steamers. But Wilson wasted another two days in the useless reconnaissance upstream and downstream instead of hastening toward Khartoum, and it was only on January 24 that his men embarked, reaching the city just

291 right and bottom *Gordon, on the right in the uniform of the governor general of the Sudan, was killed and decapitated (from* Life of General Gordon *by Walter Scott, London). His head was wrapped in a cloth and taken to al-Mahdi, after being presented to the horrified Slatin (from* Fire and Sword in the Sudan *by Rudolf C. Slatin Pasha, C. B., London, 1896). It was then raised on a pike in the victors' camp (from* Seven Years in the Soudan *by Romolo Gessi Pasha, London, 1892).*

before noon on January 28. A hail of fire greeted them from both sides of the river, from the fort of Omdurman and from the walls of Khartoum. A bullet hit Wilson in the thigh; another shattered the binoculars in his hand. Artillery fire riddled the four steamers. Sixty hours earlier the city had fallen into the hands of al-Mahdi. At dawn on January 26, the dervishes took a bastion with a surprise attack and penetrated the city, overrunning the defenders. Arriving at the governor's palace, a platoon raced up the stairs, toward Gordon's suite. The door opened, and a man in a white uniform appeared upon the threshold, a pistol in his fist. "Where is al-Mahdi?" he asked. In the silence that followed, a dervish ran a lance through his breast.

A few hours later, Slatin, chained up in al-Mahdi's camp, saw a drunken crowd approaching. "At the head marched three black soldiers: one, who was called Sheta, had something bloody in his hand. Behind him crushed a crowd that filled the air with their cries. Entering my tent, they remained for a moment in front of me, smirking. Then Sheta opened the cloth that covered the thing he was carrying, and showed me the head of General Gordon."

290-291 *When Wilson's steamboats came within sight of Khartoum on January 28, they were welcomed with cannon fire, as seen in this engraving.*

291 top left *The dervishes occupied the city at dawn on January 26, and all that remained for Wilson to do was to fire a few token shots before heading back downstream.*

Following Kordofan, Darfur, and Sennar, and while Gordon was besieged in Khartoum, the province of Bahr al-Ghazal also fell into the hands of the dervishes. Its governor, Frank Lupton, ended up as a slave in al-Mahdi's camp together with his colleague, Slatin. Of all of Egypt's immense Sudanese Empire, nothing remained but the southernmost province of Equatoria, where Emin Bey had replaced Romolo Gessi as governor. Emin's real name was Eduard Schnitzer. He was a German Jew born in Oppeln, Prussia, in 1840. A graduate in medicine and an enthusiastic naturalist, he decided to seek his fortune in Albania when it was still under Turkish rule. There he entered the good graces of the governor of Scutari, Ismail Hakki Pasha, who took him along on his subsequent appointments to various parts of the world; he thus had the opportunity of traveling from Constantinople to Armenia, from Syria to Arabia.

When his patron died, Schnitzer returned home to his mother for a few months, but by then the East was in his blood, and he departed once again for Egypt, arriving at Khartoum in 1875, where Gordon employed him as a doctor. That was when he took the name and title of Emin Effendi Hakim, "the trusted doctor." He was sent to Lado to treat the sick, then on a mission to the court of King M'tesa of Uganda, and finally to Kabba Rega, the sovereign of Bunyoro; he performed so well during these delicate diplomatic assignments that in 1878 he

A MILLION POUNDS' WORTH OF IVORY: STANLEY AND THE RELIEF OF EMIN PASHA

292 bottom center
A number of Governor Schnitzer's Equatorian collaborators: from the left, the Italian Casati with his daughter born to a Sudanese woman, the Egyptian pharmacist Vita Hassan, and the Russian explorer Junker.

292 bottom *A meeting of Emin's council of chiefs in the government buildings.*

293 *The Egyptian troops parading at Dufile (above) and at Tunguru (below).*
(A. J. Mounteney-Jephson, *Emin Pasha and the Rebellion at the Equator*, London, 1890)

292 top *The Mahdist revolt completely isolated the province of Equatoria governed by the German Eduard Schnitzer, who had taken the Turkish name of Emin.*
(Gaetano Casati, *Ten Years in Equatoria and the Return with Emin Pasha*, London, 1891)

292 top center *The Italian Gessi, Gordon's lieutenant, was replaced by another Italian, Gaetano Casati, who was to become Emin's closest collaborator. Their first meeting is depicted in this drawing.*

was rewarded with the honorary title of "bey," and was then appointed governor of Equatoria.

When the Mahdist revolt broke out, Emin found himself cut off. Boats were no longer ascending the Nile from the north, and from Khartoum came news that was at times disturbing and at others encouraging but unfortunately false, like the rumor of Gordon's entry into the city with a large army and dozens of elephants. More truthful, but much more depressing, were the messages Lupton was sending from Bahr al-Ghazal as he was assailed by the dervishes of Karamallah Mohammed: "It is over for me," said the last letter. Shortly afterward the armies of al-Mahdi began to attack the most northerly outposts of Equatoria. For some time in 1884, Emin considered surrendering, but then he saw that the

(G. Casati, *Ten Years in Equatoria and the Return with Emin Pasha*)

tactics by which he was opposing the Mahdists were proving to be effective. He had in fact adopted a flexible form of defense, withdrawing his troops after each battle, inflicting heavy losses upon the enemy while enticing them ever deeper into his own territory. Forced to take one fortified post after another by storm, without ever succeeding in facing the "Turks" on the battlefield, where the overwhelming numerical superiority of the dervishes would be decisive, Karamallah Mohammed was worried that he would meet the same end as Hicks and fall into a trap prepared by the astute doctor. He thus retreated, and Emin was left in relative peace.

Emin had evacuated the most exposed stations, reducing the province to a seventh of its former size, and transformed the small capital of Lado into a highly equipped fortress, with trenches, drawbridges, bulwarks, and ramparts. He lived there as if on a desert island, immersing himself in his beloved botanical and entomological studies in the company of the Italian Gaetano Casati and a Russian-born German named Wilhelm Junker, who had

fortunately escaped the clutches of the rebels and taken refuge there in 1884. In addition to being an esteemed scientist, Junker was a brilliant administrator who profitably developed all of Equatoria's great riches—ivory, coffee, rubber, and cotton. He had formally converted to Islam and therefore enjoyed easier and more cordial relations with his Egyptian and Sudanese functionaries, who began to complain and intrigue against him only when the rebellion was well under way.

Emin still had two steamships at his disposal, the *Khedive* and the *Nyanza,* as well as a few thousand well-armed men and various artillery pieces; the dervishes were no longer pressing, and he did not lack for supplies. He was prepared to wait for developments, but he prudently transferred his headquarters even farther south, to Vadelai, some 300 kilometers from Lado.

Here in 1886, he finally received the news from Zanzibar that Gordon was dead and that all Sudan was in the hands of al-Mahdi; there was no longer any hope of help being sent from Egypt. The only possible course of action remaining open to him was to abandon the province

and evacuate his men toward the Indian Ocean. As in the case of Khartoum, this was more easily said than done: they were facing a journey of thousands of kilometers, across the warring kingdoms of Bunyoro and Uganda, as well as other hostile territories, with a caravan composed of close to 10,000 men, women, and children. This would have been an exodus of biblical proportions that could easily have finished very badly. Argument and dissent began to grow between the officers and the Egyptian and Sudanese soldiers; uncertainty and anxiety reigned, and the mild-mannered governor began to lose control over his men. Junker decided in any case to reconnoiter the route to investigate the feasibility of an evacuation, leaving for Zanzibar via Uganda. Emin in the meantime sent first his pharmacist, Vita Hassan, and then Captain Casati to the court of Kabba Rega, king of Bunyoro, to strengthen their alliance with the potentate whose land they would have to cross.

At the end of 1886, Junker arrived in Cairo, and the world, which until then had been blissfully ignorant of the

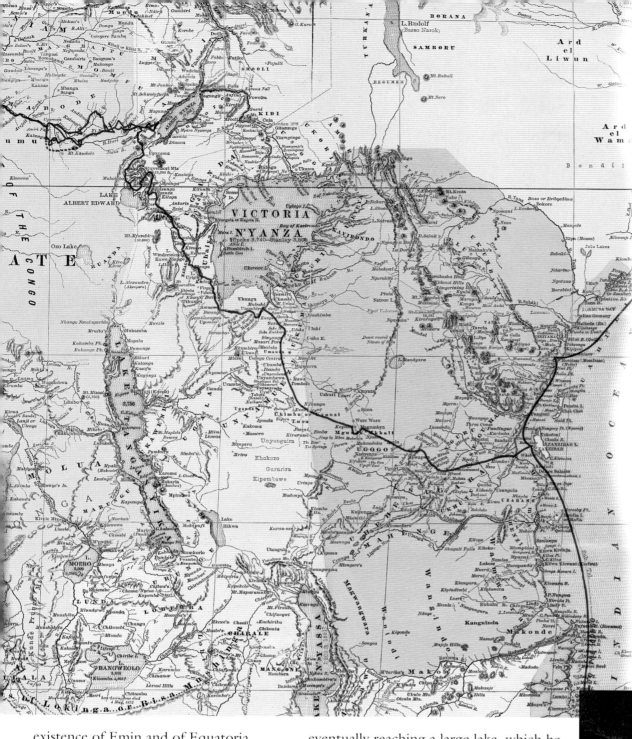

294 left *An expedition to rescue Emin was organized and led by Stanley, who chose to reach Equatoria from the west, crossing the recently constituted Congo Free State, assigned as the personal property of King Leopold II of Belgium portrayed here.*
(J. Ewin Ritchie, *The Pictorial Edition of the Life and Discoveries of David Livingstone*)

294-295 *The map shows the itinerary followed by Stanley.*
(Henry Morton Stanley, *In Darkest Africa of the Quest, Rescue and Retreat of Emin Governor of Equatoria*)

existence of Emin and of Equatoria, learned that in the heart of Africa there was a second Gordon in even worse trouble than the first. The press made Emin into the hero of the day, a fascinating and learned character, an administrator and military man who had abandoned the entomologist's magnifying glass in favor of the soldier's rifle, trapped in the tropical jungle and surrounded by fanatical savages. As in the case of Gordon, the newspapers demanded a rescue expedition. And they immediately named their man for the job—the rescuer *par excellence,* Henry Morton Stanley.

A year before Stanley completed his long journey along the Congo, King Leopold II of Belgium, with an eye to the commercial potential of the promising Dark Continent, had founded the International African Association, which in turn spawned the Study Committee for the Upper Congo that had commissioned Stanley to conduct new explorations and found trading stations along the banks of the immense waterway. Stanley completed his assignment, ascending the Congo from August 1879 to May 1882,

eventually reaching a large lake, which he named in honor of the Belgian king, and establishing settlements at every point that seemed to him to be suitable for trade with the natives. He then returned to the coast, only to leave again in May 1883 for the Upper Congo. By December he had arrived at his appointed goal, the Stanley Falls, after having overcome so many obstacles that the natives honored him with the title of Bula Matari, "breaker of rocks." By January he was back at the newly founded Léopoldville.

In 1884, on the initiative of the Germans, a conference of all the colonial powers was held in Berlin, at which Africa was effectively partitioned. The Congo was constituted as a free state and assigned as the personal property of Leopold II, who thus became the largest landowner who ever lived. The king committed himself, however, to bequeath the territory to Belgium in exchange for the financial contributions requested for its exploitation. The king would probably have assigned Stanley a government post in the new African colony, but the proposal from a committee hurriedly

294 right *One of Emin's two steamboats navigating a tributary of the White Nile.*
(Gaetano Casati, *Ten Years in Equatoria and the Return with Emin Pasha*, London, 1891)

295 top *The governor of Equatoria receiving an Arab merchant carrying a message from the coast.*
(G. Casati, *Ten Years in Equatoria and the Return with Emin Pasha*)

295 bottom *Emin in his residence, where he devoted himself to zoology and botany.*
(A. J. Mounteney-Jephson, *Emin Pasha and the Rebellion at the Equator*, London, 1890)

295

296 top left
Stanley, seen here, claimed that the Congo route was safer even though much longer and succeeded in imposing a choice *that led the expedition to cross the densest region of the great equatorial jungle.* (H. M. Stanley, *In Darkest Africa of the Quest, Rescue and Retreat of Emin Governor of Equatoria*)

296 top right
Stanley's sectioned metal boat, designed to facilitate its transportation through the jungle.

296 bottom *While navigating the Congo, Stanley used Belgian steamboats like the* Florida, *seen here at its launch.*

296-297 *This map shows in great detail the route followed by Stanley from the Congo to Lake Albert and from there, after having collected Emin and his people, to Lake Victoria.*

constituted in England to organize the Emin Pasha Relief Expedition reached him first. The British, whose collective conscience had probably been pricked by Gordon's miserable end, were far quicker to prepare this rescue expedition: donations of money poured in, and crowds of volunteers presented themselves. A total of 10,000 pounds was collected, and the same sum was contributed by the Egyptian government. The operation was cloaked in purely humanitarian motives, but the organizers also hoped that it would prove to be good business. The president of the committee, the shipbuilder Mackinnon, founder of the Indo-British Shipping Company, which traded with Zanzibar, was hoping that the march to Equatoria would open the route not only for the refugees but also for merchandise. Stories circulated about how during Emin's long years of isolation he had accumulated at Vadelai ivory worth a million pounds, a sum sufficient to transform that village of sticks and straw into a treasure chest worthy of Ali Baba.

Stanley received Mackinnon's telegram in America during a lecture tour about the Congo; he accepted command of the enterprise and traveled to England. The committee, however, was determined that he should follow an eastern route, departing from Zanzibar, while the explorer, having seen the state of perpetual war that reigned in Uganda and its neighboring countries, wanted to set out from the Atlantic coast and ascend the Congo—a longer route but one that in his judgment was safer and richer in water and provisions. He would then proceed to Zanzibar from Equatoria. Stanley insisted above all that the major risk the expedition would run was the desertion of the porters, who would flee en masse if he conducted them from Zanzibar toward the interior. He intended instead to recruit porters on the

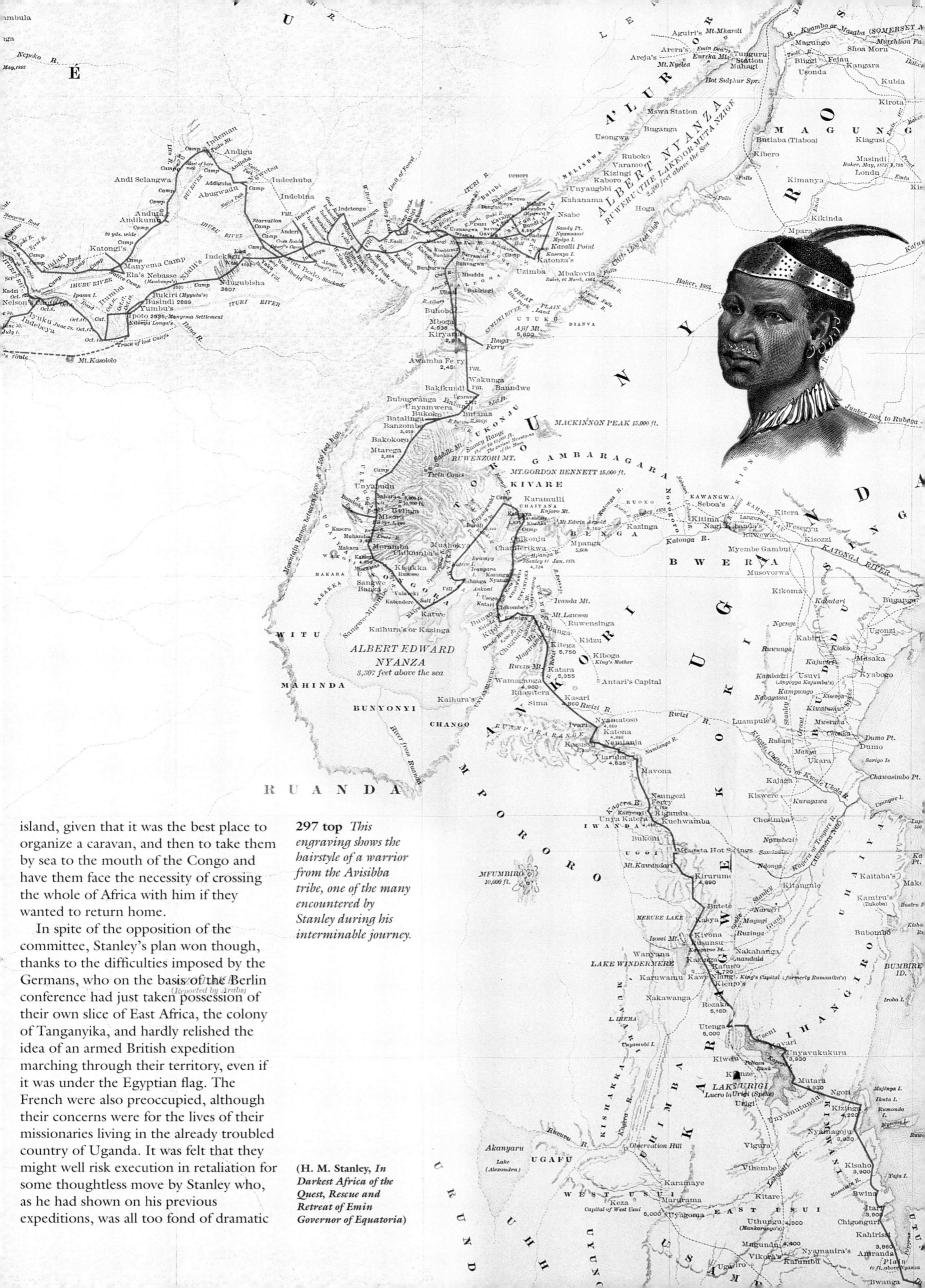

island, given that it was the best place to organize a caravan, and then to take them by sea to the mouth of the Congo and have them face the necessity of crossing the whole of Africa with him if they wanted to return home.

In spite of the opposition of the committee, Stanley's plan won though, thanks to the difficulties imposed by the Germans, who on the basis of the Berlin conference had just taken possession of their own slice of East Africa, the colony of Tanganyika, and hardly relished the idea of an armed British expedition marching through their territory, even if it was under the Egyptian flag. The French were also preoccupied, although their concerns were for the lives of their missionaries living in the already troubled country of Uganda. It was felt that they might well risk execution in retaliation for some thoughtless move by Stanley who, as he had shown on his previous expeditions, was all too fond of dramatic

297 top *This engraving shows the hairstyle of a warrior from the Avisibba tribe, one of the many encountered by Stanley during his interminable journey.*

(H. M. Stanley, *In Darkest Africa of the Quest, Rescue and Retreat of Emin Governor of Equatoria*)

298-299 *The march completed by Stanley's expedition from the Atlantic coast to the equatorial region lasted over a year and was an arduous exercise during which half of the men died of hunger and disease and as a result of the hostility of the natives. At many points the* party had to fight its way forward or procure food by taking it from the natives by force. The illustration on this page depicts an episode during the march across what Stanley called Darkest Africa, a skirmish with the Avisibba cannibals.

298

298 center left
Stanley watching a dance performed by Mazamboni warriors.

298 center right
The sound of the horn calls the men of the village of Lyugu to arms.

298 bottom *This Pygmy was captured by Stanley's expedition near Avatiko.*

299 *The Arab slave trader Tipoo Tib (bottom), who accompanied Stanley as far as the upper course of the Congo, committed himself to* *supplying a hundred porters but failed to keep his word. The illustration at the top depicts a battle with the Mazamboni tribe. In the center can be* *seen an encounter between Stanley, Emin, and Casati on the shore of Lake Albert.*

gestures made at the natives' expense.

Thus whether or not the American explorer's objections to the eastern route were well founded (some suspected that behind them was the long hand of Leopold II, who had, in fact, proposed to Emin the annexation of Equatoria by the Congo Free State), he was free to do as he saw fit. On January 21, 1887, he left for Zanzibar, where he not only recruited porters and acquired exchange goods but also took on board the man whom he considered to be the ace up his sleeve, the Arab trader Tipoo Tib, whose reputation as a slaver was cleaned up for the occasion and who was named by King Leopold as governor of the province of Stanley Falls, a territory in which he was already the de facto sultan without the need for any investiture. Stanley maintained that this man's support was essential for procuring armed protection and, more importantly, for recruiting porters to carry vital munitions to Emin and bring back the treasure of Equatoria: those famous ivory tusks that the explorer realistically valued at around 60,000 pounds, a tidy sum. Tipoo Tib agreed to join Stanley and on March 18 the expedition disembarked at the mouth of the Congo and began advancing toward the interior along the river.

From the sporadic messages that arrived from the coast, thanks to Arab

(H. M. Stanley, *In Darkest Africa of the Quest, Rescue and Retreat of Emin Governor of Equatoria*)

299

traders, Emin knew vaguely that someone
somewhere was organizing a rescue
operation. After some hesitation, he had
decided not to evacuate his territory; he
intended to remain with "his people," as
he liked to call them, where the khedive
had posted him. He needed supplies,
however, and he considered that the best
thing that could be done for him was to
reopen the route from the Great Lakes to
the east coast and restore contacts with
the civilized world. He certainly did not
imagine that very shortly the imperious
rescuer would be virtually ordering him
to allow himself to be "saved."

The skirmishes with the dervishes were
resumed on an occasional basis, but this
was perhaps the least of Emin's concerns;
what was worse was the crumbling
discipline among his already disrespectful
troops, exacerbated by the inactivity and
the increasingly evident hostility of the
king of Bunyoro, who had imprisoned
and flogged his envoy, Casati, who
managed to escape by the skin of his
teeth. However, the governor (whose
tenacious resistance had been rewarded
with the title of pasha, though he had yet
to be informed of the honor, as the
decree was being brought by Stanley),
even though he had lost his Abyssinian
wife who had given him his beloved

daughter, Ferida, and though he was
suffering from increasingly severe myopia,
was by no means pessimistic about the
future and whiled away the time
dedicating himself to his studies.

In February 1888, Emin Pasha heard
talk of white men seen in the area of Lake
Albert. He left with a boat for the
southern shore, but found nothing
concrete and turned back after leaving a
message with a tribal chief for the
eventual rescuers. Two months later one
of Stanley's lieutenants, Jephson, reached
the lake and went in search of the pasha,
disembarking at the trading station of
Msua, where the troops of Equatoria led
him to the governor. Stanley was camped
a day's journey away, after a disastrous
march lasting over a year during which he
had lost half of his men and had had to
fight frequent battles in order to pass
through the territories of hostile tribes,
not to mention the hunger and sickness
they suffered. Stanley noted acidly that as
the rescuer, he was in far worse condition
than the man he was rescuing, who,
together with Casati, presented himself
on April 29 shaved and perfumed and
dressed in a freshly washed, impeccable
white uniform. The governor further
shocked the exhausted American by
offering him and his officers a sumptuous

301 top *Emin burst into the semi-naked Jephson's room with a message from Stanley saying that he was heading in their direction with the rear column.*
(A. J. Mounteney-Jephson, *Emin Pasha and the Rebellion at the Equator*)

301 center *Intimidated by a Mahdist attack, the rebels finally decided to free Emin.*
(H. M. Stanley, *In Darkest Africa of the Quest, Rescue and Retreat of Emin Governor of Equatoria*)

301 bottom left *Emin, Jephson, and Casati embarked at Tunguru to join Stanley.*
(A. J. Mounteney-Jephson, *Emin Pasha and the Rebellion at the Equator*, London, 1890)

300 *Emin, seen in the photograph below, had no intention of leaving Equatoria and what he loved to call "my people." As he saw it, the rescue expedition should have provided him with sufficient arms and munitions to permit him to resist at length. Stanley, however, intended to "rescue" him at all costs, demanding the evacuation of the province. At this point a number of Egyptian and Sudanese officers mutinied, deposing the governor and imprisoning him together with Stanley's lieutenant Jephson (from Emin Pasha and the Rebellion at the Equator, by A. J. Mounteney-Jephson, London, 1890), who had remained with Emin while his superior turned back to recover the rear column. In the illustration above we see Stanley leading an attack against an enemy tribe.*
(**H. M. Stanley,** *In Darkest Africa of the Quest, Rescue and Retreat of Emin Governor of Equatoria*)

and refined banquet and by his sparkling conversation in perfect English; Emin spoke around a dozen languages.

Stanley immediately sowed discord in the pasha's camp with his proposal—which was in reality an ultimatum—to conduct Emin and his men to Zanzibar. He also suggested that Emin Pasha should throw in his lot with King Leopold II or the recently constituted Imperial British East Africa Company, which in a few years was to take possession of Kenya and Uganda.

Determined not to change flags, the governor intended to remain faithful to the khedive; but he was extremely uncertain as to the rest of Stanley's proposals and would probably have preferred to stay put. But timid as he was, he did not want to impose his own wishes upon his men and held a kind of referendum, the outcome of which was disastrous and sparked off a mutiny. While most of the Egyptians favored departure, the majority of the Sudanese did not see any reason to move to Egypt on an extremely dangerous march: they were quite happy where they were, better off than they ever had been at home, and they had formed families whom they had no wish to abandon.

301 bottom right *This illustration expresses all the drama of Casati's misadventure during his mission to Unyoro, where he was imprisoned and beaten.*
(**Gaetano Casati,** *Ten Years in Equatoria and the Return with Emin Pasha*, London, 1891)

Stanley left again for the Congo, to fetch his rear column and return to escort Emin Pasha, who in the meantime should have assembled the departing caravan. However, a number of officers rebelled and took the pasha and Casati prisoner. This confused situation was involuntarily resolved by the unexpected intervention of the dervishes, who at that moment decided to revive their attempts to conquer Equatoria, attacking the garrison at Dufile, the northernmost station in the province.

The panicking men freed the governor and fled to the south, toward Stanley, who had himself been faced with disaster at the rear column camp. Three of the five white officers were dead, and a fourth had returned home ill. The precious provisions, now thought to be superfluous, had been sent back to the coast, and as it turned out, the treacherous Tipoo Tib had failed to recruit any porters. Stanley returned to Lake Albert with the survivors in December 1888 and had to wait furiously until February for Emin Pasha to present himself, despite his urging for haste. Further weeks then passed before all those who intended to leave had assembled. A violent argument then burst out with the Zanzibarian porters due to the excessive quantity of baggage that the refugees intended to take with them.

Finally, Stanley discovered a conspiracy among the Egyptian officers to overpower the whites and take command; these men were subdued, Stanley reluctantly forgoing the idea of shooting them on the spot and then taking advantage of the episode to order an immediate departure.

The American's men numbered around 1,000, those of Emin Pasha not more than 600 out of 10,000. Casati, again gripped by doubts, tried to convince the governor to remain in Equatoria and not to abandon all those who had remained faithful to Egypt. Emin Pasha would have been perfectly willing to head back, but the implacable Stanley, who had no

302 *The evacuation of Equatoria was characterized by indecision and confusion. The key to the episode was Stanley's arrogance in obliging the reluctant Emin Pasha to abandon the province, abdicate from his position as governor, and leave absolute power in the hands of his "savior." Above, the exodus of Emin Pasha's men from Vadelai, from* Emin Pasha and the Rebellion at the Equator, *by A. J. Mounteney-Jephson, London, 1890. Below, Stanley berating the rebel Egyptian officers at Kavalli, from* In Darkest Africa of the Quest, Rescue, and Retreat of Emin Governor of Equatoria, *by Henry Morton Stanley.*

intention of losing the prey for which he had made so many sacrifices, brusquely ordered him to continue.

The 2,400 kilometers from Lake Albert to the coast were covered without any great problems. The Maxim machine gun carried by the bellicose Stanley took care of any hostile tribes, and on December 4, 1889, after encountering a German expedition belatedly leaving to rescue Emin Pasha, they entered the town of Bagamoyo, which then belonged to Germany. At the banquet held that evening they were toasted with champagne, and Emin Pasha received a personal telegram from the kaiser, which touched him deeply. Unfortunately, on leaving the room, the very shortsighted Emin Pasha fell from a veranda and fractured his skull. Once recovered, he put himself at the service of Germany, leading new expeditions to the interior before he was assassinated by Arab slavers in 1892 in the eastern Congo.

Of the 10,000 Egyptians and Sudanese who should have been evacuated, only 260 reached Egypt. As for the legendary ivory of Equatoria, it was acquired by an Arab merchant before it ever reached Stanley. None of this disturbed the triumphant rescuer, however. He was showered with honors and soon after married the painter Dorothy Tennant. In the gardens of the home the couple bought in England, the pond was baptized as Stanley Pool, and a hill as the Mountains of the Moon.

303 top *Prior to the definitive departure of the "rescuees" further disorder occurred, which Emin Pasha attempted to settle with what little authority he retained. The two engravings above show Emin threatened by the rebels.*
left: (Gaetano Casati, *Ten Years in Equatoria and the Return with Emin Pasha*, London, 1891)
right: (A. J. Mounteney-Jephson, *Emin Pasha and the Rebellion at the Equator*, London, 1890)

303 center *The governor bidding his final farewells to those who stayed behind. Only around 600 actually departed out of the 10,000 who theoretically should have been evacuated.*

The majority of the men died of exhaustion during the march and only 260 reached Egypt. Emin never forgave himself for having been persuaded to leave Equatoria.
(A. J. Mounteney-Jephson, *Emin Pasha and the Rebellion at the Equator*)

303 bottom *This engraving is based on a photograph of taken Emin, Stanley, and his officers, on the way to Zanzibar at Usambara.*
(H. M. Stanley, *In Darkest Africa of the Quest, Rescue and Retreat of Emin Governor of Equatoria*)

303

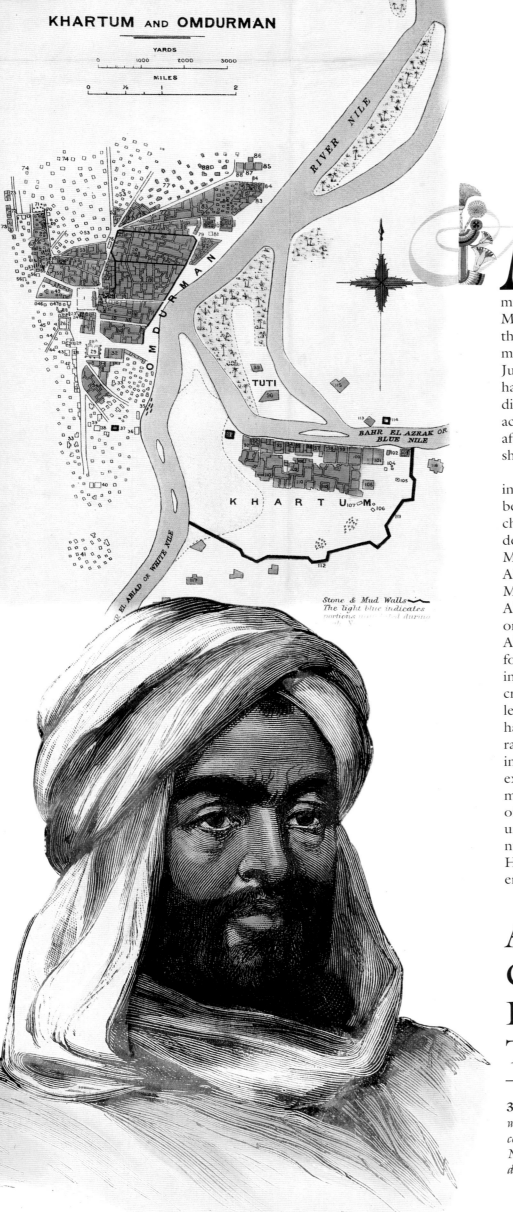

KHARTUM AND OMDURMAN

All things considered, perhaps God was on Egypt's side. The man who claimed to be his envoy, Mohammed Ahmed, al-Mahdi, died at the height of his power, just a few months after the fall of Khartoum, on June 22, 1885. He died of typhus or, as has been suggested, of the excesses of a dissolute lifestyle to which he was not accustomed, the extravagance of which after years of asceticism had cut his life short.

His death probably saved Egypt from invasion. The caliphs, though just as bellicose as al-Mahdi, did not possess his charisma, and the expansion of the dervishes to the north came to a halt. Al-Mahdi's designated successor was Abdullahi. "He is me and I am him," al-Mahdi had said before dying, presenting Abdullahi to his faithful. Coming from one of the most savage Sudanese tribes, Abdullahi was an ignorant and illiterate forty-year-old, but he was not without intelligence, astuteness, and, above all, cruelty. He was probably also among the least fanatical followers of al-Mahdi, having seen in him a political leader rather than a religious reformer. Having inherited power, the caliph manifested an extremely distrustful nature. He put the most important assignments in the hands of men of his own tribe and unscrupulously eliminated al-Mahdi's numerous relatives, one after the other. He was particularly suspicious of the emirs governing the most distant

AVENGING GORDON: THE RECONQUEST OF THE SUDAN

304 top *Khartoum was founded at the confluence of the two Niles and was defended by their* *waters and a curtain wall of beaten earth.* (Rudolf C. Slatin Pasha, C. B., *Fire and Sword in the Sudan*, London, 1896)

304 bottom *Al-Mahdi (portrayed here) died a few months after the fall of Khartoum, perhaps of typhus, perhaps due to the vices to which he had recently dedicated himself after a lifetime of abstinence.* (Walter Scott, *Life of General Gordon*, London)

304-305 *The capital of the Sudan, seen here in a bird's-eye view, at the time of al-Mahdi's revolt was inhabited by merchants, Egyptian functionaries, and a small colony of Europeans who had come to seek their fortune in the country.* (Thomas Archer, **The War in Egypt and the Soudan**, London)

305 top *Following their victory, the Madhists executed numerous infidels, hanging or decapitating them, as seen here.* (R. C. Slatin Pasha, C. B., **Fire and Sword in the Sudan**)

305 bottom *The domed tomb of al-Mahdi dominating the low, flat roofs of Omdurman, the settlement on the left bank of the White Nile that replaced Khartoum as the new Mahdist capital of the Sudan. The "Egyptian" Khartoum was razed and abandoned.* (R. C. Slatin Pasha, C. B., **Fire and Sword in the Sudan**)

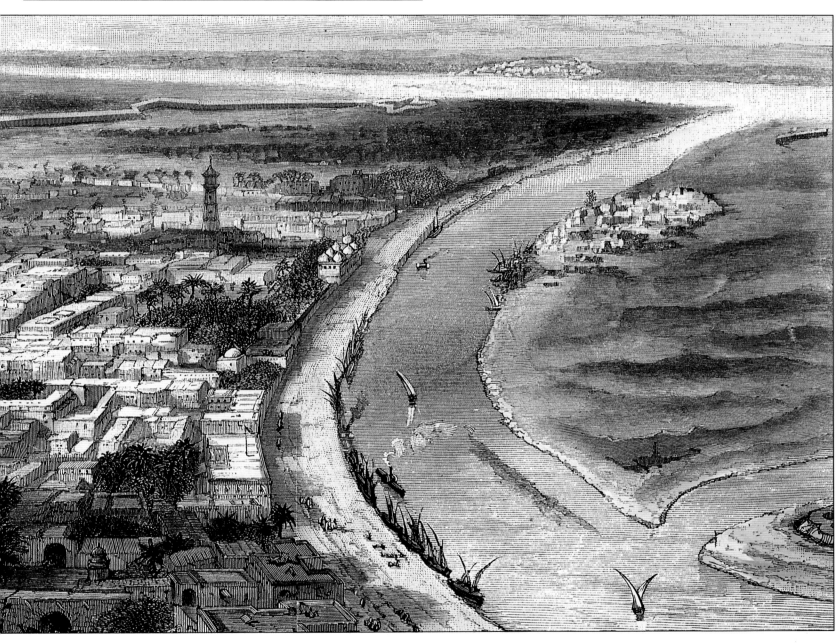

territories, who, having large armies under their command, might well have entertained notions of independence and perhaps even of seizing absolute power. He thus obliged them to leave him members of their families and property as hostages, and he punished the slightest insubordination without pity.

The ex-suburb of Omdurman, on the left bank of the White Nile, where al-Mahdi had established his camp for the siege of Khartoum, was adopted as the caliph's residence and the capital of the Sudan. It was now uninhabited and in ruins. People of all races, from all parts of the immense country, came to live in the new holy city. Huts and mud hovels were thrown together wherever there was space, extending along the riverbank for eleven kilometers. Several hundred thousand people crowded the maze of dusty lanes, over which the tomb of al-Mahdi towered. The tomb was constructed with materials torn from the buildings of the infidel Khartoum; the dome, over thirty meters high, appeared as a distant vision for those arriving from the desert or the Nile. The caliph's

palace was also built using recycled materials. It was a labyrinth of rooms and courtyards, surrounded by a high wall, composed of stables, stores, the quarters for the eunuchs and slaves, reception rooms covered in carpets, a harem of four hundred women chosen from among the most beautiful women in Africa, prisoners of war or slaves bought at the market. Slatin recounts how the caliph, who had spent his youth in the most desperate poverty, loved to surround himself with the most sophisticated European goods plundered during the sack of Khartoum and now amassed in his secret chambers: gilded iron beds with mosquito nets, tapestries, silk cushions, curtains, porcelain. And among these secondhand treasures, the poor prisoner added bitterly, the great warrior put on weight like a self-satisfied member of the bourgeoisie. But that did not stop him from leaping into his saddle again, his black banner unfurling in the wind.

During the fourteen years of his reign, Abdullahi was constantly at war. Surrounded on all sides, and deprived of access to the sea, the newborn Mahdist state was obliged to attempt to open a passage through which it could transport vital supplies, especially arms and ammunition. There were about 100,000 troops, a very respectable figure, but no more than a third of them were equipped with firearms, the Remingtons

306-307 *During the years of Mahdist domination of the Sudan, Britain restricted itself to maintaining the occupied positions and defending Egypt from the sporadic attacks of the* dervishes. *In all these skirmishes the Anglo-Egyptian forces easily dealt with their numerically superior but undisciplined adversaries. This engraving depicts the battle of Ginnes.*

306 bottom right *The Mahdists sent a number of expeditions against the Christian kingdom of Abyssinia. In 1887 they succeeded in taking the ancient capital of Gonder, burning it before returning to the Sudan with extensive spoils of war. Two years later Negus Johannes (portrayed here) attacked the dervishes at Gallabat but was defeated after his initial success and killed. His body was decapitated and the head was sent to Omdurman. The caliph Abdullahi wanted to send it to Cairo to show the khedive the end he could expect.* (Walter Scott, *Life of General Gordon,* London)

306 bottom left *The port of Suakin on the Red Sea remained in the hands of the Anglo-Egyptian forces, as did a few other bridgeheads along the coast. The rest of the Sudan fell to the Mahdists, from Aswan to Equatoria. The dervishes attempted to conquer Suakin to obtain access to the sea but were soundly defeated.* (Thomas Archer, *The War in Egypt and the Soudan,* London)

taken from their victims or old muzzle-loader shotguns. The rest had only sabers, lances, and knives. But even the rifles they did have were rapidly deteriorating, and smuggling by way of the Red Sea ports or the Nile was not sufficient to replace them. The dervishes had captured eighty cannons but were not in a position to make the necessary ammunition.

To avoid suffocation, the caliph attempted to break the circle, concentrating on Abyssinia as Egypt was proving to be too strong: as early as 1885, the year of their great victory at Khartoum, the dervishes had been soundly defeated at Suakin, a city supplied by sea and therefore impregnable, and at Ginnis on the Egyptian border. There the Anglo-Egyptian troops retreating northward

were attacked by the Mahdists, who, though superior in number, were routed, suffering huge losses. This was proof that the British could have swept away the rebels completely, if they had wanted to; but the British government was firm in its determination not to get involved in a Sudanese war, and stressed its own disinterest by leaving only the Egyptian troops to guard the border, withdrawing its own men as far as Aswan. A victory over the Christian Abyssinians, however, seemed to be one possibility, even though in that same year, the army of Negus Johannes, invited by the English to rescue the dervish-surrounded Egyptian garrisons of Cassala and Sennar, had inflicted a heavy defeat upon the Mahdist Emir Osman Digna.

After two years of continuous warring with alternate fortunes, the caliph entrusted one of his best commanders, Abu Angar, with an army of 5,000 men, two thirds of whom were armed with Remingtons. He began to ascend the Blue Nile, gradually recruiting more troops until his army had doubled in size, and then invaded Abyssinia, slipping through the mountain gorges. Arriving on the plain of Debre Sin, they

307 bottom *The encampment of the Scots Guards at Suakin.* (Thomas Archer, *The War in Egypt and the Soudan*, London)

307 right *A squadron of British cavalrymen on a scouting mission in the desert.*

found the army of Ras Adal drawn up in battle order. Actually, it was the entire population of his province, 200,000 people, including women and children; it is not known how many combatants there were. Thousands of Abyssinians were felled by the Dervishes, and after sacking and burning Gonder, Abu Angar returned to the Sudan with an immense booty.

In 1889 Negus Johannes in person marched to take revenge, arriving with his army in front of Gallabat, which he took and laid to waste. But then news of their king's death spread among the looting, triumphant victors—he had been hit by rifle fire while fighting in the front line against the already overwhelmed dervishes. Dismayed, the Abyssinians retreated during the night, taking with them the body of the fallen negus. The following morning the Mahdists, stupefied by their enemy's disappearance, threw themselves into pursuit. They caught up with the

Abyssinians, slowed down by the spoils of war, and slaughtered them. The body of Negus Johannes was decapitated, and the head was sent to the caliph at Omdurman, who momentarily considered sending it to Cairo as a macabre warning to the khedive. On the wave of euphoria provoked by this triumph over the Christians, and in spite of its enormous cost, he ordered the emir al-Negiuni to march against Egypt, but the expedition was annihilated by Anglo-Egyptian troops not far from Wadi Halfa.

Abdullahi perhaps knew that he had entrusted his emir with an impossible task, but he had decided to make the desperate attempt because the Sudan was devastated by famine. The Austrian missionary Ohrwalder, another prisoner of the Mahdists, left a frightening picture of Omdurman in those dramatic times. From the countryside that was turning to desert, the peasants flocked into the city where they were hoping for

relief from their hunger. Instead, they found streets full of bodies rotting in the open air, and all that remained for them to do was to lie down beside the dead to wait for the end. The boldest among them would gather in groups of twenty or thirty and assault the food stores, the owners of which would defend themselves by bludgeoning those living skeletons. Others rummaged through the foulest garbage or fought over the blood of animals slaughtered by the butchers; there were those who killed for a morsel of bread. Slatin recounts cases of cannibalism. Then came the epidemics: dysentery, typhoid, and smallpox.

Strangely, England did not seem to be in any hurry to set foot in a country that by that time would have accepted any liberator. It was not until 1896 that London began to take the reconquest of Sudan into consideration, for the good reason that France, while continuing its diplomatic pressure on Britain to leave

308-309 *Not until 1896 did Britain begin to consider the reconquest of the Sudan, partly as a means of obstructing France's vague plans regarding the region. This plate depicts one of the first skirmishes between the British patrols and the dervishes on the Sudanese border.*

309 top *The British expedition was entrusted to General Herbert Kitchener, who was appointed sirdar—that is, commander in chief—of the Egyptian army.*

309 center *A British soldier attempting to escape from the assault of a number of dervishes.*

309 bottom left *Father Ohrwalder, a missionary who fell into the hands of the Mahdists, together with two nuns and a slave.* (Father Joseph Ohrwalder, *Ten Years' Captivity in the Mahdi's Camp*, London)

Egypt, appeared to be intending to organize Atlantic expeditions to the Upper Nile from its Atlantic colonies. The British cabinet let them know that this would be considered "an unfriendly act," and on the official pretext of offering aid to its ally, Italy—which, having establishing itself in Eritrea, had suffered a setback at Adwa at the hands of the Abyssinians and was now being attacked by the Mahdists at Kassala— decided to forestall any French ambitions in the Sudan.

Herbert Kitchener, who had become general and *sirdar*—that is to say, commander in chief—of the Egyptian army, was instructed in March 1896 to march on Dongola. He had 22,000 men at his disposal, along with a river fleet comprising various armored gunboats. He had no fear of the dervishes, whom he defeated very easily, but was concerned about the desert, which he knew well. He wisely advanced slowly, being careful to secure supply lines. He finally entered

309 bottom right *The Ririghat warriors, the bellicose appearance of whom can be seen in this drawing, were among the most fanatical Mahdists.* (Rudolf C. Slatin Pasha, C. B., *Fire and Sword in the Sudan*, London, 1896)

310 left *A convoy of wounded British troops, exhausted by the battle, making its way behind the lines.*

R. Caton Woodville

310 bottom
Egyptian machine gunners firing at Baggara horsemen from their boat during Kitchener's advance toward Khartoum, which was slow but unstoppable. It began in March 1896, and the first phase was completed in the September of that year with the capture of Dongola. The general then had a railway laid across the desert from Wadi Halfa to Abu Hamed and reached Berber in September 1897.

310-311 *On September 1, 1898, an Anglo-Egyptian expeditionary force reached Omdurman. The following day the dervishes emerged from the city ready to fight. They were massacred: the Mahdists threw themselves against the enemy ranks and were decimated by the disciplined volleys of gun and cannon fire. A bird's-eye view of the battlefield is seen here.*

under the flapping of green, yellow, and white flags. A gigantic black banner indicated the point at which the caliph sat, cross-legged on a rug, praying while watching the battle.

The battle was reduced to a brave but hopeless frontal attack with lances and scimitars against cannons and automatic rifles: two hours of slaughter. Another witness, a certain Lieutenant Stevens, wrote that the battle, which was fought on the last day of Mahdism, was more like an execution. The dervishes, in fact, could never have won against the British, but they would not retreat. The plain that extended in front of the soldiers was white with corpses dressed in white. The barrels of the soldiers' guns were red hot and were to be exchanged for cold rifles.

Kitchener, assuming the encounter to be over, finally ordered the advance upon Omdurman, but from behind the hills, to the right of the Anglo-Egyptian troops, another formidable formation of suicidal dervishes hurled themselves forward. There was a second slaughter that, according to Churchill, was even worse than the first. After an indescribable massacre of over 20,000 men, whose bodies lay scattered across the ground, looking like mounds of snow in their white cloaks, the entire mass of dervishes disintegrated into fragments and dispersed among the fantastic mirages of the desert. (The caliph Abdullahi fled to his Kordofan territories. From there, hunted down like a ferocious wild beast, he kept the victors at bay for another year until he was killed with the last of the faithful in November 1899.)

The Anglo-Egyptian troops entered the Mahdist capital before noon. Kitchener's first order was to demolish the Guided One's tomb and to dump his ashes in the Nile. Then he wept as Gordon's favorite hymn was played while the English and Egyptian flags were raised above the ruins of the governor's palace.

At Khartoum, Kitchener opened a sealed envelope that had arrived from England with orders that its contents were to be read only after he had completed his mission. That message

Dongola on September 23. In preparation for the next advance he laid the railway across the desert from Wadi Halfa to Abu Hamed, cutting a straight line of 400 kilometers across the great curve of the Nile. Thanks to this railway, he could concentrate sufficient forces to occupy Berber easily, arriving a year later, early in September 1897.

Kitchener was moving slowly but very surely. He paused again to permit the tracks to be extended to Berber and then, in April 1898, he confronted the Mahdists near the Atbara River, there defeating them before halting again for another five months, fine-tuning his war machine for the final hurdle. At the end of August the Anglo-Egyptians were downstream of the Sixth Cataract, around 50 kilometers from Omdurman. They made their move on August 24,

marching along the Nile with the gunboats that sailed up the middle of the river. On September 1, the patrols sent to scout ahead spotted the dervish hordes advancing across the desert plain from Omdurman on a front 3 kilometers wide. They stopped in view of the invading army and camped, ready to fight the next day.

On the morning of September 2, the young Winston Churchill, then a lieutenant in the 21st Lancers, was sent on reconnaissance. From a dune he saw an immense sequence of black rows animated by an incessant flickering—the sparkling of the rising sun upon guns. As the light grew, the rows became tawny, then white, and the invocation of Allah was heard along with the rolling of drums and the raucous sound of the horns. The multitude moved in unison

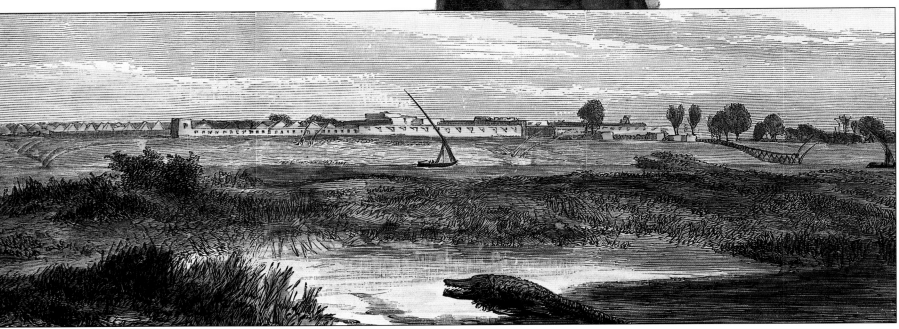

informed him that a French expedition had been sent from the Congo toward the White Nile. The *sirdar* was to locate them and throw them out of the Sudan. A few days later one of Gordon's old boats, which had fallen into the hands of the dervishes, arrived at Khartoum. Unaware that the city had been taken by the Anglo-Egyptians, the crew quietly disembarked and was captured. They reported that at Fashoda, 600 kilometers upstream, there were black soldiers commanded by whites who had shot at them; they carried an unknown flag.

Those riflemen were the Senegalese of Captain Jean-Baptiste Marchand, who had left two years before from Brazzaville, capital of the French Congo, with orders to "occupy"—with only 100 men—the Upper Nile in the name of France and to meet up with another French corps arriving from Jibuti. The second force did actually exist, but it had already retreated, having failed to find the others. The tenacious Marchand, however, had installed himself there in an Egyptian station that had been abandoned for years, perhaps the most unhealthy of all those he could have chosen. The khedive had once sent condemned prisoners there so that the climate would administer justice. Marchand's presence had now created a dramatic and potentially explosive situation. In their colonial rivalry the hackles of both Britain and France were rising, and there was a risk of war in Europe.

Kitchener left immediately with five armed steamboats and a good number of soldiers and cannons. But instead of sweeping away the impertinent Frenchmen, he displayed an unexpected talent for diplomacy. He presented himself to Marchand in an Egyptian uniform, congratulated him on his successful crossing of three-quarters of Africa, and regretfully announced that he had received orders to take possession of the Upper Nile. For the moment, however, he did not intend to attack Marchand, as this would inevitably lead to conflict; instead he asked him to consult with his government, putting at Marchand's disposal all he would need to contact his homeland. Marchand accepted, and the *sirdar* raised the Egyptian flag next to the French flag over the camp, then departed for Khartoum and then England, where he arrived at the end of October.

The newspapers of the two countries were already at war. The French were attacking the English arrogance in laying claim to a territory that had never been hers and had for many years been no-man's-land; the British ridiculed Marchand's situation—100 isolated men in the heart of the country whom the dervishes would have torn apart in a second if they had not been undone by Kitchener. The tension seemed to be growing irresistibly, but in reality France, already profoundly divided over the Dreyfus case, did not want to go to war.

Flying in the face of public opinion, the governments maintained the peace. Marchand received orders to withdraw, which deeply angered him. On December 11, 1898, his men lowered their flag and set out toward Abyssinia so as not to pass through British-occupied territory. The following year a treaty stipulated that the basin of the White Nile belonged to England, while France had a free hand in Equatorial Africa. The Sudan was officially recognized as Anglo-Egyptian, and Kitchener was named as governor general. He had Khartoum rebuilt, his palace before all else, in front of which in 1900 he erected a statue of Gordon riding a camel.

313 top left *The feat performed by Marchand and his men—traversing immense, unexplored and dangerous regions of the African continent—was truly* *remarkable. Marchand's men carried with them small dismantled steamboats. In this illustration the soldiers aboard the boats are shooting at* *the hippopotamuses that frequently made navigation difficult. The meat of the great animals served to feed the expedition's porters.*

313 right *Marchand's mission was to lay claim to the Upper Nile on behalf of France. At Fashoda the captain, seen here in a portrait by Humbert, was to meet* *up with another French party, which had set out from Jibuti but had arrived too early and had then turned back.*

LA MISSION MARCHAND

A TRAVERS L'AFRIQUE ✳ DE L'ATLANTIQUE A LA MER ROUGE

SÉRIE INSTRUCTIVE RECOMMANDÉE POUR LES ÉCOLES

N° 4

LUTTE CONTINUELLE AVEC LES HIPPOPOTAMES

C'est une des plus grandes difficultés qu'aient eu à vaincre les membres de la Mission Marchand.
La viande des pachydermes abattus servait de nourriture aux porteurs du convoi.

LES HOMMES D'ACTION

Publié sous le patronage du Comité DUPLEIX. — BONVALOT, Directeur, 29, rue de Grammont, Paris

8. — LE COMMANDANT MARCHAND FAISANT ARBORER LE PAVILLON FRANÇAIS A FACHODA.

A few slave caravans were still moving furtively along the margins of the vast territory, but by now the trade could be said to have been eliminated; there remained small clandestine rivulets but even these were soon to disappear. Almost all of Africa was now under European control and began to sprout railways like the one from the coast of Kenya to Lake Victoria. Even the impassable marshes of the Sudd were conquered in 1899, with the opening of a permanent channel. The entire course of the Nile was open for the first tourists.

313

313 bottom left *The presence of the French party at Fashoda risked provoking a war between France and Britain, which refused* *to tolerate another colonial power in the Nile Basin. However, the French government finally ordered Marchand to withdraw. In this* *engraving, Marchand can be seen with a group of porters carrying parts of the expedition's boats.*

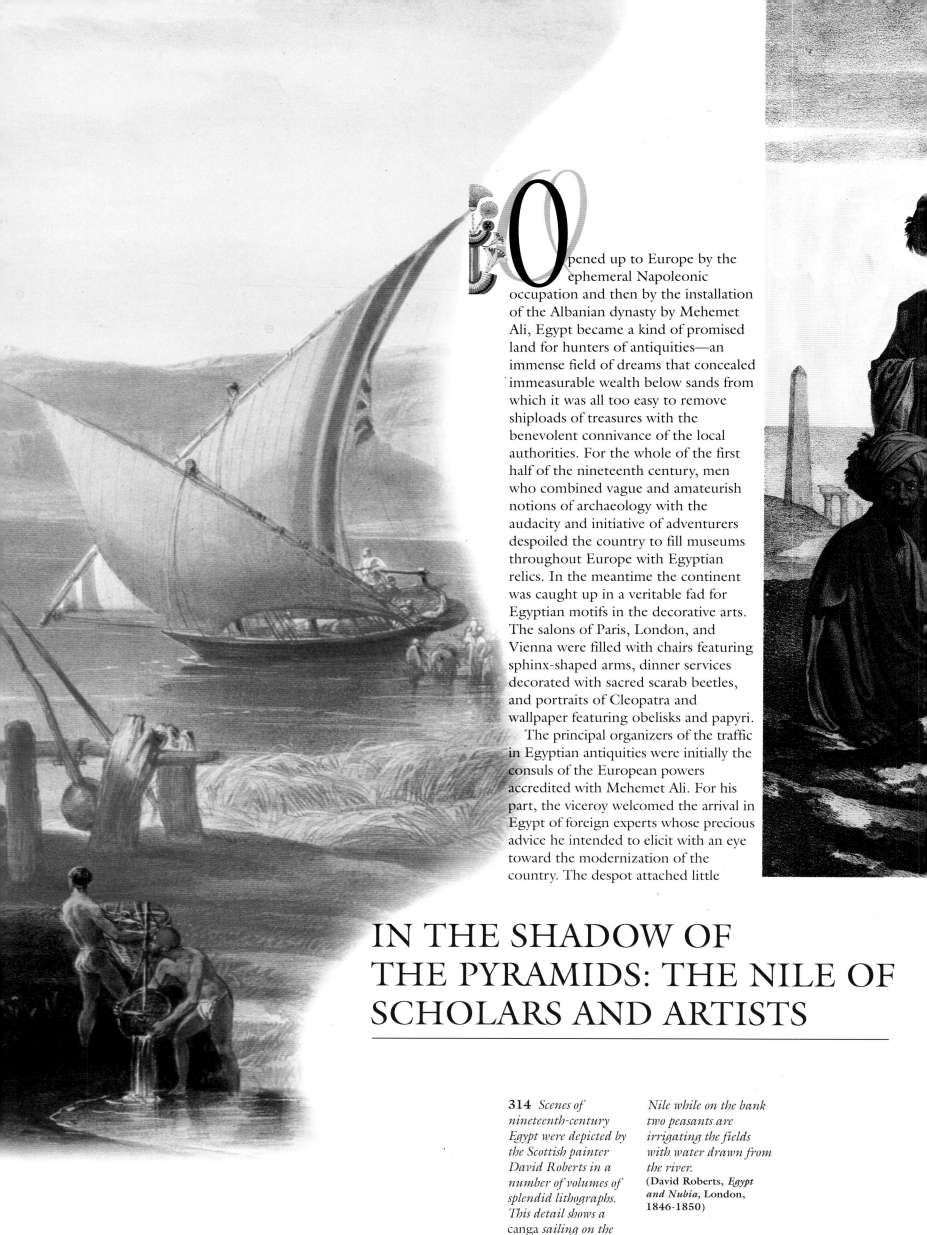

pened up to Europe by the ephemeral Napoleonic occupation and then by the installation of the Albanian dynasty by Mehemet Ali, Egypt became a kind of promised land for hunters of antiquities—an immense field of dreams that concealed immeasurable wealth below sands from which it was all too easy to remove shiploads of treasures with the benevolent connivance of the local authorities. For the whole of the first half of the nineteenth century, men who combined vague and amateurish notions of archaeology with the audacity and initiative of adventurers despoiled the country to fill museums throughout Europe with Egyptian relics. In the meantime the continent was caught up in a veritable fad for Egyptian motifs in the decorative arts. The salons of Paris, London, and Vienna were filled with chairs featuring sphinx-shaped arms, dinner services decorated with sacred scarab beetles, and portraits of Cleopatra and wallpaper featuring obelisks and papyri.

The principal organizers of the traffic in Egyptian antiquities were initially the consuls of the European powers accredited with Mehemet Ali. For his part, the viceroy welcomed the arrival in Egypt of foreign experts whose precious advice he intended to elicit with an eye toward the modernization of the country. The despot attached little

IN THE SHADOW OF THE PYRAMIDS: THE NILE OF SCHOLARS AND ARTISTS

314 *Scenes of nineteenth-century Egypt were depicted by the Scottish painter David Roberts in a number of volumes of splendid lithographs. This detail shows a* canga *sailing on the* Nile *while on the bank two peasants are irrigating the fields with water drawn from the river.* (David Roberts, *Egypt and Nubia*, London, 1846-1850)

314-315 *The first half of the nineteenth century saw the emergence of modern Egyptology and the frenetic collecting of Egyptian antiquities to be exhibited in the great museums of Paris, London, Berlin, and Turin. Among the most active seekers of archaeological treasures were the European consuls posted to Egypt, two of whom were the Englishman Salt and the French consul Bernardino Drovetti, originally from* *Piedmont. The latter is portrayed in this engraving holding a plumb line to a colossal statue. On his left, in Arab costume, is the Marseilles-born sculptor Jean-Jacques Rifaud, who combed Egypt for relics on behalf of the consul.* (Forbin, *Voyage dans le Levant*, Paris, 1819)

315 bottom *Over the centuries sand had partially buried the temple of Abu Simbel, as can be seen in this unsigned engraving.*

316 top *The Scottish antiquarian Robert Hay discovered Egypt through the views of the country painted by Frederick Catherwood, who later became famous for discovering the Mayan monuments in the jungles of South* America. *Hay completed numerous trips through the Nile Valley after 1824, and he too executed a host of drawings, among which are the panoramas of the Egyptian capital we see on these pages, taken from his* Views *of Cairo. Giza, on the left bank of the Nile in front of Cairo, was the point of departure for excursions to the Pyramids.*

316-317 *Crowded with boats of all kinds, lined with palaces, mosques, ruins, and* villages, the great river provided artists with an infinite range of picturesque subjects. Here we see the river traffic at Birkat al-Fil. *(Robert Hay of Linplum,* Views of Cairo, **London, 1840)**

317 bottom *The northern quarter of Bulaq was Cairo's river port, the depot and market for the goods transported along the river from the Mediterranean and the Sudan.* **(R. Hay of Linplum,** *Views of Cairo)*

318-319 *Before becoming the British consul in Egypt in 1816, Henry Salt had painted and had completed a long and difficult journey in remote and inaccessible Abyssinia from 1809 to 1811. This magnificent view of Old Cairo with the* *Nile and the Pyramids visible beyond the long aqueduct is his. Salt painted this scene in 1809 during his first stay in the country.* (Henry Salt, *Twenty Four Views taken in St. Helena, the Cape, India, Ceylon, Abyssinia and Egypt,* London, 1809)

importance to the traces of the great historical and artistic past of a non-Muslim culture. He willingly conceded permits for excavations and the recruitment of laborers to the diplomats from those countries whose political support was essential to his attempts to free himself of the yoke of the Ottoman Empire. Henry Salt, the British consul from 1816 to 1827, and the Piedmontese Drovetti, who was the French consul general from 1810 to 1815 and then again from 1820 to 1829, were thus able to hire capable and conveniently unscrupulous agents who

for years combed the Nile Valley in search of objets d'art. Among them, Jean-Jacques Rifaud, a sculptor from Marseilles, earned a degree of fame during the forty years he spent traveling and investigating throughout Egypt, where he executed a number of splendid drawings of landscapes and monuments.

On behalf of Drovetti, Rifaud collected a great deal of material, above all statues on which with scant respect for artistic integrity he used to inscribe his name and the date of discovery. The French consul then tried to sell the impressive collection to Louis XVIII, but

the king declined the offer, claiming that the price was excessive. Drovetti thus turned to the sovereign of his true homeland, Carlo Felice, the king of Sardinia, who bought the magnificent collection of over 1,000 pieces for the sum of 400,000 lire on behalf of Piedmont. The collection formed the initial nucleus of the Egyptian Museum of Turin. Subsequently, and again through the services of the indefatigable Rifaud, Drovetti compiled two more collections, which he sold to Charles X of France for the Louvre and to the king of Prussia for the Berlin Museum.

In competition with the French

consul, who concentrated mainly on the ruins of Thebes and Tanis, the Englishman Salt also sent men to the most promising archaeological sites. Over the years he too put together three collections. He sold one of them to Charles X and brought the Louvre collection up to the same standard as the one in Turin. The other two were acquired by the British Museum.

Salt's best agent, the prince among the excavators of Egyptian antiquities, was an Italian named Giovanni Battista Belzoni, an extraordinary character. Born at Padua in 1778, he emigrated to England, where he earned his living as

320 top *The most famous of the artists who depicted ancient and modern Egypt was undoubtedly David Roberts, thanks to the 247 lithographs worked up from his watercolors and published between 1842 and 1849. Roberts ascended the Nile as far as the Second Cataract and obtained permission from the viceroy to paint the interiors of mosques, usually forbidden to infidels. This plate shows two men of Cairo anxiously watching the water level while waiting for the flood.* (David Roberts, *Egypt and Nubia*, London, 1846-1850)

320 bottom *A boat loaded with passengers descends the river with the current near Saqqara.*

320-321 *The ferry from Cairo to Giza waiting to transport passengers to the far side of the river. In the background to the right can be seen the Pyramids.*

321 bottom left *A 5-kilometer-long aqueduct led from the right bank of the Nile in front of the island of Roda and carried water from the river to the Citadel. This lithograph shows the pumping station.*

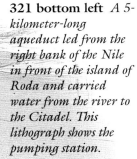

321 bottom right *A group of Egyptian men, women, and children pleasantly passing time on the bank of the river against the backdrop of the Pyramids of Giza.*

(D. Roberts, *Egypt and Nubia*)

321

the circus performer Samson of
Patagonia. During his strongman act he
would lift and carry around the stage ten
or twelve people sitting on a metal
frame. He then decided to head east
and, on his way to Constantinople,
heard that Mehemet Ali was looking for
experts in hydraulics, a field in which he
could boast a certain degree of
experience.

Belzoni landed in Egypt and presented
to the viceroy a project for an innovative
waterwheel that would take water from
the Nile, but it was rejected, probably as
a result of petty court jealousy. Now
penniless, he had the good fortune to
meet Salt, who suggested he put his
mechanical talent to good use by
removing the extremely heavy granite
bust known as *The Young Memnon* from
the Ramesseum of Thebes. Having
brilliantly completed this task, Belzoni
ascended the Nile to search other sites.

323 top *A woman crossing the Cairo market carrying a bundle of papyrus canes.*

323 bottom *This watercolor shows an exchange of looks between a water carrier and an attractive unveiled woman carrying a jug on her head.*

322-323 *A Maltese noble of Italian origins, Count Amadeo Preziosi found his true vocation in the field of art. After having studied at Paris he settled at Constantinople in 1842, where he married a Greek woman with whom he had four children. In the Ottoman capital he became famous as a watercolorist depicting* *Turkish figures and costumes. His paintings were acquired by wealthy European travelers. He also traveled to Egypt and executed numerous drawings of the local people. This plate shows a number of merchants waiting for their boat on the shore of the island of Bulaq in the port of Cairo.*

322 bottom left *A Cairo noblewoman, richly dressed and followed by a maid carrying bolts of fabric.*
(Amadeo Preziosi, *Souvenir du Caire*, Paris, 1862)

322 bottom right *Amadeo Preziosi carefully studied the smallest details of the local costumes. This illustration depicts a babouche seller.*

(A. Preziosi, *Souvenir du Caire*)

324 top *Prior to becoming one of the most faithful and able spokesmen of the Prussian chancellor Bismarck, Julius Hermann Moritz Busch dedicated himself to journalism and literature after graduating in philosophy from the University of Leipzig. He traveled in America and, between 1853 and 1855, in the Middle East, an experience he put to good use by publishing books on Egypt, Palestine, and Greece. In 1864 at Trieste, he published a richly illustrated volume,* Bilder aus dem Orient. *This plate shows an evocative image of Cairo seen from the sandy emptiness of the desert. To travelers reaching the city from the desert, the minarets and cupolas of Cairo appeared like a mirage.*

(Moritz Busch, ***Bilder aus dem Orient*, Trieste, 1864)**

324-325 *With its lush vegetation, the island of Roda, today almost completely built over, was a small earthly paradise where the residents of Cairo went to escape the summer heat.*

The list of Belzoni's discoveries is quite stunning: he opened the great temple of Ramses II at Abu Simbel; he discovered many tombs in the Valley of the Kings, including the most beautiful, that of Seti I; he excavated at Karnak and many other sites; and he was the first man to penetrate the Chephren pyramid, which since ancient times had been thought to be a solid mass of stone. On his return to London he received a triumphant welcome and organized an exhibition of his relics and the casts that he had made, along with drawings he had completed during his long stay in Egypt.

Shortly afterward he decided to depart for Africa once again, but with a very different goal: he intended to discover the sources of the Niger, one of the many problems that were perplexing the geographers of the age. On this occasion fortune was not on his side; he fell ill with dysentery and died at Gato in the Benin region in 1823.

In that period large numbers of people began to visit Egypt for academic motives or out of sheer curiosity. We could hardly ignore another Italian, Girolamo Segato, who arrived in Cairo in 1818 and entered the service of the

325 top *A caravan with a number of camels resting in the shade of a palm grove on Roda.*

325 bottom *An infinite number of views of the pyramids were executed by European artists. In this plate Busch has framed them between palm trees.*

viceroy as a topographer, accompanying Ibrahim's expedition to Sennar where his brother Ismail was conducting his campaign of conquest in the Sudan. Segato was sent back to Cairo halfway through the expedition, the victim of internal squabbles, but during his trip he accumulated a great quantity of drawings and surveys. A few years later he explored the archaeological area of Saqqara and discovered the entrance to the first step pyramid.

Mention should also be made of two Englishmen, the architect Charles Barry, who in 1818 traveled into Nubia and brought back a splendid album of drawings, and John Gardner Wilkinson, who arrived in Egypt in 1821 and remained there for twelve years completing numerous excavations around Thebes, thanks to which he is recognized as one of the fathers of Egyptology, a discipline that at that time was taking its first hesitant steps.

(Moritz Busch, *Bilder aus dem Orient*)

326-327 top *The Marseilles-born Jean-Jacques Rifaud lived in Egypt for forty years, working for the antiquarians and procuring for them pieces of all kinds and sizes. He had the deplorable habit of inscribing his name and the date of discovery on the statues he found. It was Rifaud who supplied the consul general of* *France, Bernardino Drovetti, with the immense collection of relics that was subsequently acquired by the king of Sardinia, Carlo Felice, and formed the nucleus of the collection in Turin's Egyptian Museum. A few years later he put together, again for Drovetti, a second collection, which he sold to Charles X of* *France, who assigned it to the Louvre. During his long stay in Egypt, Rifaud executed over 14,000 drawings, some of which were published in his* Voyage en Egypte, en Nubie, Paris, 1830. *This plate portrays Kalib Bey of Al-Faiyum lying in his tent in the camp pitched by his soldiers near a village.*

In 1821 this science, the birth of which can be attributed to the work of the savants who accompanied Bonaparte to Egypt, was covered in unexpected glory when a fundamental discovery was made: a thirty-two-year-old French academic, Jean-François Champollion, published the results of long years of hard work and spirited intuition demonstrating that he had succeeded in deciphering hieroglyphics. Two years later he was able to describe in another book the rudiments of ancient Egyptian grammar.

In 1828 Champollion, who had never visited Egypt but had studied the inscriptions on the relics conserved in the museums of Europe or copied by the explorers, was appointed leader of the so-called Franco-Tuscan scientific expedition financed by Charles X of France and the grand duke of Tuscany, Leopold II. The expedition was to complete the first systematic exploration of monuments. Ippolito Rosellini, from Pisa, the French scholar's most promising disciple, took part in the expedition and later, between 1832 and 1844, published a large collection of illustrations entitled *Monuments of Egypt and Nubia*. Other drawings were executed by the Frenchman Nestor L'Hôte. The team ascended the Nile as far as the Second Cataract, and during the two-year expedition Champollion, who was unfortunately to die prematurely in 1832, saw the validity of his deciphering system confirmed in the field.

In addition to archaeologists interested in studying the monuments or in stripping them for financial gain, Egypt began to attract artists whose work, published on their return home, would in turn stimulate others to follow in their tracks. In 1823 the Nile Valley was painted by Frederick Catherwood

326-327 bottom
The houses of the village of Benalasal in the delta region reflected in the waters of a branch of the Nile.
(Jean-Jacques Rifaud, *Voyage en Egypte, en Nubie*, Paris, 1830)

328-329 top *This illustration by Jean-Jacques Rifaud shows a dense thicket of dovecotes characterizing the village Gessay in Lower Egypt.* (Jean-Jacques Rifaud, *Voyage en Egypte, en Nubie*, Paris, 1830)

328-329 bottom *Arching along the banks of a branch of the delta, around a dozen kilometers from the sea, the city of Damietta was the port of preference for ships from Syria.* (J.-J. Rifaud, *Voyage en Egypte, en Nubie*)

who, years later, became famous for discovering the lost cities of the Maya. The Scottish antiquarian Robert Hay, who met Catherwood in Malta, was seduced by the beauty of his work and traveled to Egypt to draw. A large number of impressive plates were produced by the Frenchman Prisse d'Avennes in his spare time while he worked as an engineer for Mehemet Ali from 1826 to 1836. He wrote and illustrated the invaluable *Histoire de l'art Egyptien d'apres les monuments*, a work still consulted today. A bizarre character, he cruised the Nile in his own boat, flying the British flag to mark what he claimed were his Welsh origins. From 1836 onward he devoted himself exclusively to archaeology, dressing in Turkish costume and taking the name Edris Effendi. His favorite area for exploration was Nubia, and he made a particular study of the temples of Abu Simbel.

The first artist to arrive in Egypt with the precise aim of executing drawings and sketches in the field that he would later work up into pictures for the domestic market was the Scot, David Roberts. He landed at Alexandria in August 1838 and left the country in February 1839, crossing the Sinai Desert to visit Petra and then Jerusalem. At Cairo he acquired a boat that became his home and studio as well as a means of transport that carried him up the Nile as far as Abu Simbel. He was also interested in contemporary Egypt and spent a

330-331 *The work of the Berliner Richard Lepsius, who arrived in Egypt in 1842, marked a turning point in the study of the antiquities of the country: thanks to him Egyptology was transformed into a precise science. The over 15,000 pieces he took back to Germany formed the Egyptian Museum he founded at Berlin. The twelve volumes of his* Denkmäler aus Aegypten und Aethiopien, *published between 1848 and 1859, are still essential reading. The 894 plates illustrating them were executed by Ernst Weidenbach. This illustration depicts the colonnade of the Temple of Seti I at Thebes standing against the slopes of a hill; to the left can be seen the sphinxes, now seriously eroded, that once lined the access road. In the background to the left the flooded Nile is lapping at the Colossi of Memnon.*

331 bottom
Together with nearby Luxor, the monumental complex of Karnak conserved memories of ancient Thebes.
(Dominique Vivant Denon, *Voyage dans la Basse et la Haute Egypte*, Paris, 1802)

fortnight in the capital painting mosques and scenes of daily life. He dressed as a Turk and took care to not use hog's-hair brushes, which might have offended Muslim religious sensibilities.

Louis Haghe used the material he collected during his trip to produce a splendid series of lithographs. Those with Egyptian subjects were published in color and in a large format between 1846 and 1850 and were reissued on a number of occasions.

Following the *Description de L'Egypte* compiled by the academics of the Napoleonic expedition and published at

the beginning of the century, another major work of great erudition was published by a German, Richard Lepsius: *Denkmäler aus Aegypten und Aethiopien,* twelve folio volumes issued between 1849 and 1859 and still considered essential reading today. Lepsius, born in Saxonia in 1810, studied in Paris and visited all the European collections of Egyptian antiquities. From 1842 to 1845 he directed a major expedition sponsored by king of Prussia, who was interested in procuring new works of art to add to the Egyptian halls of the Museum of Berlin.

Among the king and Lepsius's most ambitious objectives was the Chamber of the Kings in the Temple of Karnak. However, this plan was discovered by Prisse d'Avennes, who got there ahead of the Germans and had the blocks of stone cut, packed, and loaded aboard his boat to be taken back to Cairo. During the trip the would-be Welshman encountered Lepsius's boat ascending the Nile. The German came aboard d'Avennes's vessel and confided to him that he had come to Egypt especially for the bas-reliefs, quite unaware that he was sitting and drinking coffee on the chests

332 top *The nineteenth century saw the publication of numerous illustrated books on Egypt that enjoyed great success throughout Europe such as* The Nile Boat, *by the Englishman William Henry Bartlett, published in 1858. This plate depicting camel drivers on the banks of the Nile near the Temples of Luxor is taken from Bartlett's book.*

332-333 *The spectacular ruins of Luxor left Roberts breathless. In addition to sketching them, he spent hours measuring the columns.* (David Roberts, *Egypt and Nubia,* London, 1846-1850)

333 top *The almost surreal light of dawn embraces and drenches in warm reflections the Colossi of Memnon surrounded by the waters of the Nile.* (David Roberts, *Egypt and Nubia,* London, 1846-1850)

333 bottom *The German Karl Werner published* Le Nil *in 1882. This plate depicts the time-worn lion-headed statues of the goddess Sekhmet at Karnak.*

that contained them—and of course Prisse d'Avennes took care not to tell him. Today the Chamber of the Kings is one of the treasures of the Louvre. While Lepsius's predatory ambitions may have been foiled on that occasion, thanks to his academic work he was later recognized, along with Champollion, as one of the founders of modern Egyptology.

It was a Frenchman, Auguste Mariette, who was to be given the rather unexpected task of bringing to a halt the plundering that had continued for half a century and to found the Service des Antiquités Egyptiennes and the Egyptian Antiquities Museum at Cairo. In 1842 Mariette, who was Nestor L'Hôte's cousin, was ordered to catalog the drawings and notes Nestor made during the expedition with Champollion; while Mariette was working he contracted the so-called Egyptian virus. He had arrived in Egypt in 1850 with the modest task of acquiring Coptic manuscripts for the Louvre. However, once in the country he began a series of excavations at Saqqara that led him to the discovery of the Serapeum of Memphis, one of the most important ancient monuments to have been uncovered.

Having made his name in Europe through this discovery, Mariette returned to Egypt in 1857 to receive from Viceroy Said a mission to excavate not for foreign sovereigns but for the long-exploited country of Egypt. His labors, which lasted for over two decades and were conducted throughout the Nile Valley, from Giza to Saqqara, from Thebes to Abydos and Elephantine, were to result in the creation of the Museum of Egyptian Antiquities in Cairo that contains the accumulated antiquities discovered from then onward.

334-335 *When Champollion visited Egypt between 1828 and 1829 with Ippolito Rosellini to begin the first scientific exploration of the monuments, he took with him a young student named Nestor L'Hôte, who executed a series of excellent drawings. This watercolor of the Nile cataracts represents a little light relief from the labors of Egyptology.* (**Nestor L'Hôte,** *Panorama d'Egypte et de Nubie,* **Paris, 1841**)

336 left *The island of Philae, with its temples dedicated to Isis, Horus, and Hathor, was one of the most sacred sites of ancient Egypt. Its evocative situation and the beauty of the buildings made it one of the* favorite subjects for the painters who ascended the Nile. In this painting by David Roberts we can admire the exceptional state of conservation of the murals of the Temple of Isis, of which we see the hypostyle hall.

336 top right *A magnificent panorama faced those who contemplated the river valley from the tip of the island.* (William Henry Bartlett, *The Nile Boat*, London, 1858)

336-337 *This extraordinary view by David Roberts (1838) shows the Temple of Isis complex seen from the top of the island of Bigga from where it is visible in all its majesty.* (David Roberts, *Egypt and Nubia*, London, 1846-1850)

337 top *The perfect colonnade of the Temple of Trajan is partially concealed by the palms flourishing on the banks of the Nile.* (Owen Jones, *Views on the Nile*, London, 1843)

338 top *All of the great illustrated books on Egypt printed in the nineteenth century rightly paid tribute to the Temples of Philae. This plate by Karl*

Werner published in Le Nil, *Paris, 1882, depicts the curtain wall of the temple above the waters of the Nile in the dry season.*

338 bottom *This panoramic view of the Nile at Philae is taken from* The Nile Boat, *by William Bartlett, London, 1858.*

It was by no means an easy task, in spite of the support of the viceroy: the peasants and the local authorities had been accustomed for decades to earning what by their standards were vast sums by selling relics to foreigners. They used all the means at their disposal to hamper the work of Mariette and his successor Gaston Maspero, another great French Egyptologist.

The suspicions of Maspero, who had been appointed director of the excavations following the death of Mariette, were aroused by the appearance on the antiques market of objects from royal tombs, and he began to investigate. The trail eventually led him to the discovery of the so-called hideaway of Deir el-Bahri, where the ancient priests had concealed remains and objects belonging to the pharaohs to prevent them from falling into the hands of grave robbers.

Another extraordinary discovery that gave rise to another bout of Egyptian fever, this time in association with the Art Deco movement, was made in 1922 by the English archaeologist Howard Carter, who penetrated the tomb of Tutankhamen.

Excavations continue throughout Egypt, albeit with less spectacular results, under the aegis of both the Egyptian authorities and foreign institutions.

338-339 *Three Egyptians resting along the Nile and admiring the sacred island of Philae. This poetical illustration was published in* Denkmäler aus Aegypten und Aethiopien, *by Richard Lepsius, Berlin, 1849-1859.*

339 bottom *Miriam, the daughter of Abdallah, the guardian of the Temple of Philae, is sitting on the remains of the temple itself in an illustration taken from* Le Nil *by Karl Werner.*

339 right *The Temple of Trajan rises austerely on Philae's eastern shore.* (W.H. Bartlett, *The Nile Boat*, London, 1858)

339

340-341 *The smaller temple at Abu Simbel. Duke Maximilian of the reigning Wittelsbach family loved traveling to the extent that he was known as a "migratory bird." In 1838 he visited the Middle East and published a lavish illustrated book about* his trip entitled Malerische Ansichten aus dem Oriente Gesammelt auf der Reise Sr. Hoh. des Herren Herzogs Maximilian in Bayern, nach Nubien, Aegypten, Palaestina, Syrien und Malta im Jahre 1838, *from which this plate is taken.*

340 bottom *Four seated statues in the naos of the Great Temple of Abu Simbel. This temple complex, which still stuns visitors today, was described by David Roberts as "the* *monument that on its own justifies a journey to Nubia." The Scottish artist executed numerous drawings of the complex.* (David Roberts, *Egypt and Nubia*, London, 1846-1850)

341 top *The moon shining on the waters of the Nile and the great statues of Ramses II.* (William Henry Bartlett, *The Nile Boat*, London, 1858)

341 bottom *The sand accumulated over the centuries from which the ruins emerged lent an extremely romantic air to the temples.* (Jean-Jacques Rifaud, *Voyage en Egypte, en Nubie*, Paris, 1830)

342-343 *The colossal statues of Ramses II at Abu Simbel, partially buried in sand blown by the wind. "The beauty and dimensions of this temple are exceeded by no other Egyptian monument," wrote the impressed David Roberts executing this drawing.* (David Roberts, *Egypt and Nubia*, London, 1846-1850)

Front Elevation of the Great Temple of Aboosimbel Nubia

THE NILE

The Nile is 5,611 kilometers long–6,677 kilometers if you include the most remote source stream, the Kagera–from Lake Victoria to the Mediterranean Sea, making it the world's longest river. Its hydrographic basin covers an area of 2,850,000 square kilometers.

The origin of the river is considered to be the Luvironza-Ruvubu that rises in the highlands to the northeast of Lake Tanganyika and forms the Kagera after joining the Nyaborongo. The Kagera eventually flows into Lake Victoria from the west. The river draining this lake, the Victoria Nile, issues from its northern tip, forms Lake Kyoga, and proceeds westwards, flowing over the magnificent 122-meter-high Murchison Falls before entering Lake Albert. From here the river flows from the northern extremity as the Albert Nile and heads north into the Sudan where it is known as the Bahr al-Gabal, the "River of the Mountains." It then forms the swamp region of the Sudd which it crosses via a number of different branches, the principal stream identified as the Bahr al-Zeraf, the "River of the Giraffes."

The enormous loss of water through evaporation in the swamps is compensated for by the two great tributaries, the Bahr al-Ghazal, or "River of the Gazelles," which joins from the left and the Sobat which joins from the right. After the confluence with the Bahr al-Ghazal the river takes the name Bahr al-Abyad or White Nile until it is joined by the Bahr al-Azraq, or Blue Nile, at Khartoum. From there onwards it is known simply as the Nile.

The Blue Nile rises in Ethiopia as the Abay Wenz, crosses Lake Tana, and turns west to meander through the narrow gorges of the Sudan; the Blue Nile is itself 1,610 kilometers long. To the north of Khartoum the Nile, the course of which is interrupted by cataracts, flows through a narrow valley flanked to the east by the Nubian Desert and to the west by the Libyan Desert. It is joined by another great Ethiopian tributary, the Atbara. After a great curve to the south and then another back to the north the river enters Egypt forming the artificial lake created by the Aswan Dam. The Egyptian section of the Nile is 1,530 kilometers long. Beyond Cairo it splits in two to form a vast fan-shaped delta covering an area of 24,000 square kilometers. The two branches flow to Rosetta to the west and Damietta to the east.

The Nile is characterized by regular summer floods that begin in June and culminate in September, inundating the surrounding terrain and fertilizing it with silt from the volcanic highlands of Ethiopia that has been eroded by torrents during the wet season. As regularly as they occur, the magnitude of the floods varies widely; at one time the prosperity or poverty of Egypt depended on the floods but in this century the construction of the great dams has done much to protect the country from the caprices of nature.

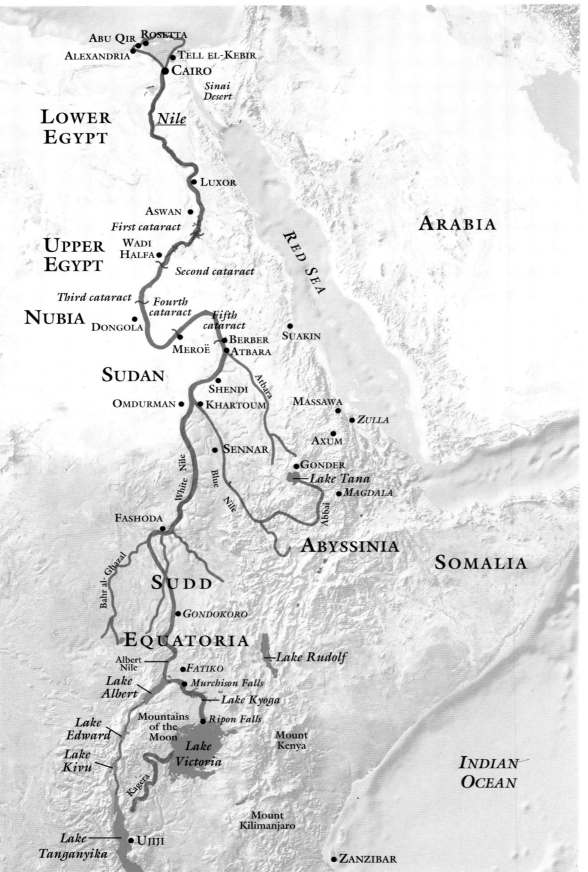

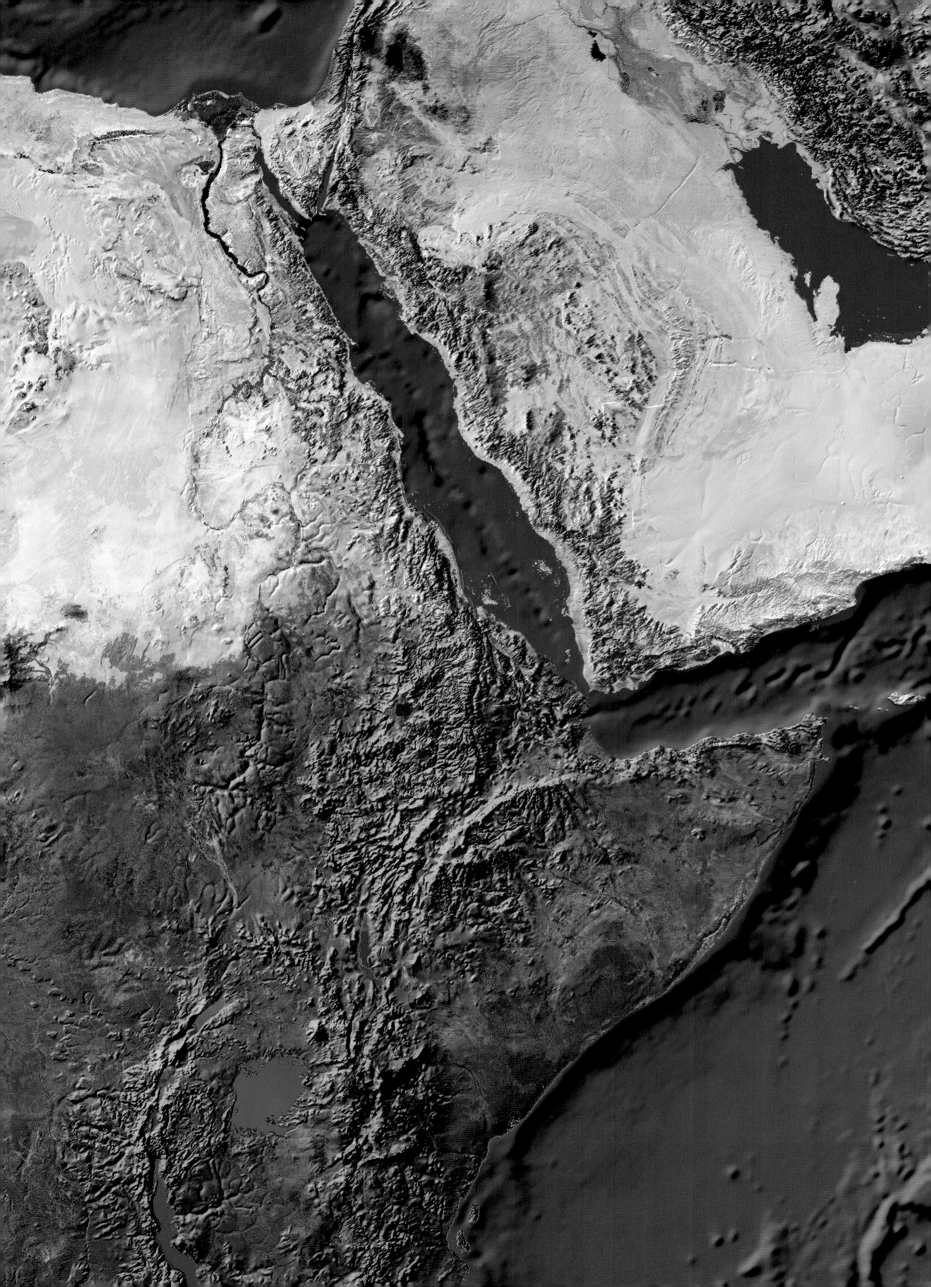

BIBLIOGRAPHY

ote

ere is a vast bibliography regarding the
le and its sources. Here we have cited
ly the principal works written by the
otagonists themselves or by eye-witnesses
d the more specific studies are used as
erence material.

eneral works

bbert, Christopher *Africa Explored:
ropean in the Dark Continent 1769-1889*,
ndon, 1982.
hnston, Harry *The Nile Quest*, London,
'03.
dwig, Emil *Der Nil. Lebenslauf eines
romes*, Amsterdam, 1935.
oorehead, Alan *The Blue Nile*, London,
'62.
oorehead, Alan *The White Nile*, London,
60.
verin, Timothy *The African Adventure:
0 Years of Exploration*, London, 1973.

troduction

Hôte, Nestor *Panorama d'Egypte et de
ubie*, Paris, 1841.
aximilian in Bayern, *Bilder aus dem
rient*, Stuttgart, 1846.
anley, Henry Morton, *Through the Dark
ntinent*, London, 1878.
arious Authors *The Life and Explorations
Dr Livingstone the Great Missionary
aveller*, London.

hapter 1

osellini, Ippolito *I Monumenti dell'Egitto e
lla Nubia*, Pisa, 1832.

hapter 2

aeu, Johannes *Atlante*, 1635.
aeu, Johannes *Nova et Accuratissima
tius Terrarum Orbis Tabula*, 1662.
omann, Baptista *Atlas Novum Terrarum
bis Imperia Regna et Status Exactis
eograpie Demestrans*, 1710.
omen, Diogo *Atlante*, 1559.
rtelius, Abraham, *Theatrum Orbis
rrarum*, 1592.

hapter 3

rtlett, William Henry *The Nile Boat*,
ndon, 1858.
lzoni, Giovanni Battista *Egypt and Nubia*,
ndon, 1820.
non, Dominique Vivant *Voyage dans la
sse et la Haute Egypte*, Paris, 1802.
ers, G. *Egypt: Description, Historical and
ctoresque*, London, 1884.

Mayer, Luigi *Views in Egypt*, London,
1805.
Prisse d'Avennes, Emile, *L'Art Arabe*, Paris,
1877.
Rifaud, Jean-Jacques *Voyage en Egypte, en
Nubie*, Paris, 1830.
Various Authors *Description de L'Egypte*,
Paris, 1809.
Volney, Constantin-François *Voyage en Syrie
et en Egypte*, Paris, 1787.

Chapter 4

Bruce, James *Travels to discover the Source of
the Nile in the Years 1768, 1769, 1770,
1771, 1772 and 1773*, London, 1805.
Tellez, Balthasar *Travels of the Jesuits in
Ethiopia*, London, 1710.

Chapter 5

Cooper, William *A Voyage up the
Mediterranean*, London, 1802.
Denon, Dominique Vivant *Voyage dans la
Basse et la Haute Egypte*, Paris, 1802.

Chapter 6

Baker, Samuel *A Narrative of the Expedition
to Central Africa for the Suppression of the
Slave Trade* London, 1874.
Baker, Samuel *Albert Nyanza–Great Basin
of the Nile*, London, 1886.
Cailliaud, Frédéric *Voyage à Méroé*, Paris,
1826.
Dodwell, Henry *The Founder of Modern
Egypt*, Cambridge, 1931.
Ebers, G. *Egypt: Description, Historical, and
Picturesque*, London, 1884.
Forbin, L.N.P.A. *Voyage dans le Levant*,
Paris, 1819.
Gessi, Romolo Pasha *Seven Years in the
Soudan*, London, 1892.
Ghorbal, Shafik *The Beginnings of the
Egyptian Question and the Rise of Mehemet
Ali*, London, 1928.
Hoskins, G. A. *Travels in Ethiopia*, London,
1835.
Maximilian in Bayern, *Bilder aus dem
Orient*, Stuttgart, 1846.
Rifaud, Jean-Jacques *Voyage en Egypte,
en Nubie*, Paris, 1830.
Waddington, George *Journal of a Visit
to Some Parts of Ethiopia*, London, 1822.

Chapter 7

Burkhardt, Johann Ludwig *Reisen in
Arabien*, Weimar, 1830.
Cailliaud, Frédéric *Voyage à Méroé, au
Fleuve Blanc, au-delà de Fazoql dans la midi
du Royaume de Sennar*, Paris, 1826.

Chapter 8

Archer, Thomas *The War in Egypt and the
Soudan*, London.
Bartlett, William Henry *The Nile Boat*,
London, 1858.
Burton, Richard *Zanzibar, City, Island and
Coast*, London, 1872.
Ebers, G. *Egypt: Description, Historical, and
Picturesque*, London, 1884.
Godio, Guglielmo *Vita africana. Ricordi
d'un viaggio nel Sudan Orientale*, Milan,
1885.
Le Brick le Ducovëdic, *Voyage a la côte
orientale d'Afrique*, Paris, 1846-48.
Maximilian in Bayern, *Bilder aus dem
Oriente*, Stuttgart, 1846.
Roberts, David *Egypt and Nubia*, London,
1846-1850.
Salt, Henry *Twenty Four Views taken in
St. Helena, the Cape, India, Ceylon,
Abyssinia & Egypt*, London, 1809.

Chapter 9

Burton, Richard *First Footsteps in East
Africa*, London, 1856.
Burton, Richard *The Lake Regions of Central
Africa*, London, 1860.
Ritchie, J. Ewin *The Pictorial Edition
of the Life and Discoveries of David
Livingstone*.
Speke, John Hanning *What Led to the
Discovery of the Source of the Nile*, London,
1863.

Chapter 10

Grant, James August *A Walk across Africa
or Domestic Scenes from my Journal*,
London, 1864.
Speke, John Hanning *Journal of the
Discovery of the Source of the Nile*,
London, 1863.

Chapter 11

Baker, Samuel *The Albert Nyanza–Great
Basin of the Nile*, London, 1866.
Baker, Samuel *Exploration of the Nile
Tributaries of Abyssinia*, London, 1867.
Baker, Samuel *The Nile Tributaries of
Abyssinia*, London, 1868.

Chapter 12

Livingstone, David *Last Journal*, London,
1874.
Livingstone, David *The Life and
Explorations of Dr Livingstone the Great
Missionary Traveller*, London.
Livingstone, David *Missionary Travels and
Researches in South Africa*, London, 1857.

Livingstone, David *Narrative of an
Expedition to the Zambesi and its Tributaries*,
London, 1865.
Stanley, Henry Morton *How I Found
Livingstone*, London, 1872.
Stanley, Henry Morton *Through the Dark
Continent*, London, 1878.

Chapter 13

Lefebvre, Théophile *Voyage en Abyssinie*,
Paris, 1845.
Sabelli, Luca dei *Storia di Abissinia*, Rome,
1936.
Salt, Henry *Twenty Four Views taken in St.
Helena, the Cape, India, Ceylon, Abyssinia
& Egypt*, London, 1809.
Salt, Henry *A Voyage to Abyssinia*, London,
1814.
Stanley, Henry Morton *Coomassie and
Magdala; The Story of the British Campaigns
in Africa*, London, 1874.
Viscount Valencia, George *Voyages and
Travels to India, Ceylon, the Red Sea,
Abyssinia and Egypt*, London, 1811.
War Office, *Views in Abyssinia*,
London, 1867.

Chapter 14

Dainelli, Giotto *Esploratori italiani in
Africa*, Turin, 1960.
Johnston, Harry *The Nile Quest*, London,
1903.
Schweinfurth, Georg *The Heart of Africa*,
London, 1873.

Chapter 15

Baker, Samuel *Ismailia: A Narrative of
the Expedition to Central Africa for the
Suppression of the Slave Trade*, London,
1874.
Ritchie, J. Ewin *The Pictorial Edition
of the Life and Discoveries of David
Livingstone*.

Chapter 16

Allen, Bernard M. *Gordon and the Sudan*,
London, 1951.
Archer, Thomas *The War in Egypt and the
Soudan*, London.
Casati, Gaetano *Ten Years in Equatoria and
the Return with Emin Pasha*, London,
1891.
Chaillé-Long, C. *Central Africa: Naked
Truths of Naked People*, London, 1876.
Gessi, Romolo Pasha *Sette anni nel Sudan
Egiziano*, Milan, 1891.
Gessi, Romolo Pasha *Seven Years in the
Soudan*, London, 1892.

Hand Atlas, Gotha, 1850.
Pictorial Africa Its Heroes, Missionaries and Martyrs, London, 1890.
Ritchie, J. Ewin *The Pictorial Edition of the Life and Discoveries of David Livingstone*.
Salt, Henry *Twenty Four Views taken in St. Helena, The Cape, India, Ceylon, Abyssinia & Egypt*, London, 1809.
Scott, Walter *Life of General Gordon*, London.
Slatin, Rudolf C. Pasha, C. B., *Fire and Sword in the Sudan*, London, 1896.
Viscount Valencia, George *Voyages and Travels to India, Ceylon, the Red Sea, Abyssinia, and Egypt*, London, 1811.

Chapter 17
Archer, Thomas *The War in Egypt and the Soudan*, London.
Baring, Sir Evelyn *Modern Egypt*, London, 1908.
Maximilian in Bayern, *Bilder aus dem Oriente*, Stuttgart, 1846.

Chapter 18
Archer, Thomas *The War in Egypt and the*

Soudan, London.
Casati, Gaetano *Ten Years in Equatoria and the Return with Emin Pasha*, London, 1891.
Gessi, Romolo Pasha, *Seven Years in the Soudan*, London, 1892.
Ohrwalder, Father Joseph *Ten Year's Captivity in the Mahdi's Camp*, London, 1892.
Scott, Walter *Life of General Gordon*, London.
Slatin, Rudolf C. Pasha, C. B. *Fire and Sword in Sudan*, London, 1896.

Chapter 19
Casati, Gaetano *Dieci anni in Equatoria e ritorno con Emin Pascià*, Milan, 1891.
Mounteney-Jephson, A. J. *Emin Pasha and the Rebellion at the Equator*, London, 1890.
Ritchie, J. Ewin *The Pictorial Edition of the Life and Discoveries of David Livingstone*.
Schweitzer, Georg *Emin Pasha: Eine Darstellung seines Lebens und Wirkens*, Berlin, 1898.
Stanley, Henry Morton *In Darkest Africa of*

the Quest, Rescue and Retreat of Emin Governor of Equatoria, London, 1890.

Chapter 20
Archer, Thomas *The War in Egypt and the Soudan*, London.
Churchill, Winston *The River War*, London, 1899.
Holt, P.M. *The Mahdist State in Sudan 1881-89*, Oxford, 1958.
Ohrwalder, Father Joseph *Ten Years' Captivity in the Mahdi's Camp*, London, 1892.
Scott, Walter *Life of General Gordon*, London.
Slatin, Rudolf C. Pasha, C. B., *Fire and Sword in the Sudan*, London, 1896.

Chapter 21
Bartlett, William Henry *The Nile Boat*, London, 1858.
Duca Massimiliano Wittelsbach, *Malerische Ansichten aus dem Oriente Gesammelt auf der Reise Sr. Hoh. des Herren Herzogs Maximilian in Bayern, nach Nubien,*

Aegypten, Palastina, Syrien, und Malta im Jahre 1838, Munich, 1838.
Forbin, L.N.P.A. *Voyage dans le Levant*, Paris, 1819.
Jones, Owen *Views of the Nile*, London, 1843.
Hay of Linplum, Robert *Views of Cairo*, London, 1840.
Lepsius, Karl Richard *Denkmaler aus Aegypten und Aethiopien*, Berlin, 1848-1859.
Moritz Busch, Julius Hermann *Bilder aus dem Orient*, Trieste, 1864.
Preziosi, Amadeo *Souvenir du Caire*, Paris, 1862.
Rifaud, Jean-Jacques *Voyage en Égypte, en Nubie*, Paris, 1830.
Roberts, David *Egypt and Nubia*, London, 1846-1849.
Salt, Henry *Twenty Four Views taken in St. Helena, the Cape, India, Ceylon, Abyssinia & Egypt*, London, 1809.
Werner, Karl *Le Nil*, Paris, 1882.

ILLUSTRATION CREDITS

n Egypte, en Nubie", Paris, 1830.
© Private collection.

Chapter 9
42 J. Ewin Ritchie , "The Pictorial dition of the Life and Discoveries of avid Livingstone". © Private collection.
42-143, 146, 147, 148, 148-149, 50, 151 Richard Burton, "The Lake egions of Central Africa", London, 860. © Private collection.
43 center © National Library of cotland.
43 bottom © Private collection.
44-145 © Royal Geographical Society.
44 bottom © Royal Geographical ociety.
45 © Royal Geographical Society.
49 bottom © Royal Geographical ociety.

Chapter 10
52 top © Royal Geographical Society.
52 bottom, 154, 155, 156, 156-157, 58 top, 160, 161, 162, 163, 166 ohn Hanning Speke, "Journal of the iscovery of the Source of the Nile", ondon, 1863. © Private collection.
53 left © Private collection/National ortrait Gallery, London.
53 right © Royal Geographical Society.
57 © Royal Geographical Society.
58-159, 159, 164, 165, 166-167, 67 top, 167 bottom © National ibrary of Scotland.

Chapter 11
68, 169, 170-171, 171, 172-173, 72 bottom, 173 bottom Samuel Baker Exploration of the Nile Tributaries of byssinia", London, 1867.
 Private collection.
70, 173 top, 176 bottom, 178, 179, 82, 183 © Royal Geographical Society.
74, 175, 176-177, 177, 180, 181 amuel Baker, "Albert Nyanza–Great asin of the Nile", London, 1886.
 Private collection.

Chapter 12
84-185 © Royal Geographical Society.
84 bottom © Royal Geographical ociety.
85, 187 top left, 188, 189, 190, 191, 92, 193, 194, 195, 196 top, 200-01 "The Life and Explorations of Dr ivingstone the Great Missionary raveller", London.
 Private collection.
86 © Royal Geographical Society.
87 © Royal Geographical Society.
87 bottom © Royal Geographical ociety.
96 bottom © Science and Society icture Library.
97 top (two photos) © Royal eographical Society.
97 bottom (three photos) © The avid Livingstone Centre.
98, 199, 200 top, 201, 202 bottom, 03 Henry Morton Stanley "How I ound Livingstone", London, 1872.
 Private collection.
00 bottom, 202 bottom right Pictorial Africa, Its Heroes, Missionaries nd Martyrs".
 Private collection.
02 top © Royal Geographical Society.
04, 205, 206, 207, 208, 209, 210, 11 Henry Morton Stanley "Through e Dark Continent", London, 1878.
 Private collection.

Chapter 13
12, 218 bottom left Henry alt"Twenty Four Views taken in St. elena, The Cape, India, Ceylon, byssinia & Egypt", London, 1809.
 Private collection.
12-213, 217 top, 217 center, Henry alt "A Voyage to Abyssinia", London, 814.
 Private collection.
13 bottom left © Private collection.
13 bottom right © Private collection.
14, 215, 216 top, 217 bottom, 218

top, 220, 221, 222 top, 222-223, 224, 225, 226, 227 Théophile Lefebvre, "Voyage en Abyssinie", Paris, 1845. © Private collection.
216 bottom © Private collection/ Illustrated Travels.
216-217 War Office, "Views in Abyssinia", London, 1867. © Private collection.
218 bottom right George Viscount Valencia, "Voyages and Travels to India, Ceylon, the Red Sea, Abyssinia and Egypt", London, 1811.
© Private collection.
218-219, 229 top, 229 center right, 229 bottom, 230 bottom, 230-231, 231 bottom, 232-233, 233 top right, 233 center right, 233 bottom right The Illustrated London News. © Private collection.
222 center © Private collection.
222 bottom, 228 bottom left, 228 right, 233 top Henry Morton Stanley "Coomassie and Magdala; The Story of the British Campaigns in Africa", London, 1874.
© Private collection.
228 top left © Private collection.
229 center left © Fotomas Index.
230 top © HQ Mess of the Royal Engineers.
232 © Private collection.

Chapter 14
234 top, 234 bottom, 235, 236, 237, 238, 239, 240 top right, 240-241, 240 bottom, 241 Georg Schweinfurth, "The Heart of Africa", London, 1873. © Private collection.
234 center "The Nile Quest", London, 1903. © Private collection.
240 top left © Accademia dei Concordi, Rovigo.

Chapter 15
242, 243, 244, 245, 246, 247, 248, 249, 250 top, 250 bottom, 251 Samuel Baker, "Ismailia: A Narrative of the Expedition to Central Africa for the Suppression of the Slave Trade", London, 1874. © Private collection.
242-243 © Private collection.
250 center © Royal Geographical Society.

Chapter 16
252 top © Private collection.
252 center, 264 center, 265 top, 265 center The Illustrated London News. © Private collection.
252 bottom © Mary Evans Picture Library.
253 Hand Atlas, Gotha, 1850.
© Private collection.
254 left Rudolf C. Slatin Pasha, C. B., "Fire and Sword in the Sudan", London, 1896. © Private collection.
254 right, 267 bottom Gaetano Casati, "Ten Years in Equatoria and the Return with Emin Pasha", London, 1891.
© Private collection.
255 top, 266 top Walter Scott, "Life of General Gordon". © Private collection.
255 center, 255 bottom J. Ewin Ritchie, "The Pictorial Edition of the Life and Discoveries of David Livingstone".
© Private collection.
256, 257, 258, 259 C. Chaillé-Long, "Central Africa: Naked Truths of Naked People", London, 1876. © Private collection.
260 top, 260 bottom, 260-261, 268, 269 Romolo Gessi Pasha, "Seven Years in the Soudan", London, 1892.
© Private collection.
262 top © Private collection.
262 bottom, 264 top Henry Salt "Twenty Four Views taken in St. Helena, the Cape, India, Ceylon, Abyssinia & Egypt", London, 1809. © Private collection.
262-263, 263 bottom left, 263 bottom right George Viscount Valencia, "Voyages and Travels to India, Ceylon, the Red Sea, Abyssinia and Egypt", London, 1811. © Private collection.
265 bottom left © Private collection.

265 bottom right "Galérie Iconographique Egyptienne".
© Private collection.
266 bottom"Pictorial Africa, Its Heroes, Missionaries and Martyrs", London, 1890. © Private collection.
267 top Thomas Archer, "The War in Egypt and the Soudan", London.
© Private collection.

Chapter 17
270, 271 top right, 271 bottom, 273 top, 273 bottom Thomas Archer, "The War in Egypt and the Soudan", London. © Private collection.
271 top left Maximilian in Bayern, "Bilder aus dem Orient", Stuttgard, 1846. © Private collection.
272-273, 272 bottom, 274, 275/278 The Illustrated London News.
© Private collection.
273 top © Private collection/Le Monde Illustré.
273 center © Private collection.
279 The Pictorial World. © Private collection.

Chapter 18
280 top, 281 bottom, 283 center left, 286 top and bottom, 286 top, 286 center right, 287 top Thomas Archer, "The War in Egypt and the Soudan", London.
© Private collection.
280 bottom, 283 bottom, 286 center left, 289 top, 291 bottom left Rudolf C. Slatin Pasha, C. B., "Fire and Sword in the Sudan", London, 1896. © Private collection.
281 top, 282 top, 282-283, 283 top, 284-285, 285 bottom, 286-287, 288 top, 288-289, 289 bottom, 290-291, 291 top left The Illustrated London News. © Private collection.
283 center right, 292 top, 292 center top, 292 center bottom, 292 bottom Gaetano Casati, "Ten Years in Equatoria and the Return with Emin Pasha", London, 1891.
© Private collection.
291 top right Walter Scott, "Life of General Gordon", London.
© Private collection.
291 right bottom Romolo Gessi Pasha, "Seven Years in the Soudan, London, 1892. © Private collection.

Chapter 19
292, 294 right, 295 top, 301 bottom right, 303 top left Gaetano Casati, "Ten Years in Equatoria and the Return with Emin Pasha", London, 1891. © Private collection.
293, 295 bottom, 300 bottom, 301 top, 301 bottom left, 302 top, 303 top right, 303 center A. J. Mounteney-Jephson, "Emin Pasha and the Rebellion at the Equator", London, 1890. © Private collection.
294 left J. Ewin Ritchie , "The Pictorial Edition of the Life and Discoveries of David Livingstone".
© Private collection.
294-295, 296, 297, 298, 299, 300 top, 301 center, 302 bottom, 303 bottom Henry Morton Stanley, "In Darkest Africa of the Quest, Rescue and Retreat of Emin Governor of Equatoria", London, 1890.
© Private collection.

Chapter 20
304 top, 305 top, 305 bottom, 309 bottom right Rudolf C. Slatin Pasha, C. B., "Fire and Sword in the Sudan", London, 1896.
© Private collection.
304 bottom, 306 bottom right Walter Scott, "Life of General Gordon". © Private collection.
304-305, 306 bottom left, 307 bottom Thomas Archer, "The War in Egypt and the Soudan", London.
© Private collection.
306-307, 307 right, 308-309, 309

center, 310, 312 bottom The Illustrated London News.
© Private collection.
309 top © Mary Evans Picture Library.
309 bottom left Father Joseph Ohrwalder, "Ten Years' Captivity in the Mahdi's Camp", London. © Private collection.
310-311 © Private collection.
312 top © Giovanni Dagli Orti/Musée des Arts Africains et Océaniens.
313 top left © Collection Kharbine-Tapabor, Paris.
313 bottom left Petit Journal © Giovanni Dagli Orti.
313 right © Collection Kharbine-Tapabor, Paris.

Chapter 21
314, 320 top, 320, 321, 332-333, 333 top, 336 left, 336-337, 339 right, 340 bottom, 342-343 David Roberts, "Egypt and Nubia", London 1846-1849. © Library of Congress, Washington.
314-315 L.N.P.A. Forbin, "Voyage dans le Levant", Paris, 1819. © Private collection.
315 bottom © Private collection.
316, 317 Robert Hay of Linplum "Views of Cairo", London, 1840. © Private collection.
318-319 Henry Salt "Twenty Four Views taken in St. Helena, the Cape, India, Ceylon, Abyssinia & Egypt", London, 1809. © Private collection.
322, 323 Amadeo Preziosi, "Souvenir du Caire", Paris 1862. © Private collection.
324, 325 Julius Hermann Moritz Busch, "Bilder aus dem Orient", Trieste, 1864. © Private collection.
326, 327, 328, 329 Jean-Jacques Rifaud, "Voyage en Egypte, en Nubie", Paris, 1830. © Private collection.
330, 331, 338-339, 341 bottom Karl Richard Lepsius, "Denkmaler aus Aegypten und Aethiopien", Berlin, 1848-1859. © Private collection.
332 top, 336 top right, 338 bottom, 341 top William Henry Bartlett, "The Nile Boat", London, 1858. © Private collection.
333 bottom, 338 top, 339 bottom, 339 bottom Karl Werner, "Le Nil", Paris, 1882. © Private collection.
334-335 © Edimedia, Paris.
337 top, Owen Jones, "Views on the Nile", London, 1843. © Private collection.
340-341 Duca Massimiliano Wittelsbach, "Malerische Ansichten aus dem Oriente", Monaco, 1838. © Private collection.
344 © WorldSat International Inc. Jim Knighton, 1996.

The maps and old prints were hand colored by Old Church Galleries, London and by Franca Tegliucci, Rome.

CHOROGRAPHIA
ORIGINIS NILI *Fol. 55*
iuxta obseruationem Odoardi Lopez

CHOROGRAPHIA ORIGINISNILI
SEVFONTIVM IPSIVS *Fol. 53*
EX Arabum Geographia deprompta

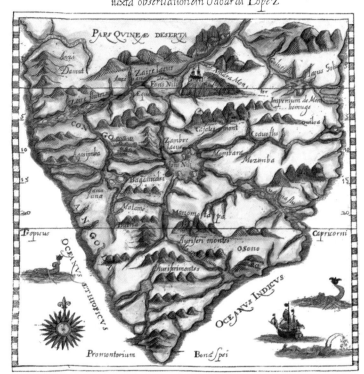

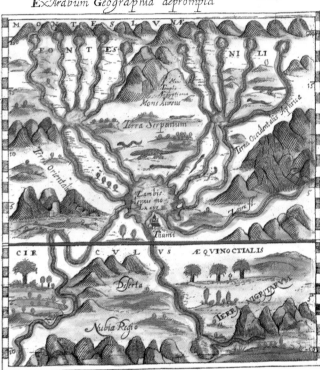

VERA ET GENVINA FONTIVM NILI TOPOGRAPHIA
facta a P. PETRO PAIS: Societ IESU Anno 1618: die 21. Apeilis in praesentia Imperatoris... Fol 56

Athanasius Kircher
Obelisci Aegyptiaci, Rome 1666